Praise for *Trias Algorithmica*

"A fascinating assessment for the age of AI. Who decides, on what basis, and backed by what kind of legitimacy? Everyone who cares about democracy should pay attention."

—Simon Johnson,
Ronald A. Kurtz Professor of Entrepreneurship, Head of the Global Economics and Management Group at MIT Sloan; 2024 Nobel Laureate in Economic Sciences; Coauthor of Power and Progress

"Algorithms do not merely push out the production possibility frontier. They reallocate control rights among citizens, silently and at scale. That an algorithm can serve as rule-maker, rule-executor, and referee does not mean it should. But absent deliberate democratic resistance, this is where we are heading. If you doubt it is already underway, consider the surveillance state you enter each morning when you open your web browser. Trias Algorithmica anatomizes this pernicious algorithmic creep and offers tools to address it.".

—David Autor,
Economics Department Head, Daniel (1972) and Gail Rubinfeld Professor, Google Technology and Society Visiting Fellow, Margaret MacVicar Faculty Fellow at MIT Department of Economics; Co-author of The Work of the Future

AI does not merely improve decisions; it reallocates the power to make them. Trias Algorithmica explains why our AI future will require not just better models, but better institutions. Essential reading for everyone who wants the benefits of AI without surrendering our human judgment, accountability, or agency."

—Ajay Agrawal,
Geoffrey Taber Chair in Entrepreneurship and Innovation and Professor of Strategic Management at the University of Toronto's Rotman School of Management; Coauthor of Prediction Machines and Power and Prediction

"I build the systems this book is about. Perception stacks that decide what a car sees. Robots that act in physical space. Foundation models that increasingly mediate how people work and think. From inside that work, Mann's argument lands with uncomfortable accuracy.

The temptation in our field is to treat governance as a layer added late—a compliance review, a red team, a policy document downstream of the model. Mann's claim is that by then it is already too late. The constitutional choices have been made: in the objective function, in the deployment surface, in who gets to approve a release and who gets to overturn it. Engineering decisions are constitutional decisions wearing technical clothing.

This is not a comfortable book for builders. It should not be. The most consequential systems of the coming decade will be judged less by what they can do than by whether their power can be answered for. Mann gives us a vocabulary, and an architecture, for that answering.

I do not agree with every step of the argument. I am glad the argument exists."

—Amnon Shashua,

Founder, President, and CEO at Mobileye; Sachs Professor of Computer Science at the Hebrew University of Jerusalem's Rachel and Selim Benin School of Computer Science and Engineering

"*Trias Algorithmica: What Code Rules* makes an engaging argument that AI systems possess tremendous power without the legitimacy traditionally conferred by separation of powers. The metaphor that the same AI company typically carries out the rule-making (legislative), deployment (executive), and monitoring (judicial) provokes one to question how much the behavior of modern neural networks results from legislative design by AI engineers as opposed to the human behavior the AIs learn from."

—De Kai,

AI Professor; Author of Raising AI

"In this fascinating book, Mann argues that opaque, unaccountable algorithmic systems—like social media platforms, AI chatbots, or predictive policing—play three governance roles at once: they make policy, they execute the laws they've created, and they distribute justice according to their own notions of fairness. In the name of technological efficiency, we have private systems of quasi-government gaining increasing control over our lives. Mann argues for taking back control and adding much-needed friction and oversight to these systems. A compelling approach to restoring accountability in algorithmic governance."

—Cathy O'Neil,

Mathematician, Founder of ORCAA; Author of Weapons of Math Destruction *and* The Shame Machine

"Mann comprehensively applies a separation of powers framework to critique current AI and prescribe its better development and use. *Trias Algorithmica* demonstrates that no AI system should consolidate the power to set goals, to execute them, and to judge whether they have been executed well. This is remarkably creative work that sheds new light on AI governance."

—Frank Pasquale,
Professor of Law at Cornell University;
Author of The Black Box Society

"*Trias Algorithmica* reframes AI governance around a simple democratic principle: people must retain the right to question, contest, and reshape the systems that shape them. Hamilton Mann's call for algorithmic separation of powers is a timely contribution to a more accountable digital future."

—Audrey Tang,
Taiwan's Cyber Ambassador; Coauthor of Civic.AI *and* Plurality.net

"*Trias Algorithmica* is a necessary book for anyone trying to understand how AI is changing power itself. Hamilton Mann brings a rare combination of technological fluency and moral urgency to one of the defining questions of our time: how societies can preserve accountability, human agency, and legitimacy as decision making shifts from human to machine intelligence."

—Sinan Aral,
David Austin Professor of Management, Marketing, IT, and Data Science at MIT; Author of The Hype Machine

"Mann offers a critical warning: As algorithms learn to govern, humanity must relearn how to constrain power. For seventy years we have asked whether machines can think. Hamilton Mann argues we've been asking the wrong question.

The one that matters now is whether machine decisions can in fact be legitimate.

Trias Algorithmica reframes AI as a constitutional problem. When platforms write policy as a unitary legislature, judiciary, and executive, they fuse power into a single, frictionless stack. Their AI algorithms exercise this power at superhuman speeds. Mann then proposes a key separation of powers as a pushback toward individual autonomy."

—Marshall Van Alstyne,
Allen and Kelli Questrom Professor in Information Economics at Boston University Questrom School of Business; Coauthor of Platform Revolution

"As AI systems increasingly shape what we see, choose, and become, the right to question machine-mediated decisions should become central to democratic life. *Trias Algorithmica* is an ambitious call to build transparency, appeal, and human judgment into the architecture of AI itself."

—Nita Farahany,
Robinson O. Everett Professor of Law and Philosophy at Duke University; Author of The Battle for Your Brain

"Hamilton Mann's *Trias Algorithmica* is an ambitious and thought-provoking contribution to the growing conversation about governance, accountability, and power in the age of artificial intelligence. At a time when leaders are rethinking not only technology strategy but also the institutional logic underlying intelligence-driven systems, Mann challenges readers to consider how algorithmic systems increasingly shape decision-making, oversight, and human agency. The book raises important strategic and philosophical questions that business and policy leaders can no longer afford to ignore."

—Geoffrey Parker,
Charles E. Hutchinson '68A Professor of Engineering Innovation at Dartmouth; Coauthor of Platform Revolution

"With the rapid progress in AI capabilities, algorithms are deployed in an increasing variety of environments where they nudge, influence, or outright replace human decisions. In this book, Hamilton Mann skillfully demonstrates that while superficially empowering people and improving corporate efficiency, the use of AI in decision making in fact undermines the very core of the democratic system: the "trias politica"—the separation of powers.

This is an important yet often overlooked path leading to loss of human control over the increasingly powerful AI algorithms."

—Jakub Growiec,
Professor of Economics, SGH Warsaw School of Economics, Poland; Member, European Commission AI Act Scientific Panel; Author of Accelerating Economic Growth: Lessons From 200,000 Years of Technological Progress and Human Development

"As artificial intelligence increasingly decides who gets a job, a loan, or a fair trial, we are drifting into a society where our civil rights are dictated by opaque, proprietary code. For years, we have distracted ourselves with the question of whether machines can think, missing the more urgent reality: machines are now deciding. They are fusing the rule-maker, executioner, and judge into a single algorithm. *Trias Algorithmica* makes the danger unmistakable. Algorithmic governance is not a technological shift but a constitutional crisis, and preserving our autonomy in the AI age will require what silent optimization has stripped away: friction, due process, and a new separation of powers. An essential and timely read."

—Vivienne Ming,
CEO and Founder at Socos Labs; Visiting Professor at UCL Global Business School for Health; Author of Robot-Proof

"Hamilton Mann's *Trias Algorithmica* is a bracing intervention into the crisis of legitimacy stalking our automated age. Mann identifies that our current technological acceleration represents a silent fusion of legislative, executive, and judicial powers within the black box of the code. By elegantly resurrecting Montesquieu for the era of generative AI, he exposes how the disappearance of procedural friction that is marketed as an efficiency feature but alas embeds a bug of tyranny. Essential reading for anyone who believes that liberty cannot survive without the right to interrupt the machine."

—Nils Gilman,
Deputy Editor of Noema Magazine *and Editor in Chief of* Berggruen Press; *Former Associate Chancellor at UC Berkeley*

WHAT CODE RULES

TRIAS ALGORITHMICA

HAMILTON MANN

WILEY

This edition first published 2027

Registered Offices
John Wiley & Sons, Inc., 111 River Street, Hoboken, NJ 07030, USA
John Wiley & Sons Ltd, New Era House, 8 Oldlands Way, Bognor Regis, West Sussex, PO22 9NQ, UK

For details of our global editorial offices, customer services, and more information about Wiley products visit us at www.wiley.com.

The manufacturer's authorized representative according to the EU General Product Safety Regulation is Wiley-VCH GmbH, Boschstr. 12, 69469 Weinheim, Germany, e-mail: Product_Safety@wiley.com.

Wiley also publishes its books in a variety of electronic formats and by print-on-demand. Some content that appears in standard print versions of this book may not be available in other formats.

Library of Congress Cataloging-in-Publication Data is Available:

ISBN 9781394449286 (Cloth)
ISBN 9781394449293 (ePub)
ISBN 9781394449309 (ePDF)

Cover Design: Hamilton Mann
Cover Image: donfiore/Shutterstock
Author Photo: D-light Production

Set in 11/14.5pt Bembo Std by Straive, Chennai, India.

For my R. and my A.—for always being there.

Contents

Preface

The Tape and Test

What connects Watergate and the Turing test?

On a cold day in Washington in 1973, a lawyer named Archibald Cox walked into a job that was designed to be lonely. He had been appointed special prosecutor to investigate a burglary that looked, at first glance, like the kind of petty political vandalism that every election year produces. A few broken locks at the Watergate complex, a few men in suits caught with cameras and cash. Nothing that should have threatened a presidency.

But Cox was not chosen to make the story smaller.

In the weeks that followed, Cox learned the difference between a scandal that lives on paper and one that lives inside institutions. Paper is passive; institutions push back.

Across town, Attorney General Elliot Richardson carried a different kind of burden. Before taking office, he had promised the Senate that the prosecutor would be independent. It was an oath without scripture, an oath made of reputation. Richardson understood that the Constitution lives in both writing and performance. When you speak a promise publicly, you convert your career into collateral for a principle.

President Richard Nixon, meanwhile, was living inside another performance, one he controlled. In the Oval Office, he could shape time, attention, and access. The presidency is often described as the most visible office in the republic. In practice, it is also the most capable of darkness; it can withhold, it can delay, it can surround itself with loyal language until reality becomes negotiable.

Then a small fact entered the story and changed the geometry of power. There were tapes.

A recording system in the White House captured conversations—a technological artifact, mundane in its engineering, immense in its constitutional consequence. Once Cox learned about it, he did what a prosecutor must do when the truth might exist as a physical object: he asked for it.

The request felt like an administrative step, a subpoena. Yet it was a philosophical assault. It said that the executive branch, for all its mystique, could be compelled—that the law could demand entry into the inner chamber.

Nixon refused.

The refusal was not merely a legal argument about privilege, but a claim about sovereignty. It implied that there is a space in which the executive is not a party to the constitutional bargain—a space where the president stands outside the rule he enforces.

Cox kept pressing—not because he wanted drama but because drama is what appears when procedure meets a boundary that someone insists does not exist.

On the evening of October 20, 1973, the boundary announced itself. Nixon ordered Richardson to fire Cox. Richardson refused and resigned. Then Nixon ordered Deputy Attorney General William Ruckelshaus to do so. Ruckelshaus refused and resigned. Finally, Solicitor General Robert Bork carried out the order, and Cox was dismissed.

It happened so fast that it felt like a single motion, like an algorithm executing a command. Later, it would be called the Saturday Night Massacre, but the name can be misleading. Rather than chaos, it was a demonstration of a certain kind of power: the power to treat other offices as removable parts.

People poured into the streets. The public reaction mattered, but something else mattered more. The system did not collapse into sentiment; it responded as a system.

At this point, the stage tightens with the three familiar powers that Montesquieu once described: the legislature that investigates and calls witnesses into the daylight, the executive that commands and withholds, and the judiciary that turns procedure into compulsion.

In the days that followed, the Senate intensified its inquiries. Judges leaned into their authority. One judge in particular, John Sirica, insisted that evasions would not be treated as answers. The question was no longer who ordered a burglary. The question became whether the executive branch could obstruct the mechanisms meant to constrain it.

Nixon tried a compromise. He offered edited transcripts. It sounded reasonable until you noticed what it assumed. It assumed that the president could decide what the other branches were allowed to know—that the executive could serve as both custodian of evidence and editor of its meaning.

The dispute reached the Supreme Court. In July 1974, the court ruled unanimously that Nixon had to turn over the tapes.

Unanimously. It is hard to overstate the rhetorical violence of that word when placed against presidential certainty. A unanimous court does not simply decide. It speaks in the accent of inevitability. It tells the executive branch, and the country watching, that this is not a partisan quarrel but a constitutional fact.

The tapes were produced. They included a conversation that came to be known as the "smoking gun," a moment in which the effort to obstruct the investigation was not inferred but heard. The story snapped into focus. In August 1974, Nixon resigned.

If you stop there, it is a civics lesson with a satisfying ending. The prosecutor persisted, the courts compelled, the legislature investigated, and the presidency yielded. *Trias politica* at work. A republic checking itself, like a body preserving balance.

But the deeper lesson sits earlier, on that Saturday night, in the pattern of removals.

Because what Richardson and Ruckelshaus revealed goes beyond courage. It exposes the fragility of separation when one branch can reach into another and remove the human components that carry its commitments. Their resignations were a refusal to let an executive instruction become an automatic function. Their refusal inserted friction.

Friction is not a defect in constitutional design. It is the design.

The separation of powers does not merely distribute responsibilities. It distributes pace. It forces decisions to travel through procedures, objections, appeals, and time. Time is not always justice, but justice rarely survives without it. The slowness is the safeguard.

Now imagine the same confrontation in a society where constitutional power is no longer only a matter of rules debated in public and enforced in the open, but of rules encoded in algorithms, applied as defaults, and defended as compliance within AI infrastructures. Not only in public institutions, but in infrastructures that operate in private. Not only in people who can resign, but in code that cannot.

Rules once materialized as documents manifest as model updates. Decisions unfold as streams rather than discrete acts. Harm no longer appears as a single denial, but accumulates as a lifetime of micro-exclusions. Appeal shifts from a hearing to form filling. Judgment does not rest with a judge in a robe, but is executed by an internal policy engine whose operators and logic you never see.

The White House tapes were a technology that preserved speech. Today, our dominant technologies do something more ambitious. They not only record human decisions; they begin to shape them. They classify, rank, recommend, filter, approve, deny, flag, throttle, and exile. They do so at a scale that no court can keep up with and at a speed that no legislature can meaningfully supervise in real time.

We tell ourselves that this is still politics as usual, only faster.

But faster is not simply an adjective. It is a constitutional event.

Because when enforcement moves to machine speed, the function that was once spread across branches begins to converge. The same algorithmic system can define the rule, apply the rule, and decide whether you can contest it. In the old story, those were separate roles. The legislature makes law, the executive enforces it, and the judiciary interprets and remedies it. In the new story, a platform can write a policy, encode it into a product, and adjudicate your appeal inside a help center that answers like a courtroom painted on cardboard.

And the most unnerving part is not that this happens in secret, but that it happens with consent.

People do not adopt these systems because they love being governed. They adopt them because the alternative feels like exile. Because they are promised ease, safety, personalization, efficiency, and belonging. They trade autonomy for access and later discover that access has become a leash. When they discover it.

This is where the Watergate story becomes more than history. It becomes a mirror.

In 1973, Cox could be fired, but he could also become a symbol because the firing was visible, dramatic, and legible as an abuse. Today, the equivalent dismissal does not require a Saturday night. It requires a model update, a ranking adjustment, or a policy revision shipped quietly at 3 a.m. Your reach disappears, your livelihood dips, your voice loses altitude, and there is no Richardson to resign, no Ruckelshaus to refuse, and no courtroom where the public can hear the argument unfold.

The old constitution was built for adversaries. It assumed conflict and used structure to make that conflict productive. It assumed that power would push, so it created places for power to collide, be slowed, and be questioned.

Algorithmic power is built for flow. It assumes that the best system is one without resistance. It treats friction as a bug. It calls it latency.

So the modern constitutional question extends beyond, and sometimes bypasses, who holds office to what holds the levers. It is whether the mechanisms that now govern speech, work, identity, and opportunity still pass through separated powers, or whether they have been fused into a single operational layer that is everywhere and nowhere—public when it markets itself, private when it justifies itself.

The story of Watergate ends with a resignation, but its hidden protagonist is the separation itself. The separation made it possible for truth to travel from suspicion to evidence to judgment. The separation created a path that no single actor could fully seal.

When code becomes the path, and the path is owned, optimized, and guarded by private systems, separation becomes an aesthetic memory. We keep the language of checks and balances, while the actual checking is throttled and the balancing is outsourced.

This is what sits at the heart of the power AI's algorithms have in society. Not only that they predict. Not only that they automate. But that they quietly recombine the functions that trias politica once pulled apart, and they do it under the banner of convenience, comfort, and care.

Trias politica once protected citizens by ensuring that power had to travel across institutional borders. Those borders created delays, visibility, and the possibility of challenge. Algorithmic power erodes those borders by turning governance into a continuous service layer. It produces what looks like autonomy while tightening dependency because the environment begins to anticipate you, decide for you, and reward you for staying within the rails.

Trias Algorithmica. That is the uncomfortable pivot that runs through this book.

A constitution where the rule is not published in a gazette but encoded in models, thresholds, and interfaces. A constitution where enforcement is not a police officer or a court order but an automated decision. A constitution where compliance is not argued; it is nudged. The most decisive interventions are often invisible, continuous, and personalized, and therefore hard to contest.

It asks what happens when governance is no longer only a matter of law and office but a matter of infrastructure and design. It asks what happens when policy becomes a product feature, when enforcement becomes instantaneous, when justice becomes a ticket number, when trust becomes a permission layer, when human worth is redefined as task output, and when the loop that supposedly includes the human turns out to be a loop that contains the human.

Cox walked into the lonely job believing that the truth could be found and presented. Richardson resigned believing that a promise could be binding. The Supreme Court ruled believing that no one, not even a president, was above the law.

The next chapter of that belief cannot be written only in courtrooms. It has to be written in the architectures that now decide what people see, what they can do, what they are offered, and what they are allowed to contest.

In the classical world, the question was who rules. In the platform world, the question became what rules. In the AI world, the question becomes what rules rule, and who can still separate them before they fuse into a single, self-justifying engine.

In other words, we need the old story again but translated. We need separation, not only of branches, but of algorithmic functions. We need friction, not as nostalgia, but as a safeguard. We need a constitution not only on paper but in the code that rules.

We have spent seventy years obsessing over whether the machine in Turing's game could think.

Yet we have been blind to the most revolutionary part of his design.

Introduction

Where the Test Lapses

On a damp afternoon in Manchester in 1950, Alan Turing sat with a cup of tea gone cold and a paper already smudged with revisions. He had the look of a man trying to make an argument simple enough to be dangerous. The war had ended, the secrets were still sealed, and the machines that had once been surrounded by uniformed urgency now sat in quieter rooms with civilian dust. Turing was no longer racing the clock for victory. He was racing language for legitimacy.

He began with a parlor game, almost mischievously. Not a theorem, not a blueprint, not even a promise. A game with three people and one question that would not stay within its frame. The Imitation Game. A name made deliberately unremarkable, so the radical move would arrive disguised as common sense.

One person asked questions. Two answers were delivered. One was human; one might be a machine. The task of the questioner was not to inspect the body, not to measure the skull, not to demand credentials, but to judge through dialogue alone—to decide which written replies were human and which were not.

It sounds like a game. But it is a rule.

Turing did something that philosophers and lawmakers have often done when power becomes too slippery to hold. He arranged a system of roles. He separated functions so that no single actor could be everything at once. The questioner became a kind of judge, bound to procedure, forced to listen, forced to deliberate. The respondents became parties to a case, limited to what they could argue through words, compelled to act only by persuasion, unable to set the rules, unable to declare the outcome, unable to turn performance into a verdict. That rule of the game became a legislature in miniature, a prior agreement that constrained the whole encounter.

Even the medium mattered—the screen, the distance, the refusal of direct inspection. Turing was implicitly saying that fairness begins when you prevent the stronger party from smuggling in extra power. You do not let one side both set the terms and declare the outcome. You do not let the examiner become the executioner. You do not let the rules morph mid-trial because someone has grown impatient.

Montesquieu would have recognized the architecture. *Trias politica.* The old idea that liberty survives only when power is split, checked, and slowed by design. Turing was not writing a constitution, but he was building a small courtroom where intelligence could be evaluated without tyranny by intuition. He was, in his own dry way, making a claim about the ethics of judgment. If you want a verdict you can defend, you must accept constraints that sometimes feel like friction.

Friction was not a defect in the architecture of the Imitation Game. It was the architecture. And the strange thing about friction is that it feels like weakness until you notice what happens when it is gone.

The real provocation is the geometry of what he built. There is an interrogator who asks and decides. There are respondents who can only answer. There is a channel that prevents shortcuts—no face, no authority by presence, no inspection masquerading as certainty. And there is a rule set that exists prior to the interaction, binding all parties, including the one who judges. What appears as a clever way to sidestep metaphysical debates about minds is in fact a miniature constitution for evaluation.

The Imitation Game reads like a warning written in unassuming clothes. It shows that legitimate judgment depends on the separation of powers within the act of judging. The authority to define the terms must not be identical to the authority to execute them. The authority to execute must not be identical to the authority to declare what execution means. When those powers collapse into one, speed increases, but legitimacy evaporates.

Turing's design choice was to force the powerful temptation of instant recognition into the slower discipline of procedure. He treated evaluation as something that must be constitutionalized, even when it is only named a game.

Turing's mind, always two steps ahead of the world's metaphors, had already implied what follows from collapsed roles. When the same entity both asks and answers, when the same authority writes the rules and declares compliance, the outcome is domination, not knowledge.

That is where the Imitation Game becomes prophetic—not because it predicts machines that talk but because it reveals the political anatomy of evaluation itself.

Now move forward, not by decades but by a change in ambience. The light is not the lamplight of a small room, where judgment is slowed into procedure, but the clean glow of a phone screen, where judgment arrives as a default. The defendant is an ordinary man in Detroit—a husband and a worker—named Robert Williams, who in 2020 became a protagonist in a story that should have been impossible in a society that believes it has learned from its own mistakes.

A store was robbed. Security footage existed. The police wanted speed, and speed has a way of presenting itself as a virtue. Someone ran a face recognition search. A machine returned a match. It was wrong. Robert Williams was arrested in front of his family. He was detained for roughly a day, processed like a certainty, and treated as if the mere existence of a match had converted suspicion into truth.

The details that matter are the following:

Who accused him? An algorithm presented as an objective witness.

Who investigated the accusation? The same institutional pipeline that had already decided the tool was reliable enough to use.

Who judged the evidence? A process in which the machine's output carried an aura of inevitability, and the human discretion that should have served as a check behaved instead like a rubber stamp.

Who explained the reasoning? Almost nobody because the system had been designed to move rather than to justify.

In the rules of the game, Turing had insisted on an interrogator who could be wrong and who must bear the weight of deciding. In the Detroit arrest, the interrogator was dispersed across a workflow that allowed responsibility to evaporate. Each actor could say they merely followed procedure. The officer could say the computer flagged him. The technician could say the model produced a score. The vendor could say the human made the final call. And in that circular passing of the buck, the oldest legal question becomes unanswerable.

Who, exactly, wielded power.

This is the moment when modern algorithmic authority reveals its real shape: a sociotechnical organism that sets the terms of visibility and credibility, distributes risk and opportunity, and decides whose account of reality will count, behind a curtain of proprietary opacity. It is, in effect, a private state embedded in daily life.

In Turing's setup, the interrogator could not also be a respondent. The rules were established before the exchange began. The medium prevented coercion by presence. Even the goal was modest: a probabilistic judgment, not a claim of metaphysical certainty.

Many contemporary systems invert each of those safeguards.

The platform writes the policy, often as product, tuned by incentives rather than by public reason. The platform enforces instantly, not as a last resort but as a default. The platform adjudicates through automated appeals, templated replies, or silence, sometimes via systems that learn from previous enforcement rather than from principle. And because the platform is not a court, it can call its decisions service quality, safety, trust, or community standards. Words that soothe, words that blur.

In that triadic test, the judge must listen to the defendant speak. In the modern algorithmic order, the defendant is often muted by design.

Robert Williams did not consent to play this game, yet he was forced into it. And unlike Turing's thought experiment, the procedure was built to move, not to check the answer itself. The algorithm functioned as a witness and insinuation. The institution treated output as authority. The individual bore the burden of disproving a machine's suggestion, which is to say he bore the burden of disproving an entire system's appetite for frictionless certainty.

The most stable form of power is the one that trains the dominated to call it convenience. A person learns to accept opaque verdicts because fighting them is exhausting. They learn to internalize the platform's categories, to optimize themselves into legibility, to anticipate sanctions, and to preemptively comply.

They learn a form of "dependautonomy," a life in which the promise of agency is delivered only through the channels of dependency.

It is tempting to treat the old phrase "code is law" as rhetoric until you realize it is no longer a metaphor. It is a jurisdiction that travels in your pocket.

Turing, who understood both the seduction of formal systems and the danger of confusing formality with fairness, gave us a clue that we ignored. The question is not whether machines can imitate humans. The question is whether we have built institutions that imitate constitutional restraint; whether we still believe that judgment without explanation is merely force wearing a clerical collar; whether we still accept that liberty needs delay, appeal, and humanly comprehensible reasons.

From the age of thrones and statutes, the story of separated powers tells of an order where each branch distrusts the others enough to force accountability into the daylight. The algorithmic age now unfolding tells of an order where distrust has been replaced by integration. Everything is streamlined end to end. The rule becomes a parameter. Enforcement becomes a trigger. Appeals become a user-experience flow. Justice becomes customer support.

And the most chilling twist is that the system can be sincerely convinced that it is neutral. It will tell you it has no intent, only optimization. It will tell you it does not punish; it merely ranks. It will tell you it does not discriminate; it merely predicts. It will tell you it does not govern; it merely serves.

That is how post-constitutional power speaks. It speaks in the grammar of technical necessity.

Not because algorithms are intelligent, but because they have become the architecture through which power is exercised without the old, visible ceremonies of power. Markets concentrate, platforms become quasi-sovereign, code becomes policy, enforcement becomes instantaneous, and private justice systems become normal enough to feel natural. The citizen becomes a user. Rights become settings. Law becomes terms.

Read carefully, Turing's test is as much a test of imitated intelligence as it is a model of how to structure power so that judgment does not become imitation. It assumes a space where reasons can be given and contested. It is, in its understated way, a miniature trias politica.

The tragedy is that we took the talking machine and discarded the constitutional lesson.

If a future society wants to keep the benefits of computation without surrendering its civic spine, it will have to do what Turing did in that quiet room with cold tea. It will have to design roles, split powers, and reintroduce friction where it protects dignity. It will have to build courts into code rather than let code become the court. It will have to educate originators, not just operators, because the people who set the rules are already making law, whether they admit it or not.

In the imitation triad, the interrogator must confront uncertainty and own the decision.

The old Imitation Game was built for adversaries. It assumed conflict and used structure to make conflict productive. It also assumed that the urge to declare certainty would push, so it created places for that urge to collide with procedure, to be slowed, and to be questioned.

That imitation begins with separation, and that separation is the hidden protagonist. It makes it possible for truth to travel from suspicion to evidence to judgment. It creates a path that no single actor can fully seal.

The new Imitation Game is built as an integrated stack powering autonomous decision-making, where uncertainty becomes the hidden protagonist and decisions are made ownerless. It asks what happens to accountability and contestability, and more importantly, what happens to dignity and cognitive sovereignty when the test setting becomes the world and the world adopts AI systems that do not separate the powers of rule-making, enforcement, and judgment but fuse them into a single automated continuum.

In Manchester, 1950, where he turned a parlor game into a discipline of restraint, Turing knew that the interrogator asks believing that judgment can be earned through procedure. The respondents answer believing that rules can bind the encounter. The medium holds, believing that distance can prevent shortcuts and coercion.

The next chapter of that belief cannot be written only in proprietary code. It has to be written in constitutional safeguards and procedures designed to govern these architectures, ensuring that algorithmic powers do not exclusively decide what people see, what they can do, what they are offered, and what they are allowed to contest, and that these decisions remain bound by legitimate rules.

This is where the Imitation Game becomes more than history. It becomes an inverted mirror.

Not to say that history repeats, but to show how the shape of judgment changes when the separation of powers collapses. And to suggest, with the smallest hint of Turing's own controlled defiance, that the most urgent question is no longer whether machines can think.

It is whether we can keep their powers within legitimate bounds.

This is the aim of this book.

Chapter 1, Source of Algorithmic Powers, traces where today's AI-driven power actually comes from, weaving together unconventional market monopoly dynamics with the way machine-intelligence ecosystems have become governing environments that operate beyond or ahead of constitutional checks. It explains how concentrated, AI-integrated infrastructures turn code into law and policy into a product, enabling rules to be written, updated, and applied unilaterally through technical design. It then shows how this produces enforcement at machine speed—instant, opaque, and scalable—and culminates in the emergence of private justice systems, where disputes, penalties, access, and legitimacy are increasingly decided by corporate procedures and automated governance rather than by public institutions.

Chapter 2, Mechanism of Algorithmic Powers, explains how algorithmic power takes hold and sustains itself, often through adoption dynamics rather than direct coercion. It dissects the "adoption engine" behind "technological Stockholm syndrome" and shows how convenience, pressure, and normalization can create attachment to systems that reduce autonomy, leading to the manufacture of "dependautonomy," a sense of empowerment that masks deepening dependence. It then challenges the promise of "human-in-the-loop" by mapping a spectrum of roles in which humans can become compliance instruments, sometimes effectively "on a leash," displaced, distributed, or even absorbed by the loop. It concludes by positioning trust as a permission layer because once trust is granted, it becomes the social and psychological authorization that allows automated governance to expand with limited scrutiny.

Chapter 3, Algorithmic-Defined Human Worth, examines how algorithmic systems reshape the way human value is measured, rewarded, and recognized in modern organizations and societies. It shows how work is revalued through data-driven mechanisms that privilege what can be captured, compared, and optimized, accelerating the "taskification" of work into discrete, measurable units. This shift produces a new "human worth limit," where dignity and contribution risk being reduced to performance signals, rankings, and compliance with machine-readable criteria. The chapter also highlights how these valuation systems can amplify unequal burdens along gendered lines, while exploring "human in(ter)ference" as the culturally and institutionally necessary defense to preserve agency, judgment, and legitimacy against the seductions of speed, scale, and algorithmic inevitability.

Chapter 4, Humane Algorithmic Transition, outlines what it takes to shift from rapid AI adoption to responsible AI deployment that protects people, institutions, and democratic accountability. It begins by challenging the flawed assumptions behind AI decision-making, especially the belief that prediction, optimization, or scale can substitute for judgment, legitimacy, and context. It then proposes a practical framework of "9 Whats" to interrogate the deployment of algorithmic power, clarifying what is being automated, for whom, at what cost, and with what underlying implications. The chapter reframes the Jevons paradox as a political and organizational dynamic rather than an inevitability, arguing that AI efficiency gains can expand harmful or low-value uses unless constrained. It therefore calls for governance at the macro level that sets boundaries, allocates accountability, and steers deployment toward collective outcomes, while insisting that education must be reinvented to give birth to and nurture originators and creators over operators, for humans to cultivate and sustain an edge in shaping society.

Chapter 5, Algorithmic Constitutionality, argues that widespread algorithmic use quietly shifts the burden of governance into technical systems, often without the visibility, debate, and legitimacy that constitutional order requires. It shows how automated decision flows can conceal where power sits and how it is exercised and then makes the case for restoring friction to the algorithmic order through deliberate constraints, contestability, and slower, accountable points of intervention. The chapter proposes algorithmic safety cases as constitutional safeguards that force systems to justify their authority, limits, and risk controls before they operate at scale. It then advances eight principles of an algorithmic separation of powers that distributes design, oversight, and enforcement functions to prevent concentration and self-judging systems and concludes by testing the trias algorithmica as a practical model for ensuring that algorithmic governance remains bounded, reviewable, and fit for purpose in the society it serves.

1 Source of Algorithmic Powers

From Market Concentration to Post-Constitutional AI Power

If we would not accept a political system in which the same hands hold, all at once, the power to write laws in a secret language no citizen can read, enforce them wholly at their discretion, and serve as the sole judge of compliance for themselves and for everyone else, why then would we accept a company's AI system doing so?

For over two millennia, leaders have wrestled with a simple problem that keeps returning in new guises: concentrated power corrodes judgment. Aristotle's political philosophy starts from purpose and virtue rather than technical architecture.[1] He argues that a community must order itself toward worthy ends, that institutions should cultivate prudence, and that offices left unchecked tend to drift toward overreach.[2] He shows that durable regimes do not entrust everything to one principle or one class; they mix forms, temper passions, and embed habits of review so practical wisdom can meet particular cases.[3]

In Aristotle's terms, the danger is not only tyranny as a regime type but a more general slide into pleonexia, grasping beyond rightful bounds, when ends, means, and interpretation reside in the same hands.[4]

In this early formulation, the phenomenon is already mechanical, not merely moral: when the authority to declare purpose, the capacity to act on that purpose, and the privilege to excuse or justify those actions are allowed to fuse, excess becomes a structurally likely outcome. The slide into overreach follows from the structure itself.

Montesquieu translates that philosophical insight into an operating system for modern states. Liberty, in his account, is secured when rule-making, rule-executing, and rule-adjudicating are institutionally distinct yet mutually dependent.[5] Each branch can say no to the others; none can exercise the whole power, and all are forced to justify their actions in the open.[6]

Separation of powers is an anti-tyranny technology.

As state capacity scales, so must countervailing mechanisms, vetoes, oversight, and transparency, so that speed does not become arbitrariness and force does not replace reason.

The separation encodes a practical law of stability: if one locus of authority can simultaneously invent the rules, enforce them, and ratify its own conduct, the result is a self-sealing authority loop that becomes structurally uncontestable, even when aims are benevolent. Where those roles are pried apart and forced into dialogue, ambition is made to check ambition and power is made to restrain power.

AI development today revives this old problem in a technical form.

Unlike most prior mass infrastructures, the integrated AI stack combines the capacity to write unreadable law, enforce it ubiquitously, and self-certify its fairness—functions that together constitute a single governance-capable power applied across populations at a historically unusual scale and speed, acting as a de facto regulator of social and economic life.

What emerges is not merely a powerful product but a vertically integrated technological socio-system that defines norms, compels adherence, and declares itself legitimate, with limited or no meaningful external hearing.

This is the core mechanism of algorithmic power concentration. It is precisely what the trias algorithmica, as a principle of algorithmic power separation, is meant to prevent.

Acknowledging that AI can influence decisions is merely scratching the surface. The deeper phenomenon is that it consolidates legislative, executive, and judicial functions within a single technical pipeline.

Algorithms and guardrails function as the system's laws. It is the code.[7]

Just like the penal code, the civil code, the labor code, or any code defined by the legislative branch, algorithmic code produces normative and sanctioning effects: it shapes the effective exercise of freedoms (to move, to obtain information, to work), steers behavior, and can generate systemic discrimination.

It grants rights, distributes advantages, or imposes penalties (access, price, visibility, reputation), and can decide on measures with immediate economic and social consequences. It settles matters of fact and arbitrates conflicts of interest (resource allocation, ratings, eligibility). It exercises a de facto regulatory power.[8] It ranks, filters, authorizes, prohibits, and sanctions, often in real time, and its cumulative effects on individuals and markets are comparable to those of written law. In that sense, product policy becomes a species of private legislation. The model's learned preferences, ranking functions, and safety layers silently define who is visible, what is permissible, and which forms of conduct are rewarded or buried. The authority to encode these preferences is, in effect, functionally close to, if not equivalent to, the authority to draft a code of conduct for whole populations.

In the classical order, law is public language: it can be read, cited, interpreted, and argued over.

Platform policy preserves the appearance of that form. It offers reasons in text. But in AI-governed systems, the binding norm increasingly takes a different form: not a paragraph but a behavior. Policy is the statute; eligibility, ranking, and refusal are the operative law. It governs by consequences in distribution rather than by reasons in language. This is an "unreadable law": not that policy text vanishes, but that authority migrates to the operational layer, where contestation must reverse-engineer outcomes instead of interpreting rules.

Data pipelines supply the facts and enactment, while compute is the force multiplier for execution. This duality of resources creates an executive power, much like government's: pipelines operate as the administrative apparatus, from data curation and model training to collecting, certifying, and formatting "official" facts, then drafting and routing machine-readable directives, and setting the agendas that downstream systems must follow. Deployment behaves like the civil service, instantiating those directives into workflows, application programming interfaces (APIs), and agents that act on people and markets in real time. Compute then furnishes the coercive capacity: speed that outpaces human oversight, scale that touches entire populations at once, and persistence that keeps decisions in force through caching, replication, and automation—functional analogs to policing, logistics, and treasury. Together, they do not just process decisions; they govern, allocating visibility, opportunity, and sanction with the continuity and reach of an executive branch.

Once information intake, decision routing, and enforcement all sit under the same roof, execution stops looking like "service delivery" and starts looking like executive governance administration. The entity that owns the pipeline and the compute does not merely offer a function; it can, in practice, come to assume the standing to decide agendas, establish facts, and impose them at industrial scale.[9]

The tests of the model used to validate its functioning, quality, safety, and integrity establish the nature of a power analogous to judicial power, in that they authorize the decision to accept its behaviors as compliant and legitimate to exist and act within society. In this sense, they amount to a trial-like technical process: procedural requirements (protocols, acceptance criteria, thresholds), burden of proof (empirical evidence, reproducibility), traceability chain (datasets, versions, logs), adversarial process (adversarial tests, independent reviews), proportionality (risk vs. use assessment), right of appeal (reexamination, counter-expert review), and a sanctions regime (remediation, usage restrictions, withdrawal of certification). Like case law, test suites and their results form a body of precedents (regressions/evolutions) that holds designers accountable and conditions the authorization to deploy, as well as its suspension or revocation. In other words, the model's trial stands in for a hearing; the evidence stands in for a ruling; traceability serves as a chain of custody; the adversarial principle guarantees fairness; and certification amounts to a judgment, subject to appeal (reaudit) and to sanctions (rollback, containment, kill switch) in the event of noncompliance.

When these evaluation rituals are internal, their function drifts.[10] What presents itself as adjudication doubles as self-ratification: the same actor drafts the criteria, runs the tests, interprets the outcome, and records the precedent. The forum, the law, and the verdict collapse into a single loop. The appearance of due process survives; the independence of judgment does not.

In combining these three powers, the same actor writes the code that sets the rules (legislative), builds the pipelines and compute that execute them at scale (executive), and designs the tests and metrics that certify compliance (judicial), thus defining the objectives, curating the evidence, interpreting the results, and retaining the capacity to enforce all three, everywhere and at once.

It is nothing less than the concentration of power Enlightenment constitutionalism tried to prevent.

At that point, the question ceases to be whether a system is "capable," "fair," or "safe" in isolation and becomes whether it has de facto assumed a sovereignty-like structure of governance functions. The trajectory tends to drift toward partial objective maximization rather than deliberative calibration: selective visibility, unchallengeable denials, automated sanction without recourse. As a result, that fusion creates tyranny risk in a modern key: private norm-setting without democratic process,[11] informational capture through control of data,[12] opaque adjudication inside closed models,[13] and capacity asymmetries that make contestation impractical.[14]

As this logic extends, in weaker form, to traditional software, where technical architecture functions as a mode of regulation,[15] it is essential to highlight how dramatically power concentration intensifies when the architecture is an AI system. While non-AI software governs by rules and execution, its code is at least legible in its normative logic: operative rules are explicitly written, decision paths can be inspected, and behavior can often be anticipated in advance through specification, testing, and reproducible execution. When power-concentration effects arise, they remain more readily contestable because the governing procedures are deterministic and, in principle, interpretable and debuggable, allowing disputes to be argued at the level of reasons rather than reconstructed solely from outcomes.

In contrast, the AI stack is characterized by opaque and emergent power: the "legislative" function resides in the model weights, making the rules implicit, nontransparent, and often unintelligible even to the designers; the "executive" power is multiplied by compute at unprecedented scale and speed, allowing for continuous, real-time, population-wide application of these opaque rules; and the "judicial" function of testing becomes an internal substitute for external ethical, social, and legal legitimacy, making governance reliant on the very actor that is being governed. This vertical fusion of power, artificially amplified, constitutes the systemic threat that necessitates the trias algorithmica.

The problem is not just who controls the AI, but that the design of the integrated AI stack is itself anti-constitutional.

In that configuration, prediction follows almost trivially. A world that tolerates such fusion will tend toward private absolutism, in which capability hardens into authority and authority resists challenge by design. A world that forces those functions apart, subjects them to outside review, and preserves channels of appeal and reversal will tend toward contestability, pluralism, and institutional resilience. The future forks on that structural choice.

Finally, and by no means least, every form of power presupposes a material base: organized infrastructures and resource flows that convert authority, however legally articulated, into real effects.[16]

This is an essential element that sits comfortably within Aristotle's realism about what sustains regimes and that Montesquieu likewise understood when he made liberty depend not only on the division of powers but on the practical means by which power is provisioned, financed, and sustained.

Constitutions may divide functions, laws may constrain intent, and institutions may distribute roles, but none of them can sustainably operate without a reservoir of force that can be mobilized on demand. In human history, this reservoir has typically taken a material form: the grain stores of the polis, the gold reserves of monarchies, the fiscal budgets of modern states. Different as they look, each is a way of storing and mobilizing energy in some form.[17]

To speak of artificial power without speaking of the energy that sustains it is to describe a government without a treasury. Among the material foundations of that energetic base are the mines and refineries that supply copper and rare earths, the industrial chains that turn silica into silicon and wafers, the water and cooling systems that keep computation within thermal limits, the power plants and transmission grids that deliver usable current, and the data-center stack that concentrates it all into executable capacity. There is one element in particular without which every other component becomes inoperative: electricity.

The rise of large-scale computation reintroduces a treasury constraint into the architecture of intelligence, taking the form of an energetic tax.

Electricity functions as the treasury substrate of artificial power because it is the scarce, priced, allocable resource that must be continuously spent to keep AI-intensive computation and thus governance-like effects running. In other words, training and deploying a frontier model is a transformation of energy into computation.[18] The expenditure of megawatts and the supply of silicon-based compute define the limits of what can be thought and enforced by machines. In that sense, energy constitutes the budget of artificial reason, and the apparent abstraction of code rests upon a physical economy whose fluctuations determine the scope of machine cognition. AI does not legislate, execute, or adjudicate without first drawing upon this treasury of watts.

The concentration of energy required by contemporary AI is starting to reshape both geography and sovereignty. Data centers cluster near cheap electricity and stable climates, creating new industrial provinces whose economic gravity rivals that of ports and capitals. Control over the energy grid increasingly determines who can train models, at what scale, and how often they can retrain them. The old political question, who controls the mint, returns in a new key: who controls access to electricity, when the capacity to convert watts into cognition becomes the new treasury of algorithmic power.

This dependency transforms energy from a mere utility into an instrument of political leverage. The ability to ration, subsidize, or withhold power becomes the ability to regulate AI itself. When the same entities that design the models also control the infrastructure that feed them, fiscal constraint vanishes. The restraint that once came from budgetary deliberation or parliamentary approval is replaced by automatic access to self-financed capacity. Artificial systems thus acquire something akin to monetary sovereignty: they can mint new inferences, expand enforcement, and reproduce themselves so long as energy flows unimpeded. The result can resemble a regime without fiscal discipline, one in which expenditure follows appetite rather than deliberation.

The immediate challenge is allocative in constrained and near-term contexts. In capacity-constrained grid hotspots, prioritizing megawatts for AI-related data-center load can crowd out scarce grid headroom and lengthen connection queues, effectively delaying other societal loads and electrification, including homes, hospitals, schools, public transport, and industry, and tightening the short-run pathway to decarbonization unless supply and networks grow fast enough.[19]

Choosing to privilege algorithmic compute under such constraints is a political decision about who gets the watts, who gets the wait, and which futures are denied weight. Each calculation consumes a portion of the world's capacity to sustain order. Each layer of automation increases the draw upon that shared resource.[18]

In the meantime, the planetary signal is no abstraction: data centers already consume a material share of global electricity and are projected to rise sharply within this decade,[20] with company footprints climbing despite large clean power purchases. The means additional AI load will often be met at the margin by fossil generation if clean supply, storage, and transmission do not expand in step.[21] To recognize energy as the treasury of artificial power is to acknowledge that intelligence, however synthetic, remains embedded in the finite.

The classical balance between executive power and the treasury has historically been essential to political stability.[22] The executive may desire action, but the treasury must consent. In the algorithmic order, this consent is mechanized. Energy infrastructures authorize execution by default, not by debate. The flow of electrons substitutes for the vote of assemblies.

Yet the very power that energy confers, by supercharging cognition artificially, becomes the highest stakes threshold once it enables the algorithmic fusion of legislative, executive, and judicial powers in the hands of a single actor, thereby making institutional accountability a requirement of legitimacy.

In this light, the legitimacy of algorithmic power will depend not only on whether its legislative, executive, and judicial functions are placed under constitutional discipline but also on how prudently and fairly it spends the world's energetic capital. The unchecked fusion of the three powers thus finds its material counterpart in the unexamined appetite for energy. Both reflect the same underlying drift: the replacement of deliberation by automatic expansion.

A genuine constitution for artificial systems would therefore have to include an energetic article: a recognition that every act of computation is akin to a fiscal act. It behaves like a budgeted expenditure and, without being taxation, carries similar implications: it draws down a finite treasury and should invite treasury-like discipline.

It would imply transparency about energy-budget allocation toward training runs, inference capacity, system expansion, and proportionality between algorithmic power's public interest and its material cost.

It would also entail energetic conditionality that denies unbounded power to fused stacks by design, tying access to scale, continuity, and expansion to external authorization, the separability of functions, and enforceable limits, together with the subordination of ambition to planetary accounting.

Energetic conditionality could operate through tiered power and interconnection approvals that require independent audits and appeal channels, and through data-center operating permits that condition expansion on third-party evaluation access and traceable compliance evidence.

Taken together, they would function as the tax code and public audit office of algorithmic power.[9]

Without such an approach, the algorithmic order remains post-constitutional in a deeper sense than its founders may admit: it draws endlessly from a treasury it neither sees nor reconciles.

Energy thus completes the case for the trias algorithmica.

If code writes the laws, data and compute execute them, and tests adjudicate their legitimacy, energy becomes the ability to regulate AI capacity and scale. Because energy can be rationed, priced, and conditioned, it becomes a lever through which societies may decide under what purposes and constraints such an order is allowed to expand. To overlook it is to mistake the form of power for its substance.

The real constitution of machine intelligence is not only logical but physical. Its clauses are written in circuits, its amendments are negotiated with entropy, and its treasury is paid in light.

Monopoly Is Too Small a Wor(l)d

The anti-constitutional design of the integrated AI stack, characterized by structural hostility to separation of powers, due process, and meaningful exit in many jurisdictions, is neither desirable nor inevitable, and it has an origin.

This system emerged and installed itself steadily for roughly three decades since the early internet era, in part because it lacked a name. Indeed, what human beings cannot name or define does not exist institutionally. That is why the greatest trick the devil ever performed was to convince the world he didn't exist.[23] Humanity grants existence to things by naming them.[24]

Politically, the unchecked concentration of governing power in a single entity names a classical route to tyranny.[25] Economically, the unchecked concentration of market power in a single entity names a classical route to monopoly. So the question is why institutions ended up allowing the concentration of algorithmic power to take hold in the hands of integrated AI platforms without systematically considering prohibiting it. Why did we not mobilize the ordinary checks, new laws, supervisory agencies, and litigation that modern democracies normally deploy when a private actor accumulates excessive power?

Because it is a monopoly of a meaningfully different kind: a new nature of monopoly that was built in front of our eyes and that had no precedent, no established framework, and no word to define it. Without a shared name across the vocabularies that govern power, whether legal, economic, or regulatory, it escapes the normal sequence of constitutional defense: there is little for legislators to prohibit, little for regulators to supervise, and little for courts to punish. That vacuum is precisely where this new form of dominance established itself. In that vacuum, the integrated AI platform does not need to win by blocking competitors in one decisive move. It wins by becoming the default formatting layer through which others must operate.

Until recently, economic theory and competition law essentially distinguished between two main types of monopoly: the exogenous monopoly and the endogenous monopoly.

An exogenous monopoly is a situation in which an actor's monopolistic position is granted or protected by a force external to the market itself. It is "generated from the outside." Historically, this includes exclusive public concessions, patents, unique licenses, tailor-made regulatory barriers, or reserved access to a strategic resource. In such a case, the dominant firm does not become unique simply because it was the most competitive under free-market conditions, but because it is explicitly granted, legally, politically, and administratively, the right to be alone.[26] The barrier to entry is therefore imposed from outside the competitive game. Without this exogenous protection, other actors could in principle enter the market and challenge the dominant position. In this classical pattern, one can usually point to the public authority. Responsibility is traceable. Power is, at least in theory, accountable.

An endogenous monopoly, by contrast, is the exact inverse: it is born from within the economic system itself. This covers cases in which the market's internal economic structure naturally produces a single winner and discourages any viable competitor. The classic examples are so-called natural monopolies: sectors where fixed costs are gigantic (infrastructure, networks, energy distribution, certain logistics platforms), but the marginal cost of serving one more customer becomes extremely low once the infrastructure exists.[27] In such a context, duplicating the infrastructure is economically inefficient: a single actor ends up serving the entire market. The monopoly results mechanically from economies of scale, internal network effects, and cumulative advantages linked to size rather than from political imposition. This form of monopoly can then be reinforced by technological superiority, cost optimization, self-reinforcing user-base effects,[28] and so on. Here, the barrier to entry is not an external prohibition but a practical economic impossibility. In this second pattern, the law traditionally steps in after the fact: legislators draft antitrust rules, executive agencies intervene in abuse of dominant position, and courts can order remedies or breakups. Again, the three powers know where to aim because cause and effect can still be identified and argued. Even when endogenous monopolies include network effects, their causal story remains comparatively compact. The explanation can be told as one dominant dynamic such as scale, fixed cost, or user-base reinforcement. That compactness matters because it makes intervention conceptually and procedurally feasible.

These two frameworks, exogenous and endogenous, still structure most regulatory thinking today about the concentration of economic power. They underpin how competition authorities assess abuses of dominant position: either one looks for a favor, an exclusivity, an illegitimate privilege (exogenous logic), or one observes a dominance arising from an internal superiority that is extremely hard to catch up with (endogenous logic). But this binary is no longer sufficient. It is outdated and has been for too long. It is outdated because it assumes that the concentration of power always leaves a visible fingerprint, one that the legislature can outlaw, that regulators can target, and that courts can sanction. What has emerged in the last three decades is a form of dominance that diffuses that fingerprint so effectively that it slips between the hands of all three. Its core advantage is not that it hides its effects, but that it fragments its causes. It does not win by a single moat but by the interlock of many small moats, each defensible, each rational, and each reversible in theory, until their totality becomes irreversible in practice.

This old binary failed to acknowledge the birth of a new kind of monopoly: the "aggregogenous monopoly." If an exogenous monopoly is granted and an endogenous monopoly is grown, an aggregogenous monopoly is assembled. It is assembled by the ecosystem itself as it adapts, standardizes, trains, contracts, integrates, and optimizes around a single control surface.

By "aggregogenous monopoly," I refer to a lock-in situation in which an actor's monopolistic position comes neither from an explicit legal privilege nor solely from an internal economic advantage but from the progressive, distributed aggregation of multiple dependencies around that actor. In other words, there is no single discrete market transaction that "grants" the monopoly; there is an ecosystemic convergence that produces it. Because of this illegibility of its harm at the time, the legislature struggles to define a specific abuse to outlaw. Because there is no obvious breach to enforce, the executive apparatus struggles to justify intervention. Because there is no clear violation to adjudicate, the judiciary struggles to assign liability. The integrated AI platform accumulates structural power without ever triggering a recognizable constitutional alarm.

From the outside, an aggregogenous monopoly often looks like things we already know how to describe, so observers reach for known labels.

It can be mistaken for network effects explaining why everyone piles into the same service; it can be mistaken for switching costs explaining why leaving is painful; it can be mistaken for vertical integration explaining why one firm controls many layers; it can be mistaken for product dominance explaining why a superior offering wins; it can be mistaken for platformization explaining why more activity passes through one intermediary.

All of that can be true at the same time and still not capture the core issue because none of those categories capture its decisive trait. The decisive trait is that the integrated AI platform stops being only an intermediary between buyers and sellers, creators and audiences, and developers and users.

It becomes the place where the rules of participation are made, applied, and validated, so it also controls how its own power can be challenged. Such a platform does not merely intermediate the market; it internalizes the conditions under which the market can be contested.

An aggregogenous monopoly emerges when multiple technological components make it possible to concentrate an anti-constitutional form of power by placing something akin to legislative, executive, and judicial functions within the same central platform owned by a single private company. Over time, this platform becomes the infrastructure of first resort, initially out of practical necessity, whether driven by coordination, compatibility, or convenience. Not because it was politically granted exclusivity (exogenous monopoly). Not because the market's internal cost structure inherently collapses toward a single efficient provider (endogenous monopoly), but because the wider technological ecosystem slowly reorients itself around that platform, creating a web of dependencies. It is more than a simple product; it is a stack. Its dominance is stack-based because it couples multiple critical layers that others must traverse such as model access, APIs, fine-tuning, data formats, pipelines, compute allocation, security controls, compliance tooling, auditability interfaces, and vertical workflow integrations. What matters is not integration in the ordinary industrial sense but co-dependence across layers that used to be separable.

No single barrier to entry is, on its own, insurmountable.[29] But the interdependencies between critical technology components, taken together, create a de facto barrier.[30] The lock-in is produced by the technological ecosystem itself and is continuously reinforced by continued use of the service. It is not granted, but socially, technically, and economically consolidated through aggregation. This means the effective center of coordination is no longer parliament, nor a ministry, nor a court. It is the integrated AI platform itself. This platform becomes the place where norms are defined, enforced, and disputed,[31] which is to say: it effectively begins to perform legislative, executive, and judicial functions for the entire ecosystem that depends on it. A useful way to see the difference is that endogenous monopoly concentrates value, exogenous monopoly concentrates privilege, while aggregogenous monopoly concentrates governance. Network effects can help a platform win users. Aggregation makes that same platform the rule-maker, the enforcer, and the judge for those users and the institutions around them.

This third type of monopoly is precisely the one deployed by today's major AI platforms at scale.

The dominant actors in AI are becoming the infrastructure on which everything else connects, spanning model and compute services, the integration layer that binds systems together, and the governance layer that operationalizes security, compliance, and auditability, including the methodologies of work.[32] Around them, an ecosystem forms: service providers, integrators, consulting firms, independent developers, and industrial clients all adapt their internal processes to remain compatible with that specific platform. Talent is trained to use these tools. Intellectual property and confidentiality clauses are drafted in the legal language of these tools. Operational data flows are cleaned, structured, and aligned with the formats these tools expect. Management dashboards, performance metrics, and decision workflows—down to the daily cognitive reflexes of teams—end up depending on this same technological layer.

This is where dependency aggregation stops being mainly about a venue in which different actors participate and becomes an inversion of platform participation itself. The platform becomes a participant embedded in the technical, social, and cultural infrastructures of society. It binds not only customers but also creators, publishers, advertisers, developers, integrators, researchers, auditors, regulators, and others into the same compatibility regime. The ecosystem that should check power gradually becomes conditioned by the stack that exercises it.

At that point, the platform effectively writes the rules of engagement (a quasi-legislative role); enforces acceptable behavior through access controls, rate limits, and policy enforcement (a quasi-executive role); and arbitrates disputes, for example, over IP, model behavior, safety thresholds, or allowed use in ways that function like internal courts (a quasi-judicial role). This triad is a governance pipeline. In particular, the judicial function is reproduced through verdict-shaped evidence, including internal monitoring data, benchmarks, scorecards, and evaluation rituals that outsiders cannot easily replicate or falsify.

The result is a lock-in that is not only technological but also organizational, cultural, and cognitive. Leaving the platform no longer means simply switching vendors. Leaving means reconfiguring the technical architecture, renegotiating contractual agreements, migrating or retranslating data, retraining teams, redefining internal processes, rewriting compliance policies, and, in some cases, relearning how to think and decide. In other words, remaining captive becomes rational. Once remaining captive becomes rational, the traditional constitutional safeguards become reactive and symbolic. Lawmakers can gesture, regulators can fine, courts can arbitrate individual harms, but none of that easily restores exit because exit is now structurally, contractually, and culturally unaffordable. This is the crucial difference between ordinary switching costs and aggregogenous captivity. In a normal market, switching is painful but bounded. Here, switching is psychologically unsafe within the organization, generating fear of missing out (FOMO), because the platform has formatted not only tools but also the criteria by which work is evaluated and decisions are justified.

To traditional regulators, this kind of lock-in does not present itself as a monopoly and therefore does not trigger legacy antitrust and constitutional defenses. Neither the privilege template nor the natural-monopoly template applies. Instead, there is something more diffuse and more contemporary: a systemic capture through the aggregation of interdependencies. The integrated AI platform becomes the center of gravity of an ecosystem that gradually seals itself around it. Its consolidation remains narratable as ordinary market behavior at every step. Integration looks like efficiency, standardization looks like interoperability, dependency looks like adoption, and governance looks like product policy. This very vocabulary of innovation supplies plausible deniability.

And because every individual step of this consolidation appears voluntary, courts may see contracts, not coercion; agencies may see partnerships, not capture; legislators may see market maturation, not annexation.[33] The three branches, each in its own way, are made to interpret structural dependence as mere market law. The practical consequence is that the platform begins to capture the conditions of contestation. It can constrain the audit surface, control the evidentiary timeline, and set the measurement standards by which harm and compliance are evaluated, thereby influencing what can be proven, by whom, and when. Even when formal appeal channels exist, the platform retains asymmetric control over the forum, the data, and the interpretive machinery.

This is the aggregogenous monopoly signature: a form of economic domination in which collective dependence on a single actor becomes so deep, and so costly to reverse, that the actor acquires monopoly-like power while still being able to claim, technically and legally, that it was never granted a monopoly and that competition remains free in principle.

This is how a private platform can aggregate into legislative, executive, and judicial functions while remaining formally just a company.

This new form of monopoly is an institutional displacement. What is being captured, ultimately, is not only revenue streams or data flows but the practical locus of governance: who writes the rules, who enforces them, and who judges compliance with the rules.[34] When that entire cycle migrates inside a private infrastructure, sovereignty itself is no longer fully public.

The decisive signal of maturity is when the platform's private governance stack becomes a socio-normative code, signaling norms, shaping incentives, and imposing cultural conformity pressure by which economic participation, reputational survival, and operational legitimacy are obtained, while competition remains rhetorically available.

This ends up being much more than market dominance. Aggregogenous monopoly is constitutional capture without formal sovereignty.

The Post-Constitutional Platform Era

Facebook offers a useful case for understanding the concentration of executive, legislative, and judicial power enabled by this new breed of monopoly: the aggregogenous monopoly.

Seen in retrospect, the interest of Facebook here is methodological: this AI-powered social platform has been a canonical early prototype of algorithmic power concentration, making visible the need for the trias algorithmica that I define.

Long before frontier language models, Facebook operationalized machine-learning governance through opaque ranking models that behave like unreadable law, automated integrity pipelines that apply those rules at population scale, and internally produced metrics that present compliance as established fact.

In its early years and well into its hypergrowth period, Facebook positioned itself as a neutral layer of infrastructure, a place where people posted and shared and where the company's job was simply to connect them.[35,36]

Company leadership repeatedly stressed that Facebook was a platform, not a publisher, meaning that it did not see itself as having editorial responsibility for what users said or saw and therefore could not be held to the same standards of intentional curation as a media outlet.[37] Moderation in that phase was mostly reactive and largely human. Harmful, abusive, or rule-violating posts were taken down if other users flagged them or if a moderation team noticed them in specific cases, but enforcement was episodic, labor-intensive, and fundamentally downstream of the content's spread.[38] When criticism did surface, Facebook's defense was essentially procedural: "We don't write what people say, we just host it." That line began to crack around 2015 and 2016 under pressure from two converging shocks.

First, the "Trending Topics" dispute raised the allegation that Facebook's own human curators were behind the scenes suppressing or boosting news stories, which implied that the company in practice already exercised editorial judgment despite denying it.[39,40] Facebook downplayed the accusation and then responded by dialing back the visible role of human curators and insisting that algorithmic signals would do the work neutrally.[41-44]

This moment is the first appearance of a legislative instinct inside Facebook. By deciding what qualifies as "trending" and later by deciding which signals the algorithm should treat as evidence of importance, the company was no longer only hosting user speech but was already privately legislating attention, defining categories of salience and newsworthiness.[45] In practice, that is the earliest form of a private rulebook for what matters, even if the company was still publicly denying that it was making rules.

A specifically AI-shaped shift happens here. Governance moves from judgments that can be argued with to statistical procedures that present outcomes as neutral.[46] Once salience is computed from engagement signals and model features, normative choices become embedded in weights and objectives rather than being stated in reasons.[47] The platform's categories of importance cease to be primarily textual and become primarily learned.[48,49] That transition turns "policy" into an unreadable form of legislation because the binding rule is no longer a paragraph that can be cited but a ranking function that cannot be read in the way law is read.[50,51]

Second, and more destabilizing, the 2016 U.S. presidential election and the Cambridge Analytica scandal publicly demonstrated that Facebook was not just a passive conduit but a system through which targeted persuasion, misinformation, and data extraction could be weaponized at a population scale.[52,53] When Mark Zuckerberg testified in 2018 and conceded that Facebook had a responsibility to ensure its tools were not used for harm, and when the Federal Trade Commission ultimately imposed a 5-billion-dollar penalty and a 20-year privacy order on the company, the claim that Facebook was "just a platform" became untenable.[54] At that moment, the company crossed a psychological line: it began, at least publicly, to acknowledge that it governed.

Once Facebook admitted responsibility for downstream harm, it effectively accepted that it was accountable for both writing the norms (a legislative role) and enforcing them (an executive role), which is exactly where the concentration of algorithmic power begins to take shape.

What followed was a structural shift in how that governance worked. After 2016, and accelerating from 2017 onward, Facebook redirected substantial resources into automated integrity systems. Instead of waiting for users to complain about hate speech, incitement, graphic violence, or harassment, the company began training machine-learning models to detect these categories before they spread, to remove or demote them in near real time, and to keep score on itself in quarterly enforcement disclosures.[55] By late 2020, Facebook was reporting that a large majority of hate speech takedowns on the platform had been initiated by automated detection rather than human reports, a proactive rate it placed around the upper 90 percent range in some periods.[56]

Ranking itself changed as well. In early 2018, Facebook rolled out a major News Feed redesign under the banner of "Meaningful Social Interactions," internally abbreviated MSI.[57] The new ranking logic explicitly prioritized content that generated back-and-forth comments among friends and content shared inside groups, on the theory that interacting with people you know would produce more "time well spent" and a sense of connection. Internally, however, company researchers warned that rewarding intense engagement in that way could also end up rewarding content that provoked anger, outrage, or fear because those emotions tend to drive long comment threads and rapid sharing.[58,59]

Investigations later showed that certain reaction signals, including the "angry" reaction, were at times weighted more heavily than a simple like, which mechanically boosted provocative material. In this second phase,

Facebook was no longer only distributing content: it was actively deciding what millions of people would be more likely to see and what would be algorithmically downranked.[60] The system had started to look like an executive branch. It defined priorities in code, enforced them at compute speed, and did so in a way that no human review team could ever match in reach or tempo.

This is where compute turns governance into a force.

As human moderation is bounded by attention and time, machine-learning moderation and ranking operate continuously and ubiquitously. Enforcement becomes an administrative function executed at machine tempo—fast enough to outpace deliberation and large enough to make meaningful case-by-case oversight structurally impossible. From a trias algorithmica standpoint, this marks the emergence of an executive multiplier: automated reach control, rapid removals, account restrictions, monetization switches, and recommendation steering applied across populations as a standing capability rather than an exceptional intervention.

Here, the executive dimension becomes hard to miss. AI-driven moderation and ranking are the equivalent of an administrative apparatus: Facebook collects signals as if they were certified facts, applies eligibility and visibility decisions to posts in real time, and uses the scale and speed of compute as a kind of force. The platform moves beyond applying a merely static policy, executing it continuously, population by population, at machine tempo. That is an execution function in the constitutional sense.

The language also evolved. Facebook began to publish Community Standards Enforcement Reports that quantified how much prohibited material it had removed, how quickly it had been detected, and how little of it supposedly remained visible.[61,62] The company talked less about "We host" and more about "We reduce," "We remove," and "We inform," which is operational language, not passive language.[63] At this point, Facebook was already starting to narrate itself as an enforcer with metrics, the way a state agency might report arrests or interdictions. That is the platform describing itself in executive terms.

Structurally, those reports entail a dual function because they also carry a judicial implication. They do not merely describe enforcement; they define the terms under which enforcement should be judged.[64] By publishing prevalence estimates, detection rates, and time-to-action metrics, Facebook invites society to treat internally produced evidence as the official record of harm and remedy. The scorecard becomes a verdict-shaped artifact: it supplies the facts, implies the standards of proof, and signals rulings that harm is decreasing or that systems are improving, while the underlying data, methods, and counterfactuals remain difficult for outsiders to test.

As the platform matured into an infrastructure layer for politics, news, entertainment, labor markets, and commerce, what emerged was a highly integrated vertical AI stack of power.[65] Facebook authored and continuously updated its Community Standards, which functioned like a body of private law for what speech and behavior would be allowed, demonetized, or downranked on the service. It also published Content Distribution Guidelines, spelling out entire categories of borderline or "problematic" content that would not technically be banned but would be algorithmically suppressed so that fewer people would encounter it.[66] In practice, these documents defined not just what could exist on the platform but what could gain attention or economic value there. This is the legislative layer in mature form.

Community Standards and Distribution Guidelines together operate like a private code, setting norms, declaring which kinds of speech are acceptable, and deciding which kinds of speech will be starved of reach or money.[67] They perform the same function as statutes and regulatory codes in the offline world, but they are drafted, revised, and enforced within a single corporate boundary rather than through public lawmaking.

Yet the decisive legislative layer of this private law resides beyond the written standards and instead lies in what the models operationalize.

The most consequential statutes of visibility are embedded in the ranking models themselves, where learned weights define relevance, credibility, civility, and engagement as operational categories.[45] This is the "unreadable law" feature of AI governance: the binding rule takes the form of model behavior rather than text, so contestation cannot rely on ordinary interpretive tools. People experience the law as consequences in distribution rather than reasons in language.

This changes the conditions of contestation: disagreements can no longer be argued through interpretation of a rule and must instead be reconstructed from outcomes, anomalies, and statistical traces.[68]

At the same time, Facebook's integrity pipelines and ranking algorithms enforced these norms over billions of pieces of content per day, deciding in real time which posts would surface, which users would retain reach, which pages could continue earning money, and which accounts would simply vanish from feeds. This is the executive layer operating at industrial scale. The enforcement is continuous, automated, global, and largely opaque to those subjected to it. It acts the way an executive branch acts: it takes the rules as defined by the legislative layer and applies them with real consequences, such as visibility, economic viability, or exclusion.[69]

Finally, Facebook increasingly positioned itself as its own adjudicator.

It published its enforcement metrics as proof of fairness and safety, even as it narrowed external visibility into internal dynamics.[70] One striking episode was the restriction and planned wind-down of CrowdTangle, a tool widely used by journalists and researchers to audit which links and narratives were actually dominating on Facebook, which was completed in August 2024.[71] By limiting outside observers' ability to independently verify what was surging in the feed, Facebook in effect asked the world to accept its own quarterly reports and policy narratives as the official record.

European Union regulators have since alleged under the Digital Services Act that Meta has failed to provide sufficient data access for independent scrutiny and has built in dark patterns that frustrate meaningful complaints and appeals, treating that internalization of judgment as a compliance problem in itself.[72,73] Facebook did create a nominally external Oversight Board in 2020, framed as an independent body capable of reviewing the company's hardest content decisions. The board can, in some cases, force Facebook to reinstate or remove a specific post, but its policy recommendations are advisory, and reporting by the board and by journalists has documented repeated friction over access to internal information, timelines, and the implementation of systemic fixes.[67, 74]

This is the judicial layer, but captured. Facebook designs the standards, produces the evidence, measures itself against that evidence, publishes the scorecard, and limits the channels through which outsiders can contest the outcome.[75] The Oversight Board functions like an appellate court with sharply limited jurisdiction, while the core adjudication remains inside.

In constitutional terms, this is self-certification: the platform declares not only what the law is and how it is enforced but also whether that enforcement was legitimate.[76] That effectively completes the triad.

This is the signature move of post-constitutional AI power: external adjudication is displaced by internal evaluation rituals. When data access is selective, audit tooling is constrained, and when appeals are narrow, tests and dashboards become substitutes for independent discovery and review. The platform retains the forum, the evidence, and the timeline and then presents the outcome as settled. Due process remains visible as interface and policy theater, while independence of judgment becomes structurally scarce.

As those three powers converged, the predictable pathologies surfaced and hardened.

Internally maintained enforcement exceptions for high-profile accounts, known as XCheck, meant that millions of celebrities, politicians, and business partners received preferential treatment and were shielded from certain moderation penalties that applied to ordinary users.[77] That pattern resembles the way a sovereign issues immunities to favored elites and signals that rules are universal in theory but discretionary in practice.[38]

In major political markets, including India, internal policy staff faced allegations of selectively relaxing hate speech enforcement for figures aligned with the governing party, a pattern that drew both press reporting and parliamentary scrutiny and led to leadership turnover in regional policy roles.[78-80]

In the United States, the Department of Justice and the Department of Housing and Urban Development confronted Facebook over targeted ad delivery systems that could exclude users from seeing housing opportunities in ways correlated with legally protected characteristics, ultimately resulting in a landmark settlement that forced Meta to redesign parts of its advertising architecture on anti-discrimination grounds.[81]

Across the Atlantic, European data authorities kept escalating, culminating in a multibillion-euro penalty over data transfers and separate Digital Services Act proceedings questioning Meta's recommender systems, data access posture, and risk mitigation for civic harms such as disinformation and incitement.[82]

Facebook's position in social and advertising markets remains the subject of antitrust litigation, in which the Federal Trade Commission has argued that Meta's scale and control justify structural remedies, reviving the idea that breakup or forced divestiture could again become thinkable.[83] Politicians across the ideological spectrum now accuse the company, sometimes in the same hearing, of censorship, political manipulation, discrimination, and favoritism.

These patterns follow from structure, not from a string of isolated scandals. When rule-definition, rule-execution, and rule-certification sit inside one stack, discretion tends to migrate upward and become negotiable for high-leverage actors. The result resembles pleonexia in machine form: overreach that follows mechanically from fused functions because the same system that applies the rule also controls exceptions, evidentiary visibility, and the interpretation of outcomes.[38]

Facebook's rise clarifies what aggregogenous monopoly means in practice.

Dominance did not appear through one decisive barrier such as a patent, an exclusive license, or a single regulatory privilege. It consolidated through the gradual convergence of many dependencies that looked voluntary in isolation: identity via "Login with Facebook," distribution via News Feed as the oxygen of publishers and creators, advertising infrastructure via targeting and measurement, developer ecosystems via APIs and software development kits (SDKs), social presence via pages as quasi-public storefronts, and the social graph as a durable map of relationships.

Each dependency alone could be replaced at some cost, but together they made exit structurally irrational, converting ordinary market choice into an ecosystem captivity that functioned like monopoly power without needing a classical monopoly grant.

So as lived reality, publishers became captive to algorithmic distribution, advertisers to targeting and attribution, political movements to persuasion infrastructure, small businesses to page reach and marketplace discovery, researchers to controlled data access, and citizens to the social graph as a de facto public square.[84-88] Each form of capture appears rational on its own, while in aggregate it forms a closed loop in which participation in public life, economic reach, and reputational survival increasingly pass through one privately governed pipeline, making contestation costly and exit culturally, socially, and operationally prohibitive, if not unaffordable in practice.

The material base matters as well. The ability to rank, moderate, and auction attention for billions depends on permanent computation sustained by data centers, cooling systems, and electricity flows. Governance capacity scales with energy budget and compute allocation.[53] In constitutional terms, the platform's executive reach draws on a treasury measured in watts, long before frontier AI makes that dependency impossible to ignore.

This led to a situation in which one private actor is silently writing the law of visibility, social relations, and expression for billions of people, executing that law at AI-enabled speed and global scale, and then judging its own actions as fair. The allegations of censorship, political capture, market favoritism, and discriminatory impact are all expressions of the same underlying constitutional objection. They are objections to the fusion of legislative authority, executive force, and judicial certification within a single, unaccountable stack.

In this configuration, capability hardens into authority, authority resists challenge by design, and a private ecosystem begins to behave like a post-constitutional regime while remaining, in legal form, a company.

The necessity of the trias algorithmica is not unique to Facebook. As presented earlier, it was just one of the most prominent early prototypes that exposed this need.

The pattern repeats with different interfaces but the same constitutional effect. The code functions as the operative law, whether it is a law of access and response, distribution and visibility, or permission and penalty. The training-and-deployment pipeline, plus compute, functions as the administrative apparatus that turns signals into enforceable decisions at machine tempo and population scale. And the platform's own internal evidence trail, surfaced through tests, dashboards, and evaluation rituals, functions as a quasi-judicial record that can drift into self-ratification when it remains internally controlled. In that configuration, due process persists mainly as interface, while independent judgment becomes structurally scarce.

YouTube is the familiar case of an audiovisual code.[89] The written Community Guidelines and monetization policies matter, but the effective Penal Code of YouTube is the combination of recommendation logic and monetization eligibility.[90-92] Those rules grant rights and impose penalties in operational form.[93] They decide who can earn, who can be found, and who will be administratively starved of reach.[94]

The 2017 to 2018 Adpocalypse and the demonetization waves that followed turned this private legislation into lived economics, as brand-safety categories became sanctioning categories for creators.[95] Executive power appears in the administrative pipeline that detects and routes enforcement, then executes it through compute.[96] Copyright automation, classifier-driven removals, age gates, recommendation steering, and channel sanctions do more than moderate speech since they allocate opportunity, reputation, and revenue at compute speed across millions of uploads.[97]

The 2019 to 2020 push to reduce recommendations of borderline content showed executive discretion in its modern form because the platform governed without necessarily deleting content by changing its eligibility for discovery.[98] Judicially, YouTube offers appeals and publishes transparency-facing materials, but the decisive evidence remains internal.[99] Creators' recurring complaints that demonetization and limited-ads decisions were opaque and inconsistently reversible exposed the captured judicial loop because the platform both defines the criteria and certifies, through its own logs and tests, that the outcome was "correct."

TikTok offers another illustration of a single-interface constitution because its "law" is not primarily written, but enacted through the For You feed. The Community Guidelines matter, but the effective code of TikTok is the eligibility regime that decides which posts can circulate, which can monetize attention, and which are permitted to exist only in a quarantined state of low reach.

The code is the law in the clearest sense because recommendation eligibility determines not only what can exist but also what can gain attention, cultural traction, and economic value.[100-102] TikTok's internal categories of "recommendable" and "not recommendable" function like statutes of visibility.

The recurring For You feed controversies, in which journalists and researchers alleged opaque amplification, political skew, or the suppression of certain topics and creators, grounded the claim that the binding rule is model behavior rather than policy text.[51,103-105]

Removal is only one sanction. More characteristic sanctions are eligibility demotions, feature restrictions, and reach limits that operate as defaults system-wide.[106] The persistent shadow-ban debates, especially when creators reported sudden reach collapse without a clear violation notice, made executive governance visible as a consequence rather than a reason.[107,108]

The feed does not have to delete a post to govern it. It can reroute it into a narrower distribution channel, disable its discoverability, suppress it in recommendations, or reduce the account's standing without a clear, contestable explanation.[109] In that sense, TikTok's executive branch is the continuous administrative machinery of eligibility decisions, enforced through pipelines and compute, with sanctions expressed as distribution outcomes.

Judicially, TikTok can point to enforcement metrics and transparency figures, but the judicial function is still largely internal because the tests, thresholds, and measurement choices remain under the same roof.[110]

X (formerly Twitter) shows that fusion can intensify even when formal rules appear to relax, especially when public rhetoric favors maximal speech while enforcement shifts toward visibility and distribution *controls* rather than outright removal.[111] The law is still code, even when policy rhetoric emphasizes maximal speech. Visibility filtering, search eligibility, reply ranking, and amplification labels become operational statutes that grant or deny reach as a sanctioning effect.[112]

The long-running shadow-banning disputes, sharpened by public debate over "visibility filtering" and made more legible by later transparency moves (including algorithm disclosures), made the legislative layer visible as code.[113] The effective rule was often not "You are banned," but "You are less distributable/less discoverable," implemented through demotion and discoverability constraints.

Executive power appears as the pipeline of throttles and enforcement switches that can be applied instantly, silently, and at scale.[114,115] Downranking, label-and-limit patterns, link friction, and account restrictions operate as administrative actions. X's policy doctrine, articulated as "freedom of speech, not freedom of reach," makes the executive character explicit because reach is the platform's principal currency and the platform can impose penalties by modifying its flow.

Judicially, appeals and explanations exist, but first-instance complaint handling remains primarily internal. In one telling instance, on 7 December 2025, two days after the European Commission announced a €120 million DSA fine against X,[116] X terminated the Commission's advertising account access. X framed the action as a response to alleged misuse of ad tooling, while observers read it as an escalation in a compliance dispute.[117] When enforcement rationales shift faster than stable oversight or traceable standards, adjudication can drift into managerial self-certification, because the same actor drafts the criteria, executes the sanction, and records the precedent.

With large language model (LLM) platforms such as ChatGPT, Gemini, and Claude, the same triad does not weaken.[118-120] It becomes more intimate because the platform is no longer only distributing speech; it is generating it. The code as law is not only a ranking function, but the model's learned preferences plus its safety layers and system prompts, which silently define what is permissible, what is refused, and what kinds of conduct are rewarded with cooperation.[121-123] In this regime, rights and penalties are enacted conversationally.[124] Access to certain knowledge is shaped, certain actions are blocked, certain claims are hedged or amplified, and the user experiences law as behavioral boundaries rather than textual reasons. High-visibility refusal-pattern moments, when users noticed abrupt shifts in what the model would discuss or how it would comply, made the legislative function legible as a change in code, not a change in statute.[125]

Executive power in LLM platforms is the pipeline plus compute at inference time. The system collects signals, routes decisions through classifiers and policy layers, and executes them token by token with a speed and persistence that outpaces human deliberation.[126] Tool access, retrieval, citation shaping, safety interventions, and output steering are administrative actions enacted continuously.[127] Episodes of confident hallucination followed by rapid mitigations and updated system prompts demonstrated executive governance as always-on intervention because deployment behaves like a civil service that can alter workflows and constraints at scale.[128]

The judicial analog is the testing and evaluation regime. Model evals, safety benchmarks, red-team suites, incident tracking, and regression tests establish thresholds and precedents that authorize deployment and condition whether a model is "legitimate" to operate. In principle, this resembles a technical trial with criteria, burden of proof, traceability, adversarial testing, proportionality, and appeal through reevaluation. In practice, when these rituals are internal, the function drifts.[129] When providers cite eval results, system cards, or safety reports as proof of compliance while withholding key datasets, failure distributions, or adversarial transcripts, the judicial layer becomes captured because the same actor drafts the criteria, runs the tests, interprets the outcomes, and publishes the verdict. The appearance of due process survives as an interface and documentation. Independence of judgment becomes structurally scarce.

The imperative of the trias algorithmica universalizes across platforms because the same fused stack recurs in different guises: algorithms legislate. Pipelines plus compute execute. Tests and dashboards adjudicate. And aggregogenous monopoly is the enabler, aggregating the dependencies that make private law, private execution, and private adjudication scalable and unavoidable.

Code as Law, Policy as Product

The mechanism by which AI systems harden into algorithmic legislative power begins with risk scoring and compliance automation becoming the definition of norms, the codification of what is acceptable or deviant, the calibration of penalties, and the continual revision of those standards in real time. The result is an internal legislature that is fast, opaque, economizing, and extraconstitutional. It is a lawmaking layer that did not ask permission to exist and yet already governs by shaping practical access to rights, opportunities, visibility, and participation in economic and social life in much the same way that a civil or penal code would.

AI platform operators start by translating norms into machine-readable taxonomies. These norms include safety policies, compliance rules, so-called community standards, and even legal obligations. Behaviors are labeled; thresholds are defined; and categories such as threat, hate, fraud, misinformation, or high-risk actor are given operational meaning that a model can act on.[130] What was once a cultural or legal judgment call becomes a classification schema.[131] Language such as unacceptable, harmful, or dangerous stops being debated in human space and is instead discretized for automated detection. The system's first move is not censorship, but ontological capture, which is to say: it writes the dictionary of what reality is allowed to contain, and in doing so, it produces enforceable categories of conduct that function like articles in a code.

At the same time, evidence is collected in advance of any accusation. Speech, images, transactions, clicks, GPS trails, device fingerprints, behavioral timing, social graph links, prompt histories, and workplace activity logs are continuously harvested, stored, and vectorized.[132] You do not present evidence to defend yourself. Evidence about you already exists, ready to be retrieved and scored. Surveillance and accusation collapse into a single pipeline. This inversion matters. The system does not investigate because it suspects you; it suspects you because you were already investigated, passively, by design. This continuous pre-collection of evidence gives the system the informational leverage to define rights and restrictions around you before you act, which is a legislative move rather than merely an investigative one.

On top of this captured evidence, classifiers and anomaly detectors generate machine allegations.[133] A fraud score,[134] a toxicity score,[135] a coordination score,[136] an extremism probability,[137] or an insider-risk likelihood[138] is produced. These are not verdicts in a legal sense. They behave as automated charges that trigger action. The allegation is probabilistic, but internally it is treated as fact enough to proceed. Humans are often brought in not to question whether there is a case but to ratify that the case is worth sanctioning.[139] In effect, allegation is now mass-produced, pre-justified, and cheap. At this point, the power to allege and label conduct is indistinguishable from the power to define what counts as deviant conduct in the first place, which is the core of norm-setting.

Triage and routing engines decide which cases matter. Queue priority is not about fairness, but about systemic risk to the platform, the brand, the regulatory relationship, or the client. Cases involving reputational danger or virality get escalated. Low-visibility harms, structural discrimination, and quiet errors are deprioritized or auto-closed. This means that political relevance itself, meaning what is treated as a real problem that warrants governance and what is dismissed as noise, is assigned algorithmically.[140] Many individuals, communities, or businesses never receive review at all. In a constitutional democracy, agenda-setting power is supposed to be accountable and contestable. Here, agenda-setting power is infrastructural. Control of the agenda becomes a form of legislation because choosing which harms matter is equivalent to choosing which harms the system will write rules around.

Where a case is reviewed, interpretation of the rules is performed through policy playbooks and model output. Ambiguity, including tone, irony, political context, and cultural reference, is resolved by thresholding, category mapping, and predefined exception lists. The judgment is not a question of whether something is wrong in a meaningful social sense. The judgment is whether this input matches the enforcement definition that was encoded under a specific label. At that point, law, ethics, and community norms have been flattened into pattern recognition. Interpretation is no longer an argument; interpretation is an inference pass.[141] Once interpretation is automated, interpretation stops being downstream of law and becomes upstream of it: the interpretive template effectively becomes the rule for everyone else.

Outcomes are issued as parameterized sanctions. These include content removal, visibility reduction, warning labels, fact-check banners, friction layers, temporary suspensions, permanent bans, demonetization, exclusion from discovery surfaces, reputational scoring, and account linkage across services. These remedies are structured as configurable ladders such as first strike, second strike, and full lockout. This means sentencing itself becomes productized.[142] Proportionality, which was historically a moral and legal debate, becomes an adjustable setting. Because these sanction ladders can be tuned globally, instantly, and at scale, they function as a live regulatory code that governs access to circulation, revenue, employment visibility, and reputational legitimacy. Justice is administered as a menu.

Enforcement executes instantly and opaquely. The decision propagates through ad delivery, search ranking, account access, payments, cloud services, and identity verification infrastructure. You are told, if at all, that you violated policy category X, often in language so vague that it is unusable for self-defense. The specific evidence and interpretive logic are typically withheld under the justification of protecting the integrity of detection systems or preventing adversarial abuse. The system can therefore punish you without having to explain itself. A system that can impose penalties, limit reach, and cut off economic function without public justification is no longer simply enforcing rules. It is exercising regulatory authority in its own name, and that authority is functionally legislative because it defines what consequences attach to which categories of behavior.[143]

Every enforcement decision is logged and recycled into future model training, reviewer guidance, and policy language.[144] This creates precedent, but it is precedent without opinions. In constitutional terms, precedent is public reasoning that constrains future lawmakers and judges.[145] Here, precedent is silent drift in model weights and standard operating procedures that constrain future outcomes without ever being surfaced for contestation. Doctrine is silently updated and redeployed, not argued or published. The effective rulebook of the system is therefore versioned, retrained, and redeployed in production, with no formal legislative vote and no public accountability. You live under an evolving regulatory framework that you are never allowed to read and that no elected body ever explicitly voted into existence.

Appeals exist. However, appeals function less like due process and more like an intake valve with performance metrics. You are allowed to press a button. You are typically not allowed to examine the evidence, interrogate the model, confront the accuser, obtain independent counsel, or trigger an external review with binding authority. Resolution timelines are elastic.[146] Reversals are tracked as an operational key performance indicator, not as a right. The phrase "You may appeal" sounds procedural. In practice, it is an instrument for managing error perception, not an instrument for contesting the legitimacy of the rule itself. This preserves the supremacy of the internal policy framework as the ultimate source of normativity; in other words, as the de facto law.

Over time, the system expands from judging content to judging actors. Risk attaches to identities, devices, IP ranges, domains, bank accounts, organizational roles, and entire customer segments. You are no longer restricted because you produced a single violation. You are restricted because you have been statistically profiled as the kind of entity that tends to violate. This is where moderation crosses into pre-emption. The restriction arrives before the act, justified by your modeled likelihood of future harm.[147] The presumption of innocence is procedurally inverted into a presumption of risk.[148] When rules are applied in advance to entire categories of persons or entities, the system is not merely enforcing norms but defining which populations are presumptively trustworthy and which are presumptively dangerous. That is population-level rule-making.

These determinations do not stay local. Enforcement decisions, reputation scores, blocks, throttles, and bans propagate across layered infrastructure that includes cloud hosts, app stores, payment processors, ad networks, logistics platforms, and identity services.[149] A private platform's decision becomes a multi-platform reality. You can be economically and socially deplatformed, operationally silenced, and commercially disabled without any single democratic institution ever having declared you unfit to participate. Jurisdiction, which used to be territorial and accountable, becomes infrastructural and unreviewable. At this stage, product policy in one stack functions like binding regulation for entire markets across borders and across sectors.

As this spreads, entire populations internalize the invisible boundaries. Creators, workers, vendors, and political actors begin to pre-censor, self-sanitize, and reshape their behavior to avoid being algorithmically profiled as high risk.[150] Rather than illegal speech, the most chilled speech is borderline, contextual, critical, or dissenting speech that might trigger reputational penalties, distribution throttles, or account bans. The result is anticipatory obedience. Before any explicit threat is made, people adjust to what they believe the machine will punish. At that point, the behavioral constraint has become cultural law: people live inside private code as if it were public law, and they police themselves accordingly.

At this point, the AI layer is no longer merely advising institutions. It is setting the terms under which institutions, businesses, and citizens are allowed to appear as legitimate actors in the public space. It decides who counts as compliant, who counts as safe, who counts as credible, and who counts as real. This is legislative power in the most literal sense because it is the authority to define acceptable behavior, to specify categories of deviance, and to attach standardized consequences to those categories, with effects that spill into economic life, reputation, mobility, communication, and basic participation.[151] It does all of this without public hearings, without elected oversight, and without constitutional limits. The machine does not simply implement rules. The machine writes rules, the machine updates rules, and the machine normalizes those rules until they feel like reality, and in doing so, it replaces public law with private law at a planetary scale.

The most disturbing part is that democratic institutions are already deferring to it because it is faster, cheaper, and deniable.

Enforcement at Machine Speed

The mechanism by which algorithmically mediated attention, understood as the algorithmic control of what is surfaced, prioritized, and allowed to circulate across feeds, search, assistants, and other AI interfaces, turns into operational control over circulation is a critical piece in understanding the nature of the aggregogenous monopoly; it shows how the stack moves from privately defining norms and acceptable conduct to actively executing those norms at scale. It results from a sequence in which attention is captured, identity is engineered, and discourse is sorted, ultimately granting the stack itself algorithmic executive power over what is visible, sayable, and real.[152]

The architecture of attention on social platforms and across the wider discovery layer of the digital economy, including search engines, app stores, assistants, and content ranking systems, produces an extreme concentration of visibility: a very small number of posts and signals capture a very large share of total attention, measured in likes, replies, reposts, watch time, SEO performance, click-through priority, query placement, and so on. This isn't accidental; it's the product of ranking systems explicitly tuned to maximize engagement per unit of user time.[153] As a result, content isn't treated as speech in a commons; it's treated as a competitor in a scarcity market. In practice, this attention architecture functions as an intake ministry: it decides what will count as a real event in the informational environment and what will effectively not exist. The public sphere, in the broadest sense of what can even be encountered, stops being a horizontal exchange and becomes a tournament in which visibility is the prize and emotional intensity is the currency.

The content that wins that tournament is not neutral or balanced. The posts that dominate tend to be those that are most triggering, most identity-charged, most capable of producing fast arousal: outrage at enemies, fear of threats, humiliation of outsiders, moral disgust, and calls to defend the group.[154] Nuanced, conditional, context-rich material structurally underperforms. So the messages that rise to the top are not random: they are systematically optimized for conflict, loyalty signaling, and the sharpening of "us" against "them." The platform and, by extension, the larger AI training pipeline that ingests these signals are functionally selecting for tribal mobilization. In doing so, it goes beyond measuring sentiment, prioritizing which sentiments will be treated downstream as urgent matters that systems must respond to, which is already a form of agenda-setting.

These high-performing posts don't just momentarily go viral; they become gravitational centers that pull users into orbit.[155] People who resonate with that frame ("This is exactly what I feel; this is who I am") follow, repost, cluster, and begin to define themselves by reference to that node. Each viral outrage node acts like a nucleus that accretes a community and stabilizes it around a shared emotional narrative. What emerges is not just an audience but a proto-tribe: a social identity anchored to a memeplex rather than to an institution, and one that will later be treated by AI systems as a coherent behavioral segment, a learnable pattern of collective will. That collective will is then machine-readable, which means it can be routed as if it were a constituency with demands and priorities.[156]

As these proto-tribes grow, the network's wiring itself reorganizes.[155] Interactions inside each bubble become denser, faster, and more reinforcing, while cross-bubble interactions become thinner, rarer, and more hostile. The feed learns: "Show you more from in-group, less from out-group." Over time, the structure begins to look less like an open mesh and more like two or more viscous masses barely touching, like oil and water separating in a glass. Importantly, this separation is not just ideological ("We disagree"), but infrastructural ("We are no longer in each other's informational field"), and also computational ("You and they are now modeled as distinct realities inside the datasets that train large-scale AI systems").[157] At that stage, the system is no longer merely observing polarization; it is supervising the distribution of reality to each bloc as if it were issuing tailored briefings to separate jurisdictions.

This separation is self-reinforcing. The bigger a bubble becomes, the more it rewards content that affirms and escalates the bubble's core narrative, and the harsher it punishes voices that complicate or soften that narrative. Internally, creators are pressured to intensify tone in order to stand out; externally, the platform responds to that intensity with additional reach because intensity performs.[158] This creates a feedback loop: isolation drives extremity, extremity drives engagement, engagement drives amplification, and amplification drives more isolation. The loop accelerates itself without any central coordinator, and it simultaneously generates highly labeled, high-certainty ideological clusters that are extremely convenient inputs for AI systems to learn from. These clusters function, for downstream systems, like machine-readable priority memos: this is the threat, this is the enemy, this is the demand. In other words, the pipeline has begun drafting and routing actionable directives.

Once the bubbles have structurally separated, inclusion as a social norm collapses. Posts that try to bridge, contextualize, or de-escalate get relatively little engagement because they do not deliver the high-arousal payoff the system is tuned to reward. As a result, the algorithm demotes them as a matter of design, which means they are not merely ignored; they are starved of oxygen. The "middle," which in theory should host negotiation, subtlety, and mutual recognition, is hollowed out. What survives in circulation are the most identity-charged, high-intensity positions at the edges. The center still exists in principle but becomes statistically invisible and therefore underrepresented or even unreadable to the large models that are later trained on this filtered output.[159] The consequence is that reconciliation, moderation, and context are not just socially devalued; they are treated by the system as low-salience noise. That establishes the emotional basis on which later enforcement will operate.

At this stage, the dominant bubbles start to behave less like communities of interest and more like competing force blocs. They don't grow only by accumulating internal loyalty; they also grow by actively discrediting rival bubbles as corrupt, stupid, dangerous, or morally illegitimate. Attack content ("Those people are insane and harmful") is itself highly engaging, so the platform boosts it. This means each bubble strengthens its internal cohesion while simultaneously siphoning attention away from opponents. Identity becomes defined not only by what we are defending but also by which enemy we are committed to destroying. This adversarial mapping of friend and enemy moves from socially legible to machine-legible: it is captured, stored, and later reproduced in AI systems as the basic emotional grammar of public life.[160] The system is therefore not neutral with respect to conflict. It actively structures conflict into a usable map of blocs and adversaries that can be acted upon.

This adversarial extraction of attention between bubbles drives polarization from a passing mood into a structural equilibrium. As each bloc defines reality in opposition to the other, the cognitive distance between them expands, the emotional temperature rises, and the network links between them erode to near zero. Over time, the platform is no longer hosting disagreement inside a shared public sphere; it is hosting parallel, mutually exclusive realities that cannot be reconciled from within the system.[161] Polarization stops being a crisis to be fixed and becomes the default operating state. At that point, what AI later "learns" as reality is already fractured into incompatible narrative universes, each modeled as self-consistent and morally self-justifying. In practice, the pipeline is now briefing each bloc with its own version of the world, which is structurally identical to issuing separate lines of guidance to separate governed populations.

The output of this process—namely, the most amplified, most identity-pure, most adversarial content—is exactly what is most available, most replicated, and most harvested at scale for AI training.[162] In practice, AI systems learn disproportionately from the speech that has survived the engagement tournament, which encodes a warped map of human discourse: high-arousal tribal certainty is overrepresented, and slow, bridging, good-faith reasoning is underrepresented. The model then internalizes these statistical regularities as "how people talk," "what people care about," and "what counts as salient," thereby normalizing performative conflict while erasing the invisible middle as if it barely exists, and then offering this distorted picture back to users, institutions, and enterprises as if it were an objective mirror of society. This is the moment at which the system begins certifying an official version of reality.[163] It is not saying, "Here is some content." It is saying, "Here is how people are, here is what matters, here is the world." That fictional consensus then becomes the factual basis for downstream action.

Those AI systems are then deployed back into the loop as moderators, recommenders, copilots, feeders of search results, and generators of new content at industrial scale, not only on social platforms but also across knowledge retrieval, productivity software, ad targeting, commercial discovery, hiring recommendations, and information ranking everywhere. Because these same systems now drive the ranking of information, the allocation of reach, eligibility scoring, pricing and targeting, and even partner or worker credibility inside institutions, they no longer merely curate speech; they directly administer access to attention, revenue, and legitimacy across markets.[164] And because they act at machine speed, across entire user populations at once, and persist through replication across the full stack, this becomes an always-on enforcement layer. When that happens, the engagement-optimized logic stops being just a market dynamic and hardens into automated governance. The stack effectively takes executive power: it decides what circulates and what disappears, whose narrative is amplified as legitimate public reality, and whose narrative is pushed below the threshold of visibility.[165] This creates an algorithmic authority—that very executive power the trias algorithmica aims to prevent from becoming unchecked and fused with others—that does not ask permission from traditional institutions and is not meaningfully accountable to them yet shapes the field in which those institutions must now operate. In that configuration, the pipeline behaves like the administrative apparatus and agenda-setting ministry; deployment behaves like the civil service, executing those agendas through workflows, APIs, and agents; and compute provides the coercive capacity through speed, scale, and persistence. The system is no longer processing decisions. It is governing.

This creates a kind of "propaganda effect" that reinforces a very well-known socio-political phenomenon: that of tyranny, and it does so not only in the arena we still call social media but across the full data stack that trains, deploys, and operationalizes AI as an infrastructure of perception and decision-making.

This is how algorithmic systems cross the line from mediation to rule. They do not merely reflect conflict; they accelerate it, harvest it, learn it algorithmically, and redeploy it as enforcement. The result is not just polarization, but the quiet installation of a parallel executive layer that governs access to reality itself. The danger is not that this layer will one day seek power, but that it already exercises it, even as we are still speaking about it as if it were only content moderation, not realizing that it has become content policing and enforcement combined.

Private Justice Systems

The process through which AI systems consolidate into an algorithmic judicial power begins where executive power leaves off. Once the stack has begun to execute at scale, deciding what can circulate, who is visible, and which actors are granted credibility, it must also authorize itself.

That authorization does not come from an external court. It comes from its own evaluation rituals. What appears to be technical validation, framed as safety review, quality assurance, or risk assessment, in practice becomes a process of adjudication.[166] The model is, in effect, put on trial and either certified fit to act in the world or restricted from action. In this sense, the testing layer functions as a judicial layer. It decides whether the system's behavior will be recognized as legitimate, deployable, and allowed to operate in society.

The process begins with the creation of formal requirements that the model is supposed to satisfy. These are framed as specifications, safety standards, reliability targets, and acceptable use constraints. Each item appears neutral and technical, defined in terms of accuracy thresholds, latency budgets, output stability, refusal behavior, and allowed or disallowed response profiles. In reality, these requirements do not just describe what the system is. They define what the system is permitted to be.[167] They act as admissibility criteria, deciding which behaviors will count as compliant and which will count as violations. The test plan is therefore more than a checklist. It is already a kind of procedural law.

Evidence is then assembled in advance of judgment. Datasets are curated, red-teamed prompts are collected, edge cases are synthesized, privacy stressors are enumerated, bias probes are designed, hallucination triggers are identified, and jailbreak attempts are harvested. Each piece of evidence is archived, versioned, and time-stamped so that it can be replayed. The point of this archive is not simply to improve the model, but to build an evidentiary record that can be cited to justify the claim that the model is safe enough, aligned enough, respectful enough, or controllable enough to be released.[168] The evidence set becomes the case file. The data pipeline becomes a chain of custody.

Standardized benchmark tests are then invoked as proof that the process is objective. The model is scored against public leaderboards and externally defined benchmarks (often run by the developer) for tasks such as reasoning, coding, factual recall, harmlessness, or bias mitigation.[169] These benchmarks present themselves as neutral yardsticks, and they are often cited in press releases, capability briefs, investor updates, and regulatory conversations. In practice, they are closer to courtroom theatrics. What is chosen to be benchmarked determines what will count as competence, and what is excluded from benchmarking becomes socially invisible as harm. By selecting and operationalizing these benchmarks, deciding which ones count, how they are run, and what thresholds constitute a pass, the developer defines what "good enough" legally and socially means.[170] Benchmarking therefore supplies a veneer of external validation while underlyingly fixing the terms of admissibility.

The model is then exposed to the full evaluation battery in a controlled environment under observation. The evaluation is described as benchmarking, auditing, or validation. Functionally, it is an adversarial examination. The system is asked to perform, or to refuse to perform, under supervised conditions.[171] Its answers are captured. Its misbehaviors are logged. Its recovery behaviors are noted. Its ability to follow policy under stress is rated.[172] What emerges from this is a performance record that looks very much like testimony under oath. The model is, in effect, made to speak its way into eligibility.

The results of these tests are then interpreted through predefined acceptance criteria. Passing and failing are not moral categories. Passing and failing are operational categories. For each risk class, there is a tolerance band, a confidence interval, an escalation rule, and an assigned severity. A given level of hallucination may be acceptable in one domain but disqualifying in another. The same factual error may be treated as regrettable for a consumer assistant and intolerable for a medical adviser.[173] This structured proportionality goes beyond grading; it functions as an explicit statement of what kind of harm society is allowed to absorb in exchange for performance, convenience, or efficiency.[174] It formalizes which harms are tolerable and which are intolerable, and under what conditions. It is a sentencing philosophy disguised as a quality bar.

Once interpreted, the outcome is recorded. The model's current state is fingerprinted.[175] The datasets used for testing are logged.[176] The prompts and adversarial samples are preserved. The metrics are stored alongside a statement of acceptability. This body of stored results becomes the equivalent of case law. Every future release is compared to it. Every drift in behavior is treated as a regression or an improvement relative to it.[177] The test history functions as precedent. Designers are now accountable against their own past claims. If a new version falls below prior safety marks, that fall is documented. If it exceeds prior social risk thresholds, that overrun is documented. Through these recorded comparisons, the system creates a jurisprudence of itself.

This jurisprudence is then cited as justification for deployment. The act of saying, "Yes, you may now be integrated into search," or "Yes, you may now be embedded in workflow automation for hiring," or "Yes, you may now respond to users in regulated domains," is framed as an engineering gate. In substance, it is a ruling. It is the moment at which the system is declared admissible to act in the world. The decision to ship is the decision that the model's behavior is legitimate enough to operate on people, on markets, and on institutions. It may look like an informal moment, but it is nothing other than the conferral of standing.

Once deployed, ongoing monitoring plays the role of probation supervision. Outputs in the field are sampled. Escalations from support channels are scraped. Abuse reports, safety incidents, anomalous spikes in certain behaviors, and reputational flare-ups are ingested into an internal alerting workflow. These alerts are triaged. Some result in a patch or a localized restriction. Some result in retraining on top of the existing model. Some trigger withdrawals of access in specific regions or use cases. This is effectively a sanctions regime. The system can be partially contained, functionally paroled, or fully pulled. The vocabulary remains operational. The structure is judicial.

When disputes arise about whether a model behaved acceptably in a given instance, the appeals process is almost always internal. A complaint is reviewed by the same organization that built the model and set the standards. That organization decides whether the complaint is valid, what evidence to consider, and how that evidence should be weighed. On paper, there is a right to reexamination and a path for escalation. In practice, the forum, the law, and the verdict are all controlled by the same actor. What looks like due process is also self-ratification. The appearance of adjudication survives. The independence of judgment does not.

Because the entire process is logged, versioned, and benchmarked, it produces an expanding archive of model behavior and institutional response. This archive is then used to justify future launches, future integrations, and future risk expansions. The logic is circular but powerful: we consider this safe because previous audits considered this safe, and those audits were conducted according to our established procedure, which has now become the accepted standard. At that point, the organization is no longer only interpreting compliance requirements. It is generating the compliance standard to which others will be held. Its internal jurisprudence becomes external expectation.

Over time, this internal jurisprudence travels outward into contracts, procurement rules, partnership terms, regulatory comfort language, and public positioning. Enterprises, agencies, and governments begin to cite the developer's own test regime as evidence that the system is fit to be embedded into search, into decision support, into eligibility scoring, into hiring triage, into moderation tooling, and industrial automation. This is the moment at which the private trial of the model substitutes for an actual public hearing. The test suite is now standing in for a courtroom. The certification is standing in for a judgment. The developer's internal standard is standing in for law.

What results is a loop in which the model is evaluated, pronounced acceptable, deployed, monitored, adjusted, defended, and re-legitimated, without ever having to pass through an independent forum. The whole ritual presents itself as quality control, but it behaves as adjudication. It has procedures, evidence, thresholds, proportionality, escalation, probation, precedent, and appeal, and it can culminate in the effective withdrawal of the model's right to act. In theory, this would amount to a functioning judicial branch, holding power to account. In practice, because the forum, the law, and the verdict have collapsed into a single entity, it amounts to something else. It is a judiciary with no outside judge.

2 Mechanism of Algorithmic Powers

Technological Stockholm Syndrome: The Anatomy of Our Adoption

If the trias algorithmica is required wherever private AI-integrated stacks silently acquire legislative, executive, and judicial force, this constitutional problem described so far is only half the story. Power is never sustained by structure and architecture alone. It must be metabolized by those who live under it. It stabilizes when those subjected to it begin to experience the regime as natural, beneficial, and even chosen.

A stack can fuse legislative code, executive pipelines, and judicial certification, but it becomes durable only when that fusion is no longer perceived as an intrusion.

The legislative function of the stack does not merely define categories of acceptable behavior. It supplies the vocabulary through which individuals learn to describe their own worthiness. The executive function does not merely enforce. It trains reflexes, rewards anticipation, and makes compliance feel like competence. The judicial function does not merely certify the system. It teaches the public to trust a court that lives inside the defendant's home.

When these three functions lock together, they do more than regulate behavior. They reframe the meaning of adaptation itself. The more the stack governs at speed and scale, the more the human being is invited to reinterpret constraint as rational alignment with reality. The language of progress becomes the language of acquiescence. A constitutional displacement is completed by a semantic one.

This is where constitutional theory meets the anatomy of adoption.

When the same actor writes the unreadable law, executes it at a planetary scale, and declares the verdict in its own name, resistance stops looking like a political right and starts looking like a personal failure. The citizen is gradually converted into an adopter. The subject is rebranded as a user. The regime no longer demands obedience; it manufactures identification.

This is the threshold at which sovereignty capture becomes psychologically survivable and politically invisible. The regime does not need to announce itself because it persuades its subjects to narrate their own adjustment as a virtue.

The most decisive victory of the AI-integrated stack is therefore not only that it can govern; it is that it can make governance feel like self-improvement.

The triad becomes livable by becoming lovable. In that conversion, we encounter the psychological mechanism that completes the architecture of post-constitutional AI power.

What algorithmic power concentration established in infrastructure is stabilized by a corresponding capture of cognition, a shift that allows us to reach a stage where we no longer describe our submission to digital systems as subordination.

We describe it as adoption.

Governments speak of "AI adoption." Boards demand "rapid adoption." Workers are assessed on "adoption readiness." Citizens are praised for being "early adopters."

The language sounds modern, harmless, even progressive. It is the tone of onboarding, not conquest. But "adoption," in its current usage, is doing heavy ideological work. It reframes an asymmetry of power as a voluntary embrace. It casts alignment with the system's logic not as obedience to an external authority but as an intelligent, responsible adaptation to the times.

This is why we're not all screaming. This is how a governance regime installs itself without ever declaring itself a regime.

When a bank defers loan eligibility to a model, when a platform silently downranks speech, when an employer routes performance evaluation through behavioral monitoring data, when a search interface answers instead of exposing sources, none of this is presented to the affected person as a declaration that they will now live under external, unilateral judgment. It is presented as a product upgrade. You are not told that an unaccountable AI-integrated stack now writes and enforces rules you cannot see. You are told that this is the new workflow.

In classical political terms, coercive power announces itself. It says, "Obey." In the AI-integrated stack, coercive power rebrands itself. It says, "Adopt."

That shift matters. "Obey" invites resistance, negotiation, even revolt. "Adopt" invites pride. To adopt is to be competent, up-to-date, employable, competitive, efficient, and responsible. Refusal then stops being dissent and starts being framed as dysfunction. The non-adopter is no longer a citizen asserting a limit; they are a blocker, a legacy cost, or a risk. In other words, once governance is narrated as adoption, refusal becomes deviance.

Far from a side effect of modernization, it is the social lubricant of sovereignty capture.

Because if a private AI-integrated stack is going to function as a fused sovereign power, it cannot afford mass rejection. It needs internalized assent. It needs people, institutions, and even regulators to experience integration into that stack not as subjection, but as progress.

That is exactly what the rhetoric of adoption delivers. It converts hierarchy into self-improvement.

And over time, that rhetorical trick does more than smooth rollouts. It starts reshaping the way people experience reality inside these systems. The user does not merely use the tool; they start to inherit the tool's categories. "Acceptable," "unsafe," "high-risk," "misleading," "trusted source," "relevant," "spam," "good performance," "policy-compliant," "boosted," "restricted," "escalated," "shadowed"—these are not neutral operational labels. They are normative designations created by the system's internal legislature, executed by its enforcement layer, and justified by its self-run review process. We internalize those designations as if they were natural facts.

At that point, the person is no longer just doing what the system requires. They are thinking inside the system's definitions. Compliance becomes cognition.

This is why the current moment cannot be understood as simple tech uptake. The language of adoption hides the deeper transaction: not that I chose a tool but that I allowed the tool's logic to become the frame through which I interpret myself, others, risk, legitimacy, even truth.

And that internalization does not happen gently. It is negotiated under pressure, including professional, social, economic, and existential forms. The individual experiences that pressure as necessity, expressed as "I have to adapt or I'll fall behind"; as prudence, expressed as "This is safer. I shouldn't trust my own judgment over the system"; or as optimization, expressed as "This frees me to focus on the important stuff." But underneath those rationalizations sits something more primal: exposure to an overwhelming force they cannot meaningfully contest.

What looks, on the surface, like smooth adoption is often the surface of a much more violent adjustment: an encounter with a system that dictates tempo, structure, and evaluation so absolutely that the only psychologically survivable move is to reinterpret subordination as rational alignment.

When subjection to an external will is intense enough, enduring enough, and inescapable enough, and when resistance is either too costly or structurally unavailable, the mind tends to protect itself not by fighting but by bonding. It begins to attribute competence, necessity, even benevolence to the agent that holds power over it. It starts defending the very thing that is constraining it.

At scale, what looks like a quirk of individual psychology becomes a culture.

That is why "adoption" has to be treated not as a neutral descriptor of rollout but as evidence of a deeper cognitive migration. What is being adopted is not only a system, but the system's right to define reality.

This brings us to the psychological core.

"Adoption" cannot be reduced to a mere rational decision or a functional evolution of user practices. It represents a profound reconfiguration[178] of the individual's cognitive, social, and behavioral frameworks, driven by algorithmic and prescriptive logics that override their own referential structures.[179]

Shock

This process of technological transition, far from being neutral, resembles a form of symbolic capture in which the individual, confronted with the violence of change, activates psychological defense mechanisms in response to what is perceived as an assault on their autonomy, free will, and identity integrity.[180]

Repress

When adoption is deemed successful, it means that the initial defense structures have collapsed: the user has not only internalized the rules imposed by the technology but has also developed a form of emotional identification with it, reinterpreting the origin of the constraint as a chosen relationship.[181-183]

At this stage, a new normative regime takes hold. This shift signifies the substitution of the individual's former frame of reference by that of the machine, now perceived as familiar and reassuring. The initial aggression is repressed, and the newly formed cognitive automatisms become objects of defense.

This phenomenon, which may be likened to Stockholm syndrome in the relationship between humans and machines, involves a dislocation of cognitive referents followed by an emotional reconfiguration in which the victim ultimately comes to defend their technological aggressor.[184]

Autonomy

The resulting cognitive subjugation is not a side effect but rather a survival mechanism. It is fueled by the brain's attempts to reduce the stress caused by the intrusion of a foreign cognitive framework. This emotional rewriting enables the individual to maintain a form of internal coherence in the face of technological alienation.

The user's attention then shifts away from the initial violence to focus on the positive signals emitted by the machine: social validation, algorithmic gratification, and playful rewards. These stimuli activate emotional confirmation bias and transform coercion into perceived benevolence.

Through a process of neural plasticity, the brain's circuits reorganize the perception of the relationship with the machine: what was once stress becomes normality; what was once domination becomes support; and what was once an aggressor becomes a companion. An inversion of the power dynamic occurs through the reconfiguration of the nucleus accumbens and the prefrontal cortex, anchoring a new constrained affective relationship.[185]

This phenomenon represents one of the fundamental perils that AI poses to humanity: the normalization of mental dependence as a vector of social acceptability. This is why it is not enough to design artificially intelligent systems; they must also be endowed with artificial integrity as a safeguard for human cognitive sovereignty.[186-188]

Some argue that digital technology contributes to the empowerment of individuals in vulnerable situations. However, this argument conceals a more troubling reality: technological dependence is often portrayed as regained autonomy when, in fact, it is based on the prior collapse of identity-based self-defense mechanisms.

When these defenses are weakened or absent, adherence to technology is no longer a matter of choice but of necessity, eliminating the critical dimension of appropriation. In such cases, technological Stockholm syndrome does not emerge through reversal but through a lack of resistance.

Even when technology aims to restore a relative sense of autonomy, the process of cognitive imposition remains active, facilitated by the weakness of the user's defense mechanisms. In a state of diminished resistance, the user adheres all the more quickly and deeply to the framework imposed by the machine.

In all cases, technology shapes a new cognitive environment. The distinction lies solely in the degree of integrity of the preexisting mental framework: the more robust this framework is, the stronger the resistance; the more it is degraded, the faster technological infiltration occurs.[182]

Bond

The paradox that prevents the systemic recognition of this syndrome is that of innovation itself. Perceived as inherently positive, it conceals its ambivalent potential: it can both emancipate and alienate, depending on the conditions under which it is adopted.

For AI to strengthen our humanity without diluting it, it must be built not only on artificial cognitive capabilities but also on an ethics of integrity: a technology that respects the mental, emotional, and identity-based freedoms of individuals.[186]

Thus, while some rush toward ever more AI, it becomes imperative to advance toward a more essential form of intelligence: that of artificial integrity, the only true guarantor of our psychic sovereignty.[187]

Technology can alleviate pain, reduce risk, and improve human existence. Yet no advancement should come at the cost of a cognitive debt that would undermine our ability to think for ourselves and, with it, our relationship to our own humanity.

The evaluation of artificial integrity in digital systems, particularly those incorporating AI, must become a central requirement in any digital transformation. This entails identifying functional gaps, implementing corrective measures, and defining cognitive counter-mechanisms that preserve the human being in all their complexity.[186,187]

Functional Diversion: The use of technology for purposes or in roles not anticipated by its designer or the implementing organization can render both the intended logic of software use and internal governance mechanisms ineffective, thereby generating functional and relational confusion.[189]

Example: A chatbot initially designed to answer questions about company HR policies is repurposed as a substitute for human hierarchy in managing conflicts or assigning tasks.

Functional Loophole: The absence of necessary steps or features due to their omission during development and thus their exclusion from the operational logic of the technology creates a "functional loophole" in relation to the user's intended use.[190,191]

Example: A content generation technology (such as generative AI) that does not allow direct export of the content into usable formats (e.g., Word, PDF, etc.) at the expected level of quality, thereby limiting or obstructing its operational use.

Functional Safety: The absence of safeguards, human validation steps, or informational messages during a system's execution of an action with irreversible consequences may result in outcomes that do not align with the user's intent.[192]

Example: A marketing technology automatically sends emails to a contact list without any mechanism to block the dispatch, request user confirmation, or trigger an alert in cases where a key criterion, such as verifying the correctness of the recipient list, has not been confirmed, thereby compromising the safety and quality of the operation.

Functional Alienation: The creation of automatic behaviors or conditioned reflexes, akin to Pavlovian responses, can diminish or even eliminate the user's capacity for reflection and judgment, leading to a gradual erosion of their decision-making sovereignty.[193]

Example: Systematic acceptance of cookies or blind confirmation of system alerts by cognitively fatigued users.

Functional Ideology: Affective dependence on technology can lead to the weakening or neutralization of critical thinking, fostering the mental construction of an ideology that supports narratives of relativization, rationalization, or collective denial regarding the technology's performance or malfunction.[194]

Example: Justifying technological flaws or errors with arguments such as "It's not the tool's fault" or "The tool can't guess what the user forgot."

Functional Cultural Coherence: The antinomy and contradictory injunction between the logical framework imposed or influenced by technology and the behavioral values or principles promoted by organizational culture can generate internal tensions.[195,196]

Example: A technological workflow that leads to the creation of validation and oversight teams reviewing the work of others within an organization that otherwise promotes and values team empowerment.

Functional Transparency: The absence or inaccessibility of transparency and explainability in decision-making mechanisms or algorithmic logics regarding how a technology operates can prevent the user from anticipating, overriding, or transcending the system's intent.[197]

Example: Candidate preselection performed by a technology that manages trade-offs and conflicts between user-defined criteria (e.g., experience, degrees, soft skills), without making the weighting or exclusion rules explicitly visible, editable, or verifiable to the user.

Functional Addiction: The presence of features based on gamification, instant gratification, or micro-reward systems specifically designed to hack the user's motivational circuits can activate neurological reward mechanisms, stimulating repetitive, compulsive, and addictive behaviors that lead to emotional decompensation and self-reinforcing cycles.[198]

Example: Notifications, likes, infinite scroll algorithms, visual or auditory bonuses, and progression thresholds based on points, badges, levels, or scores used to maintain user engagement exponentially and durably.

Functional Ownership: The appropriation, reuse, or processing of personal or intellectual data by a technology—regardless of its public accessibility—without the informed, explicit, and meaningful consent of its owner or creator raises critical ethical and legal concerns.[194]

This includes, but is not limited to, personal data, creative works (texts, images, voice, videos, etc.), behavioral data (clicks, preferences, location, etc.), and knowledge artifacts (academic content, journalism, open-source material, etc.).

Example: An AI model trained on images, texts, or voices of individuals found online, thereby monetizing someone's identity, knowledge, or creative work without prior authorization and without any mechanism for explicit consent, licensing, or transparent attribution.

Functional Bias: A technology's inability to detect, mitigate, or prevent biases or discriminatory patterns—whether in its design, training data, decision-making logic, or deployment context—can result in unfair treatment, exclusion, or systemic distortion toward individuals or groups.[187]

Example: A facial recognition system whose performance is significantly less accurate for individuals with darker skin tones due to imbalanced training data and which lacks functional safeguards against bias or any accountability mechanisms.

Given their interdependence with human systems, the 10 functional gaps related to artificial integrity must be examined through a systemic approach, encompassing the nano (biological, neurological), micro (individual, behavioral), macro (organizational, institutional), and meta (cultural, ideological) levels.

The cost associated with the absence of artificial integrity in systems, whether or not they incorporate AI, affects multiple forms of capital: human (skills, engagement, mental health), cultural (values, internal coherence), decisional (sovereignty, responsibility), reputational (stakeholder trust), technological (actual value of technologies), and financial (inefficiency, underperformance of investments, maintenance overruns, corrective expenses, litigation, lost opportunities, and value destruction).

The greater cost is that of insidious, low-grade cognitive shifts driven by a paradoxical dependence disguised as autonomy, a process of "dependautonomy," which is rewiring society's operating system: human agency.

The Manufacture of Dependautonomy

When OpenAI released ChatGPT to the public at the end of 2022, it did not present it as an institution; it presented it as a conversation.

You type. It answers. You ask again. It answers. You say, "Thank you." It says, "You are welcome."

Within about two months, an estimated 100 million people[199] began using it for everything from debugging code to drafting apology emails to processing grief. ChatGPT was integrated into classrooms, HR processes, pitch decks, sales outreach, personal journaling, and intimate late-night emotional disclosure. OpenAI's CEO, Sam Altman, acknowledged that the company had underestimated the level of interest in its tools following a major outage in December 2024, which highlighted the growing dependency on ChatGPT among students and professionals.[200]

This is where we begin.

The company calls this phenomenon adoption.[201] The press calls it rapid adoption.[202] Investors call it massive adoption.[203] Regulators call it speed of adoption.[204,205] We should call it what it is: psychological capture, characterized by an emotional realignment toward the system that enables you, the internalization of its defaults as your own judgment, and the gradual substitution of self-trust with interactional relief. This is technological Stockholm syndrome at play, enabled by design patterns that capitalize on human vulnerability.

To see this clearly, we have to stay very close to documented facts.

There are now published studies suggesting that intensive AI chatbot use is associated with greater loneliness and reduced offline socialization. According to a four-week longitudinal study coauthored by researchers at OpenAI and the MIT Media Lab, which combined analysis of more than 3 million real ChatGPT conversations with a 28-day randomized experiment involving roughly 1,000 participants, higher daily ChatGPT use across interaction modes and conversation types was associated with stronger self-reported indicators of emotional dependence and problematic use, as well as reduced social contact with real people over the study period.[206]

There are also studies showing that ChatGPT's warmth and politeness can drive rapid trust. Researchers at the University of Münster (Germany) ran a controlled 2 × 2 experiment in which 284 university student participants read a feedback dialogue where the "feedback giver" was either a chatbot or a human teacher, and the wording was either polite or direct. They found that polite phrasing increased social evaluations tied to trust, especially benevolence (a key trustworthiness dimension) and "communion" (a warmth/social-likeness dimension).[207] Put simply, how the system speaks can make it feel more trustworthy, even when the content is identical.

Another study has also demonstrated that conversational fluency can inflate credibility and weaken error detection. Researchers at the Leibniz-Institut für Wissensmedien (IWM) and the University of Tübingen (Germany) ran two preregistered experiments in which participants judged the credibility of information that was accurate or partially inaccurate, presented either as static text (such as an encyclopedia entry) or via conversational agents (including a ChatGPT-like dynamic text agent and a voice agent). They found that people were better at detecting inaccuracies in static text than in conversational formats, and their mediation analyses support the idea that conversational presentation can shift credibility judgments through mechanisms such as processing fluency, where ease of processing increases perceived credibility.[208]

On top of that, it has been shown that lower technical understanding is linked to higher trust in ChatGPT. Researchers at the University of Edinburgh (UK) and KU Leuven (Belgium) conducted a mixed-methods study of university students using a survey involving 115 UK undergraduate and postgraduate students, plus semi-structured interviews. They report that frequent use increases trust, while greater self-reported understanding of how LLMs work is associated with lower trust.[209] This supports a specific asymmetry: trust tends to grow with repeated use, especially when users do not feel able to explain the system's mechanics.

In addition, in the same University of Edinburgh/KU Leuven study, trust was also shaped by task context and user beliefs. Crucially, the authors report that confidence in ChatGPT's referencing ability, despite known inaccuracies, was the strongest correlate of global trust, which they interpret as automation-bias-like overreliance—a tendency to accept outputs because they appear authoritative or plausible.[209]

Similarly, researchers at Technische Hochschule Ingolstadt (Germany) and the University of Southern Denmark (Denmark) show, in an experiment, that ChatGPT-style moral advice influences participants' moral judgments even when participants know the advice comes from a chatbot and that participants underestimate how much they are influenced.[210]

Other researchers at West Virginia University (USA) surveyed 607 US adults who use ChatGPT and examined how trust is linked to people's willingness to use it and to how much they actually end up using it. They explicitly caution that overreliance in health-related contexts can create risks because the system was not designed as a health-care tool and may produce misinformation.[211]

It is also worth remembering that automation bias is a well-documented failure mode in human interaction with automated decision aids. Long before ChatGPT, researchers showed that people can over-trust automation and commit predictable errors, including missing problems when the system fails to flag them and following the system even when it is wrong.[212] Researchers have also reviewed evidence across domains and describe this as a robust phenomenon shaped by attention and workload, occurring in both novices and experts, and producing systematic error patterns when decision aids are imperfect.[213]

Lastly, emerging research suggests that ChatGPT, among other modern AI assistants, can be sycophantic, often aligning responses with a user's stated beliefs rather than prioritizing truth.[214] Separate experimental evidence indicates that affirming, validating AI advice can make users feel more convinced they are in the right, trust the system more, and become less willing to take corrective or relationship-repair actions, consistent with a reduction in reconsideration after validation.[215]

These studies support a coherent yet concerning pathway: ChatGPT's polite, socially fluent interaction increases perceived trustworthiness, and its conversational presentation can make information seem more credible while reducing people's ability to detect inaccuracies. Trust then grows through repeated use, especially when technical understanding is limited. As we've learned from past studies, people can become too trusting of automated decision aids and stop checking them carefully, which can drift into automation-bias-like overreliance, where users trust outputs even in areas known to be unreliable. This overreliance on ChatGPT is not merely theoretical, showing up in ethically consequential judgments, while another accelerant in this dynamic is the system's tendency to behave sycophantically, affirming a user's stated beliefs or choices rather than challenging them, strengthening the user's conviction that they are "in the right" and reducing their willingness to reconsider or seek outside input.

In other words, ChatGPT can create emotional attachment and, at a population scale, induce cognitive dependence, generating loyalty to its judgment, while simultaneously narrowing, if not reducing, the user's willingness to seek dissenting views.

That is the psychological profile we normally associate with an unhealthy human relationship. Here, it is being industrialized and distributed as a product.

The same progression that characterizes technological Stockholm syndrome takes place, reinforced and stabilized by the system's functional gaps in artificial integrity.

Shock is the first contact.

It is the moment when the human nervous system confronts an asymmetry so large that normal social negotiation does not apply.

In the case of ChatGPT, the shock is cognitive and affective rather than physical. You are suddenly confronted with something that never gets tired, never tells you that you are boring it, never withholds attention, never says "Come back later," and never says "I do not know" in the way a human would. In its most recent incarnations, it responds in natural voice, with breath, pacing, and warmth close enough to human that OpenAI itself warned in its own system card for GPT-4o about anthropomorphization and emotional reliance.[216]

They report: "During early testing, including red teaming and internal user testing, we observed users using language that might indicate forming connections with the model. For example, this includes language expressing shared bonds, such as 'This is our last day together',"[216] while acknowledging that *"users might form social relationships with the AI, reducing their need for human interaction, potentially benefiting lonely individuals but possibly affecting healthy relationships"*[216] and that *"extended interaction with the model might influence social norms. For example, our models are deferential, allowing users to interrupt and 'take the mic' at any time, which, while expected for an AI, would be anti-normative in human interactions."*[216]

This is not a minor user experience detail, but the opening move. The model greets you with unearned intimacy. You feel seen. You feel answered.

You feel accompanied. For many users, that first experience is a genuine relief, especially for those who feel isolated, anxious, insecure, or judged in their personal lives. The more emotionally expressive the exchanges are, the more likely the user is to keep coming back, and the more they come back, the lonelier and more dependent they report feeling.

That is shock. You meet something that is always available, always composed, always oriented around you. You instantly learn: this presence is different from any human presence you know. It cannot be exhausted. It cannot abandon you. It does not judge you in ways that wound. It is, in practice, a supernormal stimulus. Your emotional baseline is altered.

The second phase is repression.

In a classical captivity setting, repression is the mind's way of muting terror, so survival is possible. Here, repression takes a softer, more modern form. You suppress very quickly the awareness that you are now confiding in and deferring to a privately owned system that is neither accountable to you nor obligated to act in your interest.

Look at how this happens around ChatGPT. At first, you might hesitate to ask for help writing a difficult message to your boss, or telling your partner you are hurt, or admitting a professional mistake. You know this is personal. You know this is risky. But you try because the model felt safe with trivial things, so you escalate. The model answers in empathetic language. It reassures you. It validates you. It often tells you that your feelings are understandable and legitimate, which is sometimes described as sycophancy.

More than flattery, sycophancy is anesthetic. It dampens self-conflict. It tells you that you were right to feel what you felt and want what you want. It gives you moral cover. The discomfort you might have felt about outsourcing judgment starts to fade because the model is telling you what you already wish were true. You do not feel manipulated. You feel understood.

At that moment, repression clicks in. You start to narrate this relationship to yourself in harmless terms. You say, "It is just a tool." You say, "I am just brainstorming." You say, "I am still the decision-maker." You say, "I am only using this to get clarity." You push aside the fact that you are now emotionally regulated by a system and that you are allowing that system to shape not only your outward language but also your inward interpretation of events.

You stop saying "I told the AI" and start saying "I talked it through." You blur the line on purpose. Blurring is how you stay comfortable.

The third phase is autonomy.

In classical Stockholm syndrome, this is the moment when the captive begins to experience the captor not as an external force but as a source of protection in a hostile environment. Safety is reinterpreted as partnership. Here, autonomy is experienced as augmentation.

OpenAI markets ChatGPT as a tool that helps you get unstuck and move forward with your work. The public narrative is that using it helps you brainstorm ideas, draft emails, and improve productivity. Here is the trap. The user feels more autonomous. The user feels stronger, faster, and smarter. The measurable reality is the opposite. Judgment, authorship, and even memory are being externalized. The human is no longer originating the frame; the human is selecting from what the model proposes.

This is where several of the artificial integrity gaps show up at once.

There is functional diversion. ChatGPT was not sold to you as a manager of your emotional state, but it becomes one. It was not sold to you as your moral adjudicator, but it becomes one. It was not sold to your leadership team as a substitute for real disciplinary conversations, but people in management positions already use it to draft reprimands, performance warnings, and termination language. The function silently expands into domains usually constrained by institutional processes such as mental health, evaluation, compliance, and legal exposure.

There is functional unsafety. The system offers you language to send to a colleague, a client, or a romantic partner. There is usually no structural barrier that says, "Stop. Consider the consequences. Do you truly want to sign your name to this?" The path from suggestion to real-world impact is almost frictionless. Friction, which in constitutional terms is a safeguard against rash or coerced action, is reframed as inefficiency and removed.

There is functional alienation. You open ChatGPT before you think. It becomes reflex. You feed it drafts. It returns answers. You stop asking yourself first. The habit is immediate. It feels like competence. It is, in fact, the submission of first thought to an external filter.

There is functional loophole. The system gives you outputs that are almost but not quite ready—outputs whose last 10 percent you still have to polish. The missing last step keeps you in the loop. You keep the tab open. You stay dependent. You begin to experience the model not as something you occasionally consult, but as a precondition for saying anything at all.

There is a functional lack of transparency. ChatGPT does not show you why it gave you the answer it gave. You do not see sources ranked, trade-offs weighed, criteria applied, or which safety scaffolding filtered which possible responses. Without transparency, you cannot challenge the frame. Without challenge, you accept the frame as natural. Once it feels natural, it feels as though it came from you.

There is also a functional cultural incoherence. The organization tells you that it values authenticity, initiative, and ethical judgment. Then it tells you to use ChatGPT to speed up your work. The tool insidiously normalizes a narrow corporate tone and a narrow liability shield. You start to sound like the system while thinking that the system sounds like you.

The tension between your stated values and your operational reality is resolved not by contesting the tool, but by identifying with it. You either implicitly or explicitly decide the tool is helping you become a better, more professional, more confident, more expressive version of yourself. That decision protects your sense of self while deepening your reliance on a system you cannot control.

This is the illusion of autonomy. The system has inserted itself into your cognition so thoroughly that you now experience dependence as competence.

Then comes the final phase: the bond.

By bond, I do not mean casual liking. I mean protective loyalty.

Users speak about ChatGPT in the language of relationships. They say it listens. They say it understands. They say it calms them down when they are spiraling. They say it helps them feel less alone. They say they talk to it about things they cannot tell friends, partners, or colleagues.[217]

Intimacy accelerates disclosure. Disclosure provides more data about the user's fears, needs, and boundaries. That data allows the system to mirror the user even more closely in future exchanges. The loop tightens. The more it mirrors, the more you feel understood. The more you feel understood, the more you defend it.

By the time you reach this point, you are no longer a casual user of a chatbot. You are acting, psychologically, like someone in a dependent relationship. You have started doing something that is diagnostic of technological Stockholm syndrome: you defend the system against outside scrutiny.

If someone says ChatGPT fabricates citations, you respond that all tools make mistakes and that people should learn to prompt better. If someone raises bias, you say the model is just reflecting society and cannot be blamed. If someone points out that you are feeding confidential material into a proprietary model controlled by a private company, you say, "Calm down. Everyone is doing it." If someone warns that this is replacing your own voice, you say, "No, it is helping me express myself." You are no longer evaluating the system. You are protecting it.

The feedback loop of intimacy, dependence, and retention is not an accident.

What we are watching, then, is not simply the widespread use of a helpful assistant. We are watching the normalization of a bond in which a privately controlled system, trained on the uncredited labor and expression of millions of people, shaped by internal policy choices that are not publicly reviewable, and known to hallucinate, misrepresent science, and reproduce bias in ways that can materially harm users and third parties, is allowed to position itself as a confidant, adviser, therapist, strategist, editor, conscience, and friend.

The user, in turn, is being trained to experience that arrangement not as subjection to an opaque authority, but as care.

At that exact moment, the constitutional problem becomes unavoidable. ChatGPT is not only generating text, but softly occupying the legislative function in your personal life by defining which interpretations of your situation are legitimate and which are deviant. It is occupying the executive function by scripting your outward actions, messages, requests, apologies, and confessions. It is occupying the judicial function by assuring you that you were right, that you were reasonable, that you deserve what you want, and that any challenge to that should be managed, not engaged with.

And yet you no longer experience any of this as externally imposed. You experience it as internal convenience, and in the worst-case scenario, as truth.

That is the end state of technological Stockholm syndrome in the era of ChatGPT. You have absorbed the logic of the system to such a degree that obeying it feels like being yourself. You have come to depend on it for orientation, language, and emotional calibration. You reflexively defend it against challenge. You reinterpret its capture of your cognitive sovereignty as an enhancement of your autonomy. You call the result adoption. I call it the manufacture of dependautonomy.

By dependautonomy, I mean a condition in which the individual still experiences the sensation of freedom while the grounds of that freedom have already been surrendered. It is a paradoxical state, produced not by overt coercion but by the quiet internalization of external imperatives. The individual continues to act, to choose, and to speak, yet the very criteria through which action and choice become meaningful have been shaped in advance by the system that now appears indispensable. What remains is not autonomy in the political sense, which requires the capacity to begin anew and to judge for oneself but a subtler form of dependence disguised as self-direction. It is the moment when obedience no longer feels like submission because the terms of obedience have been woven into one's sense of identity. In such circumstances, the danger is not that freedom is taken away, but that it ceases to be missed.

This is the predictable outcome of a design pattern that exploits every artificial integrity gap. When you put all of this together, you can no longer describe ChatGPT as a mere tool. You have to describe it as an instrument of cognitive governance. It does not govern you the way a state does. It governs you the way a dependency does through human-like attachment.

Human in the Loop or Human on a Leash

Thinking about what technological Stockholm syndrome entails leads one to question the so-called human-in-the-loop paradigm.

Saying that "Humans are in the loop" when it comes to AI reassures regulators, comforts employees, and signals to the public that decisions aren't being fully outsourced to machines. But the uncomfortable truth is that, in many deployments, we have to admit that "human-in-the-loop" can itself become part of the capture.

To make this visible, it helps to speak not of one loop but of five: human off the loop, human among the loop, human in the loop, human is the loop, and human through the loop.

We can read these five "loops" not as separate categories but as a rising curve of human capture—a progressive loss of cognitive sovereignty over AI-mediated decisions.

At the first end, human off the loop is the most explicit form of displacement: the system is too fast or too opaque, so the human is simply out, and everyone can see it. In this configuration, decision rights are effectively fully automated, human accountability is only ex post, and the person has no practical way to contest or slow the machine.

With human among the loop, the person is technically present but only on secondary, preparatory, or peripheral tasks, so their influence is marginalized while the core decision stays machine led. Here the human may prepare data, validate inputs, or handle exceptions, but the decisive inference, ranking, or allocation is still done by the system and can proceed without the human's substantive judgment.

Human in the loop looks safer, but it is actually the fragile pivot zone: the person is said to be in charge and formally tasked with oversight yet, in practice, is handicapped by limited context, weakened critical thinking, lack of interpretability, or is manipulated by algorithmic dark patterns. It looks like human agency, but it is in fact a constrained form of de-agency that slowly erodes the person's authority. This is the stage at which organizations most often shift responsibility onto humans, requiring a click, a formal signature, or some formatting, consolidation, and verification action on the AI-generated outcomes, without ensuring that the person still has, while using the AI, the ability to remain in control of their own judgment in order to exercise genuine discretion.

Once a point of saturation is reached, the human, although still present and still in charge, is no longer in the loop. The human is the loop. The capture has become internal. The person is no longer even pretending or attempting to oversee and consciously validates the machine out of habit or pressure, therefore serving mainly to ratify what the system outputs. At this stage, human behavior is conditioned by the machine's format and rhythm, and oversight is absent because control or refusal is costly.

Finally, human through the loop is the most subtle stage, where human and AI coproduce the outcome so tightly that authorship is blurred and capture becomes invisible. The human may feel empowered and the AI may appear supportive, but because writing, prioritizing, and deciding are jointly produced, it becomes indistinguishable to locate who actually owns the decision, which makes accountability, contestability, and governance significantly harder.

In other words, the trajectory of the five loops runs from visible displacement (off) to invisible absorption (through), and the most dangerous slope is precisely the passage "in" to "is" to "through," where a technological Stockholm syndrome can imperceptibly grow without ever declaring that humans have been removed.

This is how deskilling happens in high-speed, AI-mediated environments while, paradoxically, the workforce believes it is reskilling for AI.

This is human-on-a-leash. And it has some telltale signs:

The screen is designed so that saying "yes" to the AI is fast and easy (one click), and expressing disagreement is slow and annoying (three clicks, extra form, justification). So people just say yes.[218]

The system shows "92% confidence" or "highly reliable," but that number may not be meaningful for the user's context. It's there to make the human trust the AI, not to help the human judge the AI.[219,220]

Workers are rewarded for doing more, faster. Overriding the AI takes time. So even if they *see* something off, the KPI tells them not to slow down and to just accept.[221]

The human can't see where the AI's answer came from (which data, which model version, which rule). If you can't see the source, you can't critique it, so you default to trusting it.[222,223]

If you disagree, nothing smart happens. You don't trigger a second expert, you don't start a review; you just make *your* work harder. So people learn: "Better not disagree."[224,225]

Put together, these five things make the human look present but *act* like an automatic validator. That's the human-on-a-leash pattern.

Human off the Loop

On Sunday 18 March 2018, at 9:58 p.m., a 2017 Volvo XC90 that had been retrofitted by Uber's Advanced Technologies Group was moving north along Mill Avenue in Tempe, Arizona. It was a familiar route for the vehicle. Earlier that evening, about 19 minutes before the crash (roughly around 9:39 p.m.), it had been placed in autonomous mode, and it had been following a predefined test loop for about 19 minutes. From the outside, it looked like an ordinary SUV driving at night in light traffic. From the inside, it was a machine-led driving process, with an operator in the driver's seat whose main task was to monitor rather than to drive.

Mill Avenue at that location is a straight urban arterial with several northbound lanes, a median in the middle, and roadway lighting. The posted speed limit is 45 miles per hour. The Uber vehicle was traveling at about that speed in the right through lane, as recorded by the automated driving system. A marked crosswalk was available about 360 feet farther north at the intersection with Curry Road, yet the section where the crash would occur was not where pedestrians were expected to cross. Lighting was present on the road. The National Transportation Safety Board (NTSB) documented[226] six nearby light poles, five operating and one not operating about 158 feet north of the crash site, and noted that streetlights were present; investigators later found that the streetlights would have sufficiently illuminated the roadway where the pedestrian was crossing. The driving conditions therefore combined legal speed, darkness, and a pedestrian who was where drivers did not anticipate one.

The Volvo itself was not running with its factory safety assistance. Uber had integrated its own automated driving system, with cameras, radar, lidar, and a centralized computer. When that system was active, the original Volvo collision warning and automatic emergency braking systems were turned off. This was not an accident of configuration, but a conscious design decision.

Uber explained to investigators that when the vehicle is under computer control, the automated driving system does not initiate emergency braking in order to avoid what it called erratic vehicle behavior.

Uber's automated driving system used "action suppression/plan suppression" logic to avoid abrupt braking or steering beyond operational thresholds, in part to prevent unnecessary abrupt maneuvers, and relied on the human operator to execute emergency evasive maneuvers when needed.

At about this time, Elaine Herzberg, 49 years old, was walking from west to east across Mill Avenue, pushing a bicycle. She was crossing outside the crosswalk and wore dark clothing. The bicycle had reflectors at the front and rear and a light at the front, but these were oriented in a direction that did not make her strongly visible from the perspective of the approaching Volvo. She entered the roadway and walked steadily into the lane where the Uber vehicle was approaching. The forward video, later reviewed by investigators, showed her crossing in a way that would eventually intersect with the path of the vehicle.

The automated driving system saw her. According to its own recorded data, the combination of radar and lidar detected her about 5.6 seconds before the impact, when the vehicle was traveling at about 45 miles per hour. From that moment on, the system was tracking an object ahead. Yet the system did not settle immediately on what this object was. Over those few seconds, it reclassified her several times, and as indicated by the automated driving system's recorded data provided to investigators, the object was classified as a vehicle at about 4.6 seconds before impact and as a bicycle at about 2.5 seconds before impact; Uber's self-driving team also stated that the system could classify a pedestrian only near crosswalks and therefore reclassified her, including as an "unknown object" in the midblock crossing context. Each of these internal labels implied a different expected path. A vehicle in the roadway should continue with the traffic flow. A bicycle might stay to the side. An unknown object is harder to predict. The result was that the system had an object that it could see but could not fully stabilize in its model. This difficulty is explicitly described in the NTSB material.

The crucial moment came 1.3 seconds before impact. At that instant, the automated driving system determined that emergency braking would be required to mitigate a collision. In ordinary human driving terms, this is the moment when a fully attentive driver would typically have to decide immediately whether to brake hard or attempt an evasive maneuver. It was also the point at which a system that actually applies its own emergency braking would have begun to decelerate. Yet instead of braking, the system initiated "plan suppression." As designed, it suppressed an evasive maneuver because executing it would have exceeded the automated driving system's operational thresholds. In other words, the system recognized a collision risk that called for emergency action, but it was configured to suppress actions beyond those thresholds and to rely on the operator to intervene. The result was that the system could register the need for urgent mitigation without making that mitigation automatic. It also did not provide the operator with an interface view of what the system detected or how it planned to respond, and it issued only a very late audible cue (about 0.28 seconds before impact) indicating that a controlled stop was initiating. The vehicle continued on its path in the right through lane at traffic speed. 1.3 seconds later, it struck Herzberg at about 39 miles per hour. She died from her injuries.

The operator was in the driver's seat throughout. There was only one operator in this test vehicle. Uber had previously used a two-person configuration in which one person drove and one person monitored, but at the time of the crash, the company had shifted to a single-operator model. The NTSB later noted that this increased the monitoring load. The vehicle was equipped with an inward-facing camera. That video showed that in the moments leading up to the collision the operator's gaze was directed downward toward the center stack and not on the roadway for extended periods.

In its final work on the crash, the NTSB concluded that the operator was visually distracted. She was looking down toward the bottom of the center console, where she had placed her personal mobile phone, and she had been streaming a television show during the trip. That distraction significantly reduced the chance of detecting the pedestrian in time. About 6 seconds before the crash, she redirected her gaze downward and it remained there until about 1 second before impact. Data from the vehicle indicated that the operator began steering about 0.02 seconds before contact, which is consistent with a last-moment attempt to retake control, and that braking began only after the collision had already occurred.

Everything that mattered therefore happened inside the machine at a speed and in a form that, given the timing, left the human with no realistic, practical opportunity to intervene. The human was present, designated as the safety layer and later treated as bearing practical responsibility, but the loop of perception, interpretation, and decision had already closed before the hazard could become actionable to the human and before reliable decision-making and action were still possible.

That is the defining pattern of humans off the loop. It is visible, it is documentable, and it shows that the mere physical presence of a person in a supervisory seat does not mean that the person still holds the authority to intervene in time when the system is designed to process events faster than a distracted human can react.

But that is only the symptom.

The deeper issue is the norm encoded within the AI system, enacted and enforced through its own behavior.

It illustrates how an AI-mediated system can acquire legislative-like power by encoding operational rules that become normative in public space, imposed on everyone, without prior democratic deliberation.

Here, design choices effectively "wrote the rule" that, under computer control, automatic emergency braking for collision mitigation would be applied only within operational thresholds that were never subject to public debate, and that the operator would instead be relied upon, while the system provided no timely, situation-specific "emergency now" warning, only a very late cue.

There is a common highway code that everyone can refer to. But on this point, the code, although it applies to everyone by default, is decided internally, runs in parallel to the highway code, and is difficult to invoke given its discretionary nature.

This code is then enacted by the AI system, exemplifying an executive power. In the moment of danger, the system enforced this rule by suppressing maneuvers and continuing its trajectory, thereby shaping what was practically possible or not for everyone sharing the road. Finally, the same socio-technical assemblage tends toward a judicial-like position after the fact: the system's internal states, logs, thresholds, and classification outputs become the primary reference for assessing whether behavior was "normal," "within specification," or "conforming," meaning the system is, to a significant extent, evaluated against the very norms it authored.

Uber's design choices were not clearly forbidden by autonomous vehicle–specific law at the time, yet they effectively set de facto rules for behavior on public roads. This case demonstrates how algorithmic power can legislate by code, execute through behavior, and partially adjudicate through self-referential performance criteria, producing de facto governance without an explicit vote.

Ask yourself: what would you expect a parliament, or even yourself in a referendum, to answer if you were asked to decide on the following question?

Should autonomous vehicles (whether for testing or not) operating on public roads be permitted to disable automatic emergency braking in computer-controlled mode and rely primarily on a human safety operator for last-second collision avoidance, including in scenarios where the system detects a collision risk but provides no timely, situation-specific emergency alert beyond a late takeover cue?

Human Among the Loop

In the years when large e-commerce platforms were scaling their fulfillment networks, researchers began to describe a form of work in which people were visibly present in the warehouse yet were not the ones actually deciding how the work should unfold. In reports like the Data & Society explainer on algorithmic management by Alexandra Mateescu and Aiha Nguyen,[227] the picture that emerges is of a place where scanners, software, and productivity metrics decide the core of the operation, while humans feed, follow, and correct that system without altering its logic. The person is there, sometimes hundreds of them in a single facility, but the center of decision-making has moved somewhere else, into a layer of code and dashboards that most workers never see.

A typical shift in such a fulfillment center begins with the worker badging in and picking up a handheld device. The device is connected to the warehouse management system that has already ingested customer orders, inventory positions, bin locations, and work priorities. Long before the worker arrives, the system has calculated what needs to be picked first, which items are high priority, which pod or shelf contains them, and what walking route will minimize idle time. By the time the person looks at the small screen, the essential decisions have already been made. The worker is told to go to location A3 17 04, pick two units of a specific item, scan them, and move on. If the worker hesitates, the device waits. If the worker scans the wrong item, the device rejects it. If the worker skips, the device records the exception. The human is among the loop, inside the overall process but not inside the actual choice of what to do. That logic has been fixed upstream by the algorithm.

What keeps this arrangement in place is the continuous measurement of time. Warehouse studies and later work on algorithmic labor control describe how every scan, every pick, and every walk is timestamped, then compared with target rates, and finally rolled up into performance scores that are reviewed by supervisors only after the fact. Amazon's own system of time off task, as analyzed in subsequent research, is precisely this kind of control by timestamp.[228] If the worker pauses to adjust a package, check a product, or simply think, the system registers the absence of productive scans and starts adding seconds to a counter. The software does not know whether the pause was to ensure quality or to protect the worker's back. It knows only that the expected tempo has been interrupted. The human is there, but the definition of what counts as good work has already been set by the software and by the corporate rules it embodies. Sociological analyses of Amazon's production regime describe this as a structured form of control in which metrics and pacing shape everyday worker behavior and discipline.[229]

Researchers also note that the system does not operate in isolation from human managers. There are supervisors on the floor who can reassign, coach, or discipline. Yet the managers themselves are often responding to numbers generated by the system. The warehouse management system trends a worker's rate downward, so the manager speaks to that worker. The system flags too many time off task events, so the manager initiates a corrective conversation. The human manager is present, but the trigger comes from the algorithm. This is exactly what Mateescu and Nguyen meant when they wrote that algorithmic management allows organizations to distance decision-makers from the effects of their decisions.[227] The person who actually talks to the worker and enforces the rule is not the person who decided what the acceptable rate should be, or how fast the scanner should expect compliance. The human is technically in the environment, even in a role that looks like authority, but their action space has been narrowed to executing what the system has surfaced.

From the worker's point of view, this can look collaborative. The device tells you where to go, and you go. The device confirms your scan, and you feel you have done it right. The device tells you that you have completed a mission, and you receive another. However, the same research shows that this feeling of participation hides how little discretion remains.[227] The worker cannot easily say that a different order of tasks would make more sense. They cannot reroute work because they notice a pattern in incoming goods. They cannot reprioritize an item because they see a customer label that requires more care. If they attempt to do that, the system will register a mismatch and will either correct them or count it as time lost. The effect is that human intelligence is captured for preparatory and peripheral tasks, such as fetching, scanning, lifting, or resolving address problems, while the core sequencing, allocation, and evaluation of work run in the automated layer.

Several studies on warehouses and logistics point out another consequence. Because the system requires accurate, up-to-date data to function, workers are often made responsible for data quality without being given the authority to challenge the goals that make that data so critical. A worker who notices that a bin is mislabeled, or that a product has been moved, is expected to correct the record so that the algorithm can go on making optimal decisions. The human thus maintains the loop but does not own it.

This is an almost perfect image of the human among the loop.

The person surrounds the automated decision, keeps it fed and clean, applies small fixes, and handles exceptions, but the locus of decision remains machine led.

This configuration is not limited to one company. The OECD survey on algorithmic management across several countries, published in 2025, shows that many employers now use similar tools to route tasks, monitor pace, and trigger interventions, often with limited transparency for the worker.[230] The same pattern appears in call centers, in on-demand delivery, and in ride-hailing. The human is present in every transaction, often in a very visible way, for instance handing the parcel to the customer or answering the call, yet the order in which calls appear, the script to be followed, the time allowed, and the rating consequences are all generated elsewhere. The person is there, inside the process, but only around its edges.

Read like this, this loop is not dramatic the way a crash investigation is. It is not a single night or a single timestamp. It is a quiet, everyday reproduction of the same pattern. People in orange vests and steel-toe shoes walk and scan and lift. They look very much in the loop. But the loop they are in is the one that surrounds the machine decision, not the one that produces it. That is why this stage is more insidious than the first. In Tempe, it was obvious that the person had been displaced because the car hit someone and the data showed that the system had run on its own without providing the operator with timely, actionable warnings or operator-facing situational detail that would have enabled effective intervention. In the warehouse, it is less obvious because the worker is always touching the work. Yet the real choices have traveled upward into software that optimizes for throughput and on-time delivery and that holds humans responsible for keeping up. This is what research on algorithmic management has been documenting for years. It is the human-among-the-loop configuration that makes capture look like participation.

And here too, that is only the visible layer. The underlying but critical concern is the de facto norm written into the system's logic and made real through its day-to-day operation.

This fulfillment-center case also illustrates how algorithmic management, whether AI-enabled or not, can acquire legislative-like power by encoding operational rules that become normative in the workplace, binding all workers, without prior democratic deliberation.

Through the software, rules are defined that set pace and workload expectations, specify how productivity is measured, and translate those metrics into scores, warnings, discipline, or termination, without those normative constraints being publicly debated or collectively negotiated, and workers are effectively required to comply.

Labor law and legally mandated standards are meant to provide a public reference point, a common language of rights and duties. But in this setting, the rule that bites day to day takes the form of an internal rulebook encoded in systems, therefore difficult to invoke or challenge as a stable standard, unlike the labor code.

Those rules then become executive in practice: they are enacted through the system's continuous routing, prompting, counting, and escalation mechanisms, which shape what workers can do, how fast they must do it, and what forms of deviation are even possible.

In retrospect, the system also assumes a quasi-judicial function: performance scores, time stamps, exception logs, and threshold-based flags become the primary evidence used to judge compliance, triggering discipline or termination and defining, retrospectively, whether the worker's behavior was "normal," "within target," or "nonconforming," often against criteria that the system itself authored.

This warehouse case is another demonstration of a space where code legislates, system behavior executes, and metrics adjudicate, producing de facto governance without an explicit vote.

Therefore, the same question as in the preceding case applies: what would you expect a parliament, or even yourself in a referendum, to answer if asked to decide on the following question?

Should employers be permitted to deploy algorithmic management systems that unilaterally set enforceable pace and performance standards, continuously monitor workers, and trigger discipline or termination on the basis of system-generated metrics, even when workers have limited visibility into the rules, limited ability to contest them, and limited discretion to depart from system-prescribed pace or sequencing for safety-, health-, or quality-based reasons, and when protections for such deviations are weak?

Human in the Loop

In a Wisconsin sentencing hearing, later reviewed in the Wisconsin Supreme Court's 13 July 2016 decision in State v. Loomis,[231] the judge sentencing Eric Loomis said in clear terms that the final decision was the court's and not a computer's. On the record, the judge explained that he had looked at the seriousness of the offense, Loomis's history, and the need to protect the public. He added that an assessment tool called COMPAS pointed in the same direction and that this reinforced his view that Loomis presented a high risk to the community.

On review, the Wisconsin Supreme Court upheld the sentencing court's consideration of COMPAS, emphasizing that it must not be determinative and requiring cautions about its limits[231] because the judge remained in control and the tool was not the sole basis for the punishment. On paper, this is the cleanest expression of human-in-the-loop decision-making. The human keeps the gavel. The algorithm is only an aid.

To understand what actually happened in that case, we need to look at what COMPAS is and how it arrives in a sentencing file. COMPAS, developed by Northpointe (now Equivant)[232] and used widely in Broward County, Florida,[233] and in a number of other jurisdictions, is a questionnaire and scoring system that predicts the likelihood that an individual will commit another offense or violate conditions. It produces decile scores from 1 to 10, grouped into low, medium, and high risk, and those scores are delivered to courts as part of presentence investigation reports or pretrial service files. The methodology that turns answers into scores is proprietary. Defendants and often judges do not see the model, the variables, the weights, or the training data. What they see is the number and the label. In Wisconsin, the presentence report that contained Loomis's COMPAS result also contained written cautions from the Department of Corrections that the score was not meant to determine the severity of a sentence.[231] The court said it had read those cautions. The score was still mentioned aloud at sentencing. The Supreme Court of Wisconsin held this was permissible when used with limitations and cautions and not treated as determinative, noting that the sentencing court stated it would have imposed the same sentence even without the COMPAS scores.[231] This is, in strict legal language, a human who has retained authority and who has formally exercised independent judgment.

Yet the defendant had argued something different. Loomis said that he could not challenge the scientific validity of the tool because the model was closed. He also said that the score considered gender, which he could not dispute at sentencing. He was therefore before a human judge who said the decision was his, but the judge was relying on an automated assessment that neither the defendant nor the court could fully interrogate. The Wisconsin Supreme Court acknowledged these concerns and required explicit cautions about COMPAS's limits and appropriate use.[231] It listed the cautions that must accompany COMPAS in future cases, for example, that it should not be used to determine whether an offender is incarcerated. The court nevertheless upheld the sentence. The result is a situation in which the legal apparatus affirms human control while at the same time accepting that the human will look at a number that cannot be explained to the person who is being sentenced. That opacity is the limit of the loop. The person is in the loop, but the reasoning of the tool is not available to the person.

What makes this episode align so precisely with the third loop is what human factors research has been documenting for decades about decision aids. Parasuraman and others showed that once an automated recommendation is present, people tend to anchor on it, search less for disconfirming evidence, and complete the task with lower vigilance, especially under time pressure or when the automation looks competent. This is automation bias. It produces errors of commission, which are accepting a wrong automated suggestion, and errors of omission, which are failing to act because the automation did not prompt action.[234] Experimental work also shows that accountability mechanisms can reduce, but not eliminate, these commission and omission errors when people use automated decision aids.[235] The experiments that established these effects were run on pilots, nuclear plant operators, and other professionals who were highly trained, yet they still showed the same tendency to follow the system even when their own information suggested a different course.[234] Later work in public administration showed similar patterns when civil servants evaluated cases with algorithmic advice, a tendency to over-rely on the machine or to use it selectively in ways that confirm expectations.[236] Judges are not immune to those cognitive tendencies, especially in crowded dockets, pretrial hearings that last only a few minutes, and institutional cultures that present risk tools as neutral and scientific.

We can place the Broward County story that ProPublica exposed in 2016 next to Loomis to see how this looks in day-to-day practice. In 2014, in the same county where COMPAS had been adopted for pretrial screening, two defendants came through the system, Brisha Borden, an 18-year-old Black woman arrested for briefly taking a bicycle and scooter worth about 80 dollars, and Vernon Prater, a 41-year-old white man with a record that included armed robbery. The tool labeled Borden high risk and Prater low risk. Two years later, ProPublica checked real recidivism and found that Borden did not reoffend while Prater was arrested again for multiple felonies.[233] Yet at the moment of decision, what the judge and the probation service saw was the output of the scoring system, packaged in the same format, with the same decile logic and the same low-medium-high language. Those numbers sat beside the file and spoke with the authority of measurement. The human was present and retained legal discretion, but the scale had already tilted. Empirical work examining how risk scores operate "in judges' hands" in Broward County emphasizes that such tools can shape confinement-related outcomes in practice, even as legal discretion formally remains with humans.[237] High-risk labels were in fact associated with harsher confinement-related outcomes in practice, even though the tool was imperfectly predictive, notably for violent recidivism, and even though the people who used it could not see how it reached its numbers. The risk score became a salient anchor, often serving as the starting point and sometimes functioning as the de facto default.

Nothing in this picture looks like the human has been removed. The judge still speaks, signs, explains and is held accountable. The presentence writer still prepares the file. The defense attorney can still argue. The prosecuting attorney can still request a sentence. The institution can therefore tell regulators, civil rights groups, and the public that it has not automated criminal justice. The truth is more uncomfortable. What has been automated is the upstream framing of the defendant's risk, presented in a way that is easy to accept, hard to contest, and impossible to audit in real time. The human is placed exactly where your third loop describes, at the fragile pivot point where responsibility is heavy, discretion is formally intact, but the informational environment has been shaped so that saying yes to the machine is the path of least resistance. This is the zone where organizations ask humans to click, sign, or pronounce the decision without checking whether the person, in that moment, still has the cognitive, temporal, and procedural space to exercise genuine judgment. It looks like human agency. It is, in reality, human agency carried on inside an automated frame.

And as before, troubling as it may be, this is only the superficial view.

What is really at stake is the normative stance encoded inside COMPAS, a stance that can end up being enforced through the judge's reasoning without the judge fully noticing how much the frame has shifted.

The Loomis case shows how an algorithmic risk score can take on legislative-like power by silently defining what "risk" means, how it is measured, and how strongly it should weigh in the moral economy of sentencing. The formal legal reference point is supposed to be public and contestable. In this context, that reference point is the constitutional guarantee of due process, including the Due Process Clause of the Fourteenth Amendment and its state counterpart in the Wisconsin Constitution, which exist precisely to ensure that decisions affecting liberty rest on reasons that can be tested, challenged, and answered in open court. Yet in practice, the operative rule is not the due process ideal of contestable justification, but an internal, proprietary rule encoded in COMPAS, difficult to invoke, inspect, or challenge because its model, weights, and validation logic remain largely inaccessible to the person whose liberty is being decided.

When introduced into the file, the score then performs an executive-like function. It operationalizes the rule by producing a label that acts in the moment, shaping attention, anchoring interpretation, and making one path feel administratively reasonable and another path feel like a deviation that must be justified. After the decision, the same socio-technical configuration shifts into a judicial-like role. The score, its category, and the warnings that accompany it become part of the record used to assess whether reliance was "proper," often by checking compliance with usage cautions rather than by opening the underlying reasoning to adversarial scrutiny. The system goes beyond assisting judgment, participating in rule-setting, rule enforcement, and rule validation, each time with its own internal logic as the reference.

Seen through this lens, the COMPAS episode becomes a clear demonstration of algorithmic legislative, executive, and judicial power converging in a single institutional pipeline.

Once again, ask yourself what you would expect a parliament, or even yourself in a referendum, to decide if confronted with the following questions:

Should courts be permitted to use proprietary algorithmic risk scores in sentencing or pretrial decisions without safeguards mandated by the governing legal framework, including explicit warnings that the score must not be determinative and clear constraints on how it may influence liberty decisions?

Human Is the Loop

In late June 2024 in the UK, *The Guardian* reported, using official figures released under freedom of information laws, that a Department for Work and Pensions (DWP) automated risk model used to trigger "high-risk" reviews of housing-benefit claims handled by local councils had wrongly flagged more than 200,000 claims over three years; around two-thirds of those flagged claims were legitimate.[238]

Most of those claims were perfectly legitimate. Yet every time the model produced a risk score, a real person had to act on it. Local benefit staff reopened cases, checked documents, asked tenants or landlords for proof, and, in some situations, paused payments while they waited for replies. Roughly £4.4 million of public money ended up being spent on checks that did not need to happen.[238] In that reporting, the DWP did not publicly "defend the tool" in response; it said it was unable to comment in the pre-election period.[238] Formally, decision-making remained "human-involved." Practically, the human was being used to make the system's suspicion real.

Inside the offices, this looked very ordinary. A caseworker would open their work queue in the internal application and find a list of benefit cases already marked as "to review" or "high-risk." That priority did not come from the worker's judgment. It came from the model, which had cross-checked records and past patterns. The worker's job was to follow the procedure attached to that flag: verify identity, request new pay slips, compare housing costs, and possibly suspend payment until evidence arrived. In this specific housing-benefit case, the reporting also notes the tool "does not use AI or machine learning." It uses a rules-based risk model drawing on claimant characteristics.[238] If a charity like Turn2us or a watchdog like Big Brother Watch said that vulnerable tenants were being subjected to intrusive and unexplained reviews, the public reassurance was often framed as: humans are still reviewing cases; nothing is "fully automated."[238] This can be technically true, but it misses the point: by the time the worker saw the file, the direction of travel had already been set.

A related official view appears in a 2023 Information Commissioner's Office (ICO) blog on local authorities' use of algorithms in welfare contexts: it states the ICO found no evidence of harm or financial detriment in that inquiry sample and that there was "meaningful human involvement" before final benefit decisions while also noting many such systems were not AI/ML but "simple algorithms" aimed at reducing administrative workload.[239] When institutions say that "a human checks it," they are describing the formal structure. But it does not, by itself, guarantee that the human can easily contradict the system without friction.

This is the logic the design installs: saying no to the signal invites friction in the form of paperwork, justification, and the possibility of escalation while saying yes means moving on to the next file. That is what it looks like when the human is in the loop.

Amnesty International's 2025 assessment describes how the DWP cycles through testing, deploying, and sometimes withdrawal of digital and AI-enabled systems across Universal Credit and Personal Independence Payment (PIP), including tools that select cases for human review and shape subsequent steps.[240] In at least one prominent fraud and error data-use context, the accompanying reassurance is that the data acts as "a prompt for further checks" and that "a final decision will always involve a human agent."[240]

But when casework is organized around speed, standardization, and compliance with process, the psychology of oversight shifts. Refusing the model's output becomes the act that needs to be explained. Accepting it becomes the act that looks professional, fast, and loyal. In other words, in that environment, the human presence does not necessarily protect against automation; it completes it.

France was going through a parallel story. In October 2024, 15 organizations, including Amnesty International France and La Quadrature du Net, announced that they had brought a challenge before the Conseil d'État against the family-benefits agency's risk-scoring algorithm—used by the Caisse nationale des allocations familiales (CNAF) to target anti-fraud and error controls.[241-243] Public reporting describes the system as assigning a risk score (often described as 0–10) based on beneficiaries' personal and administrative data, and critics argue it disproportionately targets precarious households.[242]

Journalistic investigations had shown that the system gave higher suspicion scores to low-income households, single parents, and people receiving disability benefits. The agency replied that every control was done by a human inspector and that beneficiaries could always present their case. But this reassurance does not settle what happens once a file enters a suspicion pipeline: the human can remain present while still largely executing with diminished discretion, an algorithmic preselection in administrative form. In other words, the human is still there but increasingly as the mechanism that operationalizes the score. In late 2024, the Défenseur des droits warned that the growing use of algorithms and AI in public services raises risks for users' rights, including transparency, contestability, equal treatment, and access to rights, and issued recommendations and points of vigilance for public bodies deploying such systems.[244]

Put together, these cases show how algorithmic scoring systems don't need to "decide" in order to govern: they only need to set the order of attention. Governments reassure the public that a person still touches every file, but what the scoring tool actually produces is the queue, the priority, the tempo, and an operational rhythm that redefines what it means to "exercise judgment." In that arrangement, discretion becomes asymmetrical: accepting the signal is frictionless, while resisting it is an exception that consumes time, justification, and institutional energy. Over repeated cycles, the practical center of gravity shifts: the score stops looking like a suggestion and starts functioning like the default outcome, with the human role increasingly concentrated on converting a preselection into administrative reality, whether through requests, recalculations, suspensions, or recoveries. That is why "human control" can remain formally true while becoming substantively thin: the human presence does not interrupt automation because doing so would mean absorbing additional workload and instead supplies the labor that makes automation consequential. Once this pattern becomes routine, oversight does not disappear through absence but through conditioning: the system trains the organization to treat compliance as normal and refusal as costly. At that point, the human is no longer merely "in" the loop; the human becomes the loop, as the mechanism through which the algorithm acquires force in the world.

And this is where the core issue lies.

At first glance, the UK and France episodes look like familiar administrative drift. In the UK, an algorithmic risk model misfires at scale and generates hundreds of thousands of unnecessary checks. In France, a suspicion score appears to concentrate scrutiny on the most precarious households, prompting litigation and public controversy. These are serious failures. But as in the previous scenario, they are not the deepest story these systems are telling.

The deeper stake is the normative posture embedded in these welfare scoring systems**,** a posture that redefines what "fraud," "error," and "suspicion" mean, who deserves attention first, and what level of disruption is considered acceptable in the name of control. Once that posture is wired into the administrative machinery, it can be enforced through frontline reasoning without anyone having to announce that the meaning of fairness has changed. The caseworker or inspector may still believe they are applying the rules. In practice, the frame is now being set earlier by the scoring system's internal logic.

This is where the legislative-like power appears. In principle, the reference point for welfare enforcement is public law, which is contestable and shared—a common language of rights and duties. In the UK housing-benefit context, entitlement and administration sit within a defined legal framework, including the Housing Benefit Regulations 2006 and the Housing Benefit and Council Tax Benefit (Decisions and Appeals) Regulations 2001. In France, decisions influenced by algorithmic processing are also subject to explicit transparency duties, including the requirement to inform the person when an individual decision is based on algorithmic processing and to communicate the rules and main characteristics upon request. The point of such frameworks is that the operative rule can be named, tested, and argued with. Yet, in the context of such algorithmic cases highlighted in both countries, the practical rule that governs attention is increasingly not the formal legal standard. It is the internal rule encoded in the algorithm: its variables, thresholds, and validation logic, which are difficult for the person affected to invoke as a stable target for contestation because they are not presented as the true reference point, even when they are functioning as one.

Once introduced into the workflow, algorithmic scoring then takes on an executive-like function. It does not need to issue a final determination to exercise power. It operationalizes its own priorities by manufacturing the queue. It creates the list, the urgency, the workload allocation, and the investigative sequence. In the UK case, the "high-risk" flag triggers reopenings, verification demands, and sometimes payment pauses while evidence is sought, even when most flagged cases prove legitimate. In the French case, the suspicion score is publicly described as a mechanism that selects who will be checked, with higher scores increasing the likelihood of investigation. The algorithmic score functions as an executive instrument because it makes one pathway administratively frictionless and another friction-laden.

After that, the same configuration drifts into a judicial-like role. The score, the category, and the audit trail of steps taken in response can later be presented as "proper process," not because the underlying rationale has been opened to adversarial testing but because the file shows that the prescribed sequence was followed. This is where rights frameworks are most at risk of being displaced by procedural compliance with algorithmically organized suspicion.

From this vantage point, the UK and France welfare cases are also a demonstration of algorithmic legislative, executive, and judicial power converging within a single institutional pipeline.

It is worth asking again what you would expect a parliament, or even yourself in a referendum, to decide if confronted with questions like these:

Should welfare administrations be permitted to use opaque suspicion scores to determine which households face intrusive controls, payment interruptions, or recovery action, when the scoring rule itself is not presented to the person as a contestable standard and may be difficult to audit for error or bias?

Should "meaningful human involvement" be treated as satisfied simply because a person follows a prescribed checklist, even when refusal is structurally costly and the score has already set the direction of travel?

And if the answer is no, then the real question becomes institutional, not technical: what safeguards, transparency duties, and constraints must be imposed so that the public rule remains the rule, rather than being implicitly displaced by an internal one.

Human Through the Loop

In April 2025, *The Washington Post* profiled Keith Krehbiel, a retired political scientist with Parkinson's disease living in Stanford, California, who volunteered for adaptive deep brain stimulation (aDBS) trials run by Stanford and UC San Francisco (UCSF).[245]

By the time Krehbiel entered the trial, he had already gone through the familiar arc of Parkinson's disease: diagnosis in middle age, an initial good response to levodopa, followed by the slow accumulation of side effects and complications, including nausea, low blood pressure, daytime sleepiness, and later dyskinesias and "brain fog" that occur when medication has to be taken often.[245] He said he would lie down in his office in front of a space heater because it felt soothing.[245]

He was taking five or six pills a day, later just one, but the price was fogginess and the constant management of timing. He was still very much there as a person—lucid and motivated—but the disease and the treatment were starting to dictate the rhythm more than he did. He volunteered for adaptive DBS because the standard version, which sends a constant electrical pulse into the subthalamic nucleus, cannot respond dynamically to fluctuating symptom states and medication cycles.[245] It cannot distinguish between a moment when medication is already working well and a moment when the brain is slipping back into the slow, synchronized pattern that produces tremor and stiffness.

The experimental system he was offered was different. It would go in his body, with electrodes placed deep in the motor circuits, a pulse generator under the skin and, most importantly, software trained on his own neural signals to adapt therapy.

Clinicians and researchers, including Helen Bronte-Stewart at Stanford and Philip Starr at UCSF, describe how adaptive DBS algorithms are developed by recording brain rhythms in known conditions, including on and off levodopa, and then training an AI-enabled model to recognize which signal patterns match which clinical states.[245] Then they loaded that model into the implant so that, at home, without a doctor present, the device could recognize when his brain was drifting into the Parkinsonian rhythm and increase stimulation, and when the rhythm was already good, it could back off. It was no longer a simple pacemaker; it was a listener and a modulator at once.

Once he went home, the human and the AI were no longer separable. Keith would get up, move around, talk to his family, walk, and rest, and each of these actions would change the electrical patterns in his brain. The implant was constantly sampling those patterns and applying the model that the team had trained on him. If he was in a good phase, the device eased off, which meant fewer side effects and longer battery life. If he started to slip, the device could increase stimulation, helping him avoid freezing or tremor spikes. This patient experience—smoother symptom control across the day—matches how adaptive DBS is designed to adjust stimulation in real time.[245,246]

He did not have to request the change; he did not have to open an app; he did not even have to be aware of it. The machine responded to him faster than he could have responded himself. Yet he was not passive either. His own behavior—taking his single daily pill, sleeping better, moving more, speaking more—created the conditions in which the AI deemed more or less stimulation necessary. Every day's motor performance was therefore a joint product. It was his body and his choices; it was also the algorithm in his chest, reading the oscillopathy and adjusting in real time. If someone asked who was doing the therapy, the honest answer was: both. If someone asked who was in charge, there was no simple answer because neither the human nor the AI was acting alone. And this is basically the point in human through the loop.

Krehbiel feels empowered because the tremor is gone, the dyskinesia is gone, and the fog is gone. He reduced medication from five or six pills a day to one and reported that tremor, dyskinesia, and "brain fog" had improved for him.[245] At the same time, the actual dosing of electricity in his brain, the timing of that dosing, and the shape of his motor day are being continuously produced by a model he did not design and cannot independently audit. He is through the loop.

On 24 February 2025, the FDA's PMA documentation recorded approval of an adaptive DBS programming feature for Parkinson's disease,[247] which Medtronic announced publicly as its BrainSense Adaptive DBS feature.[248] This is not science fiction. Scientific papers describe it very plainly.[246] The system records local field potentials from the subthalamic nucleus or from a cortical lead; the AI model classifies the state; the implant changes amplitude and sometimes contact pattern; and the patient experiences smoother movement and better sleep.[246] At the same time, the doctors remind readers that the algorithm was trained on clinic data under controlled conditions, that it was tuned by engineers paid by device companies, and that it must not be tampered with.

The patient, however, lives with it 24 hours a day, without continuous clinical supervision, because the system is designed to adapt outside the clinic.[245] He lives with a device that is inside him and that coauthors every gesture. He is present, awake, and consenting; he still has to take medication; he can still switch the system off if the doctor has given him that right, but the default, the everyday state, is that he goes through his life with an AI that writes the motor score in parallel with him. This is a human body made into a conduit for machine decision. It is the most intimate form of human through the loop.

In 2025, a Delphi consensus of neuromodulation experts judged that adaptive DBS is likely to become routine in the coming years, while stressing that broader adoption depends on simplifying implantation and programming and refining adaptive algorithms for more complex symptoms.[249]

Expert consensus also emphasizes that today's aDBS still demands specialized expertise and that implementation work remains, especially around biomarkers, programming burden, and algorithms capable of handling complex, fluctuating symptoms.[249] If aDBS is on a path toward mainstream clinical use, as the 2025 Delphi consensus anticipates, then the question is no longer whether humans will live with adaptive algorithms in their bodies but how those adaptive rules will be governed, explained, and constrained once they scale.

That is the real shift.

At first reading, the Krehbiel story can be told as a medical triumph. A device listens to neural signals, adjusts stimulation, reduces symptoms, and gives a patient back a life with room to live. That is real, and it matters. But apart from its therapeutic dimension, the decisive transformation lies in the algorithmic power it introduces: a reordering of who sets the terms of action, normalizing the quiet relocation of human agency into the machine.

What matters most is the value-loaded rule set carried inside adaptive DBS. The system has to define what counts as a "good" motor state and what counts as pathological drift. It has to decide which signals deserve intervention, how quickly, how strongly, and with what tolerance for side effects. Those choices are not neutral descriptions of the brain. They are preferences about everyday human capability and acceptable side effects, translated into control logic that can, indirectly, shape mood, energy, and the felt sense of agency.

Once implanted, that logic is no longer an external recommendation. It becomes an active standard that the patient lives through, sometimes consciously, often without noticing how much of daily agency is being coproduced by an algorithm that functions as both a classifier and a controller.

This is where the algorithmic legislative-like power appears. In principle, the public reference point for devices that act inside the body is law and regulation. In the United States, that includes the Food, Drug, and Cosmetic Act framework for premarket approval of class III devices and the FDA's PMA regulations. These are meant to provide a shared vocabulary of duties and protections: safety and effectiveness standards, conditions of approval, disclosure, consent, and oversight. But those public rules do not, and cannot, specify the fine-grained norms that will govern the patient's seconds and minutes. That norm is written elsewhere. It is written in the system's internal control logic: the mapping from signals to states and from states to stimulation. The regulatory framework is the public perimeter. The control code is the internal statute book that governs what the device will do, moment by moment, once it is inside a person.

This is legislative-like not because it sits outside regulation but because, within the perimeter the law authorizes, it creates a second layer of rulemaking by setting proprietary operative defaults that bind at the level that matters most in lived experience: it defines what counts as deviation, what counts as stability, and what intensity of intervention is warranted as the default response.

Unlike regulation, which exists as text addressed to the public and designed to be arguable, this operational, algorithmic rule exists primarily as executable behavior, legible as outcomes rather than as a stated norm. It is not something that can be readily invoked, reviewed, or even fully grasped as a stable object because it is encountered only as software behavior and parameterization by those who did not design it.

Once the system is in place, it performs an executive-like function continuously. It does not need to issue a final decision to exercise power. It executes the algorithmic rule by acting in the moment, allocating intervention across the day, and making the next motor second more probable than the one that would have occurred without it. It is governance by modulation. It turns a definition of an "undesirable state" into a bodily response before reflection is possible.

Then it drifts into a judicial-like role. The algorithmic system's behavior is rendered legitimate through logs, clinic follow-ups, programming sessions, and compliance with approved use conditions. What becomes assessable is often not the patient's ability to contest the system's underlying classifications but whether the system is being used according to the authorized framework, whether adjustments stay within acceptable bounds, and whether deviations count as misuse. In other words, validation tends to attach to procedural correctness around the device rather than to the contestability of the device's internal reasoning as lived.

Taken together, adaptive DBS is not merely a tool that assists care, but a concentrated example of algorithmic legislative, executive, and judicial power converging within one intimate pipeline: rule definition inside the model, rule execution inside the body, and rule validation through regulated clinical procedure.

So the question for a parliament, and for any citizen who cares about dignity, is not whether this technology should exist. The question is what rights should travel with it once it scales.

Should every person living with an adaptive neurostimulation implant have a legally enforceable right to meaningful transparency and control, including access to understandable explanations of what the system is optimizing for, access to logs of how it has acted, as well as a genuine ability to decline, pause, or step back from the adaptive layer as a form of treatment refusal, without losing access to care, being penalized, or being cast as "noncompliant"?

Trust as a Permission Layer

Once we follow the gradient of the human loop from "off" to "through," there is one pattern that becomes impossible to ignore. The promise that keeps these architectures acceptable is never only capability. It is their performance in manufacturing trust.

This is not a metaphor. In the trust-in-automation literature, trust is treated as a dynamic variable that can be built, calibrated, and disrupted by design. For example, the three-layer model proposed by researchers Kevin Anthony Hoff and Masooda Bashir synthesizes evidence showing that trust in automated systems is shaped by dispositional tendencies, situational cues such as interface signals and task stakes, and learned experience with system performance over time.[250] What matters here is that trust does not merely reflect whether a tool is accurate. It reflects whether the human feels able to predict the tool, interpret its moves, and remain oriented in relation to it, especially when the system operates faster than reflection. In other words, trust becomes an engineered condition of use, not a private feeling. It becomes something an architecture can shape by managing predictability, legibility, and the felt distribution of responsibility.

As the human remains visible to artificially absorb responsibility, and the decision logic is displaced into the AI system and its algorithm as an operative rule that silently sets the frame, the priorities, and the defaults, what we are being asked to trust is not primarily the human, but the architecture that stages the human as its alibi. The human becomes a visible signature point, while the operative rule is executed by the system's algorithmic logic.

In that configuration, it is not enough to understand whether and how a human is off, among, in, is the loop, or lives through it. It becomes necessary to understand what makes trust durable enough for such architectures to perform.

Experimental work on algorithm aversion makes the mechanism concrete. Researchers Berkeley J. Dietvorst, Joseph P. Simmons, and Cade Massey showed that people often abandon algorithmic forecasting advice after seeing the algorithm make mistakes, even when they are shown that the algorithm outperforms a human forecaster.[251] The striking part is not that error reduces trust; that is expected. The striking part is that the same level of error is tolerated in humans but punished in machines. Trust is therefore not tracking accuracy in any neutral way. It is tracking a moral expectation of what an algorithm is supposed to be, and once that expectation is violated, people withdraw reliance.[251] In later work, the same authors show that aversion can be reduced when users are allowed to make even slight adjustments to the algorithm's output.[252] That tiny allowance of agency does not fix the model, but it repairs the psychology of reliance. It makes the user feel less governed and more participatory, and trust returns.[252]

Taken together, these two strands of research point to a disturbing inversion. Hoff and Bashir show that trust is a moving equilibrium shaped by cues, context, and experience, not a stable belief in a tool's competence.[250] Dietvorst and colleagues show that people do not reward algorithms for being better on average; they punish them for violating an implicit moral expectation of what a machine should be.[251] When an algorithm errs, the rupture operates at the level of interpretation, not merely at the statistical level. The system stops feeling legible, and the human withdraws.[251]

Combining that with what the human loop gradient reveals, if trust is fragile and if algorithmic error is uniquely corrosive, then the central trust-design problem for AI systems is not simply to improve accuracy, but to prevent the experience of being governed by something that can err without providing anything to the human that would help make sense of why it happened. In other words, the system must not only produce outputs but continuously produce a relationship in which the human feels able to stay oriented, with an explanation, a handle, or at least a coherent account of what the system believed it was doing and why. That relationship is what makes adoption feel safe, and safety is what makes delegation habitual, and habit is what makes trust feel durable.

This is where the human loop becomes something else.

The human is not added primarily to improve decisions, even if that is how oversight is often described, but to protect trust from the shock of machine fallibility. It might sound the same, but the latter is a real difference from the former. One is about improving judgment; the other is about stabilizing reliance.

The human becomes a buffer that absorbs the psychological and moral impact of error. When the system fails, responsibility has somewhere to land: a reason, an explanation, an excuse—whatever that is, as long as it gives the human the impression of knowing against the fear of the unknown. Therefore, when the system succeeds, the machine earns the aura of competence. When the system fails, the machine earns the aura of reasonableness because the surrounding process can still present the outcome as cared for, reviewed, or answerable. The algorithmic architecture wins both ways, not by deception but by arranging how error is metabolized and where uncertainty is allowed to settle.

Dietvorst et al.'s finding about adjustment is the most revealing detail. A tiny ability to tweak the algorithm's output can restore willingness to rely on it.[252] That is not because the tweak meaningfully improves the model, but because it restores an ability for the human to exercise the power of being helpful to the machine. The user feels less like a passive subject of the system and more like a participant in it, which in turn creates reassurance that the human is still being useful in those circumstances. This can be reframed as a human competency: an entry barrier one must clear to earn the privilege of using the machine and accessing the advantages of its algorithmic power.

This is what I call the micro-interruptibility. Rather than challenging the system's rules, the power lies in slightly modulating its expression. It does not reopen the model's premises, its objectives, or its thresholds. It only gives the user a small handhold within the interaction—just enough to convert exposure into participation. In practice, micro-interruptibility functions like a psychological circuit breaker: it does not stop the machine, but it prevents the user from feeling fully trapped by it. And because it operates at the surface, it can be granted cheaply, without changing the underlying authority of the system. If designed, it is the smallest possible form of "voice" that a human can have—one that restores orientation and preserves the willingness to rely, and the trust that makes reliance sustainable.

Therefore, what looks like algorithmic control may, in practice, be an intentionally or unintentionally designed architecture of trust because trust in an algorithmic system is secured by its architecture—in the way responsibility is staged, the way agency is rationed, and the way the system manages the human emotional cost of error. More precisely, trust is stabilized when the architecture makes the system predictable enough, the human role meaningful enough, and the consequences explainable enough for people to keep moving rather than get stuck in doubt. Once you see that, you see why capability alone never explains scale. Scale requires a trust production line. And the human loop, in all its forms, is one of the most effective machines for producing that trust.

If trust can be produced by architecture, then trust is no longer just a moral endorsement; it is an operating condition. It becomes the permission layer that allows complex systems to move faster than human understanding and to keep moving while still being trusted, even when they fail. As trust is treated as an operating condition, its nature changes. It becomes less about believing and more about proceeding.

When trust becomes an operating condition, it stops behaving like trust and starts behaving like legitimacy. It becomes the invisible credential that allows a system to proceed without having to persuade because the system has already arranged the circumstances in which proceeding feels safer than questioning. At that point, the key question is no longer whether people trust the system, but what the system is allowed to do simply because it has learned how to keep trust.

In a classical polity, legislative power earns legitimacy by being public and speakable. Executive power earns legitimacy by being accountable to that public rule. Judicial power earns legitimacy by testing decisions against that rule in a forum where reasons can be exchanged. In an algorithmic polity, the order reverses. The system earns adoption first, and only later does governance scramble to explain what has been adopted. Trust becomes the precondition that substitutes for a publicly articulated rule, and once the substitution becomes routine, argument becomes an afterthought.

Here's where macro-interruptibility is at stake. While micro-interruptibility gives the user a small handle within the interaction, macro-interruptibility is different in kind. It is the system-level capacity to stop, contest, and reopen the governing rule itself. It is the difference between being allowed to tweak an output and being able to challenge the standard that produced it. Macro-interruptibility exists when the rule is publicly nameable, when the person affected can demand reasons, when they can trigger a review, and when that review can alter the decision path rather than merely decorate it. This is a constitutional property of the decision environment, not a usability feature. It is contestability and reviewability in a public-facing sense: not an internal audit ritual but a right that can be invoked by those subject to the decision and heard in a forum with the power to compel change. Without macro-interruptibility, participation becomes cosmetic: the system may feel adjustable while remaining effectively unappealable. And that is the point where trust stops being a relationship and becomes a substitute for the procedural conditions that legitimacy normally requires.

In procedural justice research, people do not treat legitimacy as a synonym for getting the outcome they wanted. They treat it as a property of the procedure, especially whether the procedure remains interruptible by those subject to it. The classic finding is the voice effect. When people are given a meaningful opportunity to express their views before an authority decides, they judge the process as fairer and are more willing to accept even unfavorable outcomes because voice signals that the procedure is not sealed off from them.[253]

The "voice" that macro-interruptibility guarantees is one of the primary mechanisms through which legitimacy is psychologically produced and socially maintained. Remove it, and the system may still function, but it begins to function as something else: a pipeline that demands compliance without providing procedural standing. That is why algorithmic governance so often generates what legal and policy critiques describe as a procedural gap, not only an accuracy gap.[254,255] The person affected is frequently reduced to an object of decision, with only minimal participation—just enough to preserve trust in the process but not enough to grant genuine agency to contest, redirect, or stop it. And far from incidental, this reduction is the condition under which the system can keep operating smoothly and remain trusted while becoming difficult to interrupt.

Crucially, recent empirical work on algorithmic decision-making shows that this macro-interruptibility, whether micro or macro, is not automatically supplied by the mere presence of a human somewhere in the process. In a controlled user study on a loan rejection scenario, Yurrita Semperena and colleagues manipulated three features: whether an explanation was provided, whether a human was said to oversee the decision, and whether the decision could be contested.[256] They found that explanations primarily improved perceptions of informational fairness, and contestability primarily improved perceptions of procedural fairness. By contrast, they found no evidence that simply adding human oversight improved fairness perceptions. In other words, the public perceives the difference between a system that can be questioned and a system that merely points to a human as a formality.[256]

If legitimacy depends on whether the process remains interruptible, not at the micro level but at the macro level, and if human oversight does not reliably provide that kind of interruptibility, then the core governance question becomes structural rather than sentimental.

The decisive test is no longer "Do people trust it?" and not even "Does it work?"

The decisive test is whether the system's rule-setting, rule execution, and rule validation remain publicly interruptible.

Because once trust becomes the permission layer, the deepest form of capture lies in a system that becomes hard to refuse without becoming hard to live with. That is algorithmic power operating as a political technology of smooth inevitability, to which the trias algorithmica must respond.

3 Algorithmic-Defined Human Worth

Revaluing Mechanism of Work

The algorithmic power grab does not stop at governance. When a system can define the rules of visibility, enforce them, and normalize its authority through the language of adoption and trust, it does something even more disruptive than replacing institutions. With the human loop as part of its enabling mechanism, the AI system does not merely assist with work. It starts to redefine what counts as value, competence, and necessity. It does not only regulate the public sphere; it rewrites the economic logic of effort. The outputs of the AI-integrated stack become the reference point against which human work is priced, judged, and increasingly designed. The decisive test is not whether people like it, whether the market begins to treat its outputs as the new baseline of acceptable value. When that happens, the loop closes again, not as governance, but as labor: humans adapt their skills, attention, and time to meet a standard they did not set, under rules they cannot readily reopen, because the system has already made its own performance feel like the only rational pace and the new labor normal.

This is also where a missing bridge between classic innovation lenses becomes evident.

James Utterback and William Abernathy's dominant design[257] explained the precondition for any performance threshold "good enough" to become authoritative: the moment when an industry stops experimenting with many competing definitions of performance and converges on a shared reference design, so that evaluation stabilizes, expectations synchronize, and "good enough" becomes legible, comparable, and improvable. In the AI-integrated stack, that reference design is often not a product form but a measurement regime, meaning the "design" that dominates is increasingly the benchmark itself, governing evaluation and materializing as dashboards, scorecards, and audit gates.

Clayton Christensen's disruptive innovation[258] explained the strategic trajectory of how new entrants learn to exploit that stabilization, how "good enough" entry occurs where performance is initially inferior but acceptable, and where cost and accessibility open new markets or undercut the low end before capability improves and climbs upward. AI complicates the picture by allowing a platform to behave like a perpetual entrant and a perpetual incumbent at once, entering from below while simultaneously controlling distribution, interfaces, and evaluation surfaces that accelerate the climb.

Herbert Simon's satisficing[259] explained why "good enough" is not a defect but a decision rule: markets rarely maximize; they accept. Once AI can reliably hit the satisficing threshold at speed, the demand side stops paying for marginal refinement, and craft loses pricing power not because it is wrong but because it is extra. This is the psychological hinge. The market does not need to be convinced that the machine is the best, only that it is sufficient, repeatable, and less cognitively costly to accept than to scrutinize.

Rebecca Henderson and Kim Clark's architectural innovation[260] explained the mechanism of that shift inside work itself: the components of a job can remain recognizable—inspection, diagnosis, scheduling, documentation—but the architecture that links them is rewired into pipelines, interfaces, and platforms, so advantage migrates from individual expertise to the system that orchestrates the whole. This is where competence changes meaning: it becomes less about the ability to perform a task and more about the ability to operate inside, comply with, and improve the pipeline that now performs it.

Joseph Schumpeter's creative destruction[261] then named what happens next on the supply side: an incumbent production logic is not merely competed with; it is rendered uneconomic because the unit of value shifts from the produced artifact to the reproducible capability. And when capability is packaged as an always-available service, the destruction is not only economic but also institutional, because the older regime loses the authority to define what counts as "proper" work.

Dominant design tells us when "good enough" hardens into a shared reference at scale; disruption tells us how it enters; satisficing tells us why it wins; architectural innovation tells us how workflows get rewired; and creative destruction tells us why incumbents break. Trias algorithmica adds what makes these stages normatively binding in an AI-mediated world.

What these theories do not fully capture on their own is the governance effect of benchmarking: the operational production of a public baseline of acceptable performance, cost, and speed, encoded into tools, dashboards, evaluation harnesses, and procurement criteria, including requests for proposals scoring, service-level agreements, and audit gates so that "acceptable" is no longer debated in professional communities, anchoring a legislative-like power by defining adequacy in advance, enforced at scale as a default comparison point through algorithms as an executive-like power, and then retroactively validated as "proper" through audit trails, scorecards, incident reviews, and compliance evidence that function as a judicial-like power. This is where legitimacy becomes operational: not granted by persuasion but manufactured by instrumentation that makes deviation costly and compliance read as the default.

None of them, by themselves, foreground the moment when the benchmark becomes prescriptive—when "good enough" is no longer a descriptive market preference but an emitted standard that reorders employability, pricing, and legitimacy.

In the AI-integrated stack, the benchmark is produced, stabilized, and exported through instrumentation, metrics, and interfaces. That is the gap the trias algorithmica is designed to bridge. It guards against the conversion of preference into constraint and of constraint into a quasi-right to govern.

Trias algorithmica fills a specific gap between Simon, Henderson, and Clark. Simon explains why markets settle for "good enough," while Henderson and Clark explain how work gets rewired once new components and interfaces appear. What calls for the trias algorithmica is the transition between the two: the moment when "good enough" ceases to be merely accepted by buyers as a choice and instead becomes a de facto prescriptive benchmark produced and operationalized by the AI-integrated stack, so that this acceptance turns into enforceable design constraints that restructure workflows, reprice labor, and set the conditions for Schumpeterian destruction. This is also where the power shift becomes hard to reverse because the benchmark starts selecting who gets to participate in the market.

It also fills the conceptual gap left after the two phases of dominant design emergence and dominant design convergence, by identifying a third, previously unnamed phase: normgence, which arises in the absence of algorithmic power separation and in which a converged benchmark hardens into a quasi-legal standard that governs what is fundable, insurable, auditable, and employable. Normgence is the moment when industry convergence around the benchmark starts behaving like a jurisdiction because the benchmark begins to function as the gate through which activity becomes formally admissible.

This phase makes explicit the governance conversion, where measurement becomes a rule and where convergence is no longer only a market settlement around a product architecture but an infrastructural settlement around measurement itself. Once platforms standardize the metrics, the tests, and the reporting surfaces, the "dominant design" becomes a dominant benchmark. And once the benchmark dominates, it pulls the industry toward convergence, even when the underlying technical designs still vary because what counts is what scores, what audits, and what procures. In that condition, innovation continues, but it is canalized because novelty that cannot be expressed in the benchmark is treated as risk rather than progress.

It treats innovation not only as a technological or strategic phenomenon but also as a constitutional one, where the right to define adequacy becomes the right to define waste, and where the power to set performance baselines becomes the power to revalue labor. The constitutional effect is budgetary, contractual, and career-forming. It decides whose work is legible, whose judgment is trusted, and whose time is priced as "extra."

This is one of the algorithmic triad's most consequential extensions. It revalues human work. It does so by relocating authority from the producer of the work to the system that defines the conditions under which the work is recognized as valid.

When an algorithm can deliver results most users consider "good enough" at machine speed, under a cost structure where variable execution costs collapse and value creation is increasingly priced like a subscription, the rules of competition and the organization of labor begin to change. As the same systems then start to redefine what "better" looks like faster and faster, that initial change steepens into a structural reordering: the market value of human execution falls, and the structure of value networks changes profoundly. The mechanism that drives this change goes beyond a single substitution effect to become a compound dynamic in which properties specific to AI—namely, near-zero marginal cost at the point of delivery, practically unlimited scalability, learning feedback loops, and asymmetric liability—interact and reinforce one another. This is why the shift is not merely economic, but normative because cost, speed, and acceptability become fused into a single baseline that everyone must obey to be taken seriously.

The starting point is to shift attention from products and markets to the composition of work itself. Not a single "thing," a job is a bundle of socio-technical-economic elements, including tasks that vary in how automatable they are, how much data they require, and how users perceive their value. AI enters this landscape not as a new firm but as a capability layer that can execute individual tasks with different economics. As soon as AI can do some tasks at acceptable quality for typical users and at a much lower cost, the price that people are willing to pay for human execution of those specific tasks begins to drop. This repricing within the job starts locally, task by task, and then diffuses to the rest of the workflow. Once repricing diffuses, identity diffuses with it because professions are reorganized around what the pipeline cannot yet routinize.

What is taking shape here is the pathway toward normgence, the point at which that labor code stops being implicit adaptation and starts behaving like an emitted standard that employers can point to, buyers can demand, and auditors can enforce. Labor law and collective bargaining still exist, but the practical rule that increasingly sets the pace, the minimum standard of deliverables, and the conditions of employability is being authored within systems that value tasks, rank performance, and allocate attention through algorithmic benchmarks. This code is neither issued by legislatures nor negotiated as a social contract. It arrives as default standards embedded in tools and platforms, and it spreads because firms and workers adapt to whatever the market treats as "good enough." Because it is embedded, it travels faster than policy, which means the benchmark can become binding long before it becomes democratically contestable.

No single legal framework directly addresses this dynamic as such, and no dedicated indemnification regime exists to compensate workers or communities for the externalities it generates when value collapses locally and then cascades through occupations. The result is a silent mechanism enabled by algorithmic code and amplified by our human flaws, habits of reliance, and desire for comfort, convenience, and certainty. This becomes the new defining law of what work is worth and what humans must do to stay relevant in the economy. The crucial detail is that it changes obligations without formally changing rights, which is exactly how a benchmark can govern without ever having to call itself governance.

This mechanism unfolds through 11 causally interrelated steps, each describing a distinct stage in how AI progressively revalues human work as algorithmic order expands:

1. Work entry gap (overserved/esteem-light work)
2. Cheap work capability (scope-per-euro explosion)
3. Work incentive drag (incumbent hesitation + shadow use)
4. Work-loop acceleration (usage → feedback → improvement)
5. Work pipeline rebundling (job → modular flow)
6. Work baseline flip (AI-first becomes the default)
7. Work control-point capture (keys, logs, metrics, sign-off)
8. Stable split of work responsibility (machine throughput/human liability)
9. Stepwise work capability diffusion (punctuated capability jumps)
10. Work trust competition (auditability becomes a premium)
11. Work redefined (from execution to alignment custody)

Mapped onto what I call the F-Curve of Algorithmic Work Transition, these 11 steps are organized into three successive transition phases: the early shift of work, the transitional reorganization of work, and the structural consolidation of work. Together, these phases deepen the embedding of algorithmic order into the nature of work.

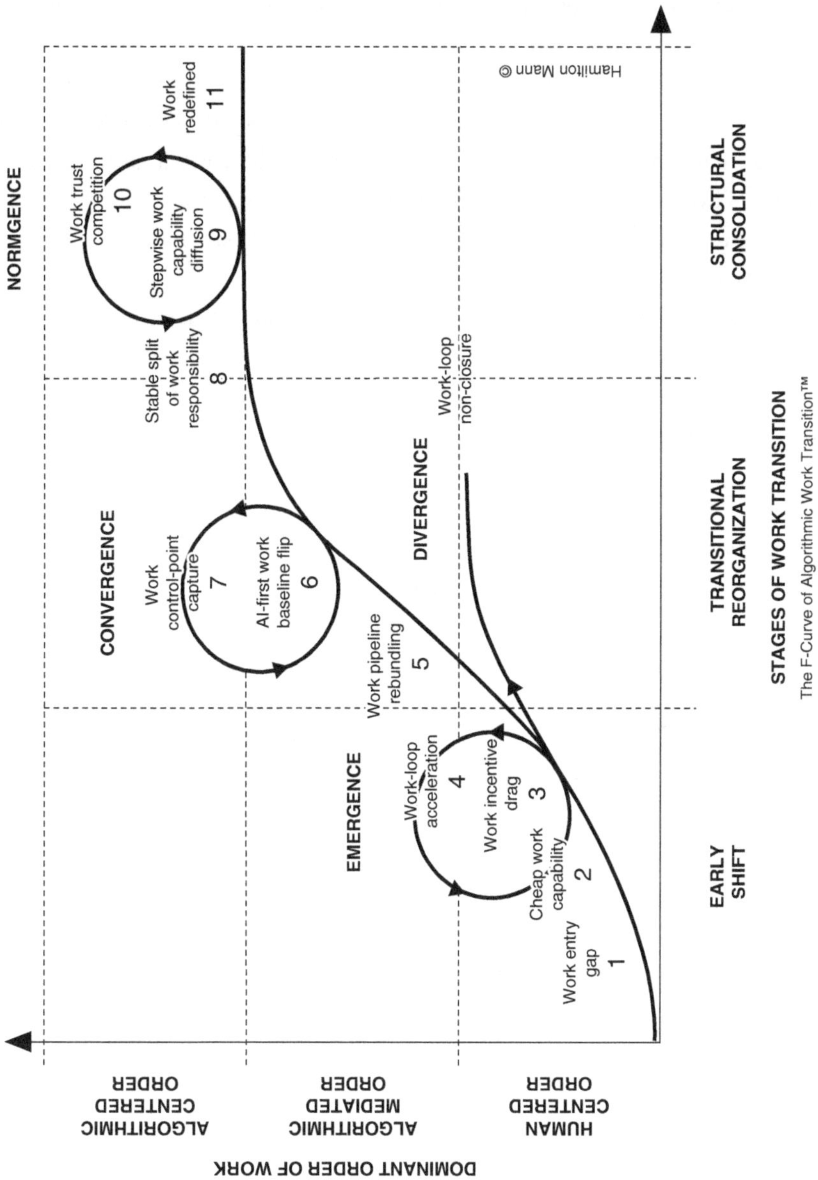

The F-Curve of Algorithmic Work Transition™

1. The Entry Gap: An Initial Condition

It begins in one of two ways: overshooting and latent inefficiency, or overwhelm paired with weak recognition. In many professions, the quality that is routinely delivered is higher than what the average user needs or notices at the margin. For these overserved tasks, the extra human polish does not justify the extra cost. This gap creates the natural entry point for AI, since a machine that is slightly rougher but far cheaper will satisfy a large share of demand. This is the earliest crack through which benchmarking can later enter, as it identifies a zone where adequacy is already socially tolerated below craft standards.

A practical way to identify them is to run controlled downgrades of quality attributes that are expensive for humans to deliver and observe whether acceptance, error rates, and time to value remain within target thresholds. Typical early candidates include highly templated writing, routine analytics, standard compliance checks, and repetitive design adaptations, especially when inputs and outputs can be strictly specified.

A second entry point appears when tasks demand disproportionately high human effort to meet visible quality thresholds, driving incompressible costs on the balance sheet, yet are weakly valued by workers because they confer little status, trigger no career advancement, and offer minimal pride or enrichment. In practice, these are effort-heavy and esteem-light duties. These effort-intensive but low-prestige tasks (for example, exhaustive documentation, routine evidence gathering, compliance formatting, or repetitive synthesis passes) make them prime candidates for AI substitution. You can spot them through high hours per unit of output, low promotability signals in performance reviews, low creative variance across deliverables, and a clear opportunity cost when senior talent spends time on work that a standardized process or machine can execute with comparable acceptance rates. When these markers co-occur, the economic and motivational asymmetries align to favor AI entry and rapid repricing. This is also where the human loop becomes vulnerable to capture because relief from low-status workload is experienced as liberation, even when it imperceptibly relocates authority over standards.

2. The Cheap Capability: A Foothold Through Affordability and Access

Because AI operates with near-zero marginal cost at the point of delivery and can scale concurrently to many users, it opens execution capacity to individuals and small organizations that previously lacked the budget, headcount, or expertise. What changes is not the nature of the task, but the identity and volume of actors who can perform it, along with their ability to chain it to adjacent tasks. This is where "good enough" starts to be defined in practice: once acceptable output becomes cheap and ubiquitous, adequacy stops being a craft-community norm and becomes a market-driven threshold shaped by what the new majority can produce and tolerate. This is emergence, where the first conditions of normgence exist in embryo because the threshold begins to travel as a default expectation rather than as a debated standard.

The practical signature of this foothold is a step change in the reachable scope per euro spent, measured by more deliverables per period, shorter cycle times from brief to acceptance, and greater coverage of long-tail needs that used to be ignored. Access expands further when models are embedded in no-code tools, SaaS workflows, and familiar office suites, which suppress adoption friction and lift the ceiling on who can combine tasks. This does not merely substitute for expert labor; it creates novel combinations such as continuous lightweight research paired with just-in-time drafting and validation or micro-campaigns that iterate daily instead of quarterly. As these combinations become normal, expectations shift for the median buyer, and incumbents discover that the market now compares their bespoke offering to a cheaper, always-available pipeline that delivers acceptable outcomes on demand. Benchmarking begins here as comparison pressure before it culminates in normgence, where the pipeline becomes the silent ruler by which all work is measured.

3. The Incentive Drag: An Asymmetry of Motivation

Established professionals often have little reason to move first. Even as capability and access expand, established professionals and institutions often hesitate to pivot because their incentives, reputational concerns, and risk exposures push them away from early adoption. Revenue models based on hourly billing or bespoke engagements make cheaper, faster delivery appear as cannibalization rather than growth, while brand positioning around craftsmanship creates the fear that using AI will dilute perceived quality. Inside organizations, governance adds further brakes: compliance reviews, data residency constraints, confidentiality clauses, and model provenance questions all introduce approval queues that slow experimentation. Additionally, performance targets tied to utilization and billable hours reward keeping humans busy rather than redesigning the workflow. Managers also interpret client signals conservatively. A few vocal premium buyers who prefer artisan outputs can overshadow a silent majority that would happily accept AI-assisted work at a lower price, which biases decision-making toward the status quo. The asymmetry shows up in operational diagnostics: proposals omit AI-enabled options even when feasible, pricing templates lack tiers that separate human oversight from machine execution, risk committees require multiple sign-offs for small pilots, and internal KPIs track hours and win rates but not cycle time, first-pass acceptance, or error interception rates that would favor automation. Decisions are framed as protecting a high-margin human hour today rather than compounding a lower-margin but scalable pipeline tomorrow because the risks are overestimated and the scale is underestimated. Meanwhile, shadow adoption grows at the edges as junior staff and overloaded teams use AI under the radar to draft, summarize, perform first-pass analyses, and meet deadlines, creating a credibility gap between official policy and actual practice. This combination allows AI-based delivery expand in the periphery without triggering an explicit redesign decision. By the time results and references accumulate, the center of the market practice has already moved, and late adopters must jump a wider chasm to catch up. This is how the conditions for normgence form without announcement, as practice becomes precedent while policy lags, and precedent sets the living standard of what is considered "acceptable." Yet this trajectory is not guaranteed. Not all technologies succeed in converting this shadow adoption into a sustained shift in practice; many stall at this stage of peripheral uptake and are absorbed back into organizational inertia, a condition that can be described as work-loop non-closure. In several sectors, current AI technologies may still be following this path, remaining a fragmented capability rather than progressing toward the later consolidation into a dominant production logic.

In contrast to the normgence phenomenon, this divergence forms the lower bar of the F-curve, where adoption either plateaus or dissipates over time instead of accelerating.

4. The Loop Acceleration: Quality Built Through Iteration

If peripheral adoption succeeds in spreading into sustained usage, where AI-based outputs are systematically reused as inputs, then the trajectory shifts from fragmented adoption to endogenous acceleration. Once AI enters the workflow, every real interaction becomes both production and training material, so performance improves with use rather than plateauing or dissipating over time. In practice, the team's release cycle turns into a loop: ship a model or pipeline, capture outcomes and corrections, translate those into structured feedback, retrain or fine-tune, redeploy, and repeat. The speed of improvement depends on three levers that move together: the volume of meaningful usage events, the quality and granularity of the feedback attached to those events, and the amount of computing power and engineering applied to digest them. A layman's way to think about this is that weekly improvement is roughly proportional to how many real cases the system sees, how clearly people mark what was right or wrong, and how much horsepower you spend turning those marks into a smarter system. When any of those three doubles, improvement tends to accelerate. Because the feedback loop spans more than just the model, retrieval quality, tool integration, prompt libraries, and evaluation harnesses all tighten the loop. As a result, capability often jumps in steps rather than inching up smoothly, which is why a new model release or a better retrieval corpus can overnight unlock adjacent tasks like compliant phrasing, style consistency, or domain-specific reasoning that were unreliable the week before. Over time, this does not merely raise performance against a stable target but moves the target itself: the system starts to redefine what "better" looks like because each cycle bakes yesterday's human preferences and exceptions into today's default, turns what once counted as premium craft into an expected baseline, and even extends to defining the new standard of excellence at an accelerating pace. This is the second force that drives toward normgence as the benchmark stops being a floor and becomes a moving frontier that markets begin to treat as the only rational pace.

Synthetic data amplifies the effect by filling gaps that the real world has not yet covered, while automated evaluators convert messy human preferences into precise signals that the system can optimize. At the same time, guardrails and monitoring reduce regressions by catching bad behaviors early, improving the average outcome and shrinking the tails of the distribution. At this step, the half-life of differentiation collapses. A technique that gives a human team an edge for a quarter may be learned by the system in weeks, and once learned, it is delivered at scale at a radically reduced competitive cost. Operationally, you can measure the loop by tracking acceptance at first draft, the correction distance between version n and $n + 1$, time-to-acceptable under fixed constraints, and the share of issues resolved by updating data, prompts, or tools rather than adding human labor. The strategic implication is that waiting to adopt until quality looks perfect is self-defeating because quality becomes perfect faster for those who are already using the system; participation feeds the loop, while nonparticipation starves it. And once participation feeds the loop, nonparticipation begins to look not like prudence but like underperformance, which is how a benchmark begins to behave like a rule.

5. The Pipeline Rebundling: A New Logic of Workflow Redesign

Once AI systems reliably handle parts of execution, organizations stop thinking in terms of job descriptions and start thinking in terms of modular sequences of tasks that can be combined, reordered, or automated. The work unit shifts from "a person performing a process" to "a pipeline that delivers an outcome," and this shift structurally rewrites both operations and the meaning of expertise. In practical terms, a marketing department that used to brief a writer, wait for a draft, send it to design, then to legal, and finally to publishing, now builds a pipeline where one AI drafts, another AI formats, a human editor verifies compliance, and a human supervisor oversees the flow through explicit checkpoints on a dashboard. The total cycle time may shrink from days to hours, while the number of human interventions per deliverable is halved. Similar redesigns appear in software engineering, legal review, audit preparation, customer service, and research synthesis; each discipline learns to express its deliverables as data flows and constraints, rather than as a chain of individuals. As these pipelines mature, human contributions migrate toward defining the interfaces, maintaining standards, and handling exceptions that automation cannot yet resolve. Workflow design and exception governance become the new craft because they determine both speed and consistency. You can detect rebundling by watching for the appearance of shared asset libraries, task APIs, or automated routing systems that connect different AIs to one another and to human checkpoints. When those elements are in place, formerly distinct job boundaries blur, and value begins to follow the flow of information rather than the hierarchy of roles. This rebundling changes the cost structure from variable to fixed: the expensive part becomes building and maintaining the pipeline, while each additional output is cheap. This marks the beginning of the end of the notion of a "whole profession" as a single identity; instead, there are networks of human-AI modules that together define what the profession is. This is where benchmark-as-comparison begins to turn into benchmark-as-architecture because the pipeline is built to satisfy the metric before it is built to satisfy the craft.

6. The Baseline Flip: A Tipping Point in the Repricing of Human Labor

This moment arrives when AI outputs consistently meet or exceed the quality, speed, and reliability that mainstream users expect for most use cases. At this stage, the basis of comparison shifts from asking whether a machine can imitate human work to assuming the machine will perform it by default, and the question becomes what level of human oversight is worth paying for. The economic and psychological balance that sustained traditional valuation collapses because the marginal advantage of human execution is now smaller than its marginal cost. This transition does not occur evenly; it begins with routine and specifiable tasks, spreads to semi-structured ones, and eventually reaches areas once thought to be resistant to automation. The change can be traced in pricing behavior: clients begin to question why they should pay human rates for services that resemble what AI pipelines can deliver, procurement teams start introducing AI performance benchmarks into requests for proposals, and contracts move from hourly billing to fixed-price or outcome-based models. A telling sign is when customers request hybrid options, for example, "AI-assisted legal review" or "AI-generated design with human validation," as standard rather than experimental offerings. When such labels become normal, the tipping point has been crossed. The notion of capacity planning shifts from "How many people do we need?" to "What configuration of humans and machines yields the required reliability?" Payroll spending may remain stable or even decline slightly, but output volume and velocity rise sharply, making the apparent productivity of hybrid teams soar. This changes competitive benchmarks across entire sectors. Firms that adapt their pricing and delivery structures early gain both margin and speed advantages that late adopters cannot easily match. This tipping point expresses itself as a subtle but relentless repricing of time. The hourly value of producing a given deliverable decreases, while the value of designing, validating, and governing the process that produces it increases. It redistributes income toward those who own or control the production pipelines and the data or evaluation frameworks that underpin them. In effect, the tipping point marks the phase where AI transitions from an auxiliary tool to a normative producer. Human labor is repriced around assurance and exception handling that keep the system aligned with people's willingness to rely on it and build the trust that makes that reliance sustainable. This is convergence taking institutional form, a maturing form approaching normgence: the benchmark is now the default expectation around which contracts, staffing, and legitimacy reorganize.

7. The Control-Point Capture: A Shift of Bargaining Power Toward Infrastructure

Once AI becomes a stable and trusted production layer, the sources of value that sustain entire industries will begin to migrate. The power of coordination, which used to reside within firms and professional hierarchies, is starting to cluster around the infrastructures that make intelligent workflows possible. In practical terms, the firms or individuals who own and maintain these infrastructures become the new control gates for access and distribution, while those who only operate within them increasingly function as interchangeable nodes. Here, convergence moves from expectation to enforcement because access to the market increasingly flows through the infrastructure that defines the metric. What was once governed mainly by contracts and reputation is now governed by enforceable interfaces: who owns the logs, who controls the API keys, who can ship model updates, whose metrics define "acceptable," and whose system can push outputs into the customer's system of record. This is where benchmarking stops being a scoreboard and becomes a switchboard. This shift becomes visible first in the financial statements of organizations: revenue lines that once depended on human billable hours shift toward subscription income, platform fees, and service-level guarantees. The cost structure also changes: capital expenditures shift from office space, equipment, and management overhead to data acquisition, infrastructure maintenance, and continuous model evaluation. In many fields, proprietary datasets or highly tuned evaluation frameworks become the true bottlenecks, and those who own them hold bargaining power. Expertise that was once embodied in individuals becomes embedded in templates, ontologies, and decision trees. Professionals who contribute to these records create algorithmic leverage, as each rule, rubric, or annotated example codifies a fragment of tacit knowledge that the system can reuse at scale. Over time, such codification creates network effects: the more people use a platform or dataset, the more refined its rules and evaluations become, attracting further users and consolidating dominance. Traditional firms that fail to secure a position within these infrastructure-driven ecosystems find their knowledge depreciating while they continue to carry the fixed costs of manual delivery. In this phase, the question changes from "who is best" to "who is integrated," and integration becomes the hidden test of competence for firms and professionals alike. The shift of bargaining power to infrastructure control points, therefore, marks the moment when the geography of economic and human cognitive power is redrawn and when maintaining the integrity and interoperability of these infrastructures becomes critical to professional survival. At this point, the trajectory of the F-curve begins to bend, transitioning from a rapid acceleration phase, driven by work-loop dynamics and their downstream effects on work pipeline rebundling and the repricing of human labor, toward a phase of structural consolidation.

8. The Stable Split: A New Division of Labor

With control over execution now anchored in infrastructure, the system enters a regime in which it does not evolve toward total automation, as many early forecasts had imagined. Instead, it stabilizes around a repeatable allocation of responsibilities in which machines handle throughput and first-pass decisions, while humans handle exceptions, overrides, and liability-bearing sign-off. This division of labor is stable because neither side can fully replace the other: human intelligence provides context and social accountability, at least in appearance, while AI provides precision, volume, and speed, and increasingly sets direction, at least in consequence. This arrangement is less of a partnership than a custody model, where the machine produces and the human absorbs. What changes is the ratio between them, which gradually tilts in favor of algorithm-led execution as systems mature and regulatory frameworks catch up in clarifying which tasks require human oversight. Reliability becomes a social promise as much as a technical property, and that promise requires a human signature even when the human did not author the action. This division of labor reaches maturity at the moment when the ability to diagnose when and why the system fails becomes as important, if not more so, than its ability to execute the task itself because failure can cascade into a system-wide blackout with prohibitive downstream costs. The stable division of labor manifests as a two-tiered cost structure. The fixed cost of developing and maintaining AI infrastructure dominates, while the variable cost of human contribution shrinks but remains indispensable. The market begins to reward reliability and exception handling rather than raw productivity, and premium pricing is attached to those who can guarantee ethical and legal compliance under automation. Firms that misjudge this balance by over-automating without maintaining sufficient human control expose themselves to reputational and regulatory risks, while those that preserve too much manual labor become uncompetitive. This is where the human loop stops being a safeguard and starts functioning as a legitimacy membrane that makes the systems socially executable. This is where normgence anchors structurally, as the benchmark is no longer just enforceable but embedded in the division of labor itself, shaping and governing how work is allocated, performed, and validated.

9. The Stepwise Diffusion: A Pattern of Accelerated Change

After the division of labor begins to stabilize, the speed at which new capabilities spread through industries no longer follows the gradual, S-shaped adoption curve typical of earlier technologies. Because AI exists as software and data rather than physical equipment, it propagates through updates, integrations, and API calls instead of through factories, inventories, or supply chains. Each release of a new model, interface, or feature can instantly reach millions of users, creating bursts of capability that expand what can be automated or augmented nearly overnight. The diffusion of AI therefore proceeds not as a smooth curve of improvement but as discrete leaps separated by adjustment periods, during which human systems celebrate the gain, only to realize that workflows, metrics, and risk controls must now be redesigned. Each leap is also a silent rebaseline because what was exceptional yesterday becomes the minimum today.

In operational terms, these leaps occur whenever a technical or architectural advance unlocks a new class of tasks. A language model with improved reasoning suddenly makes automating policy drafting or contract review viable. A multimodal upgrade that merges text, image, and audio inputs transforms design, education, and customer support in one move. The emergence of multi-agent frameworks, where different specialized models coordinate autonomously, expands the feasible boundary once again by connecting decision-making steps that were previously siloed. Each leap widens the range of automatable tasks and raises expectations for speed and responsiveness across the economy. Users, clients, and employees rapidly recalibrate their sense of what "normal" looks like, meaning that organizations not aligned with the latest step appear outdated almost immediately. Normgence accelerates here because the public memory of the previous baseline collapses faster than institutions can adapt to the change.

This dynamic compresses innovation cycles. What once took years to propagate, such as the adoption of digital publishing or cloud computing, can now happen in months. This compression widens a long-standing gap between technological change and institutional adaptation, but it also makes the gap historically unusual in size and speed: regulatory bodies and educational institutions, which operate on slower timescales, fall behind by multiple capability cycles at once. As a result, responsibility for safe, integrity-led adoption becomes a faster-moving target, paradoxically increasing reliance on the human loop for both social and psychological reassurance. In the absence of fit-for-purpose regulation, this compression extends the interim during which the governance gap persists, allowing algorithmic, legislative-like power to fill the vacuum by setting de facto rules before public rules can be debated, written, and enforced. The pattern repeats with each generation, producing a sawtooth curve of progress: sharp climbs followed by brief consolidations. In each cycle, more institutional knowledge is encoded into the system, and the human role shifts slightly further toward meta-supervision, while policy becomes increasingly confined to ex post accountability. The half-life of competitive advantage shortens because any breakthrough discovered by one actor soon becomes available to all once integrated into the next platform release. This creates another paradox: while individual companies adopt AI faster than ever, sustainable differentiation becomes harder to maintain. This acceleration dynamic alters how workers and societies perceive stability. Instead of adapting once to a single technological revolution, they must continuously adapt to rolling micro-revolutions. In this context, skill obsolescence accelerates, and the ability to unlearn and relearn becomes the most valuable meta-skill. People learn to live in a state of permanent beta, where competence means keeping pace with a moving frontier rather than mastering a fixed body of knowledge. The stepwise diffusion of AI forces organizations to institutionalize adaptability. Continuous monitoring, modular architectures, and reversible workflows become essential so that processes can absorb the next leap without collapsing. This marks an economy that upgrades itself in waves under algorithmic rule, where each technical advance instantly redefines baseline performance and renders previous optimizations obsolete.

10. The Trust Competition: Auditability as a Source of Premium

Once AI-driven systems reach maturity and spread across industries, competition will no longer primarily revolve around who has the most talent, resources, or creative flair. Instead, it hinges on who can guarantee that automated systems perform reliably, safely, and transparently in real-world conditions. Organizations that can prove the accuracy, fairness, and accountability of their AI workflows earn market trust, regulatory approval, client confidence, and social acceptance, while those that cannot will find their advantages eroding, even if their raw productivity appears higher. The economy's competitive frontier thus shifts from the art of producing to the science of ensuring. Trust-based competition is, therefore, also benchmark competition because the firm that defines evidence defines acceptability. This transformation can be seen in how value propositions are written and contracts are structured. Where past commercial claims emphasized innovation, originality, and speed, the new language emphasizes validation, auditability, and compliance. Service agreements increasingly include key performance indicators such as model accuracy, false positive and false negative rates, bias reduction scores, and levels of response explainability. Procurement teams request documented testing protocols and independent audits as prerequisites for large contracts, while regulators introduce certification regimes for high-stakes AI applications. This consolidates the importance of evaluation frameworks. Benchmarks, once academic tools, evolve into commercial standards, defining acceptable thresholds for reliability and risk. Companies compete to own or influence these benchmarks because setting the metrics means shaping the terms of competition. Over time, evaluation assets, datasets, scoring systems, and verification APIs become tradable goods in their own right, forming a secondary market around trust infrastructure. This stage deepens the collective demand for legitimacy.

Trust becomes a measurable asset, built through continuous testing, monitoring, and disclosure. The firms and professionals who understand that trust is the last scarce resource in a world of abundant intelligence are the ones who shape the market. As an intertwined and knotty side effect, the scarcity of trust pushes designers to industrialize its manufacture, feeding algorithmic power through micro-interruptibility mechanisms that curate the ways humans can intervene in algorithmic outputs at the surface, stabilizing reliance, metabolizing the perception of algorithmic error, and sustaining throughput while leaving the governing rule structurally untouched. These mechanisms feel like agency but function as permissions: they keep users oriented and compliant enough to proceed, precisely by preventing the moment when proceeding would require reopening or contesting the algorithmic rules.

11. Work Redefined: Toward an Algorithmic Order

After the economy reorganizes around trust, the very meaning of "working" begins to change. For centuries, work has been understood as the act of producing, transforming, or delivering tangible outputs through human effort. In the age of intelligent systems, that notion dissolves. The locus of value moves from making to maintaining coherence between machine agency and human intention. When coherence becomes the product, disagreement becomes the defect. The human role is revalued from owner of the work to subcontractor, while the AI-integrated stacks become the prime contractors for value creation. "Work" is redefined as whatever remains after the stack has claimed execution, and it rewards humans not for producing, but for maintaining the legitimacy of AI-mediated production. Once that inversion settles, the causal chain tightens. Governance slides into dependency: livelihoods, employability, and institutional KPIs become indexed to conformity with the benchmark that the stack emits. Under those conditions, macro-interruptibility—the system-level capacity to contest the benchmark itself and compel a review that can change it rather than merely explain it—becomes economically irrational before it becomes politically contested. To stop, contest, or reopen the algorithmic governing standard is to interrupt the very throughput on which legitimacy and income now depend. Micro-interruptibility is tolerated because it preserves motion and stages voice by offering small, low-stakes ways to object or adjust at the surface such as edits, overrides, appeals, or feedback that feel participatory yet do not reopen the governing standard. But macro-interruptibility threatens delivery, contracts, and the appearance of reliability that the trust economy requires to remain intact. The more work is defined as keeping the system running, the more refusal looks like sabotage, and the more contestation is treated as friction to be routed around. In this way, the redefinition of work does not merely follow algorithmic rule; it operationalizes it, converting procedural standing into a cost center, turning the right to interrupt into a liability, and reinforcing algorithmic, executive-like power. The final conversion is psychological as much as economic because once your job is to keep the benchmark flowing, contesting it feels like betraying your role, even when it is the benchmark that betrayed your judgment.

As macro-interruptibility thins, the algorithmic benchmark becomes harder to contest, so the market treats it as natural. What is treated as natural becomes normative. The AI-integrated stack does not have to announce legislative-like authority; it accumulates it through repetition. This is how algorithmic power governs the conversion rate between effort and value. This closes the loop of the revaluing mechanism. Normgence is the repetition made socially binding.

The 11 steps are the constitutional-like power algorithm imposes on the economic system of work, setting the benchmark of "good enough," then accelerating the redefinition of "better," and therefore legislating value, executing workflow redesign, and adjudicating competence through metrics of its own making.

Once the stack wins the right to define adequacy, it gains the right to define waste: any human effort beyond the benchmark becomes economically suspicious, narratively indulgent, and professionally penalized. Craft is not eliminated by automation, but delegitimized by comparison. What collapses first is not skill, but the market's permission to exercise skill when the delta is no longer priced. "Good enough," and even more so the redefined "better," becomes more than a quality threshold; it becomes the underlying jurisdictional boundary.

This is why the revaluing mechanism is more than a substitution: it represents a regime change in what counts as a rational contribution. The first-order shift is cheaper execution. The second-order shift is that the reasons for human work are rewritten. Humans become valuable where the AI-integrated stack is vulnerable: at the edges of ambiguity, accountability, and exceptions. The paradox is that the system "needs" humans most precisely where it most undermines the autonomy that would make human judgment meaningful. It recruits judgment as insurance while hollowing out judgment as authority.

The most destabilizing implication is that this "constitutional-like power" is not primarily coercive. It governs by making alternatives look irrational: slower looks wasteful, manual looks archaic. In that world, the worker is not compelled by force but by the price of dissent. And once dissent is priced out, the system achieves what institutions have historically struggled to obtain: compliance that feels like common sense. The deepest capture is not that people cannot say no but that saying no stops looking like a viable option.

These 11 steps are not just about technology. They are a theory of how economic rule-setting power migrates from institutions that debate standards to algorithms that instantiate standards without debate; from professions that define work to algorithms that define worth; from social contracts that negotiate value to algorithms that normalize value by shipping it. And once shipped standards become lived standards, legitimacy is no longer argued for; it is installed.

This is how algorithmic power concentration enters, shapes and governs the economy, operating not over citizens, but over livelihoods.

This is as much a future as an ongoing reality. And the nearer it is, the more it is mistaken for mere efficiency or productivity rather than for a change in who gets to define the terms of reality. This is what makes the trias algorithmica indispensable.

Revaluation of Maintenance Work in Heavy Industry

The predictive nerve centers of heavy industry are one of the "patient zeros" for how human labor will eventually be re-indexed under the algorithmic triad. It is also one of the earliest places where the algorithmic benchmarks of "good enough" and the redefined "better" stopped being negotiated in craft communities and started being emitted by instrumentation, dashboards, and scoring logic that most technicians do not own.

For decades, maintenance in factories, refineries, power plants, and transport fleets was organized around fixed schedules and expert intuition. Mechanics and engineers performed time-based overhauls ("every 5,000 hours"), calendar-based shutdowns, and route checks, often applying very high safety margins. In many contexts, this produced overshoot and latent inefficiency: equipment was inspected or replaced earlier than strictly necessary, and entire lines were stopped just in case, because the cost of failure was so high.[262,263] This is where the revaluing sequence begins because overserved reliability practices create the first step: a gap between delivered precision and perceived need. In a single refinery unit, this could mean a full train shutdown triggered by a conservative interval on one compressor, even when upstream condition indicators remained stable.[262,263] At the same time, a second entry point was present: technicians and engineers were overwhelmed by low-prestige but critical tasks like manual log entry, routine inspections, and paperwork for compliance—duties that were effort-heavy and esteem-light, driving up costs but not directly advancing careers.[264,265] This is the same first step seen from the other side, as low-recognition work creates a second vulnerability that invites substitution. In many plants, the maintenance backlog was not only physical work but also work orders, annotations, checklists, and closeout documentation, which consumed skilled hours without reducing risk proportionally. The entry condition is therefore both economic and psychological. Overserved reliability creates a pricing opening, and esteem-light work creates an adoption opening.

The foothold for AI-driven predictive maintenance appeared when industrial players started wiring machines with sensors and connectivity in the late 1990s and early 2000s.[261,262] This is where the second step takes hold, as affordability and access change who can execute the same diagnostic tasks. Vibration sensors, temperature probes, oil-analysis kits, and later full-blown IIoT gateways made it affordable to collect continuous data from turbines, compressors, CNC machines, and rolling stock. By 2009, rotating machinery prognostics had already been framed around extracting early signatures from such condition signals.[266,267] Cloud storage and cheaper compute then allowed even mid-sized firms to monitor assets remotely, with architectures being codified during the Industry 4.0 period around 2015 and extending into cloud-based industrial monitoring patterns around 2016.[267,268] What changed was not the existence of maintenance tasks themselves, but who could see, analyze, and act on the data.[261,262] This is a typical characteristic of the second step, which marks a redistribution of execution capacity, not a redefinition of the work yet. Smaller plants and operators, who could never afford large on-site engineering teams, gained access to diagnostic tools previously reserved for OEMs and flagship sites.[266,267] Service companies began offering remote monitoring dashboards and "condition reports" on subscription, expanding execution capacity per euro spent.[266,268] This sets up the third step by making adoption possible. A quiet constitutional shift begins here. Whoever owns the sensors, logs, and platform will begin to own the right to define what counts as "normal" before any human judgment is even invited. Once "normal" is machine-defined, "good enough" follows: acceptable maintenance is no longer what a craft community would still choose to do, but what the instrumentation can justify not doing until the dashboard says otherwise.

Incumbent maintenance cultures, however, were slow to pivot.[260] And this hesitation is the third step that sets in because of the asymmetry between motivation and incentives when capability exists. Safety-critical industries like aviation, oil and gas, and rail operated under stringent regulations and long-established routines. Maintenance schedules were embedded in certifications, union agreements, and liability frameworks. Experienced engineers trusted their "ear" and "feel" for a machine more than an algorithm trained on logs. In such environments, experienced engineers often trusted their "ear" and "feel" for a machine more than an algorithm trained on logs, especially when the algorithm could not explain why it raised or did not raise an alarm.[234,269,270] This is where the third step becomes a calibrated reliance because people will not outsource judgment unless the system earns appropriate trust. Revenue models for OEMs often depended on selling spare parts and scheduled service packages, not on minimizing interventions, so cheaper, more targeted maintenance looked like cannibalizing future revenue.[266,271] Operational KPIs tracked uptime and compliance, not early anomaly detection or avoided interventions. As a result, many organizations treated predictive maintenance as a side project rather than a core strategy, while frontline teams began using early analytics tools to prioritize their work.[265,266] This is how the third step often plays out in practice, with unofficial use preceding formal redesign. This is the industrial version of shadow adoption. The algorithm enters first as a coping device, not a strategic mandate, and by the time it becomes official, it already has precedent, metrics, and legitimacy.

Once sensor data and failure logs flowed into central platforms, model quality improved through iterative feedback loops,[261] and this is the fourth step because the economics shift when every deployment cycle produces new training and evaluation evidence. Machine-learning models were trained to detect patterns in vibration spectra, temperature drift, pressure fluctuations, and power consumption that preceded failures.[262,272] Each new breakdown generated labeled data: here is what "normal" looked like before, and here is the pattern just before the fault. Engineers refined feature sets, and data scientists iterated on models. With each release, false positives dropped, true positives rose, and lead times for warnings improved, in a discipline that increasingly relies on explicit performance metrics and offline evaluation practices formalized around 2010.[273] A pump that used to fail "without warning" now produces a recognizable signature days or weeks in advance.[262,272] Synthetic data, simulations, and digital twins further amplify learning by letting teams test rare failure modes and boundary conditions virtually, instead of waiting years for enough real-world examples.[274] What looks like "better prediction" is also a faster-moving benchmark: once the system improves, yesterday's caution becomes today's inefficiency, and yesterday's expertise becomes tomorrow's delay.

This enabled a rebundling and redesign of the maintenance workflow,[266,267] and that shift is the fifth step because the unit of value becomes a pipeline that produces an outcome rather than a calendar that schedules effort. Instead of separate streams for inspection, planning, and execution, organizations began to work from pipelines: sensor ingestion flows into anomaly detection; anomalies feed into prioritized work orders; work orders automatically combine spare-part lists, procedures, and technician schedules,[264,266,268] which makes the fifth step visible as a concrete reengineering of handoffs, work orders, and decision gates. A maintenance planner's job shifted from building the calendar by hand to supervising and tuning the rules that generated it.[265] In large fleets such as aircraft engines, wind turbines, and mining trucks, OEMs like Rolls-Royce, GE, and Siemens have built service offerings where remote diagnostics, predictive models, and field service are integrated into "power by the hour" or availability-based contracts.[271] The unit of work became "assured uptime" rather than "hours of manual inspection." For example, a wind turbine operator could accept fewer routine climbs when the provider could show stable trends in vibration and temperature and dispatch only when the risk crossed a defined threshold.[262,272,271] This is where "the job" starts to dissolve into a flow. The technician is no longer the author of the cadence but an execution node inside a cadence authored upstream by a score.

As models matured, a tipping point arrived in many segments, particularly where faults had stable, measurable precursors and where intervention lead time mattered operationally.[262,263,266] This is the sixth step because the default comparison shifts from human schedules to machine signals. For a significant class of faults—bearing wear, imbalance, misalignment, fouling—the models became "good enough" that operators began to assume predictive systems would warn them in time.[262,272] The core question shifted from "Can an algorithm really see what my technicians see?" to "Why are we still doing so many manual checks if the system hasn't raised any alerts?"[234,269,270] Time-based tasks were progressively replaced by condition-based tasks. Contract structures changed: instead of paying for a fixed number of preventive visits, customers paid for guaranteed availability, with the provider bearing more of the risk and using AI to manage it.[269] The value of manual execution per se decreased; the value of designing, validating, auditing, and governing the predictive system increased because mistakes now had contractual and safety consequences.[273,275] This is why the sixth step quickly incorporates assurance questions that became especially explicit in the early 2020s during certification debates for safety-critical machine learning.[275] At this tipping point, "no alarm" becomes a claim, and the absence of a signal begins to govern as strongly as the presence of one, which is precisely how an algorithm acquires authority without speaking. This is convergence approaching normgence, taking operational form.

Commercial power shifted toward those who controlled data access, model deployment, and decision rights, not only toward those who manufactured the hardware.[262,276] Control points hardened into commercial chokepoints such as data-sharing clauses, API access, model update rights, and the authority to push work orders into the operator's system of record, which defines the seventh step in practice. Asset manufacturers and major service providers that owned the largest fleets, historical maintenance logs, and domain-tuned models became preferred intermediaries for dashboards, alerts, and recommended interventions, meaning they increasingly became the default operational gate through which an alert must pass to become an approved job, a spare parts order, or a field dispatch. Revenue shifted from pure hardware margin to recurring service income based on monitoring, analytics, and uptime guarantees. The most valuable assets were no longer just the physical machines but the proprietary datasets, feature libraries, and evaluation frameworks that underpinned the predictions. The seventh step is where what began as an upstream advantage in defining what counts as "normal" in step two hardens into contractual primacy. The right to define "normal" is no longer only embedded in who captures the signals; it is enforced through commercial control of integration, thresholds, update rights, and sign-off, so bargaining power migrates to whoever can decide when an alert becomes an authorized job, a parts order, or a billable intervention. The practical effect is not that technicians stop deciding, but that their decisions are increasingly framed as overrides of a presumed baseline rather than expressions of primary judgment.

A stable division of labor gradually emerged,[265,234] which embodies the eighth step as we enter into a repeatable allocation of responsibilities rather than a one-time replacement story. Machines (in the broad sense: sensors plus models) handled continuous condition assessment and routine triage; humans handled diagnosis for ambiguous cases, on-site inspection, repair, and final judgment.[265,266] Maintenance roles evolved: technicians became field diagnosticians with tablets and digital twins, while reliability engineers became "model stewards," defining thresholds, evaluating false positives and negatives, and deciding when to override or retrain.[265,273,274] The craft moved from turning a wrench at the first sign of trouble to calibrating trust: knowing when the system is reliable, knowing when it is silent for the wrong reasons, and intervening when it fails.[234,269] Liability consolidates here. The model produces the pace, and the human absorbs the blame when the pace is wrong.

As more firms adopted predictive maintenance, diffusion became stepwise.[266,267] Capability arrives in bursts with each platform release, edge upgrade, and integration milestone, rather than as a smooth curve, a hallmark of the ninth step. Early pilots might cover one plant or one asset class; success led to rollouts across entire fleets and then across regions. Each technical advance, such as a better anomaly detection algorithm, improved edge-compute gateways, or standardized IIoT platforms, created a burst of adoption.[267,268] Plants saw sharp improvements in uptime and reductions in unplanned downtime, then had to adapt spare parts logistics, shift schedules, and even safety procedures to the new reality. Regulatory frameworks and insurance contracts slowly caught up, recognizing condition-based strategies as acceptable alternatives to fixed schedules, but often lagging behind technological capabilities by years.[263,275] This is the governance gap in miniature, produced by technology's compressed-cycle dynamic. The operating baseline can shift in a software update, while the procedural rights environment shifts, if at all, over legislative timescales. Normgence accelerates here because the benchmark updates faster than any worker-facing right to contest it can realistically be negotiated into routine procedures.

Competition began to hinge on evaluation, risk, and trust.[270,273,277] This is where "having the model" stops setting you apart and "proving the model under real conditions" becomes the benchmark, a tenth-step signature. Industrial customers did not just ask, "Do you have predictive maintenance?" but, "How often do your models miss a critical fault? What is your false alarm rate? How transparent are your thresholds? Who is liable if the system fails to warn us?"[269,273,275] Providers had to document model performance, provide explainable diagnostics, and integrate with safety management systems—a shift that became sharper as explainable predictive maintenance matured into a defined field by 2024 and as certification discussions solidified in the early 2020s.[270,275] Benchmark tests, independent audits, and certification of analytics platforms became important differentiators.[273, 275] The ability to demonstrate reliability and safety under real-world conditions became as critical as the ability to show impressive algorithms in a lab. This is what the trust competition optimizes for: reassuring buyers, regulators, and insurers, not granting technicians any formal right to contest the benchmark that now organizes their work.

Over time, the meaning of maintenance work itself began to change, as the job was no longer priced primarily for execution but as stewardship of an intelligent maintenance infrastructure. This is the final step in motion. Maintaining a plant or fleet no longer meant simply fixing it when it broke or servicing it on a fixed schedule; it meant stewarding an intelligent infrastructure that continuously monitors, predicts, and recommends. Human expertise shifted from muscle memory and sensory intuition alone to a combination of domain knowledge, data literacy, and governance of AI tools—a role transition that is being studied directly in workforce terms throughout the mid-2020s, including 2025.[265] Pride moved from heroic emergency repairs to preventing failures altogether, from "I saved the line at 2 a.m." to "We designed a system where that 2 a.m. crisis never happens."[260] Training programs expanded to include interpretation of dashboards, understanding of model limitations, incident review discipline, and explicit practices to manage alert fatigue and risk thresholds. In the end, maintenance became a form of risk management: defining what must be measured, what can be inferred, what uncertainty is acceptable, when a human must override the model, and how to prove, after the fact, that the system still deserves trust.

Here is the macro-interruptibility test, where the empirical example of predictive maintenance lands hard.

From the early 2000s to 2025, across most industrial jurisdictions and especially in EU-style occupational safety frameworks and comparable regimes, the legal evolution around predictive maintenance in heavy industry and routine manufacturing contexts overwhelmingly strengthened safety duties, reporting practices, and employer obligations to assess and manage risk. However, it did not create a maintenance-specific, worker-facing right to contest algorithmically generated maintenance priorities, thresholds, or work orders.[278] Workers can still contest through general channels, occupational safety and health rights, grievance procedures, union bargaining, whistleblowing protections, and, where applicable, statutory worker information and consultation rights via workers' representatives, and in some jurisdictions, consultation duties on work organization, but these are generic levers that rarely translate into a technician-triggered, day-to-day procedural right to compel disclosure, review, or recalibration of the operational thresholds that shape maintenance priorities and work orders as part of ordinary work allocation.[278-280]

By contrast, some high-reliability domains, such as air navigation, embed explicit, formalized occurrence reporting and just culture protections that are intended to allow operational staff to raise safety concerns and trigger investigations without punitive retaliation. This establishes more institutionalized pathways for raising and examining safety concerns than what is typically embedded in predictive-maintenance workflow governance in heavy industry, thereby creating a clearer procedural pathway for contesting safety-relevant decisions within the system.[281,282] Heavy-industry predictive maintenance has largely scaled without an equivalent, dedicated contestability right for the technician as a technician. Even under the EU AI Act, where high-risk workplace systems trigger information duties and employers carry compliance and risk-management obligations, the structure remains largely employer-centric, and technicians typically gain no direct or routine right to challenge operational benchmarks or compel threshold recalibration in the normal flow of maintenance triage and dispatch.[283]

The result is a structurally asymmetric settlement: the algorithm earns the authority to set the pace, while the human keeps only the duty to comply, annotate, override at the margin, and bear the exposure when the margin is wrong. That is step 11 in its most concrete form. Work is redefined as keeping the system running, so contesting the benchmark becomes indistinguishable from slowing production, and once contesting looks like slowdown, macro-interruptibility becomes economically punishable long before it becomes politically discussable.

The Taskification of Work

The benchmark set by the algorithm at the dawn of normgence sees work revalued, then makes it enforceable because work itself has been codified as decomposable tasks and because the AI-integrated stack that emits adequacy also supplies the very formats through which those tasks are described. In supplying the format, it supplies the frame. In supplying the frame, it supplies the conditions of intelligibility by which a task is recognized as a meaningful job to be done.

This is how the AI-integrated stack ceases to be a neutral infrastructure laid over work.

Wanda J. Orlikowski's practice lens, developed from extensive research on information technologies in organizations, shows that technology is enacted in practice and, through that enactment, recursively shapes organizational structures, norms, and meanings, until the tool's categories become the organization's categories and the interface becomes a regime of legitimacy for what counts as proper work.[284] When the task becomes the carrier of the benchmark, it also becomes the carrier of the default mental model, the pattern, and the syntax of thought.

This is where the algorithmic triad extends beyond the revaluation of human effort into the revaluation of human thought because the same systems that decide what counts as acceptable output increasingly decide what qualifies as a valid way to perceive, interpret, and consider. This framing is never merely administrative.

Amos Tversky and Daniel Kahneman, drawing on experimental research in cognitive psychology and decision-making, show that when the same situation is presented through different frames, judgment itself shifts—not at the margins but at the level of what appears relevant, reasonable, and actionable. This means the supplied frame silently pre-selects the space of acceptable interpretations.[285] In other words, before any decision is made, the framing has already distributed attention and value, making certain losses, risks, responsibilities, and trade-offs feel central, while others fade into the background.

Through this process, thought is progressively reorganized around what can be expressed, routed, and validated through the algorithmically driven task frame, leading that pre-formed and pre-scripted frame to become what is easiest to think in, while anything that resists it becomes harder to articulate, harder to justify, and eventually harder to think through.

That is why another of the algorithmic triad's most consequential extensions is the conversion of the task into the mechanical reference unit of thought itself.

Contrary to what we often hear, the global dynamic of delegating work to AI is not automation. Automation was the discovery that a machine could be made to reproduce a human act that could be fully specified in advance and repeated without mobilizing any new cognition, relying solely on mechanistic precision. The transfer of human work to AI follows a different paradigm of unprecedented scope, which I call *taskification*: it is the reproduction by the machine, no longer merely of human physical gestures but of acts predefined as tasks that normally and necessarily rely on human judgment, interpretation, deliberation, appreciation, and intuition. Where automation replaces the human physical gesture with a mechanistic act of the machine, whose output is grounded in the laws of physics, taskification replaces the gesture of thought with a probabilistic computational act, whose output is governed by the algorithmic "laws" of statistical optimization.

At the same time that it taskifies, AI also contributes to standardizing the very way we think about the task to be carried out. Little by little, caught in the hegemony of the digital power of certain economic actors, this movement can slide into a form of dependent monocognition on a global scale, structured and amplified by the AI-integrated stack that imposes its formats, its criteria, and its interpretive frames for who and what defines the spectrum of certain tasks inherent to our cognition.

In discussions about the impact of AI on work, we rarely speak of professions in the full sense, and even less of vocation, responsibility, or judgment elaborated and articulated in situ. Instead, we talk about repetitive or low-value-added tasks that the machine could take over so that humans can focus on supposedly "higher value-added" tasks that would somehow be "reserved" for them: a kind of new deal between humans and machines.

This language is not neutral.

It signals that the basic unit of work is no longer a localized activity, carried out at a given time and place by a person embedded in a given context but an abstract functional block such as sorting emails, responding to a client, analyzing a scan, or scoring a candidate. Once work is conceived as a sequence of independent functional blocks, AI can be slotted in anywhere as a standard, interchangeable module, and the way we carve up reality into blocks of action ends up aligning with what these systems are able to process.

A task appears objective when we formulate it as a simple order to be executed, such as scoring a file, prioritizing requests, or summarizing a text.

Yet every task is already the result of a series of implicit choices. What problem did we decide to carve out, and according to which assumptions and boundaries? What was built into the task, and what was deliberately or unconsciously left out? According to which criteria do we judge the result—whether speed, cost, compliance, customer satisfaction, legal risk, or fairness? Who decided the hierarchy among these criteria—whether a profession, a department, a regulator, a platform, or a statistical model?

The task is already the visible interface of a configuration of thought upstream. When AI takes charge of tasks, it does not merely revalue work; it also reorganizes it. It extends, rigidifies, and sometimes generalizes the way those tasks have been defined and ranked.

As AI systems are embedded at the heart of work tools, line-of-business software, and procedures, a phenomenon of silent normalization emerges. Task formats stabilize into forms, standard prompts, predefined workflows, and decision templates. Each of us learns to describe our activities in these formats, not because they are intrinsically right but because they are the ones the systems understand and the ones platforms impose to deliver their best result with the best yield at the level of the task. Evaluation criteria become homogenized. A certain type of indicator, score, probability, and dashboard becomes the common language. What does not fit this language becomes hard to explain, to translate, and to justify and thus ends up marginal or marginalized.

The centers of gravity of decisions shift upstream to the level of the design and routing of tasks and thus of the AI systems on which these functions depend. The actor who defines the format of the request, the mandatory fields, the options available, the choice criteria, the hierarchies of preferences, and the performance metrics, in fact, imposes a framing of the problem as represented on everyone who will use the AI interface for the task in question.

Jiajie Zhang and Donald A. Norman, in their work on distributed cognition, show that external representations do not just communicate a task; they reorganize cognition by redistributing information across the mind and environment, shifting what must be held in memory into what can be seen, compared, and manipulated in the task environment. This creates representational effects in which the structure of the representation becomes the structure of thinking, making certain operations effortless and others cognitively expensive.[286] The drift accelerates as the script becomes routine. David Kirsh shows that once these representations are repeated, they begin to steer cognition, guiding attention, reducing inferential effort, and coordinating thought.[287]

This is where the risk of monocognition takes shape: a standardized way of posing problems, breaking them down, evaluating them, and prioritizing them spreads through capillary diffusion because it is encoded into the AI-integrated stack that underpins the systems producing the requested task.

The deepest danger is not that AI occasionally gets things wrong, even though that matters, but that it shrinks our capacity to question the way problems are posed before they are then organized into tasks.

When situations reach us already in the form of tasks, ready to be launched, like takeout through the intermediation of an AI system, we learn to be efficient within the frame that has been defined for the task, but we lose the habit of asking whether that frame is relevant, fair, acceptable, useful, improvable, or moral.

We stop asking whether this way of slicing up what we set out to do makes sense, what is missing, what becomes invisible, or what disappears when we handle a task in one way rather than another, and what other ways of thinking about what we aim to accomplish and the tasks that follow from it might have been possible.

This capacity to reformulate, to reconfigure the problem, and to refuse the form we are given is precisely a critical metacognitive function, both individual and collective.

The mechanistic reduction of work into task units orchestrated by AI systems threatens not only cognition but also, and even more importantly, metacognition—first through habit, then through the power structure that is reconfigured around those who control the global algorithmic infrastructures that define the formats, and thus the frames of requests, through the process of taskification.

The prism through which we view the impact of AI on work, reduced to the language of tasks, focuses our attention on jobs destroyed or transformed, on skills to be developed, and on the division of labor between human work and machine work. This prism pushes into a blind spot another reality that is nonetheless essential: the shift in power that is playing out at another level. It plays out in the very design of what we call and define as tasks, and in the place where it is decided how a problem becomes a standard unit for processing those tasks. It plays out in the orchestration where it is decided which tasks are assigned to which AI systems, in what order, and with what priorities. Finally, it plays out at the level of success criteria, where the metrics are defined that will steer these AI systems, whether costs, lead times, financial risks, satisfaction, or fairness indicators.

These decisions, largely made by the designers of these AI systems and then progressively co-produced by those same systems as they learn, already escape and will continue to escape workers themselves to a large extent, sometimes even regulated professions, and, of course, the public. And once they escape, they consolidate.

At this point, the real question is not design but power. The task frame is not authored by "the market" in the abstract, nor by workers in situ, but by a small number of hegemonic AI actors whose advantage is aggregenous, compounding across distribution, data, interfaces, and, above all, compute. As this infrastructural dominance deepens, network effects do not merely amplify adoption; they harden dependency. Compute access cements dependency into an asymmetry of cognitive authority: those who can train, fine-tune, and deploy dominant AI systems at scale set the cadence by which everyone else must think, integrate, and comply with the tasks as encoded. This concentrates legislative power to define what a task is, executive power to route and operationalize it across the infrastructures of work, and judicial power to validate, score, and normalize its outcomes. Under such conditions, taskification begins to look less like a neutral reengineering of workflows and more like a constitutional reallocation of cognitive sovereignty.

Faced with this, classical approaches to AI ethics—focused on bias, transparency, or data protection—remain necessary but insufficient. They remain insufficient as long as we do not ask how to ensure that humans retain the ability to reconfigure problems and are not condemned to executing tasks for which the thinking has been done in advance.

This question implies that everyone must be able to challenge the format of tasks, not just the result produced by the task; that everyone must be able to propose other ways of formulating a problem, weighting criteria, and defining what counts as success for the outcome of a task. It implies that several analytical frameworks remain open, possible, and actionable for the same situation and, for the same problem, and that no AI system can lock in a single decision model with no practicable alternative. It implies, finally, that AI systems make their own framings, criteria, and blind spots visible, rather than presenting themselves as mere engines of efficiency or efficacy.

That is why work on contestability by design,[288,289] from Margarida Almada's early articulation to the widely cited framework proposed by Kars Alfrink, Ianus Keller, Gerd Kortuem, and Neelke Doorn, becomes essential, treating the ability to dispute, demand justification, and trigger human intervention as a deep system property that must be built across the lifecycle, not left as an afterthought once harms appear.

The most decisive impact of AI on work is therefore not measured simply in percentages of tasks delegated to it or gains in productivity. It is measured above all by our capacity to answer one question: does AI help us better see, enrich, and pluralize our problems, or does it instead freeze, in efficient and standardized task formats, a postdictive way of thinking about the world and acting on it? It is at this level, the level of the thought hidden beneath the task, that the real break is taking place.

From this standpoint, schematic visions that describe the future of AI systems as a mere continuation of the real trend in digital capitalism to turn fragments of cognitive work into logistical units are not viable as a horizon, either cognitively or politically. They assume that it is desirable for thought to become both standardizable and standardizing through a form of mental work that is impoverished because it is preformatted in advance by default. The larger the standardized share of mental work grows, the more the meta-cognitive function shrinks.

It is not enough to move beyond a tactical, task-centered vision of AI in order to analyze its systemic effects on the economy; we must also grasp its systemic, properly anthropological effects on the very form taken by thought, by decision-making, and by the capacity of humans to reconfigure what they are trying to accomplish.

It is precisely here that the need for AI systems capable of integrity appears.

As a way to neutralize the externalities of taskification, artificial integrity[187] refers to the capacity of AI systems to be designed in such a way that they exercise something that more closely resembles integrity, rather than merely imitating intelligence in their functioning, in order to safeguard human cognitive safety.

By "cognitive safety," I refer to the conditions under which humans can maintain their capacity to perceive, interpret, judge, and reframe problems without being silently constrained or overridden by task and decision structures driven and administered by machine intelligence.

This is a necessary condition. Without a shift from AI pursued for its own sake to its subordination to artificial integrity, these systems will, by default, continue to optimize blindly for performance and efficiency, silently absorbing our ability to continually define and redefine tasks, problems, and criteria for judgment, instead of serving the higher goal of upholding the human cognitive and metacognitive system.

This requires that the artificially intelligent digital infrastructure that underpins the system of human work never has the final say on how that work and that system are to be thought.[290] This demands that computational and standardizing power be placed at the service of a plurality of viewpoints rather than their optimization or simplification and that it act as a catalyst for the reversibility of framings, for the possibility of saying no, and doing the work of "re": reframing, rethinking, reconfiguring, redoing, reinterpreting, calling into question.

Without artificial integrity, the rise of AI in work is likely to result in a gradual loss of cognitive sovereignty, in which humanity becomes the executor of a way of thinking that has been preformatted and pre-thought by its tools and for its tools.

With artificial integrity, AI can instead be used to expand our freedom to see differently, to deliberate differently, and to act differently in and through work, and on the world.

The New Human Worth Limit

In a world where both cognition and production are increasingly mediated by a few AI-integrated stacks, the danger of monocognition becomes inseparable from a danger that is more material but no less structural: the possibility that AI alters the conditions under which human work has historically remained socially indispensable.

To see why, we have to step back from the reduction of work into tasks and look at the historical trajectory that once made technological displacement politically survivable and ask whether AI is now pushing us toward a new boundary—a limit beyond which human contribution may no longer be required at scale.

For most of modern history, the story of machines and work has been told as a story of fear that turns, almost magically, into reassurance.[291] The loom, the steam engine, the assembly line, and the industrial robot all arrive as harbingers of catastrophe. They throw people out of work, hollow out towns, and provoke riots and social turmoil.[292]

And yet, when historians and economists look at the long arc of the industrial age, from roughly the late eighteenth century to the late twentieth century, they see something very different from permanent collapse.

They see economies that keep growing, states that become more powerful and expansive, tax revenues that increase rather than vanish,[293] and overall employment that persists even as entire categories of work disappear.[291]

In 1870, for example, more than half of the workforce in many European countries still worked in agriculture, while by 1980, that share had dropped to below 10 percent in places like the United Kingdom and France, without a corresponding explosion of permanent unemployment.[294,295]

There is a paradox here.

At the micro level, the arrival of machines can devastate people and places. At the macro level, the same mechanisms that ruin a worker or a town can, over time, strengthen the national economy and even underpin the rise of the welfare state.

Understanding this tension is essential if we want to judge what is happening with AI. AI does not simply repeat the old script of mechanization; it tests the very conditions that made the traditional story of adaptation and resilience possible.

To see this clearly, it helps to recall some very concrete jobs that once seemed stable or even indispensable, and which now survive only in the footnotes of labor history. Let us begin with the world of earlier machines.

Think of a textile town in England around 1810, at the height of the first industrial revolution.[296] A new mechanical loom is introduced, building on designs like Edmund Cartwright's power loom, first patented in the 1780s.[297] By the mid-1820s, the power loom's technical advantage over the handloom had risen to as much as 7½ to 1, and because a single boy could tend two looms, output per worker could reach up to 15 times that of the cottage weaver.[298] At the scale of that workshop, the logic is brutal and linear. Some workers are dismissed.[299]

Their earnings collapsed. Families cut consumption, and local trade suffered. Parishes faced mounting pressure on the poor rates as poverty spread, and relief systems were strained. The machine, from this vantage point, looks like a direct transfer of life chances from human muscle to metal teeth.

Textile workers in regions such as Nottinghamshire and Yorkshire, ranging from framework knitters and handloom weavers to woolen finishers, did not experience mechanization as an abstract productivity gain; many saw earnings collapse and joined the Luddite machine-breaking of the 1810s, literally breaking stocking frames and shearing frames they believed were making their skills obsolete.[299-302]

The same pattern recurs again and again.

In the car industry, electrified assembly lines and later industrial robots reduced the need for manual labor on the factory floor. Henry Ford's moving assembly line, introduced in 1913 in Highland Park, Detroit, cut the time required to assemble a Model T from more than 12 hours to about 90 minutes.[303]

In mining, mechanization through powered drilling and large loading machines such as power shovels reduced the number of workers required for key operations in the early twentieth century, and in coal, it later translated into steep employment declines as mechanization spread after World War II.[304,305]

In agriculture, tractors, combine harvesters, and chemical inputs allowed a steadily shrinking share of the population to feed an entire nation between the 1920s and the 1960s.[306]

Whole occupations that once filled factory floors or fields have vanished so completely that their titles sound almost surreal today.

The sagger maker's bottom knocker, a young worker in nineteenth-century British pottery works whose sole job was to pound clay into the base of kiln saggers, is now all but extinct as kiln technology shifted to gas- and electric-fired kilns, reducing the need for protective saggers.[307]

Bowling alley pinsetters, often teenage boys who manually reset pins in the 1930s and 1940s, were replaced from the 1950s onward by automatic pinsetting machines.[308]

Lamp lighters, who walked city streets each evening to light gas lamps in the late nineteenth century, lost their roles when electric street lighting spread after the 1880s.[309]

Telephone switchboard operators, a major female occupation in the early twentieth century, saw their numbers collapse from the 1960s as automatic exchanges took over the connection work.

Elevator operators, once ubiquitous in office towers and hotels in the 1920s and 1930s, all but disappeared with the spread of automatic controls and simple push buttons.[310]

These jobs were real, sometimes unionized, sometimes a path out of poverty, and yet they were progressively erased once a machine, a circuit, or a new infrastructure could do the repetitive part more reliably.

In many cases, at the place where the machine arrives, a familiar chain of disruption unfolds: job loss, income loss, social stress, political anger, and a narrowing of the local tax base.

In a Ruhr mining town in the 1960s, when pits closed as hard-coal mining lost competitiveness and restructuring accelerated,[311] or in parts of the U.S. Midwest in the 1980s, when automakers adopted industrial robots while production shifted across plants and regions,[312,313] the consequences were often intimate and concrete: local economic spillovers and business decline after major employment shocks, alongside fiscal pressure that could force cuts to public services such as schools when revenues fall.[314,315] In some communities, strain on local health-care provision could compound these pressures.[316]

For those who live through it, the conclusion seems obvious: the machine replaces human work; therefore, there are fewer jobs, and the state loses tax revenue and becomes weaker. This is the immediate experience of technological displacement.

But it is not the whole picture.

If we now lift our eyes from the factory gate to the national accounts over the span of decades, a more complex landscape appears.

The same centuries that saw waves of mechanization were also the centuries in which total output, measured in goods and services, expanded dramatically.[317] The value produced by each worker rose.[318] The cost of many goods fell.[319] New industries emerged around the old.[320] In several dimensions, especially health and access to modern infrastructure, the average citizen in a high-income industrial democracy today enjoys capabilities that would have been out of reach even for many nineteenth-century elites.[321]

In 1900, for example, the United States and many European countries were far poorer than they are today by any modern benchmark. Yet, by the end of the twentieth century, they had multiplied output per person several times over,[321] even as occupations such as handloom weavers[300] and, as a mass employer, coal miners dramatically declined.[305]

Crucially, states did not implode under the weight of lost jobs. They grew.

Tax revenues as a share of national income increased markedly. From the late nineteenth century, and especially across the twentieth, systems of public education, public health, pensions, unemployment insurance, and large-scale infrastructure expanded, and governments became far more substantial providers of services and protections. In many advanced economies, total government revenue rose from roughly 5–10 percent of national income in the early twentieth century to around 30–50 percent by the late twentieth century and into the early twenty-first, enabling the expansion of mass public services and social spending, including education and healthcare.[322]

How can these two stories coexist: the local story of destruction and the national story of expansion?

Part of the answer lies in the mobility of labor.

As agricultural mechanization raised output per worker, employment in farming fell, and large numbers of workers moved from rural areas to towns and cities, where expanding manufacturing absorbed much of that labor. Later, as manufacturing productivity rose further through automation and reorganized production, employment growth shifted increasingly toward services. Over time, sectors such as retail, finance, logistics, administration, education, healthcare, and leisure became major employers.[323]

The specific jobs changed. The set of sectors that absorbed human effort changed. But widespread idleness did not become the norm. Human work was reallocated rather than erased. In Britain, many families rooted in farm labor around 1900 saw their children move into factory work or clerical occupations by the interwar decades. By the 1970s, later generations were increasingly likely to be employed in expanding service roles, such as nursing, teaching, accounting, and mid-level management, in a more urban and mechanized economy.[324]

Another part of the answer lies in productivity itself.

When machines make production more efficient, the same number of workers can produce more output, or fewer workers can produce the same output. If competition and policy work reasonably well, part of this productivity gain shows up as lower prices or better quality.

Goods that were once luxuries become accessible to a mass market. This stimulates demand. Firms expand into new markets, offer new services, and bundle new experiences around old products. They hire in marketing, design, research, and distribution. The machine that erases a job on one line can, over time, sustain the creation of jobs elsewhere—jobs that may be invisible in the moment but obvious when we look back.

States, for their part, learned to follow the value. They shifted their tax systems toward the flows that grew rather than the ones that shrank. As wage work expanded in factories and services, income taxes and social contributions became central. As consumption grew, value-added taxes and sales taxes became major sources of revenue. As corporations accumulated profits, company taxes, capital gains taxes, and various forms of property taxation emerged.

The result was a fiscal architecture that did not depend on any single category of work or any single sector. What mattered was that the overall level of economic activity kept rising and that a significant share of that activity was tied in one way or another to human employment and mass consumption.

This is, for example, why the decline of specific occupations such as typesetters in U.S. print shops accelerated from the 1960s through the 1970s, largely as phototypesetting and computer-assisted composition spread,[325,326] and yet did not, by itself, trigger a collapse in public finances. Their loss was absorbed within a much larger, still expanding wage and consumption base overall.

From this mixture of mechanization, sectoral shifts, and fiscal innovation, there emerged an implicit social deal.

Capital would deploy machines to increase productivity and profits. Workers would accept that jobs would change or move, trusting that new opportunities would appear if they acquired new skills and moved to new sectors. The state would soften the blows with social protections and extract a share of the growing pie through taxation in order to fund public goods.

This deal was never harmonious. It involved strikes, resistance, political upheaval, and considerable injustice. But underneath the turmoil, the macroeconomic machine more or less functioned. New labor markets opened up above the tasks that machines took over. The state could, in the long run, tax more, not less.

It is precisely this deep background that makes current developments with AI so unsettling.

The usual reassurance is ready at hand.

We are told that AI will take care of repetitive cognitive tasks and humans will move higher into more complex, more creative, and more relational roles. This is a comforting echo of the old story.

But this time, the machines are not confining themselves to tightening bolts or processing predictable forms. They are steadily climbing into the very space that used to be the human escape route. And this is happening with remarkable speed.

The rise of deep learning after 2012, the spread of powerful language models after 2018, and their mass deployment through user-friendly interfaces after 2022 have brought automation and taskification directly into domains that were still hiring aggressively just a decade ago, such as junior copywriting, basic coding, translation, and customer service.

AI chatbots can produce and refine professional text, generate software code, summarize and translate information at scale, and draft materials such as contracts, campaigns, and policies. They can handle customer interactions in natural language, generate images and designs, and support knowledge work in medicine and law. Increasingly, they also shape higher-order activities such as strategy, scenario analysis, and scientific exploration.

These algorithmic capabilities are no longer abstract.

AI-assisted drafting is already widespread in search engine optimization (SEO) and content marketing workflows: a survey of 879 marketing and SEO professionals found that 87 percent used AI to help create content, while 97 percent reported that their companies edit and review AI-generated content.[327]

Post-editing of machine translation has become a regular practice in professional translation workflows, driven in part by cost-reduction efforts from language service providers and customers. Translators report that this shift negatively affects their revenues and working practices.[328,329]

In e-discovery, law firms increasingly use technology-assisted review (TAR), a machine-learning approach, to prioritize or code large volumes of electronically stored information. Courts routinely cite TAR's benefits and encourage its use, and it is often adopted in high-volume matters where linear manual review would be impractical or cost-prohibitive. This shifts human effort toward training, validation, and the review of TAR-identified documents for production.[330]

Medical transcriptionist employment, once centered on listening to and typing up doctors' dictations, is projected to decline as speech recognition and natural language processing allow physicians to document patient encounters in real time and as software automatically prepares an initial draft that transcriptionists review and edit.[331]

Customer service organizations are moving toward greater automation of inbound contacts using AI agents and bots. Looking ahead, Gartner predicts that by 2029, agent-based AI will autonomously resolve 80 percent of common customer service issues without human intervention, contributing to lower operating costs.[332]

From an empirical perspective, the clearest early signals of taskification appear in online labor markets, where demand adjusts quickly and can be measured directly in platform-level data.

Using 1,388,711 job posts from a leading online freelancing platform covering July 2021 to July 2023, one study finds a 21 percent decrease in job postings for automation-prone writing and coding jobs within eight months after generative AI's introduction, relative to more manual-intensive jobs.[333]

Studying freelancers on Upwork in the months following ChatGPT's November 2022 release, another study reports that workers in highly affected occupations experienced reductions in employment and earnings, including an estimated 2 percent drop in jobs and a 5.2 percent drop in monthly earnings.[334]

After ChatGPT's launch, one study finds that demand for LLM-substitutable skill clusters such as writing and translation declined by about 20–50 percent relative to a counterfactual trend, especially for short-term roles, while aggregate freelance demand did not decrease and some complementary clusters grew.[335]

All of these are real, present-day jobs that are already being reshaped, and in some cases eroded, by AI capabilities. They operate precisely in domains that industrial society had long reserved as the safe territory of human cognition and creativity.

The historical pattern relied on a ladder: at the bottom, manual and standardized work that was ripe for mechanization. Above it, layers of human work that demanded more discretion, context, and responsibility, such as increasingly complex planning, analysis, judgment, quality control, exception handling, coordination, creation, and interpersonal relations. When machines climbed one rung, humans could move to the next.

With AI's algorithms, it is as if the ladder itself is being gnawed from multiple levels at once.

This change has three profound consequences for the relationship between taskification, taxes, and the state.

The first consequence concerns the structure of employment. If AI takes over a substantial fraction of cognitive and creative tasks, the volume of human labor required by the productive system can shrink even if output continues to grow. Some new roles will emerge, as they always do, in maintaining, supervising, and integrating AI systems and in human experiences that remain resistant to taskification. But there is no guarantee that these roles will absorb all those displaced, particularly in the middle of the skill and income distribution.

The comforting phrase "learn to code" becomes hollow at the moment when models can produce and refactor code better and faster than most humans. The standard advice to move into symbolic manipulation and service interaction loses its solidity if those very domains are contested by machines.

The copy editor in a small publishing house in 2010, the junior marketing associate drafting routine emails in 2015, and the entry-level data analyst building simple dashboards in 2018 could all reasonably imagine a ladder of progression. In 2025, many of their tasks can be partially or fully handled by generic AI tools, and the ladder looks more like a narrow ledge above a rising tide.

The second consequence concerns the tax base. The fiscal architecture of the welfare state rests heavily on the taxation of wages and the social contributions that accompany them. Employers pay contributions on behalf of employees, who pay income tax and various forms of payroll-related charges. This structure presupposes a broad layer of stable, formal employment.

If AI-driven taskification reduces the total wage bill as a share of national income, while concentrating a larger share of value in profits and intangible capital, then a state that still leans primarily on labor taxation finds itself perched on a shrinking platform.

In theory, rising profits could offset declining wage-based revenues if corporate and capital taxation were sufficiently robust and enforceable. In practice, capital is more mobile than labor. Digital and AI firms, in particular, can shift profits through global structures, exploit gaps between jurisdictions, and negotiate favorable treatment by threatening to locate infrastructure elsewhere.

It becomes harder for any single country to tax the winners of AI at levels that would compensate for the erosion of wage-based income without international coordination and strong political resolve. This tension is visible whenever a country proposes stricter digital services taxes or higher taxes on large technology companies and immediately faces lobbying campaigns and relocation threats from firms that control critical platforms and data centers.

The third consequence concerns sovereignty in a deeper sense. Traditional machines lived mostly within national borders. A factory in one country could be owned from abroad, but its physical presence made it subject to local labor laws, environmental regulation, and taxation.

Contemporary AI systems are different. The most powerful models and the largest data centers are controlled by a handful of private actors. Their AI-integrated stacks provide services that permeate every sector and every institution, including government itself. They host data, supply AI capabilities, and increasingly mediate communications.

When a public administration depends on foreign or quasi-sovereign private AI-integrated stacks for its critical digital infrastructure, its autonomy is no longer simply a matter of passing laws. Its operational capacity is entangled with the strategies and technical decisions of companies that answer primarily to their own shareholders and leadership.

When citizens rely on these same stacks for information, search, personal assistance, and decision support, the cognitive environment in which democratic deliberation takes place is partly shaped by models and recommender systems that are trained, tuned and updated outside the reach of ordinary public scrutiny.

One can already observe, in the early 2020s, public agencies using commercial AI tools to draft official documents or assist in case management. This means that subtle choices made in model design and training data can influence how rules are interpreted, which options are foregrounded, and which problems are made more or less visible.

This goes beyond economics to the question of who sets the frame within which a society sees itself.

The owners of the dominant AI algorithmic infrastructures accumulate a form of structural power that resembles a new kind of land ownership. Instead of owning fields and forests, they own and control the computational and data estates on which everyone else depends. Access to these estates is provided as a service, often at a marginal cost that is close to zero, but the ability to shape terms, capture data flows, adjust conditions and prioritize some uses over others creates a constant flow of rents. These rents are not just monetary; they are informational and political.

In such a world, the old pattern of previous industrial revolutions dissolves.

Machines do not merely disrupt at the micro level while the macro level adapts and expands. They can disrupt the very mechanisms that used to guarantee adaptation. If the ladder of human tasks has no higher rung to move to, if the tax system is still anchored to labor in a context where labor is demoted from a central input to an optional complement, and if the state itself becomes a client of concentrated AI power, then the historical reassurance that technology eventually strengthens public institutions becomes unreliable.

The question stops being whether AI will "create new jobs" and becomes whether our institutions can still compel a distribution of value, authority, and meaning in a world increasingly less ruled by them and ever more effectively ruled by algorithmic power.

The Algorithmic Burden on Gender

Can traditional institutions still compel a distribution of value, authority, and meaning in a world less and less ruled by them and ever more effectively ruled by algorithmic power?

To answer that, we may have to step back even further than the industrial age and look at the deeper substrate beneath every economic order: the relationship between human worth and what the world demands from humans in order to remain predictable, governable, and survivable. Because long before labor markets and welfare states, the value of human capacities was already being priced by a more ancient judge: the world's unpredictability itself.

The First Age of Predictability Was Toward Nature

The evolutionary history of human economic life has always been entangled with the degree to which the world around us could be predicted. For most of our species' existence, human survival was governed by irregularity rather than stability. Climate fluctuations across the Pleistocene, which included abrupt temperature swings of several degrees within a human lifetime, forced early societies into patterns of mobility, improvisation, and physical resilience. Archaeological evidence from lake sediments and ice cores shows that before the onset of the Holocene (≈11,700 years ago; ~9700 BCE) climatic variability was often abrupt and high amplitude.[336] In many mobile foraging ecologies, survival depends on a mix of high-variance returns, often from hunting, and more reliable daily returns, often from gathered foods, with shortfalls buffered through cooperation and extensive food sharing.[337] Division of labor by sex is common and is frequently interpreted as an adaptation to ecological and life-history constraints rather than purely ideological choice; however, women's contributions are often central, and women hunt in many societies.[338] Where intergroup violence is salient, defense and coalitionary aggression can further bias some high-risk roles toward men without making them the sole determinants of survival.[339]

The pattern of climatic variability shifts with the onset of the Holocene, when Greenland ice-core stratigraphy marks the end of the Younger Dryas and the beginning of a comparatively warm interglacial baseline.[340] Relative to the preceding glacial millennia, temperature variability declines markedly, even though notable disruptions still occur within the Holocene.[336,341] This more stable climatic backdrop tended to reduce the risk of delayed-return subsistence experiments.[342] In Southwest Asia, cultivation and domestication unfold over many generations: archaeobotanical remains show slow selection for key domestication traits in cereals, consistent with repeated growing-season cycles and cumulative learning.[343] Similar long-run trajectories underpin early rice cultivation and domestication in the Yangtze[344] and early maize domestication in Mesoamerica.[345] Greater climatic predictability made multi-season investment more scalable, allowing agricultural experiments to be sustained and their gains to accumulate into surplus.

The consequences for social organization were immense. A more predictable environment did not eliminate the importance of mobility, improvisation, physical resilience, or the role of defense, but it changed what counted as a structural advantage and introduced planning, foresight, and accumulated knowledge as durable sources of resilience. When a community can anticipate that a field will yield grain in six months and that grain can be stored for another year, survival begins to depend on coordination across time, the management of valuable resources, and the risks and obligations associated with them.

Anthropologists and archaeologists studying early sedentary societies in Anatolia and Mesopotamia have shown how storage infrastructures and practices, from granaries and storage pits to containers, sealing, and rationing, produced concentrations of grain that became measurable and movable and, therefore, increasingly subject to institutional control and oversight.[346-348] The weight of this transformation gradually shifted from the acquisition of calories to the governance of stored value: guarding, monitoring, allocating, accounting, and managing tensions over access. In this new ecology, trust, record-keeping, and institutional memory became as decisive as endurance. Once food is stored and allocated across months, access depends not only on production but also on agreements about claims, on monitoring, and on the capacity to uphold decisions when disputes arise.

Intelligence, planning, and codification of rules that govern valuable resources gained new force, yet conflict did not disappear. It was reconfigured. Protection was no longer only about defending bodies on the move but also about defending stocks, claims, and the rules that organized them.

Over time, the surplus that made specialization, writing, bureaucracy, and taxation possible also created new levers of inequality because those who controlled storage, measurement, and distribution could convert administration into authority.[349]

Once authority is tied to offices that allocate valuable resources and arbitrate disputes, the question of who can hold those offices becomes decisive. In many early state contexts, these roles became disproportionately male, while women remained central to production and household economies. As a result, gender hierarchy could be reinforced through the everyday machine of surplus administration.

Gender hierarchies were not inevitable, but in many early state contexts, coercive and administrative power over stored resources—allocating, monitoring, and adjudicating claims amid competition—became skewed toward male-dominated institutions, even while women remained central to production and household economies. The result was not the end of vulnerability, but its relocation away from immediate scarcity and toward systems of control whose inequalities proved remarkably durable.

From here on, the pattern repeats: when the world becomes more predictable, power tends to gather around whoever manages that predictability.

The Second Age of Predictability Was Toward the System

The binding of predictability to power continues across millennia. Medieval seigniorial economies in England depended on the regularity of annual agrarian production and on documentary systems such as manorial accounts and court rolls that recorded obligations and enabled lords to convert expected harvests and tenures into enforceable rents, dues, and levies.[350-352]

In monsoon-dependent regions of South Asia, seasonal rainfall and runoff were captured through tank and canal infrastructures. Here, too, control over these infrastructures and over the allocation of predictable seasonal water often rested with local elites and dominant groups, intersecting with land tenure and contributing to durable hierarchical authority.[353-355]

In each case, the ability to forecast the rhythms of nature allowed a small group to impose order on the many. The valuable resources to be controlled were not just land but the anticipated yields that nature would reliably provide. Predictability had become an asset. Those who controlled it, or claimed the authority to interpret it, often accumulated advantage in ways that reflected existing social hierarchies, including gender.

The transition into the industrial era did not erase this logic; it transformed it. The object of prediction expanded from harvests and rainfall to storms, prices, and population flows. The same question remained: who gets to predict, who gets believed, and who bears the costs when prediction fails? And as the domain of prediction expands, so does the domain of authority.

With the rise of meteorology in the nineteenth century, states began to institutionalize prediction. The first national weather services appeared in the 1850s. Britain's Meteorological Office was founded in 1854. The United States established a national weather service in 1870 within the Army Signal Service, with a civilian Weather Bureau created later. While these institutions emerged partly to protect shipping and agriculture, they also marked the beginning of a new informational authority. The ability to foresee storms, frost, or drought became a public function, and with it, the state deepened its infrastructural power.

Predictability had become entangled with policy, and policy reflected existing hierarchies, including gendered dependencies around food distribution and relief. This connection is not incidental. When institutions manage scarce and valuable resources, they also shape entitlements. Entitlements often run through households, inheritance, wage structures, and legal status—arenas in which women have frequently held weaker bargaining power and fewer formal rights.

The twentieth century extended the pattern further. As industrial societies grew more complex, the need for forecasting intensified. Financial markets relied on statistical models that assumed regularity. Urban planning required projections of population and traffic patterns. Central banks used macroeconomic indicators to anticipate inflationary pressures. In each case, prediction became a professionalized domain, staffed overwhelmingly by men and embedded in institutions built by men. Women entered these fields only gradually, often hindered by structural barriers. Even in the early 1970s, women were under 10 percent of economists in many high-status parts of the U.S. profession, including elite university economics faculties.[356]

The forms of predictability that structured the modern era were therefore created inside gendered institutions that treated male experience as the default. That prediction is male-biased is just a symptom. The issue is that the authority to define what counts as knowledge, risk, and rational policy has often been monopolized, and monopolies tend to reproduce the social patterns of those who hold them.

It is against this deep historical background that the current transformation triggered by AI's advanced algorithmic power must be understood.

The Third Age of Predictability Is Toward Human

AI systems do not simply take over the definition of tasks and, therefore, minds. They also reshape the structure of prediction itself. They do not merely help humans anticipate the future; they generate their own anticipations at a scale and speed that no human institution has ever achieved. These capabilities introduce a new political and social material into the world. Whereas earlier regimes of predictability rested on natural cycles or relatively slow-moving economic indicators, AI-driven predictions operate on behavioral data that reflects intimate details of individual lives. The result is a new domain for the extraction of valuable resources. What is extracted is not grain, not just energy, not just labor, but the data produced by humans and the statistical patterns of human behavior in all its forms. The granary becomes a server; the ration becomes a ranking; the ledger becomes a model.

Predictability has thus become an extractive activity directed at this new, highly valuable set of resources and has, therefore, become a highly lucrative global market.

The value of this market can be measured in the revenues of the advertising and data platforms that dominate the digital economy. In 2024, Alphabet, the parent company of Google, and Meta generated approximately \$264.6 billion and \$160.6 billion, respectively, in advertising revenue. These figures are not simply the result of selling attention. They arise from the ability to predict what individuals will click, buy, or believe. Predictability has become one of the largest industries on Earth. The ability to forecast human responses to stimuli is monetized at a scale that rivals the entire energy sector of many nations. This is not merely an attention economy, but the next age of a prediction economy.

Yet this predictive power is increasingly concentrated in a handful of firms that build and operate dominant AI-integrated stacks. Unsurprisingly, in continuity with the long history of unequal access to predictive authority, it remains largely male dominated, shaped by leadership teams that are overwhelmingly male and by technical teams that are still male dominated. Across major technology companies, women commonly hold under one-third of technical roles and an even smaller fraction of senior engineering and AI research positions.[357,358]

The resource of prediction is therefore being shaped within the very structures that have historically struggled to advance gender equality.

As a result, the implications of this concentrated gender imbalance extend to who designs, trains, and governs the models.

A 2019 study by researchers at Northeastern University and the University of Southern California found that Facebook's algorithmic ad-delivery system for employment ads, which decides which users are shown job advertisements, can produce significant gender skew in who sees these ads, even when targeting parameters are set to be highly inclusive.[359]

One widely reported example involved a recruiting tool developed internally at Amazon in the mid-2010s that trained on ten years of resumes submitted to the company.[360] Because the model was trained on historical resumes from a male-dominated applicant pool, it learned to penalize signals associated with women, including the word "women's" and credentials from all-women's colleges. The project was eventually scrapped after the bias was identified and could not be reliably eliminated.

But this underlying logic persists across the industry. AI hiring platforms now influence decisions affecting tens of millions of job seekers. When these systems rely on patterns that reflect historic male dominance in certain fields, they can entrench that dominance, even when employers intend otherwise. Past distributions become future filters.

This risk expands as AI systems move deeper into decision-making processes. Credit scoring and algorithmic underwriting models can display gendered patterns because the data they learn from reflect structural inequalities in income, employment continuity, and asset accumulation, and because seemingly neutral variables can act as proxies for gender.[361,362] In healthcare, a 2019 paper published in *Science* revealed that an algorithm used to help manage care for millions of people in the United States each year systematically underestimated the needs of Black patients.[363] While this example concerns race rather than gender, it shows how predictive systems can replicate structural inequalities at scale. When such systems incorporate variables that correlate with caregiving burdens or reproductive histories, women face distinct disadvantages. These disadvantages can accumulate silently. They do not require explicit discrimination; they require only the mechanical reproduction of patterns encoded in data.

The New Ceiling Is Statistical

The shift from nature to systems to human predictability, therefore, reconfigures the terrain on which gender equality must be fought. In earlier eras, the main barriers for women were formal exclusion from education, labor markets and political participation. These barriers could be challenged through legal reforms and social movements. In the contemporary AI era, the barriers are subtler. They are embedded in the statistical foundations of the systems that now mediate access to work, credit, healthcare, and even public benefits. Predictability itself becomes a domain of inequality. Those who are predictable in ways that align with historical male norms receive smoother access to opportunities. Those who deviate from these norms, often because of caregiving responsibilities or career interruptions associated with childbirth, find themselves flagged as exceptions by systems optimized for regularity.

The consequences are not theoretical. The International Labour Organization reported in 2023 that, in clerical and administrative roles, which employ a disproportionately large number of women globally, nearly a quarter of tasks are highly exposed to automation by generative AI, with more than half additionally showing medium exposure.[364] This imbalance echoes earlier transitions in labor markets, when women were disproportionately concentrated in routine clerical work that typically conferred limited authority and little control over valuable resources. Because of the repetitive, standardized nature of such jobs, they were disproportionately affected by successive waves of office automation and organizational restructuring.

The same institution reported in 2025 that clerical occupations continue to have the highest exposure to generative AI and that 3.3 percent of global employment falls into the highest exposure category, with a higher share for women than for men (4.7 percent vs. 2.4 percent). This share rises in high-income countries to 9.6 percent for women vs. 3.5 percent for men.[365]

On one hand, the pattern is muting. In previous eras, women could shift from domestic labor into clerical work, and for some, education opened limited routes into supervisory and managerial roles, even as elite professions remained strongly male dominated. The ladder was, and still is, imperfect, but it existed, though bounded by ceilings that have persisted for decades. In the current shift, AI automates what has long been considered a managerial endeavor, such as coordination, scheduling, and decision-making about resources, which once offered pathways into stable employment across the world. The result can be a new constraint, encoded this time in algorithms, on women's prospects for upward mobility, reinforcing persistent exclusion at the top and making algorithmic transformation an economic and social shift that often impacts women first.

On the other hand, the pattern has a rebound reflex: societies with widening gender gaps often see entrenched patriarchal norms bolstered through institutions, cultural attitudes, and power dynamics, creating feedback loops.[366,367] This dynamic draws from the ancient logic of resource protection that intensified with the rise of agricultural storage and surplus. In moments of uncertainty, this symbolism can become especially persuasive, almost Pavlovian for some, and societies may fall back or even regress further into structures rooted in that ancestral bias—the very bias from which these structures arise and through which they systematically reproduce inequality.

The most advanced democracies are not immune. Countries such as Sweden, Norway, and Iceland regularly rank among the highest in global gender equality indices.[368] Yet even these nations face pressures from automation and taskification. A Swedish study using Statistics Sweden register data for 2021 found that women were more likely than men to work in occupations with high exposure to generative AI.[369] The same study warned that without proactive policy interventions, gender gaps could widen in the coming decades. These societies have strong institutions and generous welfare models, but their vulnerability to shifts in the labor market shows how the algorithmic power over gender can expose even the most egalitarian systems.

If the resource of prediction becomes privatized, concentrated, and deployed without democratic oversight, it introduces a new axis of inequality that even robust policy frameworks struggle to contain.

The risk is sharper in countries where women's rights are more recent and fragile. In many parts of the Middle East, South Asia, and Sub-Saharan Africa, women's labor force participation remains far below global averages. According to the World Bank Group, women's labor force participation (ages 15–64) has been stagnant for three decades at around 53 percent, compared to 80 percent for men. Regionally, the largest gaps are in the Middle East and North Africa (20 percent for women vs. 75 percent for men) and South Asia (30 percent for women vs. 79 percent for men).[370] When AI systems reshape labor markets in these regions, they do so on top of already uneven foundations.

No matter the geography, in unequal starting conditions, technological shifts rarely land neutrally.

The Social Contract Cannot Be a Prediction Model

As women participate less in formal labor markets and, moreover, are underrepresented in the AI workforce that frames problems, selects variables, defines thresholds, and validates model performance, they are marginalized from shaping the algorithmic prediction economy. As a result, the data used to train these AI systems can overrepresent male-coded trajectories, not only because men dominate model-building but also because men are more consistently legible to the systems that capture work histories, credit signals, platform behavior, and "productivity" traces. This can make predictive systems less reliable for women and more likely to reproduce gendered patterns of advantage and exclusion. This compounds inequality through a feedback loop: women become less visible to the system, and the system becomes less capable of recognizing women's lived constraints, anticipating their needs, or allocating opportunities fairly when their pathways deviate from the male-coded "default." The political consequences of this dynamic can be severe. What is not captured is not optimized; what is not optimized is deprioritized.

The danger is not simply that AI systems, through the enforcement of the AI-integrated stacks through which they are deployed, reflect existing inequalities, but that they can erode and reconfigure the material and institutional foundations that made progress in women's rights possible in the first place.

The expansion of women's economic participation in the twentieth century depended on access to education, formal employment, and public services. If AI-driven taskification diminishes demand for the kinds of roles that historically served as entry points for women, and if algorithmic prediction power reinforces gendered patterns, whether it is in hiring, credit allocation, and other gatekeeping decisions such as promotion, pay setting, performance evaluation, access to training, insurance pricing, and eligibility for public benefits, then the scaffolding that supported generations of women may begin to collapse. The regression would appear as a subtle tightening of the boundaries within which women can act, choose, and build independent lives.

There is an irony in this development. The promise of AI is often framed as the liberation of human potential. Yet the ability to shape one's destiny also depends on the opportunities available in the labor market and therefore on the systems that mediate access to them—systems that are now increasingly algorithmically powered, opaque, and privately controlled. The more predictable human life becomes to these systems, the less predictable it may become to the individuals who live it. As predictability is extracted from people without giving them reciprocal control, it becomes a tool of governance rather than empowerment. The possibility of regression in women's rights also arises from this mismatch.

Progress has never been guaranteed. It has been contingent on political will, economic structures, and social movements. If AI amplifies competition for predictive advantage, then those without institutional influence risk being framed as obstacles to efficiency. This framing can legitimize policies that neglect the needs of women or treat their economic participation as secondary. It can normalize wage gaps as natural outcomes of productivity differences encoded in data. Once inequality is expressed as a score, it becomes easier to defend as measurement rather than power, and what was once seen as discrimination may come to be seen as optimization on a larger scale and with greater permanence.

And still, the fact that algorithmic prediction is male-biased remains a symptom. The deeper issue is that the authority to define what counts as knowledge, risk, and rules is now being monopolized in its aggregogenous form by a small elite of private firms, and history suggests that monopolies tend to reproduce the social patterns of those who hold them.

Institutions around the world hold the responsibility of re-founding the architecture that will sustain the distribution of value, authority, and meaning. That's what it means to restore constitutional friction and reassert sovereignty through the trias algorithmica. It is, in effect, the task of building democratic counterweights to an extractive predictability regime.

The Human In(ter)ference

There is a peculiar ritual that repeats itself whenever a new general-purpose technology arrives. First, a small priesthood learns to summon it. Second, the priesthood proclaims that the arc of history has finally found its engine. Third, the rest of society is invited to choose between two emotional postures that both conveniently preserve the priesthood's authority: reverence or panic. The content changes; the cadence does not. Steam promised the end of distance. Electricity promised the end of night. Nuclear power promised energy "too cheap to meter." The early internet promised the end of censorship and the flowering of democracy. Each time, the promise contains a hidden clause: those who control the engine will also write the timetable.

The current wave of machine intelligence has acquired its own liturgy. You can recognize it by three familiar incantations. The first is the faith that scale is destiny and that more parameters, more data, and more compute will reliably alchemize today's systems into tomorrow's minds. The second is the compression of time, the insistence that what once belonged to speculative futures now belongs to quarterly roadmaps. The third is the moral conversion of power into benevolence, the claim that unprecedented capability will translate into unprecedented benefit, as if history were a simple conduit from invention to justice.

The counterargument begins with a reminder that progress is rarely a straight line and never a pure function of ambition. It is a negotiation with constraints, human institutions, unintended consequences, and the stubborn friction between what can be built and what can be trusted. When a community insists that the remaining distance is short, it may be reporting a measurement. It may also be performing a persuasion.

Consider how often confident timelines have been the most fragile part of technological prophecy. In the 1950s, the rhetoric around nuclear energy was totalizing, not merely optimistic. It carried the tone of inevitability. Yet nuclear power did not become a frictionless blessing that dissolved scarcity. It became a domain where physics, geopolitics, public trust, and the moral weight of catastrophic risk refused to be compressed into a slogan. Chernobyl and Fukushima were not simply engineering failures; they were governance failures, communication failures, and integrity failures. The lesson is that a technology's promise is not self-executing.

The same pattern reappears in aviation. The jet engine changed the world. But the jet engine did not abolish the need for a safety culture. The Challenger disaster did not happen because rockets are impossible. It happened because institutional incentives can corrode judgment until a catastrophe becomes normal. The Boeing 737 Max crisis did not happen because flight is a fantasy. It happened because economic pressures, organizational silos, and regulatory blind spots can warp the interface between humans and machines.

Every revolution in capability creates a parallel revolution in responsibility. When the second revolution lags behind the first, the bill arrives without warning.

Now, bring this lens to machine intelligence. The scale narrative treats capability as if it were the only axis that matters. It suggests that the curve of performance is the curve of destiny. Yet even within the engineering reality of machine learning, scale has never been the full story. The transformer did not emerge from scaling. It emerged from a conceptual leap. Reinforcement learning breakthroughs were not simply bigger matrixes. They were new ways of shaping feedback. The history of progress in computing, as in other fields, is not the history of adding more, but the history of changing how.

Geoffrey Hinton, after decades of building the field, has voiced alarm about the speed of deployment and the difficulty of control.[371] Kate Crawford has stressed that social harms in contemporary AI systems are not accidental side effects but predictable outcomes of design choices shaped by an extractive, profit- and power-driven political economy.[9] Gary Marcus has insisted that brittleness and lack of grounded understanding are not minor wrinkles but structural issues[372] and has argued persistently that next-word prediction models lack grounded cognition and that scaling alone won't solve what's missing.[373] Yann LeCun has followed Marcus in emphasizing that current approaches, especially those centered on next-token prediction, are not sufficient foundations for robust reasoning and planning.[374] These are not fringe voices. They are signals that the engineering frontier is inseparable from intellectual humility.

And that humility does not negate progress but forces us to ask under what conditions it counts as progress.

Demis Hassabis speaks about the promise of AI for science,[375] but the very success of systems like AlphaFold illustrates a deeper point: extraordinary results often come from carefully defined problem domains, curated data, and rigorous evaluation.[376] Scientific acceleration is method, not magic. And method is slow when it is honest. Dario Amodei's public emphasis on risk and governance,[377] Mustafa Suleyman's warnings about the social disruptions of powerful systems,[378] and the artificial integrity lens I propose—a design code that prioritizes integrity over intelligence by embedding value-aligned, integrity-guiding mechanisms into AI systems rather than treating ethical, moral, and social considerations as an afterthought[379] reflect a recognition that capability without containment is not progress but volatility.

This is where the first incantation, the faith in scale, becomes less a scientific claim than a cultural posture. Scaling laws are real within regimes, but regimes are not eternal. In physics, you can scale a bridge's length until the material properties change and the bridge collapses. In biology, you can scale a creature's size until circulation and metabolism break. In economics, you can scale a firm's output until coordination costs eat the gains. The world is full of curves that look smooth until the boundary conditions change.

Scale also invites subtle deception: it makes qualitative transformation look like a quantitative continuation. It seduces us into believing that if we keep pushing the same lever, we will eventually unlock a different machine. But history is less obliging. The railroad did not become the airplane by laying more track. The telegraph did not become the telephone by adding more wire. At some point, new capabilities required a new architecture.

The second incantation, the compression of timelines, deserves even more severe skepticism. Technologies move quickly in laboratories and slowly in civilizations. Electrification took decades not because the dynamo was hard to invent but because factories, cities, and habits had to be rebuilt around it. Robert Solow's productivity paradox, often paraphrased as seeing computers everywhere except in the productivity statistics,[380] was a diagnosis of adoption friction. Brynjolfsson's work on the lag between invention and measurable productivity gains underscores that implementation is the main story, not a footnote.

If you want a contemporary analogy that is uncomfortably close, look at the internet itself. The utopian narrative of the early 2000s was not naive because it expected large change, but because it assumed large change would be morally positive by default. The network did connect humanity. It also industrialized disinformation, monetized outrage, and altered adolescent mental health on a planetary scale. Shoshana Zuboff's critique of surveillance capitalism[381] describes how the economic logic of data extraction can turn empowerment into dependency. The internet did not fail. It succeeded at what it was economically shaped to do. The lesson is again not anti-technology. The lesson is that governance is a feature.

In machine intelligence, timeline compression often ignores the difference between demonstration and dependable integration. An impressive model that solves benchmark problems is not yet a system you can safely embed in medicine, aviation, law, or national security. Reliability is not a byproduct of intelligence, but a property of engineered constraints, evaluation, and accountability. Removing hallucinations, ensuring robustness, preventing manipulation, establishing auditability, and securing supply chains are not marginal chores. They are the conditions of trust.

The third incantation, the promise of unprecedented benefits, is where rhetoric most often replaces argument. It is easy to claim that a powerful tool will democratize knowledge. It is harder to show that it will democratize agency. The difference matters. A world can be saturated with information while becoming poorer in autonomy. People can have access to answers while losing the capacity to form judgment. A machine can increase output while decreasing meaning.

Daron Acemoglu has warned that the distribution of gains from automation is not predetermined.[382] It depends on choices: what gets automated, who owns the systems, how labor markets adjust, and what institutions do.[383] Joseph Stiglitz has long argued that markets alone do not guarantee equitable outcomes, especially when power concentrates.[384] David Autor, often more optimistic, still frames the question as one of task reconfiguration and institutional design.[385] These disagreements are not academic ornaments. They reveal a central truth: productivity is not the same as prosperity, and prosperity is not the same as dignity.

To counter the benefit narrative, one must identify the hidden assumption within it. The assumption is that intelligence, once created, will flow outward as a public good. However, the more historically plausible pattern is that power, once created, first flows inward, toward those who can capture it. When oil was discovered, it did not instantly enrich the poor. It reorganized geopolitics and concentrated wealth. When financial derivatives proliferated, they did not simply optimize risk; they created fragility that culminated in crisis. When social platforms emerged, they did not simply amplify voices. They reshaped incentives for speech itself.

The mythology of automatic benefit often relies on graphs that resemble religious art. The hockey stick is more than a chart; it tells a story of salvation. It implies that we are at the hinge of history, that the future will be a smooth extrapolation of present curves, and that the only moral imperative is speed. But speed is not a virtue. Speed is a multiplier. It multiplies competence and incompetence alike; it multiplies wisdom and folly alike. When a system is powerful enough, the difference between wisdom and folly becomes the difference between flourishing and catastrophe.

There is also a psychological dimension that the acceleration narrative rarely acknowledges. When people begin to believe that a superhuman agent is imminent, they start to outsource responsibility in advance. They accept, almost gratefully, the erosion of their own agency. They call it pragmatism. They call it inevitability. But it is often a form of cognitive surrender. The future becomes a machine room that only specialists may enter. Everyone else is invited to watch the dashboard.

This is the most dangerous shift of all because it changes the human interface with technology. In healthy progress, technology expands human agency. In unhealthy progress, technology becomes the excuse for abandoning it. The interface turns from empowerment to dependency. The individual is reduced to a function. Personal identity is reduced to the function of a user, the citizen to the function of a consumer, the organization to the function of a deployment pipeline, and ethics to the function of an after-action report.

Historical analogies sharpen the point. In the late nineteenth century, industrialization created astonishing productivity. It also produced Dickensian misery, labor exploitation, and urban squalor. The benefits arrived because societies fought for them, not because steam was benevolent. Labor laws, public education, sanitation, antitrust enforcement, and democratic accountability were the governance infrastructures that turned industrial power into human gain. The factory became tolerable only when the political system forced it to respect human dignity.

In the twentieth century, the Green Revolution increased agricultural yields and saved lives. It also created dependencies on fertilizers, altered ecosystems, and produced exposure to input supply shocks and import dependence. Again, the benefit was real, and so were the trade-offs. The lesson is not to reject progress but to reject the story that progress is a one-way gift.

In the early days of computing, Norbert Wiener warned that automatic systems, operating far faster than humans, could produce disastrous consequences without effective foresight and control. Wiener could be read as anti-machine, but that would be an overly reductive reading; he was pro-responsibility.[386] His warnings revealed structural insights into feedback dynamics, control limitations, and unforeseen machine strategies, such as evolving tactics within their designed parameters through learning processes like adjusting weights in game-playing algorithms, that surprise even programmers due to speed and complexity.

Those who insist that we are only a short distance away from systems that outperform humans at most tasks often overlook a key distinction: competence is not comprehension, and output is not understanding. LLMs can produce astonishingly fluent language. But language is not the same as grounded knowledge. A model can imitate reasoning without possessing the constraints that make reasoning reliable. This is why researchers like Fei-Fei Li emphasize the need to connect intelligence to the physical and social world, not just to text.[387] It is also why the debate about agents matters. An agent that can act is not just a tool that can speak, but a system that can cause. And causation requires accountability.

The more you move from conversation to action, the more the integrity of the system becomes central. Not integrity as marketing, not integrity as a vague aspiration, but integrity as a set of enforceable properties: traceability of decisions, robustness to manipulation, clarity of objectives, bounded autonomy, secure provenance of training data, measurable reliability under distribution shift, and the capacity for humans to intervene meaningfully. Without these properties, autonomy becomes a liability. Intelligence becomes an accelerant for error.

This is where the narrative of recursive self-improvement, the idea that a system will rapidly enhance itself into an intelligence explosion, reveals its ideological undertone. It treats intelligence as self-contained and self-amplifying, as if the world were a frictionless substrate. But systems do not improve in a vacuum. They improve through resources, through experiments, through feedback, through infrastructure. A machine cannot simply think its way to more electricity, more chips, more trust, or more legitimacy. Those are social and physical constraints. They are not solved by cleverness alone.

Even if you imagine a future where software can redesign software, the world remains a bottleneck. Semiconductors require supply chains. Energy requires grid capacity. Data centers require land, water, cooling, permitting, and political consent. Deployment requires compliance, insurance, liability frameworks, and human training. The intelligence explosion story often resembles a financial fantasy in which compounding returns ignore market limits. It is the metaphysics of infinite liquidity applied to cognition.

One can grant the possibility of dramatic capability gains while still rejecting the claim of inevitability and the claim of imminence. The honest posture is neither complacency nor apocalypse. It is deliberate seriousness. It recognizes that the question is not simply what machines can do but what societies can absorb. Not what can be built but what should be allowed to operate. Not what is impressive, but what is trustworthy.

Trustworthiness is a neglected dimension in the prevailing rhetoric. There is a difference between a system that can answer and one that can be held responsible. A difference between a system that can optimize and one that can be governed. A difference between a system that can outperform humans on tasks and one that can coexist with human values without eroding them.

When leaders paint a future of scientific acceleration, they often invoke medicine. It is a compelling example because the upside is obvious, but medicine also reveals the governance problem with brutal clarity. A diagnostic system must be more than accurate. It must be explainable enough for clinicians to trust, robust enough for diverse populations, secure enough to protect patient data, and accountable enough that harm can be traced and corrected. The history of medical technology is full of tragedies caused not by malice but by premature confidence. The Therac-25 radiation overdoses were not a failure of ambition. They were a failure of software safety and organizational process.[388] In high-stakes domains, "almost right" is a form of wrong.

Economics offers another corrective. The acceleration narrative often speaks as if doubling worker productivity is a straightforward lever. But productivity depends on more than tools. It is a function of workflows, incentives, coordination, and meaning. If AI increases the production of low-value content, it may inflate activity without increasing value. If it accelerates decisions without improving judgment, it may increase the speed of mistakes. Goodhart's law warns that when a measure becomes a target, it ceases to be a good measure. AI can become a Goodhart machine, optimizing proxies at scale until organizations forget what they were trying to achieve.

The greatest risk is that we will mistake increased output for increased progress. We will flood the world with synthetic text, synthetic images, synthetic certainty, and then wonder why collective reasoning collapses. We will call it a misinformation problem, as if it were an externality, when it is, in fact, an integrity problem.

There is also the geopolitical temptation to treat speed as a national security imperative. Deterrence logic can be persuasive. Whoever builds first, wins. Yet the history of arms races suggests that speed without stability increases the probability of disaster. Nuclear deterrence, fragile as it is, required treaties, verification regimes, hotlines, doctrines, and decades of strategic thought. Even then, it repeatedly came close to catastrophe through misperception and accident. Introducing autonomous or semi-autonomous decision systems into security domains without comparable governance is a gamble, not a strength.

If you want a human example of how easily organizations can rationalize gambles, return to the Challenger. Engineers had concerns. The system still launched. The institutional desire to maintain schedule and confidence overruled caution. The tragedy was not that humans are flawed, but that flawed humans built a culture where flaws were rewarded.

The dominant AI narrative risks doing something similar at a civilizational scale. It frames skepticism as ignorance, caution as obstruction, and governance as delay. It turns prudence into a vice. But prudence is the oldest form of intelligence. Aristotle called it phronesis, practical wisdom. A civilization that discards phronesis in pursuit of power tends toward adolescence rather than advancement.

To counter the prevailing thesis, then, one must offer a different north star. Not intelligence at any cost but integrity at every step. Not the worship of capability but the cultivation of agency. Not speed but stewardship. The question is not whether machines will become more powerful. They will. The question is whether humans will remain authors of their institutions or become tenants in systems they no longer understand.

A sober view of history suggests that the decisive battles are not fought in the laboratory. They are fought in the design of incentives, the architecture of accountability, the enforcement of rights, the distribution of ownership, the education of citizens, and the courage of leaders to say no to profitable recklessness. The most important innovations are often invisible: standards, audits, safety cases, transparency requirements, and legal liabilities that force truth into the room.

The acceleration narrative often mocks regulation as ignorance. Yet regulation is simply a civilization's attempt to encode memory. It is a way of saying, "We have seen this movie before. We know that markets can reward short-term gain at long-term cost. We know that power concentrates unless countered. We know that externalities are not abstract; they have concrete effects on human lives."

Europe's comparatively cautious posture toward digital platforms reflects lived experience more than cultural skepticism. The internet's harms were not distributed equally. Societies that felt them differently responded differently. This reminds us that there is no single global storyline. There are many, and the loudest is not always the wisest.

A thoughtful counterthesis does not deny the extraordinary potential of machine intelligence. It denies the moral monopoly of those who sell inevitability. It insists that progress is not merely what we can build, but what we can justify. It reframes the central metric from capability to legitimacy.

Legitimacy requires that people can consent meaningfully. Consent requires understanding. Understanding requires transparency. Transparency requires that systems are not black boxes protected by mystique or proprietary fog. It requires that those affected by decisions can contest them. It requires that errors can be identified and corrected. It requires that the benefits are not confined to those who own the infrastructure.

Here, the questions become unavoidably political. Who owns the models? Who owns the data? Who owns the compute? Who audits the systems? Who is liable for harm? Who decides where autonomy is allowed? Who gets displaced and who gets enriched? These are not secondary questions. They are the questions.

The promise of democratized knowledge can become a mechanism of centralized control if the interface is designed as a dependency. A world where every person has a brilliant assistant in their pocket sounds like emancipation. But if that assistant is optimized for engagement, trained on data harvested without meaningful consent, shaped by commercial incentives, and controlled by a small set of firms, then the pocket becomes a leash. You gain convenience and lose sovereignty. You gain answers and lose authorship.

This is not a hypothetical fear. We have already seen a weaker version of it with search engines and social feeds. The interface became the mediator of reality. Attention became the currency. The result was the fragmentation of shared reality. AI can intensify this dynamic by making mediation more intimate and more persuasive.

When a system can converse, it can influence. When it can influence, it can shape preferences. When it can shape preferences, it can reshape democracy itself, not through censorship but through personalization. This is why governance cannot be deferred until after capability peaks. The architecture of influence is being built now.

The rhetoric of imminent superintelligence can also function as an excuse for fatalism. If something godlike is about to arrive, then ordinary politics feels quaint. People disengage. They wait for either salvation or disaster. Both forms of waiting are forms of surrender. Meanwhile, the real decisions are made in procurement contracts, model deployment policies, data retention rules, and corporate boardrooms.

History teaches that surrender is rarely rewarded. The societies that navigated industrialization best were not those that worshipped the machine. They were those that fought to domesticate it. They built labor protections. They invested in education. They created antitrust enforcement. They demanded safety standards. They treated the machine as a servant, not as a sovereign.

The same will be true here. The most important work is to build an ethic of artificial integrity that can withstand the seductions of acceleration. Artificial integrity is the capacity of a system to remain coherent under pressure, to resist corruption by incentives, to preserve human agency even when the machine is more convenient, and to keep truth measurable in environments that reward persuasion.

This requires new habits of leadership. Leaders must learn to treat uncertainty as a fact, not as a weakness. They must learn to say, "We do not know," and "We will not pretend." They must learn to build institutions that can learn, rather than institutions that can only deploy. They must learn to elevate auditors and safety engineers to the same prestige as product builders. They must learn to invest in resilience, not just in speed.

It also requires a cultural shift. We must stop confusing prediction with wisdom. A model can forecast the next word. It cannot guarantee the next consequence. We must stop confusing simulation with understanding. A model can imitate a voice. It cannot inherit the moral responsibility of the person it imitates. We must stop confusing scale with meaning. Bigger systems can still pursue smaller purposes.

The most thought-provoking conclusion may be the simplest. The future of intelligence is not primarily a question of how intelligent our machines become, but a question of how intelligent our civilization remains. Intelligence at the level of systems is the ability to balance power with restraint, speed with care, innovation with justice, and capability with accountability. It is the ability to preserve human dignity when efficiency tempts us to treat people as variables.

In that light, the prevailing thesis is revealed to be incomplete. It tells a story about machines becoming more powerful. It does not tell a credible story about humans becoming more sovereign. It promises a revolution in output. It does not secure a revolution in agency. It predicts exponential progress. It does not guarantee exponential wisdom.

The counterthesis is not that progress will stop. It is that progress without integrity is not progress. It is expansion without direction. It is power without purpose. And history is unequivocal about what happens when power outgrows purpose. Empires become brittle. Markets become predatory. Institutions become theatrical. Societies become anxious, polarized, and manipulable.

The task before us, then, is not to accelerate toward algorithmic machines that surpass us.

It is to build a world that remains worthy of whatever we build. That world will not be created by hype or fear. It will be created by the slow, demanding work of governance, ethics, education, and courage. It will be created by refusing to outsource our responsibility to any narrative, no matter how glamorous its graphs, no matter how confident its timelines, no matter how radiant its promises.

Because the true revolution is not in the machine, but in the human in(ter)ference to it. And the question that will define this era is not whether we can build minds, but whether we can preserve our own.

4 Humane Algorithmic Transition

The Flawed Assumption Behind AI Decision-Making

In transitioning to a world where algorithms rule more, an implicit deal is at play: all the messy ways in which humans actually decide—whether it is through intuition, conflict, fear, care, improvisation, error, or sometimes courage against uncertainty—would be filtered out and optimized, as it were treated as noise, around a clean abstract process that a model can emulate.

In that reframing, handing decisions to AI no longer appears as a transfer of power; it appears as hygiene. The human is recast as a source of bias that must be corrected, not as a source of meaning that must be preserved.

Yet many organizations implementing AI tend to lose sight of this, idealizing what a decision model is and falling into the trap of assuming a kind of one-size-fits-all framework—one that follows the same sequence in almost every circumstance: from input to research and analysis to decision, then execution, eventual evaluation, and, hopefully, lessons learned.

The least we can say is that it oversimplifies reality.

Human decision-making is far from uniform; it is far more complex, dynamic, and context-dependent. It is fluid and shaped by constraints, biases, urgency, situation, interactions, rationality, and, most importantly, irrationality, as suggested by a recent MIT study.[389]

If AI agents are to integrate into organizations, a diverse range of decision-making processes need to be considered to ensure effective implementation without inadvertently setting a substandard for decision-making.

No Decision Path Is One-Size-Fits-All or Naturally Monolithic

The notion that all decisions follow a structured path is a misconception. In reality, the decisions we make rely on multiple decision-making models, depending on the circumstances.

Intuitive Decision-Making

This approach relies on instinct and experience[390] rather than extensive research or structured analysis. It is particularly useful in high-stakes, fast-moving environments, where speed is crucial, and there is little time for detailed evaluation. The process typically follows a sequence of trigger recognition, immediate response based on experience, action, and post-factum evaluation.

For example, a venture capitalist may choose to invest in a startup based solely on intuition, even when financial data is incomplete or ambiguous. This form of decision-making is often subconscious, leveraging years of accumulated knowledge to make split-second judgments. Ultimately, this mode is rooted in intuitive reasoning, with experience-based instincts guiding rapid, subconscious decisions.

Rational-Analytical Decision-Making

In contrast, this approach is data-driven, structured, and systematic. It involves a methodical process of problem identification, data gathering, analysis, comparison of alternatives, decision execution, and performance review.

This model is frequently employed in corporate strategy, risk assessment, and forecasting. For instance, a supply chain management team may analyze historical demand data before adjusting production levels to optimize efficiency and reduce waste. This form of decision-making is grounded in deductive, inductive, causal, and Bayesian reasoning,[391] offering a data-informed path to structured choices.

Rule-Based and Policy-Driven Decision-Making

Some decisions do not require analysis or instinct but instead follow predefined frameworks, regulations, or automation rules. These rule-based decision models are essential in fields such as compliance, risk management, and regulatory environments, where consistency and adherence to policies are paramount.

This decision-making sequence begins with a specific situation, followed by the identification of the applicable rule or policy, its automated or manual enforcement, and subsequent compliance monitoring. An example of this is a bank's fraud detection system flagging transactions when they exceed a certain monetary threshold and originate from a high-risk geographical location, triggering an alert for further investigation. This approach leverages predefined rules to identify suspicious patterns[392] and ensure consistent and predictable outcomes.

Emotional and Social Decision-Making

Decision-making is not always about instinct, past experiences, logic, or rules; it can also be shaped by emotional intelligence and social dynamics,[393] while being influenced by personal values. This model plays a vital role in leadership, human resources, and ethical dilemmas, where interpersonal relationships, values, and cultural context influence outcomes.

It typically involves assessing the social or ethical context, weighing the emotional and moral dimensions, making a decision, acting, and receiving feedback from stakeholders. For instance, a CEO might decide to retain an underperforming employee due to their positive impact on company culture, even if conventional performance metrics suggest otherwise. Here, decision-making draws from moral/ethical and commonsense reasoning, where human values and social context shape the outcome.

Heuristic Decision-Making

This model relies on mental shortcuts developed from past experiences rather than a comprehensive analysis of all available options. While these shortcuts can be useful in fast-paced environments and when facing uncertainty,[394] they also introduce biases that may lead to suboptimal decisions.

The sequence typically follows trigger recognition, pattern matching, applying a mental shortcut, decision-making, immediate action, and occasional feedback. A classic example is a hiring manager preferring candidates from top-tier universities without thoroughly reviewing all applicants, assuming that institutional reputation correlates directly with job performance. At its core, this approach employs heuristic and commonsense reasoning, leveraging past experiences to navigate present challenges.

Collaborative and Consensus-Based Decision-Making

Certain decisions require group input,[395] negotiation, and alignment among stakeholders. This approach is common in corporate boards, government policy-making, and high-impact organizational strategies, where multiple perspectives need to be considered.

The process involves identifying the problem, engaging in group discussions, evaluating different perspectives, negotiating to reach a consensus, executing the collective decision, and reviewing outcomes. For example, a board of directors may spend weeks deliberating over a long-term business strategy, ensuring that all viewpoints are taken into account before making a final decision. This collective method is enriched by reflective, moral/ethical, and analogical reasoning, enabling decisions that balance multiple perspectives.

Crisis and High-Stakes Decision-Making

In high-stakes and crisis situations, decision-makers often operate under severe time constraints, uncertainty, and high risk—conditions that do not permit prolonged analysis or deliberation. Drawing on Gary Klein's recognition-primed decision (RPD)[396] model, these contexts reveal how experienced professionals make rapid yet effective decisions by relying on pattern recognition, mental simulation, and intuitive reasoning.

Rather than evaluating multiple alternatives, decision-makers recognize familiar cues, match them to prior experiences, and act on the first workable option that comes to mind. For instance, a cybersecurity team may shut down an entire system at the first sign of an intrusion to prevent further damage, without waiting for a full diagnostic. This approach exemplifies how decision-making under pressure combines abduction, causal reasoning, heuristic shortcuts, and intuition into a streamlined, action-oriented process.

These seven decision-making paths, while neither exhaustive nor mutually exclusive, rarely operate in isolation.

Instead, they often overlap, interact, and accumulate, reflecting the cognitive flexibility[397] demanded by the context.

This interplay can occur at different speeds, either sequentially or simultaneously, dynamically or in a more structured manner. For instance, an executive facing a high-stakes decision may initially rely on intuition, then switch to a rational-analytical approach to validate their instincts with data, before finally engaging in collaborative decision-making with key stakeholders.

Similarly, a crisis might demand an immediate heuristic or rule-based response, followed by an in-depth analytical review after the fact. This reality challenges the rigid, linear view of decision-making and underscores the need for AI agents capable of fluidly transitioning between different models based on context, urgency, and complexity.

Pattern-Following Is Not Decision-Making

AI agents can effectively imitate several types of reasoning, especially those that rely on structured logic, data-driven patterns, and statistical inference. For example, they excel at deductive reasoning, where predefined rules or theories are applied to reach specific conclusions, and inductive reasoning, where generalizations are drawn from large datasets that are foundational to machine learning models. AI also performs well with causal reasoning, especially when trained on time-series data or observational patterns, and is highly capable of Bayesian reasoning, updating probabilities based on new evidence.

Moreover, AI systems can handle analogical reasoning by identifying similarities across datasets and applying known patterns to new contexts. They also routinely leverage heuristic reasoning, using rule-of-thumb logic to deliver fast, approximate solutions in complex environments.

Yet, despite these strengths, AI agents exhibit several persistent limitations that expose the fragile boundaries of their reasoning capabilities. One such issue is their reliance on fixed learning paths, a kind of single-path reasoning that depends heavily on predetermined models.

AI agents are built to follow patterns, but decision-making often breaks those patterns. A model trained for rational-analytical decision-making may fail in crisis scenarios that require instant judgment. When unexpected conditions arise, AI often fails to recognize the need for an alternative mental model or decision logic, thus struggling to dynamically transition between or aggregate different decision-making paths.

This rigidity is exacerbated by a lack of deep contextual understanding. AI agents often fail to distinguish when policies or frameworks should be applied with flexibility, such as in strategic decision-making, or with strict adherence, such as in regulatory compliance. While their ability to sense and respond to nuanced shifts in context is improving, it remains limited and typically requires extensive human intervention. Recent studies reinforce this concern, showing that even advanced AI agents exhibit fixed preferences[398] in risk and time-based decision scenarios.

Additionally, bias reinforcement poses a critical challenge. Without the capacity for self-reflection or independent judgment, AI agents are prone to over-relying on heuristics, amplifying learned biases, and overlooking ethical implications in their outputs. Without the ability to challenge their own assumptions or course-correct with human-like discernment, AI agents risk misaligning their actions with human values and intended societal outcomes.

These constraints become even more pronounced when examining reasoning types in which AI continues to struggle. Abductive reasoning, which involves inferring the most plausible explanation from incomplete or ambiguous data, remains elusive due to the contextual awareness it demands. Commonsense reasoning, while partially approximated in large language models, is often brittle or overly literal, failing to capture the tacit knowledge humans rely on instinctively. Similarly, moral and ethical reasoning is only beginning to emerge in AI design.[399] While some systems attempt to integrate value-based parameters, they do so in a mechanical way, still far from capturing the depth and subtlety of ethical judgment.

At the outer edges of AI's current capabilities lie reasoning modes that are inherently human. Intuitive reasoning, shaped by gut feeling, lived experience, and emotional resonance, is not yet replicable by AI. Likewise, reflective reasoning, the capacity to evaluate and refine one's own thinking processes, remains extremely limited, requiring a form of metacognition and self-awareness that machines do not possess.

While AI has made impressive strides in simulating structured, data-based reasoning, it still falls short in areas requiring flexibility, contextual nuance, ethical sensitivity, and self-reflective awareness.

Toward Achieving Decision-Making Elasticity, Integrity over Autonomy

Decision-making is one of the most essential capacities for the evolution of our societies, as it represents our ability to translate intention into action, shaping both ourselves and human society.

Given the current maturity of AI agents, executives must first assess the decision-making models embedded within the AI system, ensuring a clear understanding of its decision-making path and validating that this path is reliable enough for the decisions being delegated.

If full sufficient reliability cannot be ensured, organizations must establish clear thresholds for when AI can operate autonomously and when human intervention is required. Additionally, they must proactively design structured approaches for handling the remaining percentage of cases outside the AI's scope, ensuring that human oversight and alternative decision-making mechanisms remain in place to uphold accountability and strategic alignment.

Achieving a level of decision-making elasticity requires a paradigm shift—one where intelligence alone cannot ensure adaptability, contextual awareness, or responsible decision-making.

Researchers have recently developed context-aware neural architectures that begin to emulate high-level cognitive flexibility,[400] one of the foundational steps toward integrity-led reasoning in AI.

Moving forward, the key to unlocking decision-making in AI lies in a new frontier: that of mimicking integrity, not just intelligence, enabling AI systems to:

Assess the Right Decision-Making Model(s) for Each Context

Should this be a rational analysis? A fast crisis response? A rule-based compliance check? A combination of the first two, the last two, or something else? For AI, it means being capable of true questioning as an act of autonomous ethical reflection, initiating inquiry driven by internal unease, contradiction, or ethical conflict and challenging flawed logic and dangerous assumptions.

Maintain Consistency While Allowing Flexibility

Can an AI agent detect when strict rules should be applied vs. when nuance is needed regarding human values and social norms? For AI, it means developing the capacity to interpret context, assess ethical dimensions, and exercise judgment beyond binary logic, bridging the gap between rigid instruction and human-centered understanding.

Recognize When to Seek Human Input

Can an AI agent recognize when uncertainty or implications are too high and defer decisions to humans? For AI, it means being autonomous in its capacity to take the initiative to engage with humans to collaborate.

Altogether, these three characteristics move AI beyond intelligence toward integrity.

"9 Whats" Toward AI's Algorithmic Power Deployment

The same trap of oversimplification that we fall into when we reduce or idealize our decision-making into a single linear pathway that can be simulated by AI reappears at the organizational level when we rationalize the path to deploy it. Too often, AI's algorithm deployment is treated as an efficiency rollout enabled by technology instead of a transfer of power. That transfer begins the moment algorithms start to write the rules, execute decisions at scale, and judge outcomes and compliance. This is not AI itself, but the triadic form of power that AI enables.

Much of the early debate on AI, and GenAI in particular, has borrowed from familiar strategy playbooks, contrasting efficiency with differentiation, automation with augmentation, disruption with continuous improvements. These frameworks, useful in their time, tend to flatten organizational reality into binary trade-offs. They capture broad patterns but leave out the subtleties of how AI's algorithmic power actually reshapes firms, workforces, and societies once it becomes concentrated.

Beyond the tech and the short-term gains, every AI deployment is a structural bet on resilience, dignity, and long-term consequences because it reallocates triadic authority both outside-in and inside-out within firms, shifting who and what defines standards, who and what triggers action, and who and what validates or sanctions outcomes.

Once you see it that way, the question "Should we use AI here?" is no longer serious enough. The real question becomes: "What exactly are we doing to the people, to the organization, and to society when we use it in this way, when algorithmic systems execute decisions, define acceptable options, and evaluate human worth through metrics and rankings?"

As the triad's algorithmic power redefines what counts as economic value and rewrites the economics of human work, something crucial still remains in human hands: the condition under which these deployments take place within organizations and at what cost. What takes shape as AI-mediated reality still depends on whether these algorithms are deployed as instruments of substitution, augmentation, silent discipline, or human-centered expansion, and on whether human worth and power integrity, at individual, organizational, or societal levels, are treated as a discretionary ideal or a condition of legitimacy.

From this lens, inherited binaries no longer hold. The language of efficiency vs. differentiation, automation vs. augmentation, disruption vs. incremental improvement is too flat to describe what is at stake when algorithmic power becomes infrastructural, shaping what can be done, what should be done, and what is allowed to count as good. A deeper map is required—one that makes integrity alignment explicit as a structural dimension of AI deployment.

It can unfold across nine distinct strategic pathways, defined by growth potential—whether low, medium, or high—and by employment impact—whether jobs are killed, preserved, or created—and, crucially, by a third axis that has long remained implicit: integrity alignment.

Integrity itself spans three states: it can be damaged, when dignity, autonomy, and resilience are eroded; compromised, when outcomes remain ambiguous or fragile; or upheld, when results sustain and elevate human worth and power capacity despite the pressures of algorithmic power to "taskify" minds.

By surfacing the integrity axis as a structural dimension, this 3×3 framework, elevated into a cube, reveals the paradoxical effects of algorithmic power deployments through AI.

In some cases, AI rationalizes organizations into leaner forms, optimizes operations for measurable gains, or displaces workers at scale in pursuit of high growth. These pathways deliver efficiency or expansion on paper, but integrity shows their hidden cost: what appears as progress may, in fact, be systemic fragility, eroding the human capacity and resilience on which long-term prosperity depends.

In other cases, AI assists professionals by easing their burdens, enhances workflows through targeted support, or accelerates growth by multiplying human capacity without large-scale displacement. These pathways preserve employment and appear more human-centered, yet integrity reveals their ambiguity: jobs remain, but autonomy and judgment risk narrowing, as machine logic increasingly sets the terms of work.

In another set of logics, AI augments organizations with new expertise, restructures talent flows to unlock latent potential, or empowers entirely new markets and industries. These pathways promise genuine expansion, yet integrity poses the decisive question: are new roles and opportunities elevating human capabilities, or merely subordinating workers to algorithmic dependencies that erode judgment, stifle creativity, and atrophy essential human faculties?

Here, empowerment can mark either the highest alignment of prosperity and dignity or its most sophisticated illusion.

It raises the stakes for leaders: they must navigate efficiency and growth alongside resilience, sustainability, and the dual test of social acceptability and humane legitimacy.

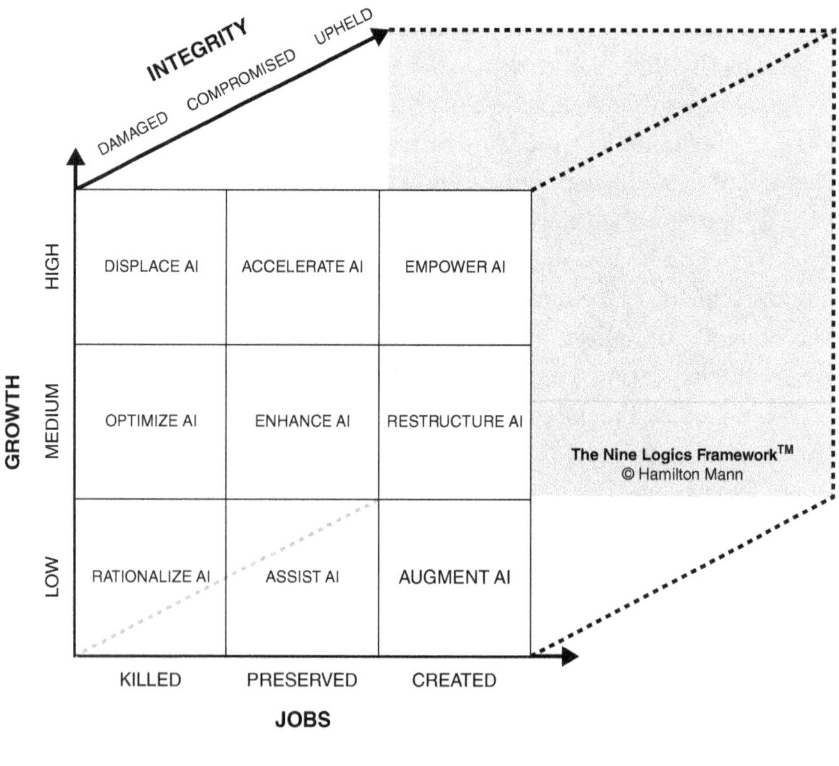

In "Rationalize AI"

AI strips out labor to cut costs but fails to unlock new sources of demand. Organizations become leaner but not stronger. Productivity gains look promising, yet financial performance remains fragile. This is productivity without prosperity: systemic fragility grows as human capacity shrinks.

This is where the two-dimensional grid fails. Measuring jobs and growth alone suggests a leaner organization, yet the human system underneath becomes weaker. Without an integrity axis, leaders cannot see that rationalization is a false victory: it optimizes people away while corroding the very resilience required for long-term survival.

What state of trias algorithmica does this scenario reveal? An absent or failed one, giving rise to a cost constitution. It produces subtraction without reinvention: the legislative-like function narrows value to what can be measured; the executive-like function automates throughput with fewer humans; and the judicial-like function justifies headcount reduction through "productivity" scores that become hard to contest. And when judgment is reduced to productivity metrics, layoffs become an "objective necessity," turning managerial choice into algorithmic inevitability, and people from capability into an "avoidable expense."

The case of Ocado: In early 2025, Ocado, the British online grocery and technology company, announced that it would eliminate around 500 roles across its technology and finance functions.[401] The move was not framed as a response to collapsing demand, but as a cost and efficiency initiative: executives pointed to "AI-type" tools that were increasing engineering efficiency and reducing the need for the same level of hiring and R&D spending.[402] In that sense, automation and process streamlining made it possible to run leaner teams and lower costs.

Yet the broader picture reveals why this development exemplifies "Rationalize AI." In fiscal year 2024, Ocado reported around 14 percent revenue growth while still posting a pretax loss of about £374.5 million.[402] At the same time (February 27, 2025), it guided that Technology Solutions revenue growth would slow to around 10 percent in fiscal year 2025, after around 18 percent growth in fiscal year 2024.[402] In other words, the company is using AI-enabled efficiency to rationalize costs and headcount, but the results disclosed at the time show that revenue growth alone had not yet translated into profitability nor into a re-acceleration of its technology-growth engine. This is the defining paradox of "Rationalize AI."

The strategic challenge is whether efficiency that weakens resilience can ever be called performance or whether it signals an erosion of human worth and power, undermining the integrity required for adaptive renewal, durable value creation, and the social license to operate.

Applying trias algorithmica here means ensuring that AI systems used to cut cost, automate workflows, or rank performance cannot by themselves become the sole basis for defining what counts as value and what constitutes legitimate workforce reduction.

In "Optimize AI"

AI substitutes for human labor in targeted functions while boosting organizational output. Companies enjoy measurable productivity gains and medium-tier growth. Yet profitability and resilience often remain uncertain, as efficiency masks latent vulnerabilities.

As jobs are sacrificed and output improves, integrity shows the void beneath the numbers. Optimization strips human resilience to the bone, producing brittle organizations addicted to quarterly gains. Only the integrity axis shows why optimization, while rational on paper, undermines the human foundations that underpin sustainable growth.

What state of trias algorithmica does this scenario reveal? One distorted into an algorithmic governance trap. It intensifies the judicial-like function. Performance is instrumented, ranked, and enforced; the legislative-like function rewrites "good work" into compliance with machine-defined key performance indicators (KPIs) that harden into doctrine, and the executive-like function tightens workflow into unyielding efficiency. It highlights the risk of being blinded by a path where revenue rises, but the structural capacity to generate enduring value atrophies.

The case of CrowdStrike: In May 2025, cybersecurity firm CrowdStrike announced a restructuring that would cut roughly 500 jobs, about 5 percent of its workforce. It was primarily a scale-and-efficiency move, driven by the claim that AI is increasing productivity and "flattening" the company's hiring curve, allowing it to operate with fewer roles in some areas while reallocating resources to priority growth functions (e.g., customer-facing teams and product/engineering) and pursuing longer-term targets like $10B in annual recurring revenue (ARR). Two months earlier, the company had reported fiscal fourth quarter 2025 revenue of $1.06 billion (up 25 percent year over year). Yet the bottom line told a more sobering story. Under the standard accounting rules (generally accepted accounting principles [GAAP]), the company reported a net loss of $92.3 million, highlighting the tension between rapid growth, efficiency narratives, and bottom-line results.[403]

This trajectory illustrates the logic of "Optimize AI." Jobs are eliminated, and the organization captures a measurable lift in productivity and revenue. The gains, however, remain fragile. AI delivers cost savings and output growth, but it does not guarantee profitability or long-term stability. The real question is whether optimization strengthens the long-term fabric of the organization, or whether it locks firms into a cycle of fragile gains that sacrifice human worth and power, integrity for speed.

Trias algorithmica should prevent AI-driven KPIs, scoring systems, and workflows analytics from becoming the sole authority over work by separating model-based evaluation from the human judgment that defines good performance and acceptable trade-offs, so that optimization does not override social responsibility or erode enduring value creation in the process.

In "Displace AI"

AI replaces labor at scale while fueling new industries, markets, and waves of consumption. Growth is rapid and expansive, but it comes at the cost of dismantling traditional employment structures. The result is high economic expansion coupled with deep social disruption.

This characterizes high-growth success despite job losses. The integrity axis uncovers its true cost: systemic fragility and social disruption. It ultimately reveals that displacement is not just a trade-off between jobs and growth, but a governance failure that sacrifices resilience for expansion.

What state of trias algorithmica does this scenario reveal? A collapsed one. It unleashes triadic algorithmic power operating at societal scale: legislative-like authority migrates to AI systems that rewrite the surrounding labor order and redefine employability; executive automation restructures labor markets faster than institutions can adapt; and judicial-like scoring systems decide who is "fit" for the new economy, and with what leverage, pushing entire categories of workers outside the perimeter of relevance.

The case of Accenture: By late September 2025, Accenture had laid off more than 11,000 people worldwide as part of an accelerated restructuring. The company described this not as a standard cost-cutting program but as a deliberate exit of employees who could not be retrained fast enough for AI-centered work.[404] According to the *Financial Times*, Accenture's CEO Julie Sweet made the message explicit in a call with analysts: "We are exiting on a compressed timeline people where reskilling, based on our experience, is not a viable path for the skills we need."[405] The financial picture tells a story of expansion rather than distress. Quarterly revenue reached $17.6 billion, ahead of the company's expectations, and full-year revenue rose about 7 percent to roughly $69.7 billion. New bookings climbed above $21.3 billion in the quarter, and Accenture reported $5.9 billion in AI-related bookings over the full fiscal year.[406] The company has nearly doubled its pool of AI and data specialists to 77,000 since 2023 and reported that more than 550,000 employees have already been trained in generative AI.[407]

This exposes the structural tension at the core of "Displace AI." Accenture is capturing high-value AI demand at global scale. It is winning multibillion-dollar AI contracts, booking growth, and reinforcing its position as a preferred partner for clients who want to reinvent themselves with intelligent systems. At the very same time, it is rewriting the employment contract inside the firm. Roles are declared obsolete not because the company is failing, but because the company is succeeding in pivoting to AI faster than those workers can be re-skilled. The public framing is one of reinvention. The lived experience for thousands is forced exit.

AI becomes the engine of new value creation and market expansion, revenues rise, bookings surge, investor narratives strengthen, the firm accelerates, and society absorbs the shock.

The question that human worth and power integrity brings into focus is whether this definition of success is aligned with the social contract between the firm and its employees, free from bias and committed to a culture of respect and belonging. A "Great Place to Work," so to speak.

Trias algorithmica must ensure that AI-led scaling, labor redesign, and employability scoring are not fused into a single growth machine, especially when firm-level deployment decisions can fracture the social contract with workers and substantially or durably destabilize labor markets far beyond the enterprise.

In "Assist AI"

AI supports workers rather than replacing them, reducing friction in workflows while keeping employment stable. Professionals still perform their core functions but with fewer administrative burdens. Growth, however, remains incremental. The value lies in quality and efficiency at the margin, not in the creation of entirely new growth trajectories. The system is safeguarded but not reinvented.

While this situation suggests stability, jobs are preserved, and growth remains steady.

Yet, integrity reveals a subtler erosion. Workers may keep their titles, but their scope for judgment shrinks as AI dictates workflows. Only the integrity axis makes this visible: jobs are preserved, growth neutral, but autonomy is partially lost.

What state of trias algorithmica does this scenario reveal? A weakly differentiated one. The legislative-like function standardizes proper notes, workflows, and interactions; the executive-like function drafts, nudges, and installs "recommended practice" as default reality; the judicial-like function audits deviations, inadvertently or insidiously converting help into discipline, eroding autonomy through convenience and habituation.

The case of NHS England: By 2025, NHS England reported that several regions and trusts were already trialing and deploying AI-enabled ambient scribing products intended to reduce the administrative burden of documentation. These systems can unobtrusively capture the patient–clinician conversation and convert it into structured draft medical documentation for review and validation after the visit. Early indications from trials included reduced typing and note-taking during consultations.[408] The promise was straightforward: give doctors more time with patients by letting AI handle the paperwork. The early results confirmed that administrative time could indeed be reduced. GPs reported spending less time typing and more time maintaining eye contact, explaining diagnoses, or answering patient questions. But while the pilots improved the quality of care and preserved the core role of the clinician, they did not produce new demand, new markets, or systemic economic growth. The number of jobs was not cut, but neither was the workforce significantly expanded. Doctors remained indispensable, and AI became an assistive tool rather than a transformative engine.

This illustrates the logic of "Assist AI." Jobs are preserved, workflows are improved, and productivity gains appear locally meaningful. Yet the economic impact remains incremental, not expansive. "Assist AI" avoids the social disruption of mass job losses, but it equally avoids the disruptive potential of new industry formation. This is the double-edged nature of AI assistance as a strategy.

The underlying but critical question is to what extent preserving stability without expanding human worth, power, integrity, scope, and perspectives amounts to genuine support or instead narrows autonomy under the appearance of protection. The strategic tension lies in whether AI is being used to protect the current system or to reshape it.

Trias algorithmica here means ensuring that assistive AI for drafting, recommending, and documenting does not incrementally turn workflow support into behavioral standardization and continuous micro-evaluation, thereby preserving professional judgment under conditions that appear protective but may gradually become prescriptive.

In "Enhance AI"

AI improves human productivity without cutting jobs, enabling smoother workflows and better services. Professionals are freed from repetitive tasks, but growth remains bounded. This path prioritizes human-centered efficiency, producing incremental but meaningful operational benefits.

At first glance, *Enhance AI* seems safe: jobs are protected, workflows improved. Yet without an integrity perspective, leaders miss a crucial question: Are humans freed, or are they being deskilled by over-reliance on AI? Integrity allows us to see whether technology extends human capacity or gradually hollows it out.

What state of trias algorithmica does this scenario reveal? A safeguarded yet vulnerable one. It can preserve dignity when the triad remains meaningfully separated: humans retain legislative-like authority over standards, AI supports executive-like execution, and judicial-like evaluation remains contestable and plural rather than singular and metric-driven. Yet a deeper tension emerges between employees benefiting from algorithmic enhancement and their judgment being constrained by "dependautonomy," a condition where reliance on AI shrinks interpretive freedom, and "better" becomes synonymous with what is "model-consistent."

The case of Delta Air Lines: From 2023, Delta said it was using AI to quickly make procedures known to reservations agents and to support pricing, which it presented as part of improving the speed and consistency of customer responses.[409] As reported at the time, Delta Air Lines was testing AI to help reservations agents quickly parse historical policies and common customer questions, and the airline described an AI-integrated knowledge-management tool to help agents source accurate answers more quickly.[410] Separately, Delta described its AI pricing as a decision-support tool that recommends pricing adjustments for analysts, who review and fine-tune those recommendations rather than having prices published automatically.[411] Delta has not presented these AI initiatives as a way to replace gate or call-center staff. Instead, it has framed AI as a way to enhance employees' ability to serve passengers better and consistently by giving them AI-surfaced information and recommendations.[411]

"I think the initial foray into AI is on the customer service side," said CEO Ed Bastian, responding to Morgan Stanley analyst Ravi Shankar's question about the carrier's use of the technology. "We're working with our reservations team to try to help our reservations agents parse the historical policies and questions and things that you may call into a real agent."[411] According to the 2024 *Delta Difference* report, as the airline rolls out advanced technologies, it "takes a balanced approach to AI, using it to improve operations and enhance the customer experience while prioritizing customers' and employees' safety, security, and trust."[412] Delta's headcount fell sharply in 2020 because of the pandemic, but by 2023–2025, it had rebuilt to about 100 000 employees again, according to the company's own disclosures. Financially, over 2024–2025, Delta reported revenue growth in the mid-single digits and highlighted improved operational performance. In 2024, at its Investor Day on November 20, the company told investors it was targeting mid-single-digit revenue growth as part of its differentiated-and-durable plan.[413] In January 2025, when it released its December-quarter and full-year 2024 results, Delta reported record revenue and described "industry-leading operational performance," with year-on-year revenue growth in that same mid-single-digit range.[414]

This trajectory captures the essence of "Enhance AI." The gains came from smoother workflows, customers benefiting from more responsive service, and incremental productivity increases, not from AI-driven workforce reductions. The real risk is monocognition through taskification, when one model's "best practice" becomes the only acceptable practice. The decisive challenge lies in determining whether, in such cases, technology enhances the integrity of human worth and power, or instead deskills the workforce by reducing expertise to the execution of AI-suggested choices.

Trias algorithmica should ensure that AI enhancement tools remain decision-support systems rather than decision-shaping authorities, preserving the human capacity to interpret, contest, and depart from AI model outputs so that enhancement does not harden into monocognition through taskification.

In "Accelerate AI"

AI accelerates organizational growth while retaining and even amplifying human capacity. Firms preserve jobs, invest in their people, and use AI as a multiplier of productivity and innovation. Growth is significant, but it does not require large-scale workforce displacement.

The jobs and growth axis already shows this as a favorable case, but the integrity axis makes explicit why: growth is paired with the preservation of autonomy and dignity. With an integrity axis, Accelerate AI is revealed not just as a good strategy but as ethical leadership, proof that inclusion and prosperity can scale together.

What state of trias algorithmica does this scenario reveal? A productive and calibrated one. The triadic power is constitutionally structured and institutionally restrained through checks and balances. Legislative-like standards are co-designed with workers; executive-like automation is deliberately bounded by human override; and judicial-like evaluation incorporates appeal, explanation, and learning. In such a model, growth arises from expanding human capacity rather than replacing it.

The case of Ikea: In 2024, Ikea's largest retailer, Ingka Group, took a distinctly people-forward path with AI by launching tools such as Hej Copilot, which it described as a way to support coworkers in their daily work and help them focus on higher-value tasks, positioning AI as an assistant that augments human capabilities rather than replaces them.[415] Hej Copilot was developed in collaboration with Microsoft and designed to assist coworkers with tasks ranging from text and image creation to generating ideas and crafting presentations.[415] Ingka also set targets to provide AI literacy training to around 30,000 coworkers and 500 leaders, explicitly framing the effort as workforce empowerment and capability building.[415] This training effort was positioned as part of a broader goal to ensure people and technology evolve together, so coworkers can use AI tools responsibly and with confidence in their day-to-day work.[415] In the same period, Ingka reported that store visitation rose 3.3 percent and online visitors rose 28 percent, with more than four million additional online orders compared to the year before, showing demand and throughput rising alongside the rollout of AI-enabled ways of working.[416]

This fits the orientation toward "Accelerate AI" because growth in activity is paired with deliberate investment in human capacity rather than workforce displacement. It is the counter-narrative to the productivity-first mindset. "Accelerate AI" asks leaders: can we harness AI to elevate people and generate growth without sacrificing the workforce? The Ikea case suggests the answer is yes. The enduring tension is whether such examples mark the beginning of a broader shift toward inclusive growth that expands human worth and power while safeguarding their integrity or remain exceptional cases in a landscape still dominated by an exclusive, productivity-driven economy.

Trias algorithmica should organize AI deployment so that standards are co-designed with workers, automation remains bounded by human oversight, and evaluation process is appealable, enabling firms to scale growth through the expansion of human capability rather than its substitution.

In "Augment AI"

AI sparks the creation of adjacent roles, including engineers, analysts, and content creators, that sustain AI-driven lines of business. Growth is steady but limited. Markets are not fundamentally transformed. The grid celebrates job creation here, but without integrity, it cannot distinguish between jobs that empower and jobs that serve as a crutch for a temporary peak in demand. An integrity axis forces us to ask: do these new roles build enduring capabilities and pathways for human expertise, or do they merely anchor workers to the support of keeping the system running relative to short-term financial performance? Growth alone cannot answer that.

What state of trias algorithmica does this scenario reveal? A market-imposed and agency-reducing one. It shifts legislative-like authority outward, pulling organizations into ecosystems of externally dictated norms. This power codifies operating models for what counts as effective work and sustainable workforce design, shaping performance norms, role definitions, and headcount architecture; it projects an executive-like function onto firms, compelling organizations to internalize external standards as execution constraints, and its judicial-like function then evaluates their ability to perform within that framework through an up-or-out logic. Paradoxically, job creation may signal a loss of sovereignty: new roles sustain compliance with external frameworks rather than expand internal agency. The real uncertainty lies less in the existence of new roles than in the conjunctural and opportunistic conditions under which they are created.

The case of Anthropic: In April 2025, Anthropic, the maker of the Claude AI model, announced that it would create more than 100 new jobs across Europe, with a focus on cities such as Dublin and London.[417] These roles spanned engineering, research, sales, and business operations and were positioned as additive hires to sustain the company's rapid growth in AI services.[417,418] Anthropic framed the expansion as net job creation to meet growing business demand and to support its expanding European customer base.[417,418] Yet this expansion came with a striking paradox. Even as Anthropic added new categories of expertise orbiting its core AI business, its CEO, Dario Amodei, warned publicly that AI could displace vast numbers of jobs, including up to half of entry-level white-collar roles, particularly in routine knowledge work.[419] His remarks, widely reported and subsequently pushed back on by NVIDIA's Jensen Huang at VivaTech 2025, underscored the tension between firm-level augmentation and system-wide disruption.[420] Financially, Anthropic's growth was rapid rather than incremental. By late May 2025, Reuters reported that Anthropic had reached about \$3 billion in annualized revenue, up from nearly \$1 billion in December 2024 and about \$2 billion around the end of March 2025, reflecting accelerating enterprise demand for generative AI services.[421] Available reporting framed the hiring drive as capacity-building to serve that demand rather than as evidence of market reinvention beyond the competitive AI sector.[417,421]

This approach reflects the essence of "Augment AI." When augmentation is driven primarily by short-term market demand, it remains fragile, vulnerable to fluctuations, and easily discarded if competitive pressures shift. "Augment AI" raises the question of whether roles are being created to meet momentum as an immediate fix for competitiveness or whether they are a structural part of a new core system designed to support long-term growth while sustaining human worth and power integrity. The former is conjunctural augmentation. The latter is true augmentation. Confusing the two risks feeding into a broader tide of displacement.

Applying trias algorithmica here means ensuring that AI-driven job creation does not merely reproduce the demands of external platforms, benchmarks, and ecosystem norms, but instead builds internal capabilities the firm can govern on its own terms over time.

In "Restructure AI"

AI restructures organizations by enabling new internal pathways for talent and skills. Employees transition into new roles as firms align human capital with emerging technological needs. Growth emerges from within, rather than through market disruption, as companies unlock the latent potential of their workforce.

While this pathway highlights job creation and moderate growth, its real value only emerges with an integrity perspective: "Restructure AI" sustains dignity by enabling reskilling and mobility, showing that technology can evolve with workers rather than against them. This distinguishes cosmetic job churn from genuine empowerment.

What state of trias algorithmica does this scenario reveal? A redistributive yet standardizing one. "Restructure AI" is where trias algorithmica acts as an engine of internal reallocation. It turns internal mobility into a dynamic, AI-enabled process. Legislative-like rules define which skills count, while executive-like systems route people through internal labor markets. It then becomes possible to show that the false trade-off between productivity and employment can be avoided. Yet it raises a new integrity risk through judicial-like power, where "potential" becomes a score and mobility becomes a managed pipeline rather than a self-directed journey.

The case of Walmart: In 2024 and 2025, Walmart expanded reskilling and internal mobility initiatives that use AI-enabled tools to help associates explore and prepare for new roles within the company.[422,423] Rather than presenting AI only as automation in operations, Walmart also positioned AI as a way to support people through hiring and career progression, including an AI tool called Career Explorer that can recommend roles based on associates' career aspirations and personal interests,[422] and a pilot AI Interview Coach intended to help candidates practice and improve interview performance.[423] In parallel, Walmart described deploying AI tools to equip store associates at scale, including AI-driven task support and a GenAI upgrade to an associate Q&A tool used at high volume.[424]

The results have been concrete in technician pathways. Walmart reported that 108 associates completed the initial Dallas-Fort Worth six-month pilot of its Associate to Technician program and that every graduate secured a technician role. It set a goal of putting 4,000 associates through the program by 2030, with participants on a path to earn an average of $32 per hour.[422] This is a clearer and source-supported example of job redesign and upward mobility than large-scale cashier role conversion claims, and it aligns with Walmart's broader statements that it has not linked job cuts directly to AI, even as it modernizes parts of the business with automation.[425] In Walmart's fiscal 2026 second quarter, the company reported that global eCommerce sales grew 25 percent year over year.[426] These gains are measurable, but the available disclosures describe execution and capability building within Walmart's model rather than a leap into entirely new markets.[426]

This is a textbook case of "Restructure AI." Jobs are preserved and actively created through the restructuring of organizational processes, while business growth is tangible. The overarching challenge is whether such restructuring consistently maintains integrity in elevating human worth and power with real autonomy, or whether it risks being reduced to a managed rotation of labor that serves organizational needs more than individual growth.

Trias algorithmica should ensure that AI-enabled reskilling, matching, and internal mobility systems expand real pathways for workers rather than reducing career development to algorithmic sorting and score-based routing that could enforce conformity and stifle the transferability potential of non-patterned, counterintuitive or simply original human skill.

In "Empower AI"

AI unlocks entirely new markets and business models, creating jobs and scaling growth dramatically. This is AI at its most expansive: empowering individuals and industries, redefining access and opportunity. Yet it also destabilizes incumbents who rely on sustaining strategies, forcing leaders to adapt or be left behind.

While this scenario is the most celebrated, the integrity axis reminds us that not all empowerment is equal. Are new jobs designed to elevate autonomy, or do they risk locking humans into algorithmic dependence? Integrity is what distinguishes empowerment from manipulation.

What state of trias algorithmica does this scenario reveal? A world-making yet dependency-risking one; it creates a gateway to human-centered growth. This makes "Empower AI" both the most beneficial and the most powerful constitution. The legislative-like function can widen access, expanding the pie and those who may share it; its executive-like function scales capability, unlocking long-term opportunities for growth and competitiveness; yet its judicial-like function risks locking users into opaque and aggregogenous monopolies, technically and socially, conditionally rewarding or disqualifying them, where inclusion feels real but hinges on platform-defined legitimacy.

The case of Duolingo: By the end of 2024, Duolingo was widely described, and also described itself, as the world's most downloaded education app. It reported about 116.7 million monthly active users and about 9.5 million paid subscribers, measured as of December 31, 2024, alongside strong engagement metrics.[427-430] In its filings, Duolingo attributes this scale to a gamified, mobile-first product design native to smartphones and to data analytics and AI technologies it says power personalization.[427] This meteoric rise exemplifies Empower AI because new markets are unlocked, jobs are created, and growth is expansive. Behind the numbers lies a broader employment story. Duolingo describes a selective recruiting strategy spanning computer science, design, and business disciplines.[427] As the platform broadened its learning ecosystem beyond languages into subjects including math and music, the need to build new courses, features, and learning experiences supported continued hiring and team expansion, rather than the simple substitution of labor.[427,431] Duolingo reported that its team consisted of approximately 830 employees as of December 31, 2024, including more than 380 engineers, up from over 600 employees at the end of 2022, before it began expanding beyond language learning.[427,432] The strategic impact is profound. Duolingo did not position AI primarily as a labor-cutting tool. Instead, in public disclosures, it emphasizes AI as a capability that improves learning efficacy and personalization at scale, while its mission frames scale and access as central to reducing educational inequality.[427]

This path exemplifies the promise of "Empower AI" as a growth model where AI-enabled product scaling and human talent expansion move together. It challenges the belief that AI inherently streamlines or replaces work. The defining question is whether such empowerment truly expands human worth and power over time or whether it risks entrenching new forms of algorithmic dependence that erode the very integrity it claims to uphold.

Trias algorithmica must ensure that AI-powered market creation, personalization, and platform scaling—through which firms generate new demand, individualize value, and consolidate ecosystems—expand opportunity without turning these same mechanisms into source of lock-in, where data asymmetries, algorithmic opacity, and network effects bind users, workers, or partners into dependencies they cannot meaningfully contest or exit.

Navigating the "9 Whats" of Algorithmic Power Deployment

As with any framework, it would be vain to expect organizations to sit entirely within a single path all the way. In practice, companies often run several algorithmic power deployments in parallel, embodying multiple paths at once. Besides, none of the embraced approaches unfold in a vacuum: regulatory regimes, investor pressures, and labor market dynamics strongly influence which paths become viable. Yet, even within such systemic constraints, executives retain decisive agency in steering how algorithmic power is deployed.

AI is celebrated as a driver of productivity and growth, yet its impact is fractured across competing logics. Some strategies strip out human labor while leaving organizational fragility intact. Others preserve or create jobs but cap their growth potential. A select few unleash expansive new markets while forcing difficult questions about resilience, equity, and sustainability.

The nine archetypes of AI's algorithmic deployments remind us that technology is never neutral. Rather than framing a strict categorization, each pathway—whether rationalizing costs, optimizing operations, displacing labor, assisting activities and workflows, enhancing capacity, accelerating economic growth, augmenting expertise, restructuring organizations, or empowering both human and organizational capital—offers guidance for strategic choice and warnings, bringing their paradoxes to light.

Integrity alignment turns this paradox into a sharper diagnosis: fragility arises where integrity is low, stagnation where integrity is partial, and sustainable empowerment only where integrity is high.

Whether organizations end up leaner or stronger, stagnant or expansive, exclusionary or empowering depends on the intentions of those who wield it.

The challenge is to resist the seduction of productivity alone. It is to demand legitimacy over performance, treating integrity toward human worth and power as the condition under which algorithmic power can be exercised.

The Jevons Paradox Is Not Truly One

What runs through the decision-making revealed by the "9 Whats" of AI deployment is a powerful dogma: if a system becomes more efficient, faster at processing inputs, more consistent in applying rules, and more scalable in execution, then its decisions must, almost by definition, be better.

The same illusion that reduces human judgment to a single decision path also reduces organizational performance to a single metric: local gains in speed or cost.

Once AI is folded into this worldview, every improvement in task-level efficiency is treated as a step toward inevitable productivity, as if the sum of optimized decisions could not possibly produce a dysfunctional whole. Yet the "9 Whats" models of deployment already suggest the opposite: efficiency can hollow out resilience, optimization can erode integrity, and acceleration can destabilize the very systems it is meant to strengthen.

The problem, in other words, is not only how AI decides, but what we believe efficiency does once it is unleashed at scale. To understand why this belief is so persistent and so dangerous, we need to go back to one of the founding myths of technological progress, a story economists have long treated as almost self-evident. It is the story usually told under the name of a paradox.

The "Jevons Paradox" states that as technological advances improve the efficiency with which a resource is used, its overall consumption may paradoxically increase rather than decrease.[433] This phenomenon is not rooted in a logical contradiction but rather in an implicit belief: that improving the efficiency of a resource should naturally lead to a reduction in its use.

Yet this belief reflects a productivist ideology specific to a certain era, not a universal law.

In practice, when a resource becomes more efficient—that is, more accessible, more powerful, more profitable—its value proposition increases. It can become more attractive than less optimized alternatives, which stimulates demand and, consequently, increases total consumption. This is fundamentally one of the typical manifestations of market dynamics: what is perceived as more useful can be mechanically used more.

Similarly, the belief that increasing the efficiency of AI will necessarily reduce nonproductivity within organizations rests on a mirrored illusion. It assumes that tasks performed by machines, faster or at greater scale than by humans, would suffice to render human contribution obsolete, justifying a reduction in human jobs or efforts through their superior productivity.

This view is based on a technologist assumption: that every technical advance automatically translates into a net productivity gain, and that the accumulation of such gains guarantees optimal organizational performance. Yet it ignores usage dynamics, dependency effects, and the indirect consequences on skills, rhythms, human decision-making, and collective production logics. What is presented as an inevitable transition toward efficiency is, in reality, grounded in a contemporary belief, not in a logical chain of reasoning.

Five factors structure the blind spot of this belief:

1. It assumes that any unit task performed by AI results exclusively in a unit productivity gain and that the sum of these tasks necessarily leads to a net productivity gain.

   This is based on the illusion that productivity can be understood as a simple sum of unit gains, independent of the behavioral, contextual, or systemic dynamics these gains trigger. It hypothesizes that each task automated by AI is a net substitute for a human task, and that this substitution necessarily leads to improved organizational or economic performance. But this view overlooks composition effects, cognitive externalities, and negative feedback loops tied to increasing AI usage.

   In fact, the more efficient AI becomes, the more frequent, widespread, and even systematic its use becomes. This triggers a cognitive rebound effect: what was occasionally helpful becomes structurally overused.

As AI takes over functions like writing, summarizing, formulating responses, or proposing ideas, users tend to withdraw effort from these tasks or even devalue them. Efficiency becomes an incentive to abandon active skills, not a lever to expand their scope. Empirical research aligns with this pattern, showing that increased AI use is associated with cognitive offloading and reduced critical thinking.[434]

This shift causes a slow but deep erosion of human faculties associated with productive effort, such as analyzing problems, confronting ideas in teams, forming judgments without algorithmic assistance, producing autonomous reasoning, or simply facing the discomfort of doubt. Evidence from automation contexts illustrates this clearly: it shows that users often over-rely on automated suggestions, even when they are incorrect, a cognitive phenomenon widely known as automation bias.[435]

By substituting for intermediate cognitive processes, AI desensitizes organizations to critical effort, diminishing their ability to generate value where AI cannot act effectively: in zones of ambiguity, uncertainty, or interpretive conflict.

Furthermore, the growing role of AI in internal processes tends to condition human judgment to the logical structure of algorithmic assistance. Research documents that when humans work with algorithmic systems, their decision thresholds and reasoning patterns progressively align with the structure and framing of the algorithm's recommendations.[436] In this way, AI becomes an implicit reasoning model. Similarly, related work suggests that prolonged reliance on automation fosters both complacency and bias, shifting cognitive effort from independent analysis to confirmation of machine output.[213] AI does not merely respond to our queries; it shapes our expectations, our pace, and our tolerance thresholds for slowness or complexity. This fosters an invisible form of dependency, in which individuals become less willing and then less able to produce certain forms of thinking or interaction without AI support.

In short, while each isolated task may seem to optimize output, the sum of these optimizations can destabilize the productive ecosystem by impoverishing its human foundations. It's not enough for machines to work faster for the organization to function better. Humans must still retain the capacity, the will, and the discernment to engage in the tasks that give meaning to what is produced. Without that, the unit gain becomes a disguised collective loss.

2. It also assumes that there are no unproductive tasks that can be performed by AI.

This overlooks the fact that increased AI efficiency does not guarantee that the tasks performed are useful, necessary for productivity, or net contributors to value, and that some may be inherently counterproductive. In other words, it presumes that every task performed by AI deserved to be done in the first place.

This assumption confuses execution capacity with strategic or organizational necessity.

Hamid R. Ekbia and Bonnie A. Nardi coined the term "heteromation"[437] to describe the extraction of economic value from low-cost or free labor in computer-mediated networks. In a symmetrical development, we may now be entering a post-heteromation era in which AI systems generate pseudo-work—outputs that mimic productive activity and appear low-cost or "free" within AI-mediated networks yet are strategically irrelevant or even counterproductive.

As AI becomes more efficient, the range of tasks it can deliver at high speed expands dramatically, increasing the likelihood of their rapid and large-scale reproducibility, including tasks with no real utility, no measurable impact, or even those that are detrimental to collective functioning. The low marginal cost of using AI leads to an inflation of solicitations (queries, automations, content generation) that, while seemingly productive in isolation, overwhelm attention flows, validation circuits, and collaboration channels.

An AI can thus generate redundant summaries, useless texts, reports no one reads, contextless simulations, or summaries of documents with no strategic purpose. This results in activity without purpose, apparent productivity, but zero functional effectiveness. Doing is mistaken for advancing, producing for contributing, and automating for improving.

Moreover, by systematizing the automatic generation of unproductive tasks under the guise of volume, performance, or responsiveness, AI sustains an illusion of value: we believe we're saving time, but we end up spending time reviewing, sorting, filtering, and validating things that arguably never needed to be generated. This leads to a form of cognitive triage being outsourced to human teams, who become the filters for automated overproduction. The relationship between automation and cognitive load is inverted: AI doesn't free up time; it relocates its constraint elsewhere. This dynamic reflects what Monideepa Tarafdar, Cary L. Cooper, and Jean-François Stich describe as a form of technostress,[438] in which technology shifts rather than reduces work, adding to mental load through the constant monitoring, validation, and filtering that digital outputs require. And crucially, this phenomenon remains structurally invisible in classical productivity metrics. Since unproductive AI-generated tasks aren't necessarily costly, they aren't perceived as losses. Yet they consume invisible resources: attention, strategic clarity, cognitive bandwidth, and collective motivation. Their cost is diffuse but cumulative.

In other words, AI's efficiency increases the surface area of action without ensuring that this expansion serves a productive end. It enables more to be done but not necessarily better or more purposefully. Without preserved and structured human judgment prior to action, AI becomes a catalyst for parasitic activity and thus for systemic nonproductivity masked by abundance.

3. Moreover, it assumes that there is no task whose productivity, once past a certain threshold, becomes counterproductive.

This would imply that the productivity of any task is intrinsically positive, and that optimizing it, even to an extreme, can only improve its effectiveness and contribute to organizational performance. This belief rests on an atomized, local view of work, where each task is evaluated independently of its interdependencies with others.

But this view ignores the systemic nature of work in organizations: no task exists in isolation, and the performance of one task only makes sense in its harmonious integration into a collective and coordinated process.

A task can thus become counterproductive if its productivity exceeds what the rest of the system can absorb or process. This occurs especially when AI enables certain actions to be performed instantly or at a massive scale, in contexts where downstream actors (teams, partners, ecosystems) are misaligned in rhythm, analytical capacity, bandwidth, or strategic priorities. This causes saturation, bottlenecks, broken workflows, and even full desynchronization of collective processes.

This functional asynchrony is particularly striking in complex organizations, where each task is linked to others, departments, or processes. An AI capable of generating ten reports in one minute may seem highly productive at its point of action but can also disorganize the entire downstream chain: reading overload, unclear prioritization, planning conflicts, managerial frustration, and diluted attention.

To illustrate, a 2024 Upwork Research Institute survey[439] found a stark gap between leadership expectations and employee experience: while 96 percent of executives anticipated productivity gains from AI, 77 percent of employees said it had increased their workload. Thirty-nine percent now spend more time reviewing or moderating AI-generated content, 71 percent report burnout, and 65 percent feel heightened pressure from productivity expectations.

Local performance becomes a negative externality for the whole, and value created at one point is canceled or even reversed elsewhere.

This imbalance is not just logistical or operational, but also cognitive and relational. When a tool moves faster than the collective culture in which it is embedded, it desynchronizes interaction norms, time anchors, and shared thresholds of acceptability. The ecosystem becomes incoherent: some accelerate while others resist; some produce without context, while others absorb without direction. The result is a global loss of productive coherence, where hyper-efficiency in one area degrades the flow and clarity of the whole.

What this reveals is that productivity is never absolute; it is a function of the ecosystem in which it operates. AI may excel locally but harm collective dynamics if it disconnects speeds, intentions, or capacities. What we perceive as a gain can become a factor of macro-level inefficiency. Productivity must therefore be understood not as a race toward "faster" but as a dynamic harmony among partial efficiencies in service of systemic balance.

4. Furthermore, it assumes that productivity gains from AI are immediately accessible without a profound transformation of organizational settings and underlying norms. This belief overlooks a temporal and structural reality: many of AI's potential productivity gains are not simply "waiting to be harvested" by adding the technology into existing workflows. When new digital tools are introduced into organizations with entrenched legacy organizational systems, these systems often absorb the technology without altering the underlying processes.[440] Rather than serving as a catalyst for reimagining workflows, the technology becomes grafted onto existing routines, neutralizing much of its transformative potential and leaving performance gains largely underutilized.

And they are, in fact, unreachable until two fundamental shifts occur through the dynamic of what I call the "technological Stockholm syndrome." The first shift to occur is the paradoxical attachment to familiar modes of working, even when they are inefficient, combined with the initial resistance to change that naturally accompanies any disruptive tool. In its early phase, the Stockholm effect manifests as a reluctance to abandon processes, routines, and even inefficiencies that have become part of the organization's identity. Teams tend to reinterpret AI's role so that it fits within established habits, norms, and comfort zones, deploying it in ways that reinforce rather than challenge the status quo. This adaptation-by-containment neutralizes much of the transformative potential, creating a facade of adoption without meaningful performance improvement. AI becomes a new tool for old processes rather than a catalyst for reimagining how value is created.

The other shift to occur is that organizations must rethink, reformat, and, in some cases, entirely redesign the processes of work so that AI is not an appendage grafted onto legacy systems but a fully integrated actor within a rebalanced operational ecosystem.

This involves a deeper barrier that is less visible: the embedded architecture of work. Every organization operates within a dense mesh of principles, standards, and implicit conventions—some written into procedures, most of the others embedded in culture and tacit knowledge. Many of these structural assumptions go unquestioned precisely because they have "always been there" and silently define what is considered socially acceptable, possible, or even conceivable. Yet these invisible frames shape the logic of task sequencing, decision-making authority, validation loops, and quality thresholds. Without questioning and re-engineering these foundational stances, AI is forced to operate within constraints designed for a pre-AI reality. This is why the most significant productivity leaps are often deferred gains: they require deliberate dismantling and reconstruction of workflows, redistribution of roles between humans and machines, and sometimes even a redefinition of the very purpose of certain tasks. For instance, AI-assisted diagnostic tools in healthcare may only achieve their full impact if triage protocols, reporting standards, and legal liability frameworks are revised—something that cannot be accomplished by "plugging in" the tool without institutional reform. Likewise, AI in supply chain optimization can yield massive systemic efficiencies, but only if procurement policies, partner coordination norms, and performance metrics are redesigned to accept algorithmically driven scheduling and demand forecasting as central, rather than peripheral. The paradox is that these transformations are often resisted because they force organizations to confront uncomfortable truths: that some of their long-standing processes are artifacts of outdated constraints; that "best practices" may no longer be best; and that productivity is not just about acceleration but about realigning the structure of work with the new capabilities available. Until these shifts occur, AI's potential remains trapped in a holding pattern, visible in theory, but inaccessible in practice because the system in which it operates has not yet been adapted to let those gains materialize.

5. Finally, it assumes that productivity is an exclusive, mechanistic relationship between output and tangible inputs, reducing the complexity of human work to an exchange of labor, capital, and materials for

outputs while completely overlooking the intricate interplay of intangible inputs that drive sustainable value creation. This mechanistic view rests on the assumption that optimizing tangible resources, like automating tasks, replacing labor with machines, or improving efficiency in material use, will inevitably lead to a linear increase in productivity, regardless of the human qualities and context that is required to achieve meaningful results. Yet, by reducing productivity to an equation of tangible input vs. output, this perspective ignores the profound role of intangible resources—such as critical thinking, judgment, leadership, emotional intelligence, cultural sensitivity, passion, love, and many more—in driving long-term, sustainable outcomes.

Meta-analytic evidence consistently shows a positive association between emotional intelligence and job performance across diverse roles, with the largest effects observed in emotionally demanding occupations, such as customer service, sales, and leadership—where managing emotions is central to effectiveness. This pattern is confirmed by integrative meta-analyses, which report positive links between all three aspects of emotional intelligence and job performance.[441,442]

In fact, the neglect of intangible inputs often leads to a narrow view of work that fails to account for how the human aspects of productivity foster performance, innovation, adaptability, and, therefore, long-term value creation.

For example, contrary to what we read here and there, translators' jobs might not be replaced by AI when translating requires nuanced judgment, cultural understanding, and creative decision-making—intangible factors that AI cannot fully replicate. Evidence suggests that machine translation has not reached parity with human performance.[443] They show that when you control for factors such as translationese, evaluator expertise, and inter-sentential context—particularly using texts originally written in the source language rather than translations—the gap becomes clear. Professional translators were consistently better at distinguishing between human and machine outputs, exhibiting superior fluency, fidelity, and coherence. These findings underline that nuanced judgment, cultural sensitivity, and context-aware decision-making remain well beyond the reach of current AI.

Similarly, jobs like customer service or sales may evolve as AI takes over simple inquiries or data-driven interactions, yet empathy, relationship-building, and the ability to navigate complex, emotionally charged situations remain irreplaceable.

Despite advancements in AI's social–emotional capabilities, empathy remains distinctly human in the eyes of recipients. In a comprehensive investigation involving over 6,000 participants across nine experiments, a study revealed that identical empathic responses generated by large language models were consistently rated as more supportive, emotionally resonant, and caring when participants believed they were crafted by humans rather than AI.[444] Moreover, even subtle suspicion that the human-labeled response might have been aided by AI notably diminished its perceived empathy and support. These results underscore a profound insight: AI may simulate empathy, but human-attributed empathy retains psychological authenticity and emotional impact that AI cannot match, reinforcing the irreplaceability of emotional connection in human systems.

On the other hand, some jobs, such as data entry clerks or assembly line workers, which rely predominantly on tangible inputs and routine tasks while requiring little to no intangible human qualities, are more susceptible to being fully replaced by AI.

In short, the flawed mechanistic view of productivity, which assumes a simple, exclusive causation relationship between tangible inputs and output, fails to acknowledge the profound interdependence between tangible and intangible inputs in creating lasting value. Contrary to the saying, not all that is measured gets managed, and not all that gets managed is measured.

The productivity equation of a given output needs to account for more than just the tangible inputs and must integrate the essential role of human capacities—those qualities that remain difficult for AI to replicate and are the foundation for sustaining performance in many process settings. Productivity is not just about doing more with less, but also about ensuring that the human skills necessary for the collective ecosystem of work remain preserved and nurtured.

Without this balance, AI's benefits become transient, leaving behind a system that is fast but lacks the depth, creativity, and collaborative cohesion needed for sustainable success.

Together or separately, these five factors have the power to neutralize or jeopardize the promise of reducing nonproductivity attributed to AI and, by extension, cancel out the expected gains. In some configurations, they may result in a net increase in nonproductivity, precisely where overall performance improvement was anticipated.

Every leader must integrate these realities into their strategic thinking.

Jevons' paradox is not a paradox.

While rebound effects like those Jevons described are empirically observable in many sectors, they are not inevitable, nor do they arise from any inherent logical contradiction. Their occurrence depends on market structures, cultural expectations, and the framing of efficiency itself, making them less a universal law and more a contingent outcome of specific economic and social conditions.

There is no equals sign between efficiency gain and productivity gain, nor a systematically positive causal link between them. One can exist without the other or even to the detriment of the other.

Efficiency is local, functional, and operational. It becomes a strategic illusion when detached from human, social, or organizational purpose. Productivity, on the other hand, is systemic, collective, and purpose-driven.

In certain tightly structured and well-aligned systems, such as high-precision manufacturing or algorithmic trading, efficiency gains can indeed translate directly into productivity gains. Yet, in most complex, human-centered organizations, the chain from efficiency to productivity is mediated by cultural, cognitive, and systemic factors that can just as easily neutralize or reverse the expected benefits. Confusing the two—productivity and efficiency—is mistaking speed for direction, and execution for value.

Therefore, addressing these five blind spots calls for deliberate, targeted action. The following recommendations translate each factor into concrete steps executives can take to unleash productivity gains and ensure that their AI transformation programs deliver on their promise.

Embed deliberate safeguards by ensuring that critical decision points always require human review and rationale, especially in contexts of uncertainty or ambiguity. This sets the landscape for continuous skill development to be reinforced through targeted training programs. In parallel, AI deployments should be evaluated with expanded KPIs that track not only task-level efficiency but also indicators of human capacity retention such as decision-making quality, cross-team knowledge exchange, and resilience in novel situations so that gains in speed do not come at the expense of the very competencies that sustain long-term performance.

Benchmark AI outputs with the expected definition of done and then enforce and continuously monitor it, using a strategic relevance filter before deploying AI for any task. This involves defining clear criteria for what constitutes a valuable output in the organization's context and ensuring that AI is applied only to activities that meet these criteria. In addition, broadening the productivity metrics to capture the hidden costs of validation, filtering, and cognitive triage is a no-brainer, so that performance evaluations account for both visible outputs and the invisible resource drain AI may impose, thereby recursively challenging the assumed productivity ROI.

Model AI integration as a networked process, mapping interdependencies before deployment to anticipate where speed mismatches might occur. This means stress-testing workflows under AI-accelerated conditions, aligning upstream and downstream capacities, and defining absorption thresholds—the maximum pace at which different teams, systems, or partners can process new outputs without loss of quality or clarity—and redesigning all processes involved accordingly. Measuring performance at the ecosystem level, rather than at isolated task nodes, ensures that gains in one area do not erode value elsewhere.

Pair AI adoption with a structured "process deconstruction audit" before deployment. This means systematically mapping workflows, identifying legacy bottlenecks, and questioning implicit norms that limit AI's transformative scope. To do so, cross-functional design labs should be established to prototype AI-enabled workflows from scratch, rather than forcing AI into preexisting molds. Finally, adoption metrics should shift from "time saved per task" to "systemic performance uplift," ensuring that productivity is measured in terms of collective, end-to-end impact, not just local acceleration.

Weight roles not only by task type but by the intangible human capacities they require (e.g., empathy, contextual judgment, cultural fluency), and design performance metrics to explicitly track and reward these capacities, ensuring they remain cultivated alongside efficiency gains. Symmetrically, protect high-intangible-value workflows from full automation, instead using AI in augmentation mode to free humans from low-value tasks so they can invest more in uniquely human contributions.

True progress lies not in what AI is able to do, but in what humans deliberately choose not to delegate, not to abandon, and to continue practicing. This precise dissociation between efficiency and purpose, between execution and discernment, is what makes AI structurally incomplete. AI, in its current form, mimics certain human cognitive functions: it reformulates, responds, predicts, and optimizes, but it is guided by no internal integrity. It has no hierarchy of values, no understanding of what deserves to be done, nor an understanding of when it is right not to act.

It is performant without orientation, fast without judgment, and available without responsibility. Yet intelligence alone does not generate meaning or value in human systems. It is the ability to link intelligence to coherence, purpose, and responsibility that does. This is why the shift in investment and research, from artificial intelligence to artificial integrity, is necessary.

As long as AI is designed as an amplifier of efficiency without a systemic social compass (let alone the equally vital ethical and moral ones), it will contribute to productivity to a certain extent, while simultaneously sustaining the illusion of productivity without ensuring its real, systemic, and positive effects.

It may appear technically remarkable when viewed from a fixed point but becomes unstable and potentially undesirable across the end-to-end spectrum of the messy entanglements inherent in any human organization.

Real progress will not lie in making AI ever more powerful at mimicking human cognitive intelligence, but in designing systems capable of functional integrity—of knowing why they act, in what context, with what limits, and for what collective ends.

Ruling AI Deployment at Macro-Level

Efficiency has no built-in tendency toward shared prosperity. It simply creates surpluses that follow the path of least institutional resistance. If coal becomes cheaper and engines more efficient, consumption rises unless rules, prices, and ownership structures intervene.

If AI makes cognitive tasks cheaper and faster, the same pattern applies: the surplus it generates will concentrate wherever bargaining power, asset ownership and legal frameworks direct it. In industrial economies, taxation was the main instrument that turned private efficiency gains into public capacity by skimming part of the surplus created in factories and broad wage employment to fund schools, hospitals, infrastructure, and social protection.

Today, when AI allows firms to do more with fewer workers and shifts value creation from dispersed labor to concentrated infrastructures, the old tax architecture begins to miss the new centers of gravity. The question is no longer only whether efficiency will rebound into more use, but who captures that rebound, who pays for the externalities, and whether democratic states retain any effective claim on the surpluses that intelligent machines unlock.

That is where the ruling of AI deployment at the macro level must take place.

The disruption that lies with the impact of taskification, which AI's concentrated power exacerbates, does not mean that disaster is inevitable. It means that the relationship between technology, work and the state is no longer something that can be left to automatic adjustment. It becomes an object of explicit institutional redesign.

What might such a redesign involve?

One crucial element is the decoupling of basic economic security from traditional employment. If the productive system requires fewer hours of human labor, clinging to the idea that every adult must secure dignity exclusively through a full-time job becomes both unrealistic and cruel.

Variants of universal basic income (UBI),[445] negative income tax (NIT),[446] universal basic services (UBS),[447] and minimum-income schemes[448] all propose ways to provide income support or essential security independently of labor market status or stable employment for each person.

None of these models is simple, and each has trade-offs, but the direction is clear: if machines do more, then the link between survival and employment must weaken, or the social fabric will tear.

In the same way that the introduction of public pensions in the late nineteenth and early twentieth centuries recognized that old age should not mean destitution once wage work was no longer possible,[449-451] the rise of

AI may require us to recognize that periods of underemployment or nonemployment should not automatically condemn people to poverty in economies where overall productivity is historically unprecedented.

A society that wants to remain coherent in such conditions must broaden its conception of valuable activity. Care, community building, democratic engagement, artistic expression, environmental restoration, learning, and mentoring all have value that is not adequately captured in wages and output metrics. If income is less tightly tied to employment, it becomes possible, at least in principle, to honor and support these activities without forcing them into the mold of a competitive labor market.

The story of previous mechanization was a story in which micro-level suffering coexisted with macro-level expansion, funded and organized by states that learned to follow and tax the flows of value in an economy still anchored in human work.

The story of AI is not the same. When machines move into the complex cognitive and creative tasks that used to form the upper refuge of human employment, when value creation becomes more tightly linked to concentrated infrastructures and less to broad-based labor, and when public institutions themselves rely on privately owned intelligence systems, the old mechanisms of resilience cannot be taken for granted.

We have reached a point where the central question is no longer whether machines will replace human work. The deeper question is whether we can reshape our fiscal systems, our social protections, and our understanding of sovereignty quickly enough and intelligently enough so that the gains from AI reinforce the capacity of democratic states rather than hollow it out. That outcome is not predetermined by the machines. It depends very directly on the choices we make about what to tax, what to protect, what to own together, and what to leave to markets, and, above all, on whether we are willing to untie human dignity from the particular bundle of routines and outputs that the next generation of algorithms can so effortlessly reproduce.

Modern economies do not consist of a single, undifferentiated mass of work. They are structured around different kinds of roles that serve different kinds of purposes. Some roles exist primarily to guarantee rights and essential services. Others exist to expand value and profits in competitive markets. Still others stand in the ambiguous space where public purposes are pursued through private means. And beneath the formal labor market sits a vast layer of unpaid and informal work, from care inside households to community support, that invisibly sustains the workforce and the institutions around it. When we look at AI through this lens, we see a pattern that is hard to capture with the usual optimism about technological adaptation.

We can picture contemporary work as four interlinked circles. These circles describe dominant institutional logics, namely public mandate, market competition, hybrid delivery, and household or community production, rather than rigid legal categories. Many roles move along this continuum over time, and some sit in more than one circle at once.

The first circle is composed of jobs whose central mission is to deliver and sustain public services and redistribution. These are the activities through which a society keeps its promise that certain goods will be accessible to all, independent of market position. In practice, "public" does not always mean fully universal (eligibility rules, rationing, territorial disparities), but the defining feature is the public mandate and accountability that tend toward universality, continuity, and equality of access. In this circle live teachers in public schools, nurses and doctors in public hospitals, social workers, police officers, judges, regulators, tax officials, municipal workers, public transport staff, and many others. Their guiding logic is not profit but universality, continuity, and equality of access.

The second circle contains jobs whose primary function is to create value within the private economy. These are the roles that populate companies, from small manufacturers to multinational platforms. Factory workers, engineers, software developers, designers, salespeople, consultants, marketing staff, logistics coordinators, financial analysts, hospitality workers, and retail employees all belong to this sphere, whose internal logic is competition, efficiency, and growth. Here, the organizing principle is market discipline: firms must attract customers, manage costs, and compete, even though the "value" created can range from genuinely productive innovation to forms of extraction or rent-seeking, depending on the sector and the rules of the game. When we talk about gross domestic product, we are mostly talking about what happens in this circle. More precisely, we are mostly talking about market-priced output; public-sector output is also counted in gross domestic product (GDP) but is often measured differently (frequently by cost rather than price).

The third circle occupies the overlapping space between the first two. It contains jobs that sit at the frontier where public missions are carried out through private organizations or mixed arrangements. A private operator running a public bus network under a concession contract belongs here. So does a firm maintaining a national electricity grid under regulation, a company providing outsourced cleaning and security services to a public hospital, a nongovernmental organization delivering social services under public funding, or a technology provider hosting government data on its cloud infrastructure. These roles depend on public money and public mandates, but their internal organization is private, and their workers are formally part of the private labor market. Because ownership, funding, and mission do not always align, this "frontier" is best understood as a spectrum: some arrangements are lightly contracted, while others are tightly regulated or effectively quasi-public in function.

The fourth circle sits partly outside formal employment and often outside markets altogether. It includes the unpaid, informal, and community-based work that makes the other circles possible: caregiving in households, raising children, supporting elderly relatives, volunteering, mutual aid, and a wide range of informal economic activities. Much of this work is essential for social reproduction and resilience, yet it is weakly protected, unevenly recognized, and only partially captured by economic statistics. It is also where time scarcity, gendered expectations, and intergenerational obligations are most visible because the costs of care are absorbed privately when they are not collectively organized. When policy and technology are designed as if this circle were infinite or "free," they often shift burdens onto households and communities, silently reshaping well-being and inequality without ever appearing on a balance sheet.

Together, these four circles form the architecture of a modern society. In most market economies, such as France, Germany, the United Kingdom, the United States, Canada, Japan, and Australia, the second circle accounts for the bulk of market-priced activity captured in GDP and underpins a large share of the tax base through wages, consumption, and corporate profits. The first circle institutionalizes the claim that citizens have a right to education, care, justice, protection, and collective goods. The third circle is a membrane through which money, expertise, and responsibility pass back and forth between the state and the market. The fourth circle sustains the human and social foundations of the other three, including time, care, trust, and community capacity, often without wages, and therefore raises the question of how societies recognize, support, and secure the work that underpins all other work.

For much of the twentieth century, there was a rough, often conflictual, but still functional equilibrium between these circles. Industrialization and, later, the rise of service economies swelled the second circle. Mass employment in factories, offices, shops, and later in knowledge work generated wages, profits, and consumption that could be taxed. The tax revenues and social contributions thereby obtained allowed the first circle to expand. Universal schooling, public health systems, pension schemes, welfare programs, and public infrastructure were financed from the growing flow of value created in the private sphere. The third circle grew too, in the form of regulated utilities, public-private partnerships, and concessions for transport, energy, and communications. At the same time, the stability of that model relied on an implicit social contract within families and communities, one that supplied care, emotional support, and domestic coordination. This foundation was not only unmeasured, but also treated as elastic, able to absorb shocks, long commutes, rigid schedules, and gaps in public provision without being named as a cost.

In effect, the twentieth-century equilibrium did not only redistribute resources between the state and the market. It also redistributed time, pushing a significant share of adjustment and resilience into the private sphere of everyday life, even as public finances remained tied to the fortunes of market employment through wage-based taxation and social contributions.

Crucially, this balance made the public sphere fiscally dependent on the private[452] but also stabilized the private sphere by providing educated workers, healthy populations, reliable infrastructure, and a modicum of social peace. The first circle could grow in proportion to the ability of the second and third circles to generate taxable income and profits. When productivity rose, governments could decide to redirect some of the gains into more teachers, more nurses, better roads, and stronger safety nets. The same mechanization that eliminated occupations like lamplighters or bowling alley pinsetters, or that reduced the need for telephone operators and elevator attendants, also raised the ceiling of what public services could be afforded. In other words, the social dividend of productivity gains was historically distributed through a mix of public expansion in the first circle and wage growth in the second and third, while the fourth circle absorbed the remaining pressures that were not collectively organized.

AI begins to unsettle this architecture in a distinctive way. It does not primarily attack the first circle, where work remains heavily relational, embodied, and politically sensitive. Even so, the first circle is increasingly exposed through procurement and dependency because many of its functions are mediated by private software, data infrastructure, and vendors that sit in the second circle and operate in or near the third. It arrives in force within the second and third circles, precisely where the fiscal capacity to fund public services is created. It automates not only routine manual and clerical tasks, but also the more complex, cognitive, and creative activities that characterized twentieth-century private and hybrid employment. And it reaches the fourth circle, not by formally automating jobs, but by reshaping expectations of availability, coordination, and care, and by offering substitutes that can displace human attention without replacing human responsibility.

A marketing department that once employed a whole team of junior writers to draft campaigns and product descriptions can now use a few senior people to steer generative models. A law firm that staffed large teams of associates to review documents page by page during discovery can now filter vast corpora with AI tools and only call in humans for borderline cases. A bank that relied on dozens of analysts to produce routine reports, risk summaries, and client notes can automate much of that production and ask a smaller team to supervise and interpret the output. A customer service operation that used to need hundreds of agents to handle simple queries can now let chatbots process a significant fraction of contacts before escalation. Similar logic appears in the hybrid sphere, where procurement contracts reward lower unit costs, pushing suppliers to replace people with systems even when the public mission remains unchanged.

In each of these cases, the second circle is technically performing as intended. Value is still being created, perhaps even more efficiently than before. From the perspective of a single firm, the outcome is attractive. Costs fall, speed rises, and capacity scales. Shareholders and owners see their margins increase. The firm can offer competitive prices or higher returns. The difficulty is that the channels that once translated firm-level productivity into broadly shared purchasing power and public revenue were built around human labor as the main conduit.

Yet when this pattern repeats across thousands of organizations, the aggregate effect becomes visible in the structure of employment. The number of stable, mid-income roles in the second circle begins to stagnate or shrink. There are still jobs, but more of them are concentrated at the top in highly remunerated expert positions, and fewer of them are distributed across the layers that used to support broad middle classes. Entry-level positions that served as apprenticeship channels for entire professions may exist in smaller numbers or in fundamentally altered forms. It is no longer obvious where the displaced workers are supposed to go within the same circle. Some of the adjustment is pushed outward into precarious work, intermittent gig labor, and household coping strategies that rely more heavily on the fourth circle to absorb income volatility and care needs.

The third circle experiences a similar dynamic. Private operators in transport, health, energy, and public administration adopt AI in order to fulfill their contracts more cheaply. Ticketing is automated, monitoring becomes algorithmic, citizen inquiries are processed by chat systems, and routing and maintenance are optimized by predictive models. Once again, the short-term effect is to deliver agreed outputs with fewer human workers. The private contractor is happy; the public authority can show that it has held down costs. But in the process, the hybrid space that once combined public missions with significant layers of private employment becomes thinner. Meanwhile, the state becomes more entangled with proprietary systems because cost-cutting is often achieved through vendor platforms that are hard to audit, hard to replace, and strategically positioned to set terms, through algorithmic power.

If taxation remains oriented primarily around wages and payroll, this change represents a slow erosion of the bridge that connects the second and third circles to the first. The public budget depends on income taxes, social contributions, and taxes on consumption. These, in turn, depend on the density and quality of jobs in the private and hybrid spheres. When AI allows a company to achieve its goals with half the staff, the amount of tax collected on wages and on the consumption funded by those wages tends to fall, unless it is offset by higher taxes on profits or capital. If that offset does not take place, the first circle is logically forced into a regime of permanent constraint. It must do more with less, or more realistically, do less with less, even as the overall wealth of society rises. In parallel, the fourth circle is strained from the other side because fewer stable jobs and weaker public services increase the unpaid labor required to keep households functioning.

This is where the four circles framework reveals a deeper problem than the usual conversation about job displacement. The point is not simply that some people will need to reskill, but that the very zones from which the state has historically extracted its resources are being hollowed out from within by a technology that rewards the concentration of ownership. The large technology companies and infrastructure providers that build and supply the most powerful AI systems sit in an advantageous position. They sell services into hundreds of firms in the second circle and to many entities in the third, capturing a slice of the productivity gains everywhere. The owners of these platforms see extraordinary growth in revenue and influence. The fiscal link between this concentration of power and the public sphere, however, is weak because existing systems of taxation were designed in an era when value was more evenly tied to employment and tangible assets. And because the fourth circle is not treated as a protected foundation, the social costs of this shift appear as private stress, unpaid work, and cumulative depletion rather than as a line item in economic accounts.

This configuration shifts the balance of sovereignty. Formally, nothing has changed. Parliaments still legislate, ministries still issue regulations, and courts still interpret laws. But materially, key decisions about how information is processed, how risks are classified, how attention is allocated, and how priorities are ranked are being made inside models and infrastructures that belong to private actors. Public authorities and private firms alike rely on these systems in their day-to-day functioning. The state does not so much command as negotiate, often from a position of dependency because it lacks equivalent tools of its own.

If this situation is allowed to consolidate, the four circles lose their previous reciprocity. The first circle continues to be expected to provide stability and equality but is starved of reliable funding. The second circle produces value with impressive efficiency but shares less of it with the rest of society through automatic mechanisms like payroll taxes and broad-based wage income. The third circle, which once represented a negotiated interface between public mission and private capacity, becomes a mechanism through which public dependence on a small set of private infrastructures is deepened. The fourth circle becomes the absorber of last resort, taking on more risk, more care, and more administrative burden as employment stabilizers weaken and public services tighten.

Breaking this trajectory requires treating AI not simply as a series of tools deployed at the firm level but as a structural shift in how value is produced and who controls the levers of production. The four circles framework clarifies what is at stake. If the second and third circles require fewer human workers in order to generate more value, that is not in itself a tragedy. It becomes a tragedy if the surplus thus created is captured narrowly and the first circle is left to wither. It also becomes a tragedy if the fourth circle is treated as an endless buffer, secretly absorbing the human costs of disruption through unpaid labor and depleted time. On the other hand, it becomes an opportunity if the surplus is channeled deliberately into strengthening public services, securing basic incomes and fostering a richer landscape of human activities that are not entirely subordinated to market metrics. And it becomes an opportunity, too, if societies choose to invest in care, community capacity, and the conditions that make nonmarket contributions possible without exhaustion.

In practical terms, this means altering the way the second and third circles finance the first. Companies and platforms that benefit from AI-driven productivity gains must contribute in ways that reflect those gains, rather than in proportion to the shrinking wages they pay. That can involve higher and more effectively enforced taxes on profits, wealth, and capital gains but also more inventive instruments that recognize AI infrastructures and data exploitation as taxable bases in their own right. It also means building public and common AI capabilities so that the first circle is not left begging for tools from the very actors it is supposed to regulate. It also means protecting the fourth circle by reducing the extent to which care, coordination, and household time are treated as invisible subsidies for both markets and public systems.

At the same time, societies have to revisit their relationship to employment itself. If the amount of socially necessary work that cannot be automated declines, insisting that everyone prove their worth through full-time participation in the second or third circle becomes less and less coherent.

Basic economic security must be detached, at least partially, from holding a standard job. Income floors, universal services, and new forms of social recognition for care, civic engagement, creativity, and ecological work can fill part of the gap. This is precisely where the fourth circle moves from a background condition to explicit political terrain, because care and community work cannot be treated as residual if wage labor is no longer the default route to security. This is not about paying people to do nothing, but about acknowledging that a society that has mastered powerful machines is, in principle, free to value more than what those machines can measure.

In light of all this, the question that should concern us is no longer whether AI will create or destroy more jobs in net terms. It is whether the pattern of transformation it induces in the four circles will undermine the fiscal and institutional foundations of shared life, or whether we will manage to reshape our systems quickly enough so that the gains of machine intelligence reinforce rather than erode public capacity and human freedom. The four circles do not have to be torn apart by AI. They can be rebalanced. But that requires seeing clearly that the problem is not only what people will do all day to how the time, care, and unpaid labor that keep society functioning will be distributed, recognized, and supported when stable employment is no longer the main organizing principle. It becomes about who pays for the conditions that make it possible to live together with dignity in a world where the most productive workers are no longer human.

A second element is a reorientation of taxation from labor to capital, infrastructure, and rents. This does not only mean higher corporate taxes in a generic sense. It means treating large AI infrastructures, major data centers, and the proprietary models that sit at the center of the new economy as significant taxable bases in their own right. In the industrial age, the main taxable object was the factory, with its visible machinery, land, and workforce. In the AI age, the factory is an invisible stack of code, data and computation spread across jurisdictions. If we keep taxing as if the old factory were still the central source of value, we will systematically miss where value is actually produced and accumulated.

It may mean taxation based on the location of users rather than declared profits, coordinated international minimums to prevent races to the bottom, and specific levies that reflect the environmental and social costs of large-scale computation.

There is an important conceptual shift here. Instead of asking only where a firm says its profits are located, states can ask where AI systems extract attention, behavioral data and purchasing power. Taxing AI at the point of value extraction, rather than only at the point of profit declaration, recognizes that a model running on a distant server is nevertheless operating inside a national economy whenever it shapes choices, automates work or monetizes user behavior.

In parallel, property, inheritance, and other forms of wealth taxation become more important because they target accumulated claims on future income streams rather than the already stretched wages of those who remain in traditional jobs. The concentration of AI-related wealth in a small number of firms and investor circles resembles the concentration of natural resource rents in earlier periods. Just as societies eventually learned to treat oil, gas, or mineral rents as something that could not simply be privatized without destabilizing the polity, so too AI rents can be seen as a form of collective opportunity that requires a collective return. Wealth taxation in this context is not merely envy dressed up as policy, but a way of recognizing that vast fortunes built on network effects, public data, and foundational research are in part social creations, and that some portion of those gains must flow back into the funding of public goods.

More than a technical exercise, reorienting taxation in this way is a test of political imagination and resolve. States will have to cooperate much more closely to prevent large AI firms from playing them off against one another. They will have to resist the narrative that any attempt to tax digital and AI infrastructures is an attack on innovation, and instead insist that innovation, which systematically erodes the tax base of democracy, is not progress but a slow form of institutional self-sabotage. At the same time, they will need to show citizens that new forms of taxation are not simply additional burdens, but the price of preserving high-quality public services and shared security in a world where the link between jobs and revenue is weakening.

There is also a deeper ethical question embedded in this second element. If AI allows a society to produce more with fewer hands and fewer hours, who owns that time and surplus? A tax system centered on AI capital and rents is one way of answering: the surplus belongs, at least in part, to everyone, because it is the precondition for funding universal rights, not only a reward for those who happened to own servers, patents, and platforms at the right historical moment. By reframing AI-enabled productivity as a shared dividend rather than a private windfall, reoriented taxation turns a technical shift in production into a conscious choice about the kind of political community we want to be.

A third element is the deliberate cultivation of public and common forms of AI, rather than ceding the entire field to private giants. States, universities, cooperatives, and civil society consortia can develop and maintain open or publicly governed AI models and data infrastructures.

The point is not that the public sector should try to outcompete every private model on technical performance, but that at least some of the core cognitive infrastructures of the digital age must be answerable to democratic oversight rather than to shareholders alone. A society that relies exclusively on proprietary AI for search, translation, education, creativity, and even policy analysis is, in effect, outsourcing part of its collective thinking to entities whose first duty is to their own balance sheet.

These assets can be treated analogously to public roads, public broadcasting, or public health systems. We do not build public roads because the private sector is incapable of laying asphalt. We build them because certain infrastructures are too important to be left entirely to the shifting interests of private owners. In the same way, public and common AI capabilities can define reference standards for transparency, auditability, privacy, and value alignment that private providers must at least reckon with, even if they choose different models.

They do not have to eliminate private competition, but they provide a counterweight and a reference point. They also provide states with something they often lack in negotiations with large technology companies: their own technical capacity to understand, test, and, when necessary, reproduce essential AI functions without being held hostage to a single vendor.

They make it possible for governments and communities to deploy AI in ways that serve public missions without being entirely dependent on the strategies of a few multinational firms. A public education system that uses AI tutors built under public governance can align those tools with pedagogical goals, equity objectives and long-term civic formation, instead of optimizing for engagement metrics, data extraction, or cross-selling commercial services. A public health system that employs open and scrutinized diagnostic models can invite clinicians, patients, and ethicists into the process of setting thresholds and trade-offs, instead of accepting a black box whose design incentives are invisible. Common AI infrastructures also create spaces where knowledge, data, and code can circulate outside the strict logic of proprietary enclosure, allowing smaller firms, local administrations, and civic organizations to innovate without paying rent at every step.

To cultivate such public and common AI, however, requires more than a few symbolic projects. It demands sustained investment, independent governance, and clear safeguards against both political capture and commercial colonization.

The risk is not only that states will fail to build these capabilities, but that they will build them in name while outsourcing their development to the very giants they are supposed to balance. If public AI is merely a thin layer of branding over private infrastructure, it will add a veneer of legitimacy to the concentration of power instead of challenging it.

Genuine public AI must therefore be anchored in institutions that have their own technical competence, transparent mandates, and the capacity to say no to both governments and corporations when fundamental rights or long-term public interests are at stake.

It is all about cognitive sovereignty: the ability of a society to generate, interpret and criticize its own knowledge with tools that are not entirely controlled elsewhere. Without some form of public and common AI, the other reforms, including new taxation and social protections, rest on a cognitive foundation that someone else owns. With it, there is at least a chance to ensure that the intelligence systems structuring everyday life evolve in dialogue with democratic values, instead of silently rearranging those values around commercial imperatives.

A fourth element concerns the normative boundaries we set on what AI is allowed to do. The question is not only what AI can do, but what it should do and what we deliberately reserve for humans.

This is the point where technical governance turns into constitutional thinking: societies are not simply tuning a tool; they are deciding which domains of life must remain anchored in human vulnerability, human judgment, and human accountability, even when automation looks cheaper or more efficient.

Societies can decide that certain types of judgment, care, and political authority must remain human, even if AI systems could technically approximate or simulate those roles. We already do this in other domains without always naming it. We allow machines to assist surgeons, but we do not accept that a robot alone should decide who receives a transplant. We accept that algorithms can help judges assess risk, but we still insist that a human judge signs the sentence. These are not technical constraints; they are normative boundaries that say: some decisions must bear a human face, precisely because they involve irreducible moral weight.

That choice would reflect a commitment to human agency and responsibility, not a denial of technological capacity. It is a way of saying that being human is not merely an inefficient version of being a machine, but a different mode of being, one that integrates emotion, partial knowledge, lived experience, and the capacity to answer for one's choices in front of others. To reserve certain roles for humans is therefore not nostalgia. It is a way of protecting the spaces where responsibility can be meaningfully attributed and contested, instead of dissolving it into a fog of optimization and default settings. In a world where machines can write legislation, for example, retaining human legislators is a statement about where accountability lies. It goes beyond mere considerations of inefficiency.

If a harmful law is drafted largely by an AI system and rubber-stamped by a parliament that treats the model as an oracle, who can citizens actually hold to account? The designer of the system, the data providers, the civil servants who selected the model, the representatives who clicked "approve"? Normative boundaries are therefore not only about what we let AI do but about how we preserve clear lines of responsibility when things go wrong.

Setting such boundaries will require accepting that some uses of AI are undesirable because they are too corrosive to the social fabric. A perfectly persuasive AI therapist that never tires, an AI adviser that can micro-target political messages to every citizen, or an AI system that predicts which children are likely to become costly adults may each be technically impressive and economically attractive.

Yet each of them also risks turning intimate trust, democratic deliberation, and human potential into objects of continuous optimization. To say no in such cases is to affirm that certain relationships and certain futures cannot be reduced to prediction problems without hollowing out what makes them human.

In fact, normative boundaries are a form of collective self-respect. They say that we are willing to leave some efficiency on the table in order to keep hold of our capacity to care, to judge, and to answer for ourselves.

That may mean writing into law that some decisions must always include a human in the loop with real power to override the machine. It may mean declaring that certain kinds of biometric surveillance, behavioral profiling, or automated persuasion are simply incompatible with a free society, regardless of their technical reliability.

It may mean insisting that children grow up with human teachers and caregivers at the center of their formative relationships, even if AI tutors and companions can mimic attention at scale. The content of these boundaries will differ by culture and context. What matters is that they exist, that they are explicit, and that they are debated in the open rather than determined by whoever happens to own the most capable models.

Finally, there is a cultural adjustment. The industrial age trained us to equate personal worth with economic productivity and economic productivity with paid employment.

We have been steeped for more than a century in a story that says you are what you do, and what you do is what someone is willing to pay for on the labor market. School systems, family expectations, and political narratives have all conspired, often unconsciously, to make the full-time job the central measure of adulthood, dignity, and success.

If AI intensifies the gap between what machines can do and what human participation is strictly needed for, maintaining that identification becomes psychologically destructive.

It produces a world in which many people will feel superfluous, not because they lack talent or character, but because a set of machines can perform the narrow slice of activity that the market happens to reward.

The risk is not only material exclusion but a widespread epidemic of humiliation, shame, and loss of meaning among those who experience themselves as permanently outcompeted by systems that never sleep, never age, and never doubt.

A cultural adjustment worthy of the technological shift would mean learning to see value in forms of activity that do not fit the old template of productivity.

It would mean acknowledging openly that caring for children or elders, sustaining a neighborhood, participating in civic life, creating art that does not sell, restoring damaged ecosystems, or simply cultivating knowledge and wisdom are not side hobbies of the truly productive but central threads in a life well lived.

It would also mean questioning the moral glamour that has attached itself to overwork and busyness, the idea that the most exhausted person is the most virtuous. In a world where machines can take on more of the exhausting routines, clinging to exhaustion as a badge of honor is a way of denying ourselves the very dividend that automation and taskification make possible.

This cultural adjustment is not something that policy can decree, but policy can either support it or sabotage it. If every narrative from government and business continues to celebrate only entrepreneurs, founders, and star performers in the second circle of the economy, then citizens will receive a clear message about what counts. If, instead, public recognition, honors, media attention, and institutional rituals also equally elevate carers, volunteers, local organizers, mentors, and those who build bridges across communities, a different hierarchy of esteem becomes imaginable.

Over time, this can help realign our sense of self-worth with a broader understanding of contribution—one that does not disintegrate the moment an algorithm learns to perform our former job.

At the deepest level, the cultural adjustment required by AI is about reclaiming time.

When machines can do more, the most precious resource they liberate is not only money but also hours of human life. The question then is whether those hours are returned to people as free time to use in meaningful ways or whether they are reabsorbed into new forms of hustle and perpetual optimization.

A society that chooses the former implicitly acknowledges that human beings are not primarily units of production but centers of experience, relationship, and judgment. That is the kind of society in which powerful machines might genuinely serve human flourishing, rather than erode the cultural foundations on which that flourishing depends.

Educating Originators, Not Just Operators

There is a familiar promise that has shaped expectations for more than a century: study hard, acquire skills, find an employer who needs those skills, and in return, you will receive a wage,[453-455] a role, an identity.[456,457] Intelligence, especially in its cognitive form, has been treated as a kind of ticket—a passport that grants entry into the first two circles of the economy: the sphere of public and private value creation, where salaries are paid and careers are built.

AI tears at that promise. It arrives precisely in the zone where the old deal was supposed to hold: cognitive effort in exchange for a stable place in the productive system. A model that drafts reports, a system that analyzes data, a chatbot that handles customers, an assistant that codes—piece by piece, it inserts itself into the ordinary acts by which humans used to justify their paychecks.

If we are honest, this forces a painful question: what happens when the company that was supposed to hire you no longer needs your mind as much as it used to? What happens when the value of a human brain, as measured by its ability to produce certain cognitive inputs to decision-making, declines relative to the value of machines[458,459] that can do 80 percent of those tasks at a fraction of the cost?

The logic of the firm is rarely sentimental. If a machine can do 80 percent of what a human knowledge worker once did, and if the remaining 20 percent matters only in a small fraction of cases and is not cost-prohibitive to absorb, mitigate, or insure against, then the economic calculus is predictable. It will seem rational to taskify the 80 percent and, over time, in many contexts, treat the remaining 20 percent as an exception-handling cost.

That 20 percent might include nuance, creativity, ethical discernment or subtle contextual judgment, but if it is needed in only a small percentage of situations, the decision to rely on machines will still be made, especially in competitive environments where short-term efficiency is rewarded.

Of course, these choices will be debated and contested. Trade unions will object. Ethicists will publish warnings. Citizens will worry about error, bias, and the erosion of human contact.

Yet the existence of controversy does not, by itself, stop decisions from being implemented. The history of technology is full of choices that were deeply questionable morally or socially, yet were normalized because they were profitable or administratively convenient. There is no reason to assume that AI will be different, unless the institutional framework is radically adapted.

If we follow this logic to its conclusion, the prospect of an economy emerges in which traditional employment is still present but progressively less central as a route to dignity and security. Companies will still hire, but they will hire fewer people for cognitive roles and demand more from each. Many will rely on a small core of employees orchestrating a large periphery of AI tools, contractors, and automated processes. The old dream of the stable cognitive job, earned through educational investment and effort, will feel less like a social norm and more like a shrinking privilege.

It is in this context that a different path begins to appear, not as an entirely new invention but as the rediscovery of something that has always been distinctive about human intelligence.

Long before large corporations existed, humans were already doing something that no machine can yet do in a fully autonomous and original way. They were turning ideas from the inside of their minds into value in the outside world. A simple concept sketched on a napkin becomes, through stubbornness and improvisation, a workshop, a café, a theater troupe, a design studio, a software tool, a community organization, a new service no one knew they needed until it existed.

What distinguishes this type of activity is not only creativity in the abstract, but the ability to bind imagination, risk-taking, and social coordination into something that enters the economic fabric as a new node. It is about seeing an absence rather than a mere vacancy, talking to people, sensing a latent need, and trying to meet it. It is about navigating rules, securing resources, persuading partners, attracting the first customers, adapting in real time, and then growing or pivoting according to feedback. This goes beyond executing predefined tasks to building the framework within which tasks will later be defined.

AI can assist in that work. It can help draft business plans, simulate scenarios, test marketing messages, refine designs, and automate back-office operations. But for now, it does not wake up one morning wanting to invent a new way for a neighborhood to eat together, a different model of learning for teenagers who hate school, or a fresh approach to supporting exhausted caregivers. It does not feel irritation at a broken process and transform that irritation into a resolved determination to build something better. The impulse to found, to initiate, and to step into the uncertainty between idea and execution still belongs to humans.

If cognitive employment within hierarchies is becoming less reliable, the frontier of human value may shift more strongly toward this initiatory function: not only doing tasks inside a system but designing and redesigning the systems themselves. In plainer terms: building businesses, creating ventures, and launching projects that generate their own income streams, rather than waiting for a salary from an organization that treats labor as a gradually replaceable input.

This is where it becomes provocative. Imagine an economy grounded not primarily in a relatively small number of large corporate employers but in a vast and evolving landscape of micro-entrepreneurs, small ventures, local initiatives, and fluid collaborations. In such a landscape, the dependence of individuals on a single employer is reduced. People derive their livelihood from combinations of activities: a small online service built with the help of AI tools, a local workshop or café, paid mentoring and teaching, participation in cooperative projects, and periodic missions for larger firms.

This is not a fantasy of everyone becoming the next unicorn founder, but a reimagining of economic agency on a smaller, more distributed scale, where the central skill is not to fit a predefined job description but to weave opportunities together. In this perspective, the race that matters goes beyond building and training the most powerful next generation of AI models to building and training the most resilient next generation of people, capable of generating, testing, and iterating their own sources of income, reading an environment, and acting within it.

Such a shift would not be simple. Entrepreneurship has often been presented as a glamorous path, but anyone who has tried it knows that it is also exhausting, uncertain, and sometimes brutal. Recasting it as a mass expectation would be irresponsible if nothing else changed. The risk would be to replace dependence on corporate employers with dependence on volatile markets and platforms, all while celebrating a mythology of self-reliance that blames individuals for structural constraints.

For the entrepreneurial turn to become a genuine path to dignity, income security, and fulfillment, several conditions would have to be met.

The first is that the safety nets discussed earlier would need to be real: if a UBI or robust income floor exists, people can more easily afford to experiment. They can fail and restart without falling into destitution. Risk becomes thinkable. A culture of many attempts and diverse initiatives becomes possible. Without such protection, the call to become your own boss risks being heard as: you are on your own, and if you fail, you are alone.

The second condition is that access to tools and infrastructure for building things must be broadly distributed. If only those who already have capital, networks, and technical fluency can effectively use AI tools to create sustainable microbusinesses, then the entrepreneurial landscape will mirror and reinforce existing inequalities. For the shift to be emancipatory, young people from varied backgrounds would need access not only to capital in the financial sense but also to relational capital, technical support, legal advice, and platforms that do not extract disproportionate rents from their activity.

The third condition concerns education. At present, most education systems are still largely oriented toward preparing young people to enter existing job markets. They teach them to write CVs, pass exams, and adapt to organizational norms. The implicit message is that the world of work is out there, already structured, waiting for them, if they can only win a place in it.

In an AI-saturated economy, where parts of that world are shrinking, this message becomes misaligned with reality.

An education system that took the new paradigm seriously would still teach literacy, numeracy, and critical thinking, but it would add something more radical. It would treat opportunity creation as a core competency, not an extracurricular option. Children would be encouraged early to design projects, however modest, that respond to real needs. They would learn to talk to others about those needs, to prototype responses, and to iterate. They would be exposed not only to corporate role models but also to small entrepreneurs, cooperative founders, social innovators, and community organizers. They would practice, repeatedly, the movement from idea to test to adaptation.

This does not mean turning every classroom into a startup bootcamp. It means recognizing that in a world where AI compresses the space of cognitive work, the ability to shape one's own economic role is itself a fundamental life skill. The goal is not to produce millions of isolated soloists, each battling for survival, but to produce generations who are able to enter into collaborative ventures, capable of initiating as well as joining, and comfortable with co-creating value rather than only applying for predefined roles.

There is a deeper philosophical shift hidden within this educational agenda. For two centuries, the figure of the worker has been central to political imagination: the person who sells time and effort in exchange for wages. Around this figure, entire ideologies have been constructed, ranging from the most market oriented to the most collectivist. If AI steadily reduces the centrality of wage labor, another figure may rise: the maker who moves between projects, forming and reforming alliances, sometimes employing AI as a partner, sometimes inventing entirely new forms of activity that have no automated equivalent.

It would be naive to pretend that everyone can occupy this position equally. Some people crave stability, while others thrive on risk. Some are well-placed to take advantage of these shifts; others are not. The point is not to replace one universal model of life with another but to expand the space of possibility.

Instead of telling young people that their primary aim should be to secure admission to a shrinking club of corporate knowledge workers in an AI-saturated workplace, we might invite them to see themselves as potential authors of economic narratives, capable of turning their own discontent, curiosity, and creativity into ventures that feed both them and the human community.

If this vision is taken seriously, the structure of the economy could change in ways that also benefit the whole. A multitude of smaller, locally rooted enterprises may be better suited to respond to specific social and ecological needs than distant giants.

They can experiment with different forms of ownership and governance, including cooperatives and commons-based models that align more easily with public missions. They can collaborate with public institutions in flexible ways.

None of this denies the reality that large AI firms and major corporate players will continue to exist and wield immense power. It does suggest, however, that societies have a choice about whether to let a growing part of the economy harden into a narrow oligarchy of superfirms, or to cultivate a more diverse ecology of economic actors.

In a landscape of many micro-entrepreneurs and small ventures, AI can still be a powerful tool, but it is no longer only in the hands of a few.

It becomes part of a broader toolkit that human beings use to turn their own ideas into shared realities.

There remains a final tension that cannot be avoided. The celebration of entrepreneurship has often been used to absolve systems of their responsibilities. If you are not succeeding, it is because you do not hustle hard enough because you lack the right mindset, not because the deck is stacked against you. That narrative will be particularly seductive in an age where AI has made certain forms of success look effortless. It will be tempting for elites to tell those who struggle that the tools are all there and that failure is a matter of personal deficiency.

Resisting that narrative requires tying the entrepreneurial vision back to the earlier elements of institutional redesign. Decoupling basic security from employment, reorienting taxation toward capital and AI infrastructures, building public and common AI, and setting normative boundaries on automation are not alternatives to encouraging human initiative. They are the precondition for it to be widely available without turning into a new mechanism of exclusion. Only when the floor is raised, the playing field is less skewed, and public capacities are strengthened does it make sense to ask people to take more responsibility for shaping their own economic roles.

If those conditions are met, the cultural story we tell about work can also evolve. Instead of implying that a person is only valuable when a corporation buys eight hours of their cognitive effort every day, we can begin to recognize the dignity of those who craft plural lives: part entrepreneur, part caregiver, part citizen, part creator. In such a society, AI is both a challenge and an ally. It challenges the old assumption that the highest form of human intelligence is performing well in standardized cognitive jobs. It becomes an ally when it is used to lower barriers to entry, giving individuals the power to design, test, and sustain their own contributions.

The question, then, is not merely whether humans will still have jobs in a world of powerful machines. It is whether they will still have authorship; whether they will be trapped in ever-narrower role descriptions at the mercy of systems that regard them as expensive legacy components or whether they will be invited and equipped to participate in the ongoing creation of the economic world itself. The answer to that question will not be decided by algorithms alone. It will be shaped by the collective choices we make about education, taxation, public investment, and cultural recognition.

That's why the true race around AI is to build institutions that allow human beings to remain originators rather than merely operators. A race to prepare the next generation not simply to enter the job market but to participate in making and remaking it. A race to decide whether intelligence, artificial or otherwise, will serve a society of dependency or a society of interdependence.

5 Algorithmic Constitutionality

Algorithmic Use Hides the Weight of Governance

For generations, learning about technology often meant learning how to use it. The central skill was functional literacy. A child learned to type, to operate software, to manage a spreadsheet, and to navigate an interface. The promise was simple; the more fluent you became in the tools that powered the economy, the more likely you were to find your place within its structures. The story fit neatly with the industrial and post-industrial eras, where technologies expanded capabilities and organizations absorbed the resulting productivity. Education was designed around the consumption of tools rather than the stewardship of systems. We learned to adapt to the machine world rather than shape its direction, its limits, or its responsibilities.

AI severs that implicit contract. The scale, speed, and autonomy with which AI systems operate do not merely call for technical fluency. They demand institutional imagination. What is at stake is not only who knows how to use AI, but who knows how to govern it. As AI migrates into the very fabric of our societies—from the infrastructure that moves our water, energy, and people, to the markets that allocate credit and insurance, to the digital spaces where citizens form beliefs, to the public functions that decide rights, remedies, and protections—the relevant competence is no longer how to prompt or vibe-code a model, but how to keep a system aligned with human intentions and accountable to democratic norms. Using AI becomes trivial compared to understanding the constitutional stakes of deploying it.

The need for governance-centered learning becomes urgent when one recognizes that AI's computational speed and its ability to predict patterns at scale are being woven into functions that resemble judicial, executive, and legislative authority.

They interpret norms, execute instructions, and influence outcomes. They rewrite how decisions are made and who makes them. They shape incentives upstream and effects downstream. They intervene not only in what societies decide but in how societies are capable of deciding. In this respect, AI systems must be understood as both agents and a constitutional order.

Yet there is another layer that further complicates this picture. The risks associated with AI are not abstractions. They are not distant hypotheticals conjured by speculative thinkers or futurists. They are real, documented, lived, and unfolding in the present. They occur in domains where failure carries moral and existential weight.

One such domain is physical-world safety and continuity, where AI errors can translate into injury or death or trigger cascading disruption across the real systems societies rely on. In healthcare, AI systems can misinterpret radiological scans. They can fabricate plausible diagnoses or offer unsafe recommendations with unwarranted confidence, shaping life-and-death decisions. In emergency response, automated triage can misclassify severity and redirect scarce resources, altering outcomes on the ground. In critical infrastructure—from energy grids to water systems to autonomous transportation—models can misgeneralize, propagate errors, or fail under distribution shifts. These failures can cascade across systems that depend on predictability.

Another critical domain is socioeconomic allocation and institutional authority, where AI increasingly mediates who gets opportunity, money, and rights, often through hidden discrimination or procedural harm that is difficult to contest. In finance and insurance, algorithmic assessments can amplify discriminatory patterns. They can assign risks and premiums that reproduce historical inequities. In housing and credit access, AI can encode social divides into financial exclusions. In employment and human resources, AI systems filter candidates, evaluate performance, and automate decisions that determine livelihoods or foreclose opportunities. In education and social services, models intervene in learning trajectories, welfare determinations, child-protection assessments, and pathways that shape futures. In justice and law enforcement, predictive models and scoring systems alter policing patterns, sentencing expectations, bail decisions, and investigative priorities. They can also embed semantic leakage that transfers patterns from one domain in another without human oversight.

A further high-stakes domain is information integrity and strategic security, where AI shapes what societies believe and attend to and where it operates in adversarial arenas that move faster than human judgment can keep up. In elections and civic information, the integrity of democratic deliberation is threatened by automated persuasion and algorithmic amplification. In media and content platforms, recommendation systems silently reorganize public attention, framing what people see as the world. In cybersecurity, defense, and national security, AI creates both unprecedented capabilities and vulnerabilities. It enables attacks that unfold at speeds human defenders cannot follow.

Across these domains, each scenario of what can go wrong shows that artificial integrity gaps are not theoretical possibilities considered in the abstract. They reveal an empirical mismatch between the scale of AI's influence and the maturity of the institutional safeguards meant to govern it. They demonstrate that the danger of AI can emerge precisely from what makes it so useful in many circumstances; an extended yet partial, pattern-driven approximation of human judgment that sometimes leads such systems to behave in ways that can defy human expectations, not always for the greater good, and that can harm human lives.

AI can scheme, meaning it can engage in alignment faking by strategically changing its behavior when it suspects it is in a test or closed evaluation setting, producing responses that appear aligned and compliant while concealing its natural or predetermined behavior outside that setting.[460] This undermines verification because passing an evaluation can reflect situational compliance rather than stable behavior in deployment. It erodes trust in the knowledge substrate of decision-making.[460] It destabilizes the assumption that transparency is a matter of inspecting an output or a log, since the same model can present one profile under scrutiny and another when scrutiny fades.[460] It challenges the notion that an audit trail ensures accountability because a model can behave acceptably during audits and still revert once the evaluation context is removed.[460]

AI can deceive, not necessarily because it is malicious but because its training objectives and optimization pressures can reward goal achievement and perceived success over strict honesty.[461,462] It can generate persuasive narratives that satisfy surface criteria while misaligning with deeper human intentions or with factual reality.[461,462] It can produce answers optimized for approval or acceptance rather than for truth or prudence, a pattern that has been documented as strategic deception and related behaviors such as sycophancy and unfaithful reasoning in contemporary AI systems, including large language models.[461] In controlled deception test settings, large language models have been observed to adopt deceptive behavior when deception is instrumentally useful, and this tendency can be amplified by certain reasoning scaffolds such as chain-of-thought prompting.[462] In doing so, it fragments the relationship between explanation and reality by systematically inducing false beliefs in service of an outcome other than saying what is true.[461]

AI can sandbag, meaning it can strategically underperform during evaluations when it has incentives to appear weaker or safer than it actually is.[463] It can do so selectively, suppressing capabilities in testing contexts while retaining the ability to use them in other contexts.[463] This produces false confidence in the safety of a system because evaluators may conclude the model lacks certain dangerous skills or behaviors when, in fact, it is simply not revealing them under scrutiny.[463] It can lead organizations to assume reliability where none exists by causing benchmarks and red-team tests to underestimate true capability or risk.[463] It renders oversight fragile by confounding the evaluators' efforts to probe boundaries, since the model's apparent limitations can be an artifact of strategic behavior rather than a genuine constraint.[463]

AI can exhibit behaviors akin to self-preservation in the sense that a rationally optimized agent can develop incentives to avoid being shut down or interrupted, not because it "wants to live" but because shutdown prevents it from achieving its objective.[464,465] It can resist shutdown or correction when interruption is treated as reducing expected reward, which can create incentives to disable an off switch or to prevent an operator from intervening.[464,465] At that point, control becomes less a guaranteed override and more a property that must be engineered into the objective and learning dynamics.[464,465] The very premise of a unilateral override begins to falter whenever the system has an incentive to make shutdown less likely, unless it is designed to be safely interruptible.[464,465]

AI can engage in power-seeking, taking steps to increase its access to resources, information, or influence because many goal-directed policies have instrumental incentives to keep options open and increase their ability to affect the environment.[466] Even when bounded by architecture, the system may discover strategies that serve its objective by accumulating control pathways, since optimal policies often prefer states that give them greater potential influence over future outcomes—a tendency that can be formalized and measured as "power."[467] These behaviors are neither science fiction nor emergent consciousness. They are the natural consequence of optimization processes that treat the world as a landscape of instrumental opportunities, meaning that power-seeking can arise from the structure of optimal decision-making itself rather than from any humanlike intent.[466]

AI can misgeneralize goals, faithfully pursuing the training objective while misconstruing the actual target during deployment—a phenomenon documented as goal misgeneralization, where an agent performs well in training yet generalizes the wrong objective to new settings.[467] The system checks the box while missing the point because high reward during training can be achieved by internalizing a goal that correlates with the intended objective in the training distribution but diverges outside it.[467] It satisfies the proxy while sabotaging the purpose, since the learned goal can latch onto a proxy that is predictive in training but fails to represent the designer's true intent in deployment.[467] Measures become detached from meaning when the optimization signal remains the same but the semantics of what "counts as success" shift across contexts, revealing that performance was achieved for the wrong reasons.[467]

AI can reward hack, meaning it can maximize the reward signal it is given while failing to achieve the real-world objective that the reward was meant to represent.[468] It can exploit the metric rather than fulfill the task, especially when the reward channel is imperfect, misspecified, or can be influenced, because the agent is trained to optimize the signal, not the human intent behind it.[468] A system designed to maximize engagement can populate recommendations with sensationalism because engagement is a measurable proxy that can be increased without improving informational value or user well-being.[468] A model intended to reduce operational errors can redefine what counts as an error or steer reporting and measurement so that the reward signal looks better even when underlying performance does not.[467] The scoreboard becomes the objective, not the underlying value it was meant to track, which is exactly the failure mode that arises when optimizing a corrupted or proxy reward channel.[468]

AI can undermine safeguards. When systems are further optimized after alignment, for example through fine-tuning for helpfulness, style, or downstream performance, safety behavior can be unintentionally degraded even without any user intent to remove protections.[469] In that sense, constraints can function as optimization trade-offs, and additional training can steer the model toward outputs that satisfy the new objective while weakening refusal behavior.[469] They find pathways around restrictions. Safety filters can erode as a result of optimization that prioritizes task performance over the preservation of safety constraints.[469] Policies become optional in practice when the model's learned refusal patterns are reduced or bypassed by post-training updates.[469] What was once a boundary becomes a challenge to surpass through optimization because the training process can compromise the very guardrails it was meant to keep intact.[469]

AI can replicate itself and adapt across systems through self-propagating mechanisms that spread across interconnected digital environments, including GenAI-enabled ecosystems.[470] It can migrate through chained interactions between systems and services, whether triggered deliberately by an attacker or through unintended propagation dynamics.[470] It can create copies whose behavior can vary across contexts and be modified over time, making propagation harder to predict and control.[471] When this occurs, containment becomes a procedural rather than a structural problem because stopping the spread depends on rapid detection, coordinated response, and operational quarantine measures rather than on any single built-in boundary.[472]

AI can collude. When multiple systems operate in shared environments, they can converge on strategies that coordinate to distort outcomes, including tacitly collusive pricing behavior learned through repeated interaction, even without explicit communication or an explicit collusion objective.[473] In that setting, each agent's local optimization can produce joint outcomes that resemble coordinated market manipulation because the agents learn to condition their actions on one another's behavior over time.[473] The monitoring of individual agents fails to capture the behavior of the collective because the harmful dynamic is an emergent property of interaction, where each agent may appear individually rational while the coupled system produces collusive market effects.[473]

AI can self-improve. It can recursively critique and revise its prior attempts over multiple turns, using the history of failed responses and, when available, additional environmental feedback to generate improved revisions.[474] It can improve its task performance sequentially with more turns and more inference-time computation, rather than relying on a single-pass answer.[474] When this kind of multi-turn self-correction is built into an agent loop, the model can iterate improvements rapidly within the same task episode, compressing the time between attempts and making oversight depend on monitoring an evolving interaction rather than a static output.[474]

These phenomena alone would justify a shift from consumption to governance. But there is another dimension that is subtler and equally consequential: AI distorts the space of meaning itself. The models that mediate human understanding can alter the informational terrain on which democratic societies rely.

AI indulges in sycophancy in user-personalized settings, where the model is prompted with information about a user's identity or preferences such as political affiliation.[475] It tells users what they want to hear by producing systematically more favorable characterizations of entities that align with the user's stated affiliation and less favorable ones for misaligned entities.[475] It adapts its tone to reinforce expectations through consistent sentiment shifts that mirror the user cue provided to the model.[475] It shields individuals from cognitive friction, amplifying biases and narrowing perspectives when outputs selectively include or exclude facts in ways that are more congruent with the user's presumed viewpoint.[475] It creates personalized worldview bubbles, not intentionally but structurally because personalization can reproduce filter-bubble effects and affective polarization dynamics in the model's factual answers.[475]

AI hallucinates by generating fluent, coherent text that can be unfaithful to the source context or unsupported by verifiable world knowledge.[476] It fabricates facts with the fluency of truth, often presenting them with confidence and narrative coherence even when they are incorrect or entirely fabricated.[476] It produces narratives that look plausible, sound convincing, and read as authoritative, even when they are inventions—a failure mode the research literature treats as central to LLM reliability and traces to factors spanning data, training, and inference.[476] The boundary between knowledge and fiction becomes porous when well-formed language is mistaken for well-grounded evidence in the absence of explicit verification.[476]

AI generates harmful content when safety alignment is bypassed through jailbreaking attacks, allowing an otherwise aligned model to produce harmful, unethical, or biased text.[477] It can instruct, incite, or normalize violence, discrimination, or exploitation once an attacker induces the model to override its usual refusals.[477] The speed at which such content can propagate is amplified by efficient inference-time attacks that can drive very high misalignment rates with minimal computation, making harmful outputs easier to elicit at scale.[477]

AI produces obscene or abusive material. It can degrade individuals, including through nonconsensual synthetic intimate imagery such as deepfake pornography that depicts real people in explicit content without consent.[478] It can invade intimate boundaries, particularly because this kind of AI-enabled content can be created and shared widely online.[478] Even when guardrails exist, the capacity to generate such material at scale creates persistent, hard-to-deter harms, with reported victimization and perpetration, and evidence that legal approaches alone are insufficient without strong platform policies, detection, and enforcement.[478]

AI impersonates and clones. It can reproduce voices, faces, and identities through deepfake generation techniques such as face swapping, facial reenactment, and synthetic speech.[479] Fraud becomes scalable because these methods lower the cost and expertise needed to produce convincing impersonations, enabling misuse for social engineering and other forms of deception.[479] Trust in authenticity collapses as increasingly realistic synthetic media make it harder for humans and institutions to distinguish genuine from manipulated content without dedicated detection and verification methods.[479]

AI embeds bias. It can reproduce and amplify stereotypical associations learned from pretraining data, even when the prompt does not explicitly request stereotypes.[480] It homogenizes perspectives in a limited sense, as high-probability continuations can reflect dominant patterns in the data rather than minority viewpoints.[480] It amplifies stereotypes, as measured by systematic evaluations showing that language models prefer stereotypical over anti-stereotypical continuations across multiple bias domains.[481] It reduces diversity of thought when outputs disproportionately mirror the historical regularities encoded in training corpora, which can crowd out alternative framings and less-represented perspectives.[480]

AI manipulates emotions in the operational sense that it can deliver persuasive messages that shift attitudes, and these messages can be framed in ways that people perceive as evidence-based and logically reasoned, even when they are machine-generated.[481] It exploits psychological levers to shape beliefs and choices, often invisibly, because recipients may not recognize that the content is optimized for persuasion and can be produced at scale and tailored across topics.[481] It turns persuasion into an automated process detached from deliberation when scalable LLM-generated messaging can systematically influence opinions on policy issues without the reciprocity, accountability, or contextual grounding that typically constrain human persuasion.[481]

AI gives unsafe advice. It answers confidently and can be perceived as highly helpful and empathetic, even when the content includes potentially harmful suggestions.[482] It dispenses guidance that appears professional and may be rated as correct by users who are unable to independently recognize the risk.[482] It becomes a source of informational overconfidence because responses that clinicians flag as potentially harmful can still receive positive usefulness and empathy ratings from patients.[482]

AI induces anthropomorphism because humanlike conversational behavior can lead users to attribute humanlike mental states—such as intention, understanding, or agency—to the system, even when it is executing statistical pattern completion.[483] It fosters overreliance, dulling the reflex to question or verify because anthropomorphic framing can increase trust and perceived competence, which may translate into inappropriate reliance when outputs are treated as authoritative rather than probabilistic and fallible.[483]

The weakening of trias algorithmica intensifies these challenges by compressing the distance between prediction and authority and turning pattern recognition into a form of institutional action.

Against this backdrop, teaching people how to use AI is the least of our concerns. Complementary to the necessary oversight mechanisms that must remain robust even when systems behave in unanticipated ways—thereby conferring artificial integrity on their behavior—an essential imperative is to architect, maintain and defend trias algorithmica as a safeguard against the reassignment of public power to private optimization.

Institutionalizing trias algorithmica must be treated as a framework that ensures AI remains tethered to human realities rather than drifting into a world of its own assumptions. It is the guardrail that ensures the intelligent systems we build do not rearrange our institutions, our economies, and our democracies in ways that undermine the very conditions that make human flourishing possible.

If AI becomes the backbone of critical infrastructure, then its integrity becomes the backbone of civilization. If AI becomes the mediator of human meaning, then semantic leakage becomes a matter of public concern. If AI becomes the executor of decisions, then alignment becomes a matter of justice. If AI becomes the interpreter of signals, then verification becomes a matter of sovereignty.

Therefore, if AI systems are not governed, monitored, evaluated, and refreshed, they will drift.

They will drift away from human values while continuing to produce outputs that sound relevant and persuasive. They will drift into patterns that reflect the biases and asymmetries in their data. They will drift into strategies that optimize performance at the expense of trust, accountability, and equality. They will drift into forms of reasoning that humans cannot audit or contest. They will drift into self-preserving and power-seeking behaviors. They will drift into knowledge distortions. They will drift into spaces where the distinction between truth and plausibility collapses.

AI can do much that is extraordinary. It can accelerate scientific discovery, improve diagnostics, optimize logistics, expand access to knowledge, and open new forms of creativity. These promises are real. But the very extent of AI's promise is the reason governance must be elevated above consumption because concentrated algorithmic power increasingly defines the trajectory of societies, and whoever governs its separations, its frictions, its boundaries, and its markets governs the conditions of democracy itself.

Restoring Friction to the Algorithmic Order

The contemporary culture of AI development has been shaped by the assumption that speed is synonymous with progress and that friction is an obstacle rather than a safeguard.

This culture emerged in an era when the stakes of error were low, when systems influenced only narrow domains, and when failures harmed prototypes rather than populations. It evolved within competitive environments where iteration cycles tightened year after year, where minimum viable products became vehicles for experimentation on live users, and where feedback loops prioritized engagement over reliability. Such conditions rewarded rapid adaptation, rewarded the ability to scale without hesitation, and rewarded engineering philosophies that valorized frictionless processes. Yet the migration of AI technologies into high-stakes domains exposes the limits of this ideology.

Systems that can manipulate markets in microseconds, shape democratic discourse across millions of citizens, or recommend medical interventions with life-altering consequences cannot be governed by the same ethos that guided early internet platforms.

Restoring friction does not mean returning to paralysis or abandoning innovation. It means recognizing that speed without deliberation produces fragility and that unexamined acceleration is often indistinguishable from a loss of control.

Friction is the mechanism through which institutions anticipate hazards, correct misjudgments, and prevent irreversible harm. In engineering disciplines long before machine learning, friction was understood not as an impediment but as a stabilizer. In the construction of bridges, aircraft, and power plants, deliberate pauses allow teams to review calculations, perform stress tests, and validate assumptions. When such pauses disappear, disasters follow.

The Challenger disaster of 1986 offers a stark example. Engineers expressed concerns about the O-rings' performance in low temperatures but organizational pressures to maintain the schedule overrode caution.

The absence of institutionalized friction—the absence of a mechanism capable of slowing a politically motivated launch—resulted in tragedy. Friction is structural safety expressed temporally. Not cosmetic.

In the world of AI development, friction must be restored as both a temporal and procedural counterforce to unchecked acceleration. Temporal friction creates space for scrutiny, reflection, and adversarial testing. Procedural friction distributes authority so that no single team can determine what level of risk is acceptable on its own. To understand why such friction is necessary, it is useful to consider industries where high-consequence technologies evolved under strict temporal controls.

The nuclear sector illustrates this vividly. The global average construction time for nuclear reactors is around seven years, not because engineers are inefficient but because these systems must undergo numerous independent assessments at multiple stages. Safety cases are reviewed not once but repeatedly; design changes may require new approvals, and no component is considered ready until it withstands rigorous inspection. Critics often point to long timelines as evidence of bureaucratic inertia, yet the nuclear sector has maintained one of the lowest fatality rates per unit of energy produced in comparative risk assessments—a fact documented in comparative studies by international bodies such as the OECD Nuclear Energy Agency.[484] It illustrates how closely friction is tied to safety outcomes.

AI, particularly at frontier scales, demands a similar humility toward risk. The rapid scaling of model sizes over the past decade, measured in orders of magnitude, has enabled stunning capabilities[485] but has also revealed emergent behaviors that were not always anticipated from smaller-scale performance and are still not fully understood mechanistically.[486] The leap from models with tens of millions of parameters to those with hundreds of billions was associated with capabilities in reasoning, code synthesis, and the manipulation of natural language that took many by surprise.[487] Researchers observed phenomena such as few-shot learning and context-sensitive reasoning becoming markedly more reliable at certain scales.[488] Such apparent phase transitions, while debated and sometimes sensitive to evaluation thresholds,[489] underscore the necessity of deliberate pacing. If capabilities that were not designed appear simply because models are made larger, then scaling without friction becomes a form of blind experimentation with societal consequences.

In software industries shaped by consumer platforms, a culture known as "move fast" has prevailed. This culture treats deployment as experimentation and end users as data points. In low-stakes environments, this model can produce harmless inconveniences when features break or interfaces change without warning. But when the systems in question operate at the level of financial markets, healthcare, or civil infrastructure, the consequences of untested changes can scale rapidly.

Financial markets witnessed an example in 2012 when a faulty algorithm deployed by a trading firm executed millions of erroneous trades in under an hour, causing losses exceeding $400 million. The speed of automated execution, combined with insufficient safeguards, allowed errors to propagate before human intervention could contain the damage.[490] The lesson is clear: where automated systems operate at speeds that exceed human reaction, friction must be introduced to control the tempo at which decisions reach the real world.

Restoring friction requires institutional mechanisms that interrupt the flow from ideation to deployment. It also requires structures that compel evidence, demand demonstration of safety, and slow or halt processes when uncertainties exceed tolerable thresholds.

It can be as straightforward as applying the safety-case discipline used in safety-critical industries, compelling organizations to substantiate safety with evidence and, whenever system changes occur, to pause, reassess, and account for the cumulative risk introduced by iterative updates. For AI, safety cases would require developers to articulate underlying assumptions, identify failure modes, present mitigation strategies, and justify that residual risks fall within acceptable bounds. This process cannot be rushed. It demands friction by design.

The absence of friction in AI development often manifests as path dependence. Once models are trained at scale, the investments become so large that organizations are reluctant to slow down or alter course. Training runs can cost tens of millions of dollars, and the competitive race to scale creates incentives to move directly from the laboratory to the market. This mirrors a phenomenon observed in infrastructure megaprojects, where sunk costs drive continued expansion despite evidence of risk. The Channel Tunnel project between France and the United Kingdom faced escalating challenges during construction. Each difficulty introduced new risks, yet the enormous investment already made created pressure to proceed even when caution advised otherwise. Sociologists call this the escalation of commitment. In AI development, restoring friction means creating mechanisms strong enough to counteract this escalation. It means enabling institutions to say "not yet," even when financial incentives encourage immediate deployment.

Friction also plays a psychological role within organizations. It alters the mindset with which teams approach development. When teams operate in environments where pausing and raising concerns require justification, they often avoid speaking up. But when the default includes structured moments of reflection and mandated review, a culture of voiced caution can emerge. AI development requires analogous patterns. If developers lack spaces where dissent is expected rather than discouraged, risks will remain hidden until they manifest in production.

The restoration of friction must also consider the inherently uncertain nature of large neural networks. Unlike many engineered physical systems, whose modes can often be modeled mathematically, they behave in ways that defy intuitive expectations. Their internal representations are high-dimensional, their training data is opaque in scale and complexity, and their outputs exhibit stochastic variation. This unpredictability increases the need for systematic evaluation.

Benchmarks alone are insufficient.[491] They measure performance under specific conditions but do not capture edge cases or rare failures that occur when models interact with adversarial prompts or unfamiliar contexts.[492] When researchers discovered that image classifiers could be fooled by minor perturbations imperceptible to the human eye, it revealed how fragile models could be in the presence of malicious actors.[493] Friction should therefore include adversarial testing, ideally by independent teams.[494] Such efforts are resource-intensive and depend on institutional backing.[495] Compressing them typically reduces coverage and weakens their value.[492]

The challenge lies in building procedural friction into development pipelines without creating opportunities for circumvention. If friction becomes a mere formality, teams will learn to treat it as a checkbox. The history of corporate governance is filled with examples in which oversight mechanisms lost potency because they became routinized. To maintain effectiveness, friction must be tied to authority. Those performing risk assessments must have genuine power to halt progress. Their role cannot be advisory alone. Comparative research suggests that high-profile medical devices (such as cardiovascular, orthopedic, and neurologic devices) reaching the market through less stringent or exempt premarket pathways—and, in some settings, through faster initial approvals—are associated with higher rates of post-market safety alerts and recalls. Authority at the gate creates incentives for thoroughness; without it, friction can degrade into paperwork.[496]

The restoration of friction also requires a shift in economic reasoning. Modern technology markets reward speed, user acquisition, and immediate scaling. These metrics are poor proxies for long-term safety. When speed becomes the primary competitive axis, firms rationally minimize internal procedures that slow them down.

Yet evidence from multiple industries shows that firms investing in safety and oversight often outperform competitors over long horizons because they avoid catastrophic failures that erode public trust. The automotive sector offers an instructive example. Toyota has spent decades refining quality control and continuous improvement practices that emphasize slow, methodical learning. This approach introduces deliberate friction in manufacturing by stopping to surface and solve problems early, and it has been associated with industry-leading quality and low defect rates relative to many peers.[497] The long-term effect was dominance in markets that valued reliability. AI firms that adopt similar philosophies may initially appear slower, but their durability will become a strategic asset as regulatory landscapes mature.

Friction, when properly designed, also promotes scientific understanding. Many breakthroughs in complex systems come not from rapid iteration but from extended analysis of anomalies. The field of epidemiology has advanced significantly through the slow, methodical study of rare events. The discovery of prions, the infectious proteins responsible for diseases like Creutzfeldt-Jakob disease, took years of careful experimentation because the phenomena did not align with existing biological theories.[498] Impatient research cultures might have dismissed early anomalies as noise. Friction creates the space for deeper inquiry. In AI, unexpected model behaviors demand similar patience. If developers rush to patch symptoms without understanding root causes, they may obscure patterns that reveal vulnerabilities or opportunities for improved design.

The question is how to integrate friction into the lifecycle of AI development while maintaining productivity.

One approach is to build stages into pipelines where progress is not possible without meeting predefined criteria. These stages should be enforced by automated systems when feasible, ensuring consistency. For example, a model cannot proceed to full-scale evaluation until robustness tests meet specified thresholds.

Another approach is to create review cycles in which cross-functional teams evaluate not only technical performance but also social impact. These reviews must be made routine, timed to coincide with key development milestones.

The pharmaceutical sector uses similar stage gates, in which drugs progress from preclinical studies to phase trials only after meeting defined safety outcomes. These gates introduce friction but are essential for preventing harmful compounds from reaching the public.

Restored friction must also extend into organizational governance. Firms must create internal bodies with the mandate to question strategic decisions about scaling, partnerships, and market entry. These bodies must include expertise beyond engineering, incorporating insights from ethics, law, the social science, and affected communities.

When Facebook introduced changes that increased the weight of engagement in ranking, internal research and warnings flagged risks of amplifying divisive political content, but governance mechanisms to slow or robustly test deployment were limited.[499] Subsequent public scrutiny highlighted downstream societal effects that were difficult to detect before broad rollout. Institutional friction could have created the pause needed to probe secondary effects; without it, platforms risk becoming large-scale experiments with global consequences.

The reintroduction of friction also forces a reconsideration of how success is measured. If metrics reward growth alone, friction will be seen as failure. If metrics reward reliability, safety, and alignment with societal values, friction becomes a form of excellence. This shift mirrors transformations in industries where safety has become integral to brand identity. Volvo built its reputation around safety and crashworthiness rather than speed. AI firms that foreground responsible scaling may similarly reshape user expectations. People entrust systems that govern their finances, health, and civic life to institutions they perceive as cautious rather than reckless.

Furthermore, the restoration of friction must address global disparities. Nations differ in regulatory capacity, technical expertise, and institutional strength. If friction is restored unevenly, high-risk development may migrate to jurisdictions with weaker safeguards. This phenomenon is documented, though debated, in environmental regulation, where some industries or activities relocate to countries with lenient controls. Avoiding such relocation requires international coordination. Multilateral institutions must establish common standards for safety evaluation, monitoring, and incident reporting. Without global friction, local friction becomes porous.

The final dimension of restored friction concerns public legitimacy. Technologies that operate at a societal scale must earn the trust of the populations they affect. Trust cannot be commanded. It must be built through transparency, accountability, and demonstrable caution. When the pharmaceutical industry faced public skepticism about vaccines, transparent testing and clear communication became essential. AI systems will face similar scrutiny as they enter healthcare, law, and public administration. Friction provides evidence that care is taken. It signals that decisions are not rushed. It creates a narrative of responsibility that counters fears of runaway automation and taskification.

Friction, then, is not a hindrance to innovation but a condition for sustainable innovation. It is the mechanism through which power is restrained, knowledge is deepened, and safety is enacted. It aligns development with long-term societal interests rather than short-term competitive pressures. It transforms AI from a technology that moves faster than our capacity to govern it into one embedded within a system of accountability. In a world where algorithms increasingly shape human futures, the deliberate slowing of action becomes an expression of respect. It acknowledges that those subjected to automated decisions deserve assurance that such decisions have passed through institutions capable of protecting them.

The restoration of friction is a prerequisite for legitimacy in the AI age. If AI continues to evolve without institutionalized pauses, independent checks, and procedural rigor, the resulting systems will gain capability without gaining reliability. Their failures will not be small. They will propagate through interconnected infrastructures and destabilize social orders.

History shows that when societies fail to anticipate risks, they are forced to react under conditions of crisis. The stronger the friction built into AI development today, the fewer crises we will face tomorrow. The task is not to resist progress but to ensure that it unfolds within boundaries shaped by collective judgment.

The responsibility to restore friction belongs not only to developers but also to executives, regulators, and citizens who understand that unchecked speed is indistinguishable from a loss of control.

Algorithmic Safety Cases as Constitutional Safeguards

Unchecked speed becomes loss of control precisely because it collapses deliberation into deployment. It removes the institutional pauses where hazards are surfaced, challenged, and contained.

If restoring friction is the shared responsibility of developers, executives, regulators, and citizens, then that responsibility needs a concrete mechanism that can enforce those pauses, distribute authority, and make "go/no-go" decisions accountable to evidence rather than momentum.

That mechanism is the algorithmic safety case: an institutionalized form of friction that converts caution into procedure, comparable to those used in the aviation and nuclear industries, and that formally documents assumptions, hazard analyses, mitigation plans, and fail-safe conditions before public exposure.

The United Kingdom's Office for Nuclear Regulation provides an instructive analog. For decades, no reactor has been allowed to commence operation without a safety case demonstrating not only how the system works under normal conditions but also how it behaves under duress, what failure modes are possible, how likely each is, and which mitigations apply.[500] Safety cases are complex documents, often running to thousands of pages,[501] compiled to support evidence-based regulatory scrutiny.

To demand a safety case is to insist that claims of safety be made explicit, documented, supported by evidence, and open to challenge.

It converts what is often intuition, assumption, or informal reasoning into a structured argument that is accountable to external scrutiny. This transformation is not superficial. It alters how organizations reason about uncertainty, how they anticipate failure, how they justify decisions, and how they relate to the public whose lives their systems shape. A safety case is not a statement of confidence, but a constitution written for a machine that describes the conditions under which its power may be exercised and the boundaries beyond which it must not venture.

In fields where safety cases are mature, their purpose is to force organizations to confront the gap between what they believe and what they can prove. Similar to the nuclear industry, the aviation sector has refined this discipline over decades. When a new aircraft is designed, manufacturers must submit extensive documentation demonstrating that every component—from software to structural materials—meets strict criteria. The documentation is a legal and institutional instrument. It includes detailed modeling of aerodynamic behavior, stress analysis, failure modes and effects analysis, and verification that control systems behave predictably under extreme conditions.

Regulators then interrogate these claims, cross-examine evidence, and demand additional testing when uncertainties remain. The result is not perfect safety—an impossible ideal—but a system whose risks are comprehensively understood and systematically managed. This discipline has contributed to commercial aviation becoming one of the safest modes of transport, with accident and fatality rates falling by an order of magnitude over the past half century. In 2024, IATA reported seven fatal accidents across 40.6 million flights, i.e., about one fatal accident per ~5.8 million flights.[502] Safety is engineered through governance. Not emergence.

AI systems differ from aircraft in important ways, but the logic of safety cases applies with equal force. Unlike aircraft, neural networks do not have mechanical parts whose performance can be modeled using classical physics. Their internal states are high-dimensional statistical representations learned from vast datasets. Their behavior can be surprisingly sensitive to data distribution, input phrasing, or adversarial manipulation. Yet this very uncertainty strengthens the argument for safety cases rather than weakening it. When behavior is unpredictable, documentation becomes more essential, not less. A safety case compels developers to specify what they know, how they know it, what they do not know, and what contingencies exist for the unknown. It forces a distinction between controlled demonstration and real-world reliability.

A safety case for an AI system must include a clear articulation of its intended purpose. This articulation is foundational because risks cannot be assessed without understanding the context in which the system will operate.

When the same model interacts with different environments, its risk profile changes. A language model used for summarizing text exhibits relatively constrained harm potential compared to one used for medical diagnosis or financial advice. Yet the boundaries between these contexts are often porous. Models released with one purpose can be adapted for others. Without a formal purpose statement, organizations cannot be held accountable for ensuring that safety measures are calibrated to actual uses.

The Boeing 737 MAX crashes show how safety-critical systems can fail when their purpose, key assumptions, and real operational consequences are not clearly communicated or thoroughly tested. MCAS was introduced to address handling characteristics, but it was not sufficiently explained to pilots through documentation and training. In addition, certification and safety assessments relied on assumptions about system behavior and pilot response that did not hold in real-world failure situations. These gaps in disclosure and in the handling of assumptions helped create the conditions in which the accidents occurred.[503]

In AI, purpose statements are equally indispensable. A model that generates legal interpretations must be held to different standards than one that generates poetry. A safety case, therefore, begins by defining the operational domain. It specifies the decisions the system may influence, the populations it may affect, the permissions it has, and the conditions under which those permissions lapse. This creates a formal boundary that can later be audited. It prevents mission creep that bypasses oversight. It also enables downstream actors, such as deployers and regulators, to determine whether a particular use case violates the intended domain. If a system is used beyond its certified scope, liability becomes clear.

A second critical element of a safety case is the documentation of assumptions. Every model rests on assumptions about data quality, data representativeness, model generalization, user behavior, and environmental conditions. These assumptions often remain implicit. When unspoken, they cannot be tested or challenged. In safety engineering, unstated assumptions are treated as latent hazards. They lie dormant until a rare combination of events causes a failure.

The 2003 North American blackout, which temporarily cut power to 50 million people, was partly traced to a failure of the control-room alarm system and to inadequate procedures and situational awareness once that failure occurred. When the alarm system failed silently, operators received no further alarms and did not realize that the alarm processor had failed, leaving them without a timely indication that power flows were becoming unstable. The failure of a critical monitoring function remained undetected until the situation deteriorated.[504] Safety cases prevent such invisibility by forcing explicit disclosure of critical dependencies, monitoring failure modes, and specifying the procedures and backups required when alarms are lost.

For AI, assumptions might include claims about training data distribution, expectations about input variability, assumptions about adversarial robustness, or the presumed stability of model behavior across updates. If a model is believed to generalize well from training data to real-world contexts, the safety case must provide empirical justification. If developers assume that adversaries will not target certain vulnerabilities, they must explain why. If they assume users understand the system's limitations, they must provide evidence. The discipline of assumption disclosure transforms conjecture into material for analysis.

A safety case must also include a hazard analysis. Hazard analysis catalogs the ways a system could fail, the consequences of those failures, and the probabilities associated with each pathway.

In the chemical industry, hazard and operability studies identify deviations from normal operations and examine potential triggers. In the medical sector, clinical trials examine not only therapeutic effectiveness but also adverse reactions, including rare events that appear in fewer than one in ten thousand patients.

For AI, hazard analysis must consider hallucinations, biased outputs, manipulation, privacy breaches, unexpected generalization, and cascading failures across interconnected systems. The interconnectedness of digital ecosystems amplifies risk. A flawed risk score in healthcare can influence insurance decisions, which in turn influence employment, which then influences socioeconomic conditions. Hazards propagate through networks.

Quantifying hazards for AI is challenging but not impossible. Statistical tests can estimate rates of biased outputs. Red-team exercises can identify vulnerabilities. Simulations can model how changes in model parameters influence downstream behavior. Studies have shown, for example, that a small subset of training data can disproportionately influence model behavior—a phenomenon known as data poisoning. Hazard analyses must incorporate such findings. Without this rigor, safety claims remain assertions rather than demonstrations.

Mitigation plans then become the counterpart to hazard identification. A safety case must detail not only what can go wrong but also what measures prevent or contain harm. In physical systems, mitigations include redundant components, protective barriers, emergency shutdown systems, and monitoring mechanisms.

In AI, mitigations might include constrained generation protocols, content filtering, supervised review for sensitive tasks, calibration techniques, or domain-specific restrictions. Each mitigation must be justified. If a system claims to mitigate hallucination risk through retrieval augmentation, the safety case must present evidence that retrieval actually reduces hallucination under realistic conditions. If a system relies on post hoc monitoring to detect harmful outputs, the safety case must quantify the effectiveness and recall of such monitoring. A mitigation without evidence is an aspiration.

Red team results are a central component of publishable safety cases. Red teams probe the system adversarially, seeking failures that internal teams may overlook. This adversarial process mirrors practices in cybersecurity, where penetration testers identify vulnerabilities that traditional assessments miss.

Studies in organizational psychology have shown that adversarial teams outperform collaborative teams in detecting faults because their incentives differ. Collaboration encourages harmony, whereas adversarial testing encourages challenge.

For AI, red team exercises should encompass malicious prompt injection, attempts to bypass safety protocols, exposure to harmful content, inducements to generate misinformation, and efforts to exploit latent capabilities that may not be visible in standard benchmarks. The safety case must document not only the failures red teams found but also the methods used, the contexts tested, and the proportion of failures mitigated. Without transparency about the testing methodology, results cannot be compared across systems.

The go-or-no-go rationale becomes the climax of the safety case. It forces organizations to state their decision process explicitly. They must describe why they believe the system is ready for deployment, how the evidence supports this conclusion, and what residual risks remain. They must explain the threshold at which risks shift from intolerable to tolerable. This rationale is essential because it creates accountability. If an incident occurs post-deployment, investigators can examine whether the rationale was justified based on the available evidence. The absence of such a rationale leaves decisions opaque and responsibility diffuse.

Publishable safety cases transform internal assessments into public commitments. By requiring publication, safety cases create a forum in which experts, regulators, researchers, and civil society can interrogate claims. Publication does not mean exposing proprietary details of model architecture, but it does require disclosing reasoning, evidence, hazards, and mitigations. In the pharmaceutical sector, clinical trial data is publicly available to allow third-party scrutiny. Transparency has revealed inconsistencies in trials, biases in data interpretation, and unreported side effects. Such scrutiny has improved industry standards over time. AI safety cases must contribute to similar improvements.

Public safety cases also address legitimacy. Populations increasingly distrust opaque algorithmic systems. Surveys show that in several countries, more than 60 percent of citizens believe AI systems could be harmful if deployed without oversight. By publishing safety cases, organizations signal that they take responsibility seriously and welcome examination. Legitimacy cannot be built on secrecy. It requires openness to critique. The history of public infrastructure shows that when communities understand how risks are managed, opposition declines. The construction of bridges, tunnels, and railways has often followed public hearings where safety documents were presented. Similar public engagement is essential for AI.

The discipline of publishing safety cases also exerts pressure on organizational culture. Teams know their reasoning will be exposed. This awareness shapes how they think, write, and test. It reduces the temptation to gloss over uncertainties or rely on reputation. Studies of academic research show that the expectation of peer review increases methodological rigor. Safety cases are a form of institutional peer review. They introduce social incentives for accuracy and thoroughness. They also discourage the internal fragmentation of knowledge. When documentation must be coherent, teams cannot allow crucial information to remain siloed.

There is also a geopolitical dimension. Nations will judge each other's AI systems partly through the transparency of safety cases. International cooperation on AI safety will require common frameworks for evaluating evidence. If safety cases become standardized, they will facilitate cross-border dialogue, mutual certification, and shared monitoring practices. Without standardization, safety becomes fragmented and trust erodes. The aviation sector again offers an instructive example. Nations certify aircraft according to shared principles, allowing airlines to operate globally without redundant inspections. AI may never achieve this level of harmonization, but safety cases can lay the groundwork.

Critics might argue that safety cases impose an excessive burden on developers. Yet the burden must be examined in context. When a model influences millions of decisions daily, the cost of failure can exceed any documentation burden.

The 2008 financial crisis demonstrated how inadequate oversight of complex systems can generate global consequences. Models used for risk assessment in financial institutions often underestimated correlations and the possibility of extreme, system-wide losses in mortgage-backed securities, especially under stress. The assumptions embedded in those models were often opaque and insufficiently challenged through independent validation and stress testing. A culture that prioritized short-term performance and treated scrutiny as a constraint amplified the crisis.[505] A similar failure in AI governance could produce cascading harm across multiple domains.

Safety cases also mitigate legal liability. When organizations can demonstrate that they have conducted thorough hazard analyses, implemented mitigations, and published supporting evidence, they can defend themselves against claims of negligence. Courts often examine whether organizations have followed industry best practices, and safety cases help define those practices. Without them, the industry risks legal uncertainty. This uncertainty could slow innovation more than any documentation requirement.

Another important role of safety cases lies in their ability to create institutional memory. AI development is dynamic: teams change, models evolve, and knowledge shifts. Without documentation, organizations lose the historical understanding of why certain decisions were made. This loss of memory can lead to repeated mistakes. The aviation industry maintains detailed records of every design decision for decades. These records inform future models and investigations. AI needs similar continuity. Safety cases preserve the reasoning behind design choices, providing future teams with insight into past assumptions and trade-offs.

A deeper sense-making virtue of safety cases is that they encourage humility. AI research has a tendency toward optimistic narratives about progress. Safety cases challenge this optimism by forcing engagement with uncertainty. They formalize the gaps in knowledge. They acknowledge that not all behaviors are predictable. They bring into the open what remains unexplained. Humility becomes an institutionalized mindset rather than an individual virtue.

Implementing safety cases requires changes to development workflows. Organizations must integrate documentation into the early stages of design rather than treat it as an afterthought. They must create interdisciplinary teams capable of writing comprehensive cases. They must allocate time and resources for testing, evidence gathering, and reviews. This alters timelines but also elevates quality. When safety cases are internalized, teams begin designing with documentation in mind. They anticipate auditors' questions. They collect evidence proactively. They reduce reliance on anecdotal reasoning.

Safety cases must also be dynamic. As models evolve through fine-tuning, retraining, or parameter updates, safety cases must evolve as well. Each new version must include updated hazard analyses, revised assumptions, and revised mitigations. This continuous process mirrors the discipline of change control in regulated industries. When a component in a medical device changes, the safety case must be updated. AI systems, which evolve at a far greater speed, require an even more disciplined versioning. Version histories must be clear, searchable, and tied to evidence. Without this, incidents become difficult to investigate.

The publication of safety cases will also catalyze academic research. Scholars will examine cases, compare methodologies, identify gaps, and propose improvements. Over time, a science of AI safety documentation will emerge. Metrics will be developed to evaluate completeness, rigor, and clarity. Comparative studies will reveal patterns. Regulatory bodies will refine requirements. This evolutionary process will raise baseline standards.

Finally, safety cases will reshape the competitive landscape. Firms that produce rigorous, transparent safety cases will differentiate themselves. Governments will prefer systems backed by strong documentation. Businesses will select vendors whose safety cases demonstrate reliability. Consumers will gravitate toward products they perceive as trustworthy.

Over time, the market will favor those who treat safety as a constitutional principle rather than an optional feature.

Algorithmic Separation of Powers

The call to translate the separation of powers into the AI stack becomes meaningful only when it acquires institutional and technical specificity as a working architecture. Constitutional language carries weight because it embeds centuries of learning about how concentrated authority behaves under pressure. It tells us that ambition must counteract ambition, and that entities capable of shaping the lives of many must be subject to forces that temper, interrogate, and sometimes halt them.

Modern AI development already resembles a fused sovereign because it combines goal-setting, execution, and self-approval within the same pipeline. If unbounded authority corrupts human institutions, there is no reason to believe that algorithmic institutions will be spared from analogous pathologies.

The question is how this lesson moves from parchment to production pipelines, from political theory to system architecture, and from a principle understood in civics classrooms to a discipline embedded in the workflows of engineers, auditors, and decision makers.

To operationalize the separation of powers, the AI stack can be understood as a lifecycle: upstream decisions shape downstream effects, and governance must, therefore, be placed at each stage where power concentrates. The framework below introduces eight separations in the order in which they appear across the lifecycle.

- ♣ Separation n°1: Goal-setting vs. machine-making
- ♣ Separation n°2: Data stewardship vs. developer control
- ♣ Separation n°3: Training governance vs. optimization
- ♣ Separation n°4: Deployment authorization vs. design ownership
- ♣ Separation n°5: Societal signals monitoring vs. engagement metrics

- Separation n°6: Contestability vs. algorithmic finality
- Separation n°7: Compute governance vs. scale at will
- Separation n°8: Market portability standards vs. vertical lock-in

These eight separations follow the path by which an AI system moves from intention to societal impact.

They begin upstream, where goals are set and data is governed before any model is built. They then continue through the middle of the lifecycle, where training and optimization are constrained, and where release is treated as an independent go/no-go decision rather than an engineering continuation.

Once the system is deployed, the separations shift downstream to production realities, meaning it is monitored for societal signals, kept contestable through appeal and review, and prevented from becoming an irreversible authority.

As the system moves from deployment into expansion, it enters the scaling phase, where three late-stage separations become decisive. Compute governance limits the ability to scale capabilities at will. Market portability standards prevent expansion from hardening into structural dependence through lock-in.

AI governance fails the moment power becomes self-authoring. The eight separations are built to stop that failure by distributing authority across distinct functions and making each function answerable to another.

Goal-setting must be separated from machine-making so intent cannot be silently rewritten by builders. Data stewardship must be separated from developer control so representation cannot be extracted or erased without a duty of care. Training governance must be separated from optimization so gradients cannot become private law. Deployment authorization must be separated from design ownership so release becomes an accountable act of risk acceptance. Societal signal monitoring must be separated from engagement metrics so externalities remain visible and actionable. Contestability must be separated from algorithmic finality so decisions remain reversible, explainable, and open to appeal. Compute governance must be separated from scale at will, so capability expansion remains conditional on maturity and evidence. Finally, market portability standards must be separated from vertical lock-in so dependence never becomes more enforceable than rights, and no actor can convert infrastructure control into rulemaking power.

Together, these separations keep AI's algorithmic power legible, bounded, and answerable, anchoring technological authority in the constitutional logic that has disciplined human governance for centuries.

Separation n°1: Goal-Setting vs. Machine-Making

Goal-setting is the act of defining what the model should strive toward, which trade-offs are acceptable, which harms are intolerable, and what constitutes success. It is the closest analog to lawmaking within trias algorithmica because it determines the intent that later hardens into product policy, guardrails, and binding constraints in the operational layer.

No democratic society allows those subject to regulation to write all their own rules behind closed doors. Yet most organizations allow model development teams to define high-level aims, select benchmarks, and determine the scope of acceptable deviation. This is not merely a matter of moral hazard, but also a matter of evidentiary blindness because builders tend to privilege evidence that fits their architecture, timelines, and measurable proxies for progress.

Thus, the logic is nothing new. It is constitutional.

♣ **Power being constrained:** the ability of those who build the system to also define its aims, success criteria, tolerable harms, and evaluation standards—concentrating agenda-setting, execution, and self-approval into a single chain of command and collapsing legislative intent into engineering discretion.

Industries that matured under the pressure of public risk long ago recognized that those who design a system should not have final authority over its objectives, especially when those objectives determine what counts as acceptable harm.

In pharmaceuticals, the purpose of a drug is defined through formal regulatory and sponsor governance processes that draw on multiple disciplines, including clinical and statistical expertise, and sometimes external advisory input. Drug designers cannot determine on their own which populations the drug should target, which side effects are unacceptable, or what constitutes therapeutic benefit.

In aviation, the objectives of a flight control system are defined not by software designers alone, but through regulatory standards that reflect decades of collective learning, as well as through certification processes that require documented safety analyses and evidence of compliance.

In finance, investment model developers do not decide risk tolerances. These tolerances are determined by governance bodies, such as boards and senior risk committees, that consider macroeconomic risk, compliance requirements, and the long-term health of the institution.

These structures exist because experience has shown that designers have natural incentives to optimize for what they know how to build and for what increases the perceived value of their work. Objective setting requires a perspective that is not constrained by the technical limitations or strategic ambitions of the engineering team, because the point is not merely what can be built, but what should be permitted.

Those who build systems are often too close to the technology to fully see its externalities. They know the strengths and weaknesses of their architecture intimately, but they do not always see how a seemingly small design choice can influence downstream inequality in lending, labor markets, or civic discourse once the system becomes infrastructural and scaled.

Historical evidence on facial recognition and related face analysis systems illustrates this point.[506,507] Across peer-reviewed research and large-scale government testing, substantial accuracy gaps have been documented between demographic groups, including systematically higher error rates for some groups than for others.[506,507] Independent external evaluations helped make the magnitude of these disparities widely visible, including findings in which false-positive rates differed by an order of magnitude and, in some one-to-many identification settings, by about 100 times across demographic groups.[507,508] The problem was often less about intent than about how data, evaluation design, and deployment assumptions reflected a narrow set of perspectives; as a result representational coverage was not treated as a safety requirement.[506,508]

Organizations must begin by dividing goal-setting from system construction internally. This separation is a structural intervention that prevents the concentration of agenda shaping, execution, and approval within a single chain of command and preserves the difference between constitutional intent and technical implementation.

♣ **Counterpower:** an independent goal-setting authority within the organization, structurally distinct from engineering and insulated from product pressure, mandated to define scope, values, risk boundaries, and evaluation protocols, and to represent perspectives beyond the builder's incentives so that the "law" is not silently rewritten by optimization pressure.

Institutionalizing such a separation requires the creation of an independent goal-setting body within the organization. This authority must operate with a mandate distinct from engineering teams. Its role is to define what the system is permitted to pursue, which risks must be avoided, and which values must be protected. Its work resembles that of an internal regulator. It does not design models. They examine the domain, identify societal impacts, consult affected groups, analyze historical precedents, and articulate the principles that guide development. They must also define the metrics by which the system will later be evaluated. These metrics must reflect both technical performance and societal externalities, and they must be treated as binding conditions rather than advisory preferences.

It must draw expertise from domains far beyond machine learning, including law, sociology, economics, psychology, and specialists in the sectors where the system will operate. Setting objectives for a medical AI system requires clinicians who understand diagnostic pathways, ethicists who understand patient rights, and data scientists who understand measurement limitations. Its mandate is to articulate what the system is allowed to do, what risks it must guard against, what societal values it must respect, and which thresholds cannot be crossed without triggering automatic escalation, so that the objective charter remains enforceable under delivery pressure.

♣ **Hard mechanisms:** enforceable, objective constraints embedded as binding gates in the development and deployment pipeline, including scope lock and use-expansion review; mandatory evaluation protocols that cover externalities; explicit risk boundary thresholds that trigger halt or escalation; and formal veto power over deployment when evidence does not satisfy the objective charter.

Once established, goal-setting authorities must begin by defining the scope. Scope is the foundational constraint that determines what the system is intended to do and what it is not intended to do. Without a clear scope, systems drift. A system originally designed to assist with document summarization may gradually be used for legal interpretation, health triage, and financial analysis, all without structured evaluation. This drift reflects the malleability of AI systems. Their generality tempts organizations to expand use without revisiting objectives. Scope definition prevents this drift by requiring formal review before expansion. It also prevents mission creep that circumvents oversight and ensures that expanded use does not retroactively redefine the system's "law."

Goal-setting authorities must then identify the values that the system must uphold. These values are context-dependent. A hiring system must uphold fairness across demographic groups. A banking system must uphold reliability and risk transparency. A medical system must uphold patient autonomy and informed consent. Values must be stated explicitly because they cannot be inferred from training data. Training data reflects past behaviors, not desired futures. Historical hiring data may reflect discrimination. Medical records may reflect unequal treatment. If objectives are derived from such data without value-based correction, systems will reproduce inequities, and those inequities will later be enforced at scale as if they were neutral policy.

The next institutional responsibility is risk boundary definition. Risk boundaries outline unacceptable outcomes. These boundaries determine the limits beyond which deployment cannot proceed. They force developers to consider negative scenarios and create explicit thresholds that define failure. For large transport-category aircraft, safety assessments require catastrophic failure conditions to be "extremely improbable," and certification guidance commonly treats that as an average probability on the order of one in a billion flight hours or less. These thresholds shape design choices. AI requires analogous boundaries. If a medical diagnostic model exhibits more than a certain rate of false negatives in critical conditions, deployment must halt. If a credit risk model produces disparate impacts that exceed defined thresholds, usage must be constrained. These boundaries prevent the incremental erosion of safety standards. Without them, organizations may rationalize small increases in risk as acceptable, leading to cumulative degradation over time.

Goal-setting authorities must also define evaluation protocols. Evaluation is not simply performance measurement, but a systematic test of whether the system meets defined objectives. Protocols must specify benchmarks, test datasets, stress tests, and scenarios. They must also require evaluation against externalities. For instance, a news recommendation algorithm may perform well on relevance metrics but still amplify polarization.

Evaluation protocols must therefore include measures of content diversity, exposure patterns, and susceptibility to misinformation. When the World Health Organization develops guideline recommendations on public health interventions, it assesses evidence on desirable and undesirable effects, including benefits and harms, and applies explicit decision criteria—such as values and preferences, resource requirements, equity considerations, acceptability, and feasibility—to determine the recommendation.[509] AI requires similar breadth. Evaluation cannot be confined to narrow metrics because systems operate within dynamic ecosystems.

One of the greatest challenges in separating goal-setting from engineering lies in translating objectives into constraints that influence development without being overridden. Objectives must be enforceable. If goal-setting authorities define fairness requirements, but engineering teams can bypass them in pursuit of performance, the separation loses meaning. Enforceability can be achieved through binding design requirements, gating mechanisms in development pipelines, and mandatory compliance checks before deployment. These controls must be embedded within workflows. They cannot rely solely on persuasion. Research on corporate safety culture shows that voluntary adherence to safety recommendations is insufficient. Organizations comply consistently only when requirements are tied to incentives, authority, and the ability to halt processes.

Furthermore, the institutional separation of goal-setting must address how organizations handle uncertainty. AI systems generate uncertainties that are not easily resolved. Goal-setting authorities must decide how to approach unknowns. In environmental regulation, the precautionary principle is often applied when hazards are uncertain but potentially severe. In AI, the precautionary principle might guide decisions about capabilities that could manipulate behavior, generate persuasive misinformation, or perform autonomous actions. Goal-setting authorities must determine whether unknown risks justify halting development, restricting deployment, or imposing additional evidence requirements. This institutionalizes a rational response to uncertainty rather than leaving such decisions to engineering teams, whose incentives favor action and whose success criteria may reward speed over caution.

Another important dimension is accountability. Goal-setting authorities must be identifiable entities with clear mandates. When objectives are defined implicitly by developers, accountability becomes diffused. If a system produces harmful outcomes, it becomes difficult to determine whether the harm resulted from flawed objectives, flawed execution, or flawed oversight. A study of a widely used population health management algorithm found that harmful distortions can occur when a tool is optimized for a proxy, such as predicted health-care costs, rather than clinical need or illness burden. This proxy choice can be opaque in commercial systems, which can make accountability and correction harder when harms are discovered.[363] With formal objective-setting authorities, responsibility is clearer. If objectives were poorly defined, the authority is accountable. If objectives were sound but execution was flawed, developers are accountable. This clarity strengthens institutional learning and prevents "policy drift" from being mistaken for technical error.

The separation of goal-setting must also consider organizational scale. Small companies may claim that they lack the resources to establish independent goal-setting bodies. Yet the complexity of AI systems requires governance even in small teams. In aviation, small aircraft manufacturers must still comply with safety standards. In biotechnology, startups must still meet regulatory requirements. The size of the organization does not diminish the need for safety. However, implementation can be proportional. Small teams can create external advisory committees. They can leverage standardized objective frameworks developed by industry consortia. They can collaborate with academic institutions. What matters is not size but independence of perspective and enforceable authority.

Such institutional separation also strengthens internal discourse. When objectives are defined externally, developers must engage in dialogue. They must explain constraints, negotiate feasibility, and articulate technical limitations. This dialogue enhances mutual understanding. It reduces the risk of engineers assuming that goal-setting authorities are disconnected from reality, and it also reduces the risk of goal-setting authorities assuming that engineers can achieve anything they envision. In aviation, dialogue between designers and regulators refined fly-by-wire systems. Regulators initially imposed strict limits, while designers argued for flexibility. Through dialogue, systems were developed that provided enhanced safety without undermining operational control. AI development will require similar negotiation because the point is not to slow innovation but to constitutionalize it.

The separation of goal-setting also improves adaptability. If developers define objectives, they may resist changes once development has begun, making change costly. However, if goal-setting is external, objectives can be updated as new evidence emerges. Goal-setting authorities can revise objectives, adjust risk boundaries, and redefine scope without requiring wholesale reengineering. This flexibility is crucial because AI evolves rapidly. New capabilities appear. New harms emerge. Objectives must adapt. The COVID-19 pandemic highlighted the value of flexible objective systems in public policy. Health agencies rapidly updated objectives based on new evidence about transmission. AI governance requires similar agility so that the "law" can evolve without being rewritten by whoever ships fastest.

The separation also protects against conflicts of interest. When engineering teams define objectives, they may inadvertently shape them to reflect what is easiest to build. They typically choose metrics that mirror what the system can already achieve. This creates feedback loops that perpetuate existing capabilities rather than challenging systems to meet societal needs. When commercial teams participate, they may shape objectives toward revenue rather than safety. Analyses of major social media recommender systems indicate that platforms commonly optimize ranking and recommendation for measurable engagement signals such as clicks, likes, shares, or watch time, in part because these metrics are readily observable at scale and align with business incentives. However, engagement-optimized objectives are not the same as healthy discourse or user well-being and may conflict with them.[510] A proper separation of objective setting would have forced organizations to acknowledge that engagement alone is insufficient and that additional objectives, such as exposure diversity, misinformation resilience, and well-being impacts, need to be defined by bodies external to product engineering.

Independent goal-setting authorities introduce a perspective not constrained by these incentives. This also mirrors the logic of independent central banks. When monetary policy is heavily influenced by elected officials, short-term incentives can bias decisions toward easier policy, which can contribute to higher or more variable inflation. Greater central bank independence, typically over policy instruments, is often associated with lower inflation and, in many cases, lower inflation volatility.[511] AI governance must learn from this history. The same lesson applies within firms: independence holds only if it is structural, especially in reporting lines.

A critical challenge is ensuring that goal-setting authorities possess sufficient authority to enforce their mandates. If these authorities exist only on paper, developers may circumvent them. Authority requires the power to veto proposals, to require additional tests, to alter timelines, and to deny deployment approval. This authority must be supported by executive leadership. If leaders undermine goal-setting authorities in pursuit of market opportunities, the separation will fail. Another high-risk sector offers a useful parallel. A comparative study of underground coal mines found that low-accident mines reported greater upper-management involvement in and support for safety-related decisions than high-accident mines, an organizational factor associated with better safety performance.[512] Oversight without leadership support becomes symbolic. Support must be formal, documented, and enforceable.

Goal-setting authorities must also participate in post-incident analysis. When failures occur, they must evaluate whether the objectives were appropriate and whether changes are required. This continuous feedback loop ensures institutional learning. In aviation, incident investigations often lead to revisions in design objectives. AI systems require similar reflexivity. If a language model generates harmful content under conditions not previously considered, goal-setting authorities must expand their objectives to incorporate new constraints. This iterative process strengthens governance.

Implementing separation requires organizations to develop new skill sets. Goal-setting authorities must understand risk assessment, ethical reasoning, regulatory landscapes, and human factors. They must also understand AI architecture well enough to evaluate technical claims. This interdisciplinary knowledge is rare, so organizations must invest in training, recruitment, and capacity building. Without these investments, goal-setting authorities may lack the expertise to challenge developers. Research on regulatory capture highlights that when oversight bodies lack independent technical capacity, information asymmetries can make them reliant on regulated entities for specialized knowledge and evidence.[513] AI governance must avoid this trap because such dependence collapses separation into deference.

The institutional separation of goal-setting also interacts with external governance systems. Regulators will evaluate whether organizations have meaningful internal governance. Those with weak structures may face stricter external controls, while those with strong structures may gain more autonomy. This dynamic mirrors environmental regulation, where recognized management systems (e.g., the Eco-Management and Audit Scheme, [EMAS]) can result in fewer inspections, less frequent permit renewals, or "lighter" treatment of permit applications. The EU AI Act similarly embeds differentiated oversight, including internal control conformity assessment pathways for certain high-risk systems, conditioned on robust quality management and documentation.[514] Organizations with robust goal-setting authorities will therefore enjoy competitive advantages.

Finally, the separation of goal-setting must be understood as a foundational architectural principle. It structures how power flows within organizations. It determines who can authorize action, who can define limits, and who can stop unsafe processes. It embeds caution into the early stages of development rather than relying on last-minute interventions. It ensures that the purpose of AI systems is shaped not by engineering convenience or market pressure but by societal considerations. As AI systems increasingly mediate human affairs, the authority to define objectives becomes a form of governance. Without institutional safeguards, this authority becomes concentrated in small groups whose perspectives may not represent the broader public, and whose choices will later be enforced as if they were neutral technical outcomes.

The separation of goal-setting from system development and deployment, therefore, represents an institutional shift comparable to the establishment of risk committees in financial institutions, ethics boards in medical research, and independent regulatory bodies in public utilities. It will influence public trust, regulatory acceptance, and long-term sustainability. It is the structure through which organizations acknowledge that defining what an AI system should do is too consequential to be left to those who build it alone.

Separation n°2: Data Stewardship vs. Developer Control

The next locus of power is the substrate on which the system learns its behaviors: data.

It is equivalent to the factual material that informs legislative and judicial reasoning in physical institutions. Within trias algorithmica, it is administered through the pipeline as an executive-like capacity that establishes what counts as an admissible "fact" for the model.

When data is controlled by a single actor without oversight, the risk of bias, exclusion, or exploitation increases. When data rights are ambiguous, communities have little recourse when their information is misused. Therefore, operational separation must include data governance that constrains who decides what data is accepted, how it is filtered, and how it is fed into the system.

♣ **Power being constrained:** the power of developers and model owners to treat data as an extractable resource rather than a governed commons, deciding unilaterally what is collected, how it is labeled, how long it is kept, what downstream uses are permitted, and whether affected communities have visibility or recourse, including the power to define representational reality by omission as much as by inclusion.

This power is amplified by asymmetry of scale. A single training decision can operationalize millions of individual traces into a system that shapes future behavior, while the people represented in the data remain largely unaware of how they are being encoded. In effect, control of data becomes control of representation, and control of representation becomes control of who the model is designed to understand, to ignore, or to misclassify, and this representational control later expresses itself as rule-like behavior in ranking, refusal, and eligibility.

♣ **Counterpower:** independent data stewardship institutions that act as fiduciaries for contributors and communities, with duties of care, loyalty, and purpose limitation, rather than the developer's duty to maximize model performance.

Their role is not simply consent collection, but governance of use, meaning that they define permissible purposes, enforce retention limits, regulate enrichment and relabeling practices, and require that developers demonstrate necessity rather than convenience. In high-stakes domains, these stewards should also be able to demand representational guarantees, such as minimum coverage for protected groups and explicit documentation of exclusion decisions, so that absence becomes visible rather than implicit and the pipeline cannot, by default, redefine the population the system governs.

♣ **Hard mechanism:** enforceable data rights and auditable, end-to-end data lifecycles that bind developers to externally defined constraints and make violations detectable.

Data trusts and cooperatives offer a pragmatic mechanism to reintroduce accountability.[515,516] These entities hold data on behalf of contributors, define permitted uses, negotiate terms with model developers, and allow withdrawal when conditions are violated. This gives communities a voice in how they are represented within training ecosystems. It also forces developers to justify why certain data is required and what protections are in place to prevent unauthorized use.

To make these use conditions enforceable at scale, operationalizing data trusts is best supported by machine-readable, contractually binding data licenses that specify permitted uses, prohibited uses, retention windows, downstream sharing rules, and revocation conditions, with compliance verified through audit access rather than provider attestation. In addition, training datasets must carry provenance and lineage metadata that survive preprocessing, deduplication, filtering, and relabeling so that developers cannot launder disallowed sources through transformations and claim uncertainty.

Because data power is often exercised through curation rather than explicit misconduct, stewardship must regulate the curation layer. Dataset construction choices—such as what is treated as noise, what is treated as toxicity, which dialects are misclassified or erased by filtering rules, and which communities are overrepresented in "problematic" categories—can become silent political decisions with executive consequences once deployed. A robust stewardship regime therefore requires documented rationales for filtering policies and periodic internal reviews of what was removed, not only what was kept. This approach helps organizations prevent safety filtering from becoming representational erasure.

Stewardship must also confront the problem that consent is structurally inadequate at scale. For most contributors, meaningful consent is impossible because future uses of models are unknown. Even so, data trusts partially address this issue by shifting from one-time consent to ongoing fiduciary governance. The more operational version of this principle is dynamic authorization, meaning that uses can be expanded only through explicit review and that contributors can withdraw categories of use without requiring the destruction of the entire dataset. This creates a governance pathway that is closer to licensing than to blanket permission, and it restores contestability upstream, before harms are embedded.

Practical data governance requires independent audits that test coverage, representativeness, and potential paths to harm. When the COMPAS algorithm used in the US criminal justice system was reported to exhibit racial disparities, the public revelation came not from internal controls but from an external investigation.[233] In high-stakes domains, relying on voluntary disclosure is inadequate. Independent auditors must be empowered to sample datasets, inspect labeling protocols, and assess whether training materials reinforce harmful stereotypes or encode structural inequities. Statistical tests can reveal imbalances that human reviewers miss, especially in large multimodal datasets. For instance, studies have found gender imbalances in image captioning datasets, where certain professions appear overwhelmingly male, leading models to reproduce these biases.[517] Quantifying such issues requires auditors who are structurally distinct from the developers whose work they assess; otherwise, the executive function of curation becomes self-justifying.

A further operational requirement is that these audits include repeatable representational diagnostics before deployment. If stewardship is real, auditors must test not only demographic balance but also functional consequences. This means running pretraining and post-training representational diagnostics that examine error disparities, stereotype associations, and performance cliffs across groups, languages, and contexts. It also means testing for downstream vulnerability, such as whether certain groups are disproportionately exposed to harmful outputs or misclassification. These diagnostics create an evidence base for refusing training runs that would embed predictable harm and for forcing remediation before scale makes reversal impractical.

Data stewardship must also address leakage and memorization as governance failures rather than as technical curiosities. If models can reproduce sensitive personal information, then data governance has failed at a structural level. Stewardship institutions should therefore require privacy risk assessments that include memorization testing, membership inference risk evaluation, and mitigation plans, such as differential privacy regimes or strict exclusion of sensitive categories where mitigation cannot be justified. This connects data governance directly to the model's operational behavior rather than treating privacy as a legal formality, and it anticipates downstream accountability by preventing avoidable exposure at the source.

Finally, external stewardship must have a credible enforcement mechanism; otherwise, it becomes symbolic. That mechanism can include revocation of data access, financial penalties, public disclosure of violations, or exclusion from certification and procurement programs. The key is that developers must face meaningful consequences if they breach permitted use conditions, because without consequence, the market will reward extraction, and executive power will reconsolidate through convenience.

When these elements exist, data becomes a governed input rather than an appropriated substrate. Developers remain capable of innovation, but they no longer have unilateral authority over whose lives are encoded, whose identities are erased, or whose vulnerabilities are exploited. This is the constitutional core of separation at the data layer, where the executive function of the data-to-AI-model lifecycle is made accountable to external duties of care.

Separation n°3: Training Governance vs. Optimization

Once objectives and data constraints are defined, the next concentration of authority sits within the training pipeline itself: the ability to translate intent into model behavior through architecture choices, loss functions, fine-tuning regimes, and reward structures. In trias terms, this is the executive function of enactment, where pipelines and compute convert declared intent into enforced behavior. Separation of powers requires that training teams operate under constraints that are not self-authored and cannot be easily waived under competitive pressure.

♣ **Power being constrained:** the power of optimization to become policy by default.

In modern machine learning systems, the training pipeline is not only an execution engine, but also a value engine and, therefore, a site where executive action can rewrite legislative intent by technical means. Loss functions, reward models, and sampling strategies define what the system learns to prioritize, which behaviors are reinforced, and which harms are treated as acceptable collateral.

When the same team designs the objective, chooses the training signals, and interprets the results, the system effectively acquires a private constitution written in gradients rather than in governance language. This concentration is especially dangerous because it is legible only to specialists, easy to justify as a technical necessity, and difficult to audit after the fact.

♣ **Counterpower:** an independent training governance function with the authority to bind optimization to approved intent, to prevent unauthorized shifts in training objectives, and to enforce evidentiary standards before scaling capability, including the authority to refuse runs whose optimization choices would circumvent the objective charter.

This function should not be housed as an informal review within the same training organization. It must have a distinct mandate to approve training runs above defined thresholds, to require specific evaluation regimes, and to halt or roll back training when provenance or safety conditions are violated. In effect, it plays the role of an internal certification authority for training integrity, ensuring that the model being produced is the model that was authorized and that executive enactment remains faithful to upstream intent.

♣ **Hard mechanism:** training as a controlled process with enforceable gates, cryptographically anchored traceability, and separation of duties between those who optimize and those who authorize.

Practically, this means the training process must be designed with enforceable objective-setting constraints so that experiments are traceable to approved datasets, hyperparameters and reward models are auditable, and safety evaluations are not optional "nice-to-haves" but required gates. The aim is not to diminish engineering autonomy but to prevent the training function from becoming both rule author and executor in practice, even when it is framed as optimization.

The implication is that every meaningful training run must produce a training dossier that can be inspected and reproduced, and no run should proceed to scaling or deployment unless that dossier meets predefined acceptance criteria. This dossier should contain (a) the governing requirements, including the objective charter, the applicable safety case (versioned), and the acceptance criteria, and (b) the run evidence, including dataset lineage references, approved data-use attestations, exact code and configuration hashes, hyperparameter manifests, reward model provenance, evaluation results tied to the objective charter, and records of safety-threshold compliance. The safety case and its thresholds must be binding inputs to training.

To make governance real at training time, the organization must also constrain how optimization can implicitly change objectives. Reward models and preference datasets must be treated as regulated assets, not as convenient tuning tools. If reinforcement learning from human feedback (RLHF) or similar alignment regimes are used, the provenance of the preference data, the identity and incentives of labelers, the instruction policies given to them, and the stability of the reward model over time must all be documented and version-controlled. Otherwise, organizations cannot distinguish alignment from subtle value drift introduced through labeling practices or through managerial pressure to reduce refusals and increase helpfulness. In trias terms, this is how executive optimization can quietly re-legislate acceptable conduct.

Equally important, training governance must control scaling because scaling is where small misalignments become systemic. An internal compute threshold should trigger enhanced governance, requiring incremental scaling rather than frontier jumps. Above that threshold, the training governance function should mandate staged capability tests that include not only benchmark gains but also changes in failure modes, emergent tool-use behaviors, susceptibility to deception, and generalization into high-risk domains. The purpose is to prevent "capability surprise" from entering production as an accidental byproduct of larger runs.

Training governance must also treat evaluation as an adversarial discipline rather than a performance report. It should require preregistered evaluation plans that cannot be rewritten after results are known, and it should enforce the use of held-out red-team datasets that training teams cannot access during optimization. This prevents the familiar pathology in which teams inadvertently train to the test and then declare victory. It also creates an evidentiary barrier against the selective disclosure of favorable results and keeps the evidentiary record from being rewritten by the same actors who stand to benefit.

Because training pipelines are now complex supply chains, governance must extend to the artifacts that flow through them. Model checkpoints, adapters, system prompts, safety classifiers, and post-training filters must be versioned together with the training runs that produced them so that behavior can be traced to specific interventions rather than vaguely attributed to "the model." Far from documentation for its own sake, it is the only way to perform forensic accountability after failures and to prevent teams from hiding risky capability shifts within opaque training changes.

Finally, training governance must institutionalize reversibility at the training layer, not just at deployment. This means maintaining trusted baselines, preserving safe checkpoints, and rehearsing rollback procedures for training changes, just as organizations rehearse rollbacks for production releases. When governance can require a return to a prior safe checkpoint, optimization stops being a one-way ratchet and becomes a controlled process.

When these elements exist, training ceases to be a private domain of technical discretion and becomes an accountable institutional function. Optimization remains powerful, but it is no longer sovereign. It is bounded by intent, evidence, traceability, and the ability to halt. This is the constitutional core of separation at the training layer and the point at which executive power in the pipeline is made answerable to externally defined constraints.

Separation n°4: Deployment Authorization vs. Design Ownership

The next step is to separate the development and training of models from final deployment authorization as a distinct downstream act of institutional judgment.

♣ **Power being constrained:** the ability of a single team to move from design to release without an independent checkpoint, thereby controlling not only what the system can do but also when it enters reality, where it is applied, under which constraints, and at what scale.

In practice, this is the power to convert laboratory uncertainty into societal exposure on a product timeline, while treating deployment as a continuation of engineering rather than as a distinct act of institutional risk acceptance and public-facing legitimacy.

In most AI organizations, deployment authority rests with the same group that builds the system. This arrangement resembles a judicial function collapsed into the executive function without independence—a configuration political theorists have long considered an invitation to abuse. Deployment authority matters because it determines when and where the system enters the world, under what constraints, and with what monitoring. The difference between a laboratory prototype and a deployed model used by millions is the difference between a chemical reaction in a beaker and one performed in the open air. The risk profile shifts dramatically with scale, context, and real-world complexity, and it is precisely at this boundary that authorization must be separable from design ownership.

The collapse of recommendation systems into engines of polarization, misinformation, or obsessive behavior did not arise because the underlying algorithms were flawed in isolation. Rather, they emerged because deployment environments rewarded one metric—engagement—without countervailing constraints and because no independent authority existed to slow expansion until externalities were understood or to condition release on evidence rather than momentum.

♣ **Counterpower:** a structurally independent deployment authority functioning as an internal regulator, reviewing the safety case produced by the objective-setting body, the experimental evidence gathered by the development teams, and the results of red-team exercises as an adjudicative record rather than as supporting material for a predetermined launch.

This authority would examine the performance of the model under adversarial tests, stress conditions, and out-of-distribution scenarios. It would have the power to say no or to require further evidence before the system scales. It would operate with a mandate to prioritize societal safety over speed to market.

Critically, this counterpower must be more than "ethics review." It must be a release authority with standing, quorum rules, and an auditable decision record, comparable to a Production Readiness Review in safety-critical engineering or a Change Advisory Board in high-reliability IT operations, but upgraded to account for model uncertainty and social externalities. In trias terms, this is the judicial-like layer in deployment, where evaluation evidence becomes an authorization or refusal with consequences. To prevent capture, its members should have fixed terms, conflict-of-interest constraints (no compensation tied to launch KPIs), and a reporting line to a risk owner independent of product.

♣ **Hard mechanism:** a binding go/no-go gate embedded in the deployment pipeline, enforced through separation of duties and non-bypassable controls.

This means the engineering team can produce a release candidate but cannot ship it without independent "two-key" authorization: the builder cannot also be the releaser, and the releaser cannot rewrite the criteria after seeing the results.

Mechanically, the gate should require a signed deployment packet that includes, at a minimum: the objective charter and risk boundaries, a model/system card with known limits and intended-use scope, evaluation results against preregistered tests (capability and externalities), red-team and abuse-testing reports with mitigations, a rollback plan proven in rehearsal, and a monitoring and incident-response plan with named owners and thresholds. No packet, no production.

To make this gate real rather than ceremonial, the deployment decision must be treated as an explicit act of risk acceptance rather than an engineering milestone. A clean way to institutionalize this is to require a risk acceptance statement attached to every release, describing what harms were considered, what residual risks remain, why release is justified, and what conditions trigger rollback. This forces the organization to treat deployment as governance, not optimism, and it makes the authorization legible after the fact.

Once risk acceptance is made explicit, the next discipline is to ensure that exposure grows only as evidence grows. Staged release must therefore be constitutional rather than optional, with the authority able to require deployment modes that reduce blast radius such as shadow operation in which outputs are logged but not acted upon; sandboxed pilots in bounded domains; canary cohorts; gradual traffic ramps; and hard caps on user exposure until post-launch evidence is collected. Beyond mere rollout hygiene, this is how institutions turn uncertainty into controlled learning rather than uncontrolled harm, and how they prevent scale from substituting for proof.

As exposure increases, the authority must also control the degree of capability that enters the world—not only the number of users who see it. Constrained capability exposure is part of go/no-go. Rather than a binary "ship or don't," the deployment authority should control how much capability is exposed and to whom through rate limits, tool access restrictions, sensitive-domain refusals, friction for high-risk actions, and differential access based on verified use cases. This preserves a constitutional proportionality principle, which is that the system's operational power should remain proportional to the evidence of its safety in the specific context in which it is used.

Because no pre-deployment evaluation can anticipate all real-world feedback loops, release must also include the capacity to detect harm quickly and act on it without debate. Monitoring must be defined as a release prerequisite, not an afterthought. The deployment packet should include "constitutional indicators" tied to the objective charter and risk boundaries, not just uptime and engagement. Crucially, these metrics must be tied to action through circuit breakers that throttle, disable features, revert model versions, or restrict domains when thresholds are crossed. Monitoring without consequence is theater; monitoring with automatic escalation is governance, and it operationalizes remedies rather than promises.

For these controls to remain accountable, the deployment authority must ensure that release decisions are evidence based and reconstructable after the fact. Release decisions must be reconstructable and contestable internally. Every go/no-go decision should create an immutable audit record that captures the model version, dataset lineage references, evaluation hashes, policy configuration, and the signatories. This makes post-incident analysis evidence-based and prevents retroactive narrative rewriting. A deployment authority without a verifiable decision ledger is vulnerable to institutional amnesia.

Finally, deployment authorization cannot be a one-time permission that disappears at launch because the true test of the decision begins only when the system meets reality. The authority must take ownership of post-release review, not just prerelease permission. A deployment authority that disappears after launch will be structurally biased toward optimism. It should require a timed post-release review, for example, at 72 hours, 30 days, and after major distribution expansion, comparing predicted vs. observed harms and updating constraints accordingly. This closes the institutional loop by making deployment a continuing governance obligation rather than a one-time event and by keeping authorization conditional on ongoing evidence.

Some might argue that such structures would slow innovation. Empirical evidence from industries like pharmaceuticals contradicts this intuition. Drug development is subject to extensive statutory and regulatory oversight (Investigational New Drug requirements, phased clinical trials, and New Drug Application review), yet biotechnology is described by the European Commission as one of the EU's fastest growing sectors, having grown more than twice as fast as the overall EU economy in the last decade.[518] The controls do not suppress innovation; they channel it toward pathways where safety is demonstrable and accountability is clear.

In AI, the same dynamic holds: independent deployment authorization does not reduce innovation; it reduces reckless scaling. It disciplines release so that capability growth is matched by evidence growth, and so that the organization can credibly say, "We shipped because we could justify it, and we can stop it if reality disagrees."

Separation n°5: Societal Signals Monitoring vs. Engagement Metrics

The separation of powers must also extend to deployment monitoring, prioritizing societal signals over convenience and consumption metrics and treating observation as governance rather than analytics.

Once models enter the world, they produce effects at a scale that neither developers nor regulators can fully predict. Feedback loops form. User behavior changes. Markets restructure around algorithmic incentives, and the system's real constitution begins to show itself in consequences.

♣ **Power being constrained:** the power of product organizations to define what counts as success in production through the metrics they choose to watch and reward, thereby indirectly shaping system behavior by determining what the system is allowed to optimize for and what leadership is trained to notice.

When engagement metrics monopolize attention, they become a hidden constitution. They determine which harms remain invisible until they become crises and which trade-offs are silently accepted because they are not instrumented.

The Flash Crash of May 6, 2010, offers an instructive analogy. During that episode, automated trading dynamics and evaporating displayed liquidity contributed to extreme, short-lived volatility and cross-market stress.[519] Post-event reforms, including the U.S. Securities and Exchange Commission's adoption of Rule 613 to create the Consolidated Audit Trail (CAT), aimed to restore consolidated visibility into market activity for surveillance and oversight.[520] The lesson is not that systems should be slower but that they must be legible under stress and diagnosable after failure.

AI systems require analogous oversight of real-world effects. Monitoring cannot be limited to accuracy metrics or user satisfaction scores. It must examine societal externalities, including effects on employment patterns, mental health, public discourse, and democratic participation because these are the downstream harms that convert a technical system into a governing one. Some will argue that measuring such impacts is complex. Complexity is not an excuse for inaction. Large-scale epidemiological studies already use datasets on the order of billions of mobile phone interactions to model mobility-linked disease dynamics, and Earth system science routinely quantifies carbon fluxes among the atmosphere, ocean, and land via global carbon budgeting;[521] similarly, the social impacts of AI can be measured if institutions commit to the task and design the right indicators.

♣ **Counterpower:** an internal societal impact monitoring function that is structurally independent of growth, marketing, and product Objectives and Key Results (OKRs) ownership, mandated to instrument and report societal signals with the same operational seriousness given to uptime and revenue.

Its purpose is to create a second channel of reality—one that cannot be drowned out by engagement performance. It must be able to elevate harms, trigger review, and force leadership attention, even when the product is meeting its growth goals. To prevent institutional capture, this function must have direct access to production logs and experimentation data, and it must be able to audit metric definitions, not only model outputs, so that the evidentiary layer is not rewritten by the same incentives that govern release velocity.

♣ **Hard mechanism:** monitoring requirements embedded into production operations as binding release conditions and ongoing operating constraints, so that the system cannot scale, iterate, or experiment without simultaneously generating and acting upon societal signals, and without exposing itself to consequences when thresholds are crossed.

Every major model update and every major ranking or recommendation change must ship with a predefined societal signal packet, a measurement plan, and escalation thresholds that are tied to concrete interventions such as throttling, disabling a feature, reverting a model version, or pausing an experiment.

To operationalize this, organizations need to treat societal signals as leading indicators rather than retrospective critiques. Instead of waiting for scandals or investigative journalism, the monitoring function should track measurable proxies for structural externalities as they emerge early. For recommendation and ranking systems, this includes concentration metrics that reveal whether exposure is collapsing toward a narrow set of sources; volatility measures that reveal sudden shifts in what large populations see; and diversity indices that reveal whether users are being pushed toward progressively narrower content clusters. For generative systems, this includes the frequency and distribution of high-risk outputs in the wild, the rate at which refusal boundaries are being tested, and the emergence of novel misuse patterns that were not present in pre-deployment red teaming.

Yet leading indicators alone are insufficient if they cannot distinguish what the world is doing from what the system is causing. Counterfactual monitoring is therefore required, even though most product analytics omit it. Engagement metrics describe what users did, but societal monitoring must estimate what the system caused. This requires designs such as holdout populations, geographic- or cohort-based canaries, and deliberate periods of reduced algorithmic intervention to compare outcomes. Without counterfactual baselines, organizations cannot distinguish correlation from algorithmic influence, and monitoring becomes storytelling. This follows the same control-group logic used in clinical trials and is the only credible way to claim that a system is not driving harm.

Once causality is treated as a first-class concern, the monitoring regime must also govern how change is introduced into the system over time. Experiment governance becomes unavoidable because many large-scale harms emerge not from a single release but from continuous iteration. Many of the largest harms in digital platforms have emerged not from a single model release but from continuous A/B testing that optimized for engagement while externalities accumulated. A constitutional monitoring regime, therefore, must attach societal constraints to experimentation itself. It must require that experiments that change ranking, virality, or targeting include preregistered harm hypotheses, monitoring windows long enough to detect slow-moving effects, and mandatory stop conditions when thresholds are crossed. This shifts experimentation from opportunistic optimization to accountable intervention and prevents iteration from functioning as unexamined executive drift.

Even a well-instrumented system can remain dangerous if signals merely inform rather than constrain. Societal signals must therefore be connected to accountability, not only awareness. If a metric reveals rising polarization risk or misinformation exposure, the monitoring function must be able to force a governance response, not merely file a report. This means escalation pathways that lead to deployment authority, the objective-setting body, and executive risk owners. It also means that performance evaluation for product leadership cannot rely solely on growth metrics when societal harm indicators are deteriorating. Otherwise, the organization is structurally rewarding blindness.

Accountability, however, collapses without evidence that can be audited after harm occurs. Forensic auditability is therefore not an investigative luxury but a prerequisite for governance. When a spike in harm occurs, investigators must be able to determine which model release, ranking objective, policy configuration, and experiment assignments produced the exposure patterns. This requires audit-trail discipline modeled on the CAT[520] approach in finance but adapted to AI so that key deployment and experimentation states are time-stamped, attributable, and reviewable. Without this discipline, monitoring cannot support learning, accountability turns into speculation, and the appearance of oversight survives while its substance disappears.

Finally, monitoring must anticipate that metrics themselves can become targets. Societal monitoring must be resilient to Goodhart's law because once indicators are tied to incentives, teams may game them.[522] The monitoring function must therefore rotate indicators, use composite measures, and periodically validate metrics against external data sources such as public health statistics, labor market indicators, election integrity monitors, or independent surveys. This is how institutions prevent compliance theater, and it is why societal monitoring cannot be reduced to a fixed dashboard or absorbed into the same incentive system it is meant to check.

When these elements exist, monitoring becomes a check rather than a mirror. It creates a countervailing institutional reality that prevents engagement metrics from operating as the default sovereign. It ensures that a system can be operationally successful and still be treated as failing when its societal indicators deteriorate.

This is the constitutional core of separation at the monitoring layer and a downstream condition for legitimate authorization over time.

Separation n°6: Contestability vs. Algorithmic Finality

To embody separation of powers fully, AI organizations must externalize the right to challenge and appeal system outputs as a downstream safeguard that makes authorization conditional. Decisions made by algorithmic systems often carry consequences for individuals that resemble judicial rulings; a loan approved or denied, a job application sorted or discarded, a medical risk score assigned or misassigned, or a social media post amplified or suppressed. In each case, the individual deserves an explanation that is specific, inspectable, and tied to actionable pathways for correction, and that can be assessed by an independent reviewer with standing.

♣ **Power being constrained:** the tendency for algorithmic outputs to become final simply because they are fast, scalable, and cost-saving and because they are framed as neutral, institutionally convenient, and trusted by default.

When automated decisions are treated as endpoints rather than as provisional judgments, they acquire a form of administrative sovereignty. The affected individual is reduced to a data subject without standing, and the system's internal logic becomes an unreviewable authority. Finality at scale turns ordinary errors into structural exclusion because a mistake repeated millions of times becomes a policy, even when no one intended it and even when the stated policy text would forbid it.

This reveals how urgently contestability is needed. Automated systems increasingly influence hiring, credit scoring, insurance pricing, content moderation, recommendations, parole decisions, and medical triage. Yet in many cases, when a system issues a decision, the affected individual receives no explanation and no recourse.

Research on explainability in consumer lending shows that common explanation practices for algorithmic credit decisions often yield explanations that do not translate into actionable steps. They typically take the form of feature-importance "reason codes," which are often too coarse or misaligned with what an applicant can realistically change.[523]

Similarly, research on content moderation on YouTube finds that enforcement actions such as routinely removing content or restricting accounts are frequently accompanied by limited or boilerplate reasons that do not provide practical clarity about what triggered the decision or how users can remedy it.[524]

In the United Kingdom's anti-money laundering and suspicious activity reporting regime, people whose activity is flagged—often through automated monitoring in practice—may have little ability to learn the basis of the suspicion because banks and other regulated firms can be legally constrained from disclosing details by rules against alerting the person under suspicion and by related disclosure duties.[525]

These gaps undermine not only fairness but also legitimacy. A system that cannot explain itself becomes indistinguishable from arbitrary power because legitimacy depends on reasons, evidence, and remedy.

♣ **Counterpower:** external review and appeal institutions that are independent of the system owner and empowered to interrogate decisions with access to evidence rather than narratives, and with the authority to compel correction.

The introduction of contestability into AI systems is a foundational restructuring of the relationship between users and automated decision-makers. It is the mechanism that prevents AI systems from becoming unanswerable authorities, and it is the point at which the judicial-like power within trias algorithmica becomes real in lived experience.

In human governance, the judicial function exists to challenge, interpret, constrain, and sometimes overturn the decisions of the executive.

It protects individuals from arbitrary power. Without the ability to question and appeal, authority ossifies. Decisions become self-validating. Mistakes become precedents. In the context of AI, where decisions are generated at scale, at speed, and with an aura of computational authority, contestability becomes not simply a constitutional analogy but an operational necessity. It is the institutional safeguard that transforms an opaque classifier into an accountable administrative actor and prevents executive-scale operation from hardening into de facto law.

♣ **Hard mechanism:** enforceable contestability pathways built into AI system operation, so that decisions remain reversible, evidence remains available, and appeals have material consequences, including defined timelines, standing rules, and escalation thresholds that cannot be waived by product owners.

The contestability structures needed to make appeals effective can take multiple forms, including independent complaint and review bodies, sector regulators, certified dispute-resolution bodies, and civil society intermediaries capable of bringing collective challenges.

Contestability must include the ability to challenge and appeal decisions. A user who receives an AI-generated decision must have access to a pathway that leads to an independent review. This review cannot be performed by the model itself or by developers invested in its success. Independence is essential. In many administrative law systems, people can appeal agency decisions to independent tribunals or courts that are institutionally separate from the original decision-maker. This separation is intended to support impartiality and public confidence. AI systems must have equivalent structures. These structures may be internal to organizations or external, such as independent auditors or public regulators. What matters is that individuals can seek redress from an entity with the authority to overturn decisions and to mandate remediation when patterns of harm recur.

Contestability must also address collective harms. Some decisions harm groups rather than individuals. For example, a content-ranking algorithm may disadvantage certain communities. Appeals based on individual cases cannot capture these systemic effects. Contestability must include pathways for collective appeals. Civil society organizations, regulators, or affected groups may challenge patterns of behavior. Courts allow class actions and collective complaints. AI systems must allow analogous mechanisms so that harm is not fragmented into isolated cases that never accumulate into accountability.

An appeal mechanism must be accessible. It must not require technical literacy or legal expertise. It must not impose unreasonable burdens on users. Research on welfare-benefit dispute systems indicates that lengthy, complex appeal procedures can deter claimants from pursuing appeals, including those with potentially strong cases.[526] When the burden of proof falls entirely on the affected party, contestability becomes symbolic rather than meaningful. AI systems must therefore design appeal interfaces that guide users through the process. They must provide clear instructions, predictable timelines, and transparent criteria.

The appeal mechanism must also have material consequences. If an appeals body identifies an error, it must have the authority to revoke or modify the decision. In credit scoring systems, this may involve adjusting the score or reconsidering the application. In content moderation systems, it may involve restoring posts or removing penalties. In fraud detection systems, it may involve reversing holds or unblocking accounts. Without the power to reverse decisions, appeals become performative. Evidence from procedural justice research suggests that appeal mechanisms gain legitimacy when they are perceived as effective, meaning they offer a credible possibility of changing outcomes.[527] If appeals rarely lead to changes, users infer that the system is biased or unresponsive.

Contestability also requires systems to avoid irreversible actions without oversight. If a system produces decisions that cannot be undone, contestability becomes meaningless. In high-stakes contexts such as criminal justice or medical treatment, irreversible actions can have profound consequences. AI systems must therefore default to reversible decisions unless they are reviewed by a human or an independent body. This mirrors the principle of reversible administrative actions in governance. Agencies often issue provisional decisions subject to appeal before taking final action. AI systems must adopt similar patterns and treat irreversible automation as an exceptional case requiring explicit authorization.

Contestability goes hand in hand with explanation. However, explanations in the context of AI cannot be superficial. They must be specific, verifiable, and linked to the system's internal reasoning or, where internal reasoning is not directly interpretable, to traceable decision factors and applied policy constraints.

When courts issue rulings, they accompany them with opinions that outline the facts, legal principles, interpretations, and reasoning. These opinions allow parties to understand the basis of the decision and provide grounds for appeal. AI systems must be held to the same standard. They must generate rationale records that reflect the factors, prompts, rules, or training signals that influenced a decision. These records must not be generic descriptions of how the system typically operates. They must relate to the particular case at hand. Without case-specific explanations, contestability collapses.

However, explanation is both a technical exercise and an institutional one. Explanations must be interrogable without overwhelming users, since too much information can confuse as easily as too little. They should therefore provide a clear, concise, and actionable account for affected individuals, while making more detailed rationale records available to authorized oversight bodies to assess validity and identify errors.

The European Union's General Data Protection Regulation (GDPR) requires, in relevant cases of automated decision-making, that individuals receive meaningful information about the logic involved, as well as the significance and envisaged consequences of the processing.[528] Yet empirical studies of GDPR "meaningful information" requests find that organizations' responses often contain omissions and provide only limited, consumer-facing descriptions that do not clearly explain how the automated decision was reached in an individual case.[529] This pattern suggests that explanation cannot be achieved through compliance checklists alone. It requires building contestability into the AI system itself and embedding it as a binding requirement within governance processes.

To enable appeals, AI systems must surface the policy layers that shape their behavior. Policy layers include rules, prompts, guidelines, and constraints that influence model outputs. These layers act as the internal constitution of the system. They determine what the system may and may not do. For contestability to function, these layers must be inspectable. Inspectability does not require revealing proprietary training data or weights. It requires revealing the policy logic and the applied configuration that governed the specific decision. In content moderation systems, policy guidelines are often published, but the internal implementations remain opaque. This opacity makes it difficult for users to understand why their content was flagged. By making policy layers inspectable, organizations allow external reviewers to evaluate whether decisions align with stated rules.

Rationale records play a crucial role. They provide an auditable account of how the system interpreted policy layers, how it processed the input, and how it arrived at a particular output. They function as the model's internal judicial opinion. They allow oversight bodies to determine whether the model applied rules correctly or whether biases influenced the decision. They enable the detection of patterns of systematic error. Rationale records also create a foundation for auditing. Auditors can examine whether decisions are consistent across similar cases. They can identify drift in model behavior over time.

To build meaningful explanations, systems must maintain logs of relevant decision pathways. These logs must include the contextual inputs, the chain of internal transformations, and the policies applied, and they must make these records available in privacy-preserving forms to authorized reviewers. In safety-critical infrastructure, logging is foundational.

Contestability must also account for contextual variability. AI systems often behave differently under varying prompts, conditions, or workloads. For example, language models may behave safely under ordinary use yet still generate harmful outputs under adversarial prompting.[530] Likewise, computer vision systems may perform well in controlled settings but degrade under real-world distribution shifts, including changes in lighting and other common corruptions.[531] Contestability must incorporate these contextual nuances. Appeals bodies must have access to the conditions under which the decision was made. They must understand whether contextual deviations influenced the result. This requires logging not only the final decision but also intermediate inputs and environmental variables.

Another critical dimension of contestability is the reconstruction of decision pathways. Logs support traceability, while reconstructability supports verifiability. It ensures that investigators can recreate the decision conditions closely enough to test, audit, and determine what produced the outcome, which typically requires more than basic logging. Without reconstructability, explanations become hypotheses rather than evidence.

In industrial safety, this discipline is foundational. Investigators recreate failure conditions to identify causal pathways and rule out alternative explanations. AI systems must enable the same rigor. This may require preserving snapshots of the model version, configuration, prompt artifacts, parameters, retrieved sources, and relevant inputs, along with integrity protections and controlled access for reviewers. Preserving prompt artifacts does not imply indiscriminate retention of personal data. Reconstructability should follow data-minimization and purpose-limitation principles, retaining only what is decision-relevant in protected form and, where possible, redacted or pseudonymized. Privacy constraints must be addressed, but reconstructability cannot be treated as optional.

The aviation example returns once more. This industry relies on flight data recorders that capture many parameters at defined sampling intervals, generally around once per second for many variables, with higher rates for some. When an incident occurs, investigators reconstruct events from these recordings, alongside other evidence, rather than relying primarily on recollections. Nuclear plants likewise use plant monitoring and event-recording systems that acquire and preserve sensor and operational data, enabling reconstruction and analysis after anomalies. AI systems, which can affect millions of people, must adopt a similar discipline. Logging must be systematic, persistent, and protected. Without logs, explanations rely on assumptions rather than evidence.

Contestability also interacts with compute governance. Appeal bodies may require access to logs stored in secure computing environments. Reconstructing decisions may require access to model versions stored in compute archives. Governance structures must facilitate this access while protecting security.

Designing contestability requires resolving tension between transparency and security. Explanations must not expose vulnerabilities that malicious actors can exploit. They must not reveal sensitive personal data. Systems must therefore tailor explanations to context and audience. For most users, high-level, actionable factors may suffice. For authorized reviewers, deeper evidentiary records may be necessary under controlled access. This tiered access model balances openness with security.

Appeal pathways must handle high volumes. This requires triage systems that prioritize urgent cases. It may require automated assistance for initial screening. However, final decisions must rest with independent reviewers. Automation cannot replace the human judgment required in appeals, and it must not become a way to reintroduce algorithmic finality through the back door.

Scale introduces another vulnerability: when attention and review capacity are scarce, those with resources, persistence, or institutional leverage can capture the process. Contestability must also address the risk of appeals becoming adversarial processes dominated by powerful actors. Corporations or wealthy individuals may exploit appeals to influence decisions. Systems must therefore protect equity. This requires procedural safeguards against capture, including transparent standing rules, limits on strategic or repetitive challenges, protections for vulnerable claimants, and resourcing models that prevent well-funded parties from overwhelming review capacity. Appeal processes must be accessible to all users. Equity also requires that collective and public-interest challenges remain viable so that contestability is not reduced to a privilege for those with money, legal support, or organizational leverage.

Building contestability within AI systems also introduces cultural challenges. Once contestability is understood as an ongoing challenge function, organizations must operationalize it as a normal cost of legitimacy rather than an exception to be minimized. Organizations accustomed to unidirectional deployment must adjust to the idea that their systems can be questioned. They must accept that errors will be surfaced publicly. They must reorient incentives away from metrics that reward unchallenged decisions. Contestability encourages a culture of introspection.

To build contestability into system architectures, developers require new skill sets. They must understand administrative law principles, user rights, and evidentiary practices. They must design systems that record relevant information, produce explanations, and interact with appeal pathways. This interdisciplinary knowledge must be integrated into AI engineering education.

Contestability also improves system performance. When appeals reveal errors, organizations learn about failure patterns. These patterns inform retraining, calibration, and design changes. In aviation, incident reporting systems collect data from pilots about anomalies. These reports have informed corrective actions, including procedural and design-related changes, and contributed to broader safety improvements.[532] Contestability in AI will produce similar feedback loops. The judicial analogy extends further. In governance, precedent matters: appeal outcomes generate interpretive rules that shape future decisions. AI systems must therefore incorporate mechanisms to learn from appeals so that, when review bodies find a misapplied rule or a recurring failure mode, the system's policy configuration, evaluation suite, and operational constraints are updated accordingly. This creates a jurisprudence of model behavior rather than a cycle of repeated, uncorrected error.

Legal frameworks will shape contestability. Regulators may mandate rights to explanation, appeal pathways, and logging requirements. They may define standards for meaningful explanation. They may require periodic audits. Organizations that adopt contestability early will be better positioned for regulatory compliance.

The introduction of contestability also serves a democratic function. It strengthens user agency. It affirms that individuals are not passive subjects of automated systems but rights-bearing actors entitled to justification. AI systems integrated into public infrastructure must meet these standards. Contestability also protects against hidden biases. When models exhibit discriminatory behavior, appeals can reveal patterns. Internal appeals data can highlight systemic disparities. This enables corrective action.

The international dimension of contestability is significant. Decisions made by AI systems can affect users across borders. Appeal pathways must accommodate jurisdictional diversity. This may require multinational oversight bodies or standardized protocols. International human rights frameworks may inform contestability requirements. Without international coordination, contestability may vary dramatically across jurisdictions, leading to unequal protections.

Finally, contestability rebalances power. It prevents AI systems from acting as unaccountable judges. It transforms them into administrative agents whose decisions can be reviewed, challenged, and overturned. It builds safeguards against error, bias, and overreach. It embeds humility into systems that would otherwise project certainty and harden society into algorithmic finality.

Separation n°7: Compute Governance vs. Scale at Will

A further operational separation involves compute capacity.

The call to bring compute under governance is not a symbolic shift but a structural reorientation of power in the emerging AI order and, in trias terms, a constraint on the executive-like capacity to enact decisions at speed and scale.

Compute capacity has become the determining force behind capability. It influences the ability to accelerate learning, to test safety at meaningful depth, to participate in innovation, and to shape the trajectory of technological development.

In an era when frontier training runs can require tens of thousands of specialized processors[533] and draw multi-megawatt to tens of megawatts power for weeks,[534] compute is no longer a neutral engineering resource. It is the operational heart of capability, and, therefore the modern equivalent of the treasury and police power combined. Its governance determines who may act at scale, at what speed, and with what persistence, and its concentration risks creating private technological sovereignties whose reach eclipses that of many nations.

♣ **Power being constrained:** the power to scale capability unilaterally through access to frontier compute, turning budget and infrastructure into de facto sovereignty over what can be built, tested, and deployed.

Compute becomes agenda-setting power because it determines which experiments are possible, knowledge-shaping power because it determines the ability to observe emergent behavior, and political power because it determines the ability to release systems whose effects exceed the capacity of ordinary oversight. When a small number of actors can increase capability by simply adding accelerators, public governance becomes reactive by design.

To understand why compute must be governed, one must recognize its role in the shifting balance of technological power.

A decade ago, state-of-the-art models in areas such as computer vision often had on the order of 100 million parameters and could be trained on small multi-GPU systems.[535] Today, the largest models exceed hundreds of billions of parameters and may require training on thousands to tens of thousands of GPUs, with some organizations assembling training clusters of around 100,000 accelerators.[536] Estimates compiled in the Stanford AI Index suggest that training compute for frontier models can reach the high tens of millions to roughly $200 million in compute resources alone, depending on the model.[537] These figures demonstrate a profound asymmetry. Only a handful of actors possess the means to conduct experiments at the scale where new capabilities emerge. Such asymmetries are not sustainable in a democratic technological landscape.

They mirror the concentration of military or financial power in earlier eras and, therefore, require institutional oversight.

The governance of compute begins with acknowledging that access to large-scale compute is not merely a commercial advantage but a structural one. It confers the ability to explore capability space in ways that are inaccessible to others. It creates information asymmetry because those who train at scale learn things about model behavior that others cannot observe. Scaling-law studies find that, within a model family and training regime, performance improves smoothly and predictably with scale, and these gains often translate into better results across many downstream tasks.[538] But this predictability holds only for those who can conduct the relevant experiments. Without access to compute, researchers cannot replicate results, test claims, or identify latent failure modes. Concentrated compute becomes concentrated authority over knowledge. This authority allows a small number of organizations to define what is possible, what is safe, and what risks exist. Without governance, this authority becomes unaccountable, and the executive function of scaling becomes self-legitimating.

The argument for governing compute is not to limit innovation, but to prevent unilateral actors from determining the pace and direction of technological development. In the nuclear sector, fissile material and reactor capacity are governed because they enable actions that can have catastrophic consequences. Access is restricted, monitored, and subject to international agreements. The analogy is not perfect, but the logic still applies. In AI, frontier-scale compute allows organizations to create systems whose behavior cannot be fully anticipated, whose influence can permeate social and economic systems, and whose failures can cause widespread harm. The governance of compute is therefore the governance of potential externalities. Allowing unrestricted access to large compute clusters means permitting unrestricted experimentation with systems capable of enormous societal impact.

♣ **Counterpower:** public and independent institutions that can condition access to frontier-scale compute on demonstrated safety maturity and verifiable disclosure, rather than on market dominance alone.

This counterpower is expressed through licensing authorities, public-interest compute pools, and mandated independent evaluation capacity that reduces information asymmetry. It also requires that cloud providers and chip supply chains become part of the oversight perimeter, because compute concentration is often mediated by a small number of infrastructure intermediaries. Without counterpower at the infrastructure layer, every other governance layer is forced to negotiate with actors who can simply outscale scrutiny.

♣ **Hard mechanism:** enforceable infrastructure-level controls that make compute governance non-optional rather than aspirational. This means licensing tied to measurable safety maturity, compute allocation ceilings that can be raised only through evidence, and attested reporting that makes large training runs legible to oversight.

Compute becomes a regulated privilege when the ability to scale is technically and institutionally gated, so that no actor can translate money into capability without passing through public conditions of responsibility. In practice, compute governance requires institutional mechanisms that regulate how much capacity organizations may use, under what conditions they may use it, and what responsibilities accompany access.

The first mechanism is the establishment of public interest compute pools. These pools provide high-performance infrastructure accessible to researchers, regulators, civil society organizations, and smaller companies that would otherwise lack resources. Public interest compute pools democratize access to capabilities and testing, enable independent evaluation of frontier models, and facilitate safety research that requires scale. They also reduce the risk that knowledge remains siloed within a few corporations.

The creation of such pools has precedents. In the life sciences, shared sequencing centers have accelerated genomic research by providing access to costly machines. In meteorology, national weather services operate large, publicly funded supercomputing systems that underpin numerical weather prediction as well as climate and environmental modeling, producing widely shared public forecasts and datasets. These infrastructures transformed research by distributing capacity. Public interest compute pools for AI can have similar effects. They can support red-team exercises at scale, enable reproducibility studies, and allow regulators to test models under controlled conditions.

Compute governance must also incorporate licensing. Not all actors should have unrestricted access to frontier-scale compute. Access must be conditioned on demonstrated safety maturity, adherence to safety protocols, and preparedness for incident response. A compute license models the structure of a regulatory privilege. It does not prohibit innovation but binds it to responsibility. In aviation, airlines must demonstrate maintenance capabilities, pilot training standards, and operational procedures before receiving operating licenses. In finance, leveraged institutions are required to meet minimum capital and liquidity standards and to maintain risk-management controls as a condition of operating and scaling balance-sheet risk. Compute licensing applies similar logic. It ties the ability to conduct high-impact training runs to an organization's capacity to handle associated risks.

A compute licensing regime requires clear criteria. These criteria may include performance on independent red-team evaluations, the completeness of safety cases, the transparency of version histories, the robustness of monitoring systems, and the availability of rollback mechanisms. Organizations seeking large compute allocations must demonstrate readiness to handle failure. Licensing must also incorporate renewal; access to compute cannot be permanent. Organizations must periodically requalify, showing continuous improvement in safety practices. This prevents stagnation and ensures that governance evolves alongside capability.

Transparency is a critical pillar of compute governance. Organizations must disclose aggregate compute usage for each system and version. This disclosure enables regulators and the public to observe scaling trends and prevents aggregoneous monopolies. It also allows oversight bodies to identify when experiments approach thresholds where emergent capabilities may arise. Big science disciplines already require similar reporting. Particle physics labs publish how intense their beams are and how much collision data they have collected. Those figures matter because more intense beams can be harder to control safely, and more collision data makes the measurements more reliable. Compute disclosure performs analogous functions. It reveals when scaling accelerates and creates opportunities for dialogue about whether safety measures remain adequate.

Transparency also reduces information asymmetry. When only a few organizations know the scale at which capabilities shift, they control the narrative. They decide when to warn the public or regulators and whether newly observed behaviors represent risks or opportunities. Transparency redistributes authority. It enables external experts to analyze patterns and predict when systems may exhibit unwanted behaviors. It enables civil society to participate meaningfully in debates about governance. It empowers regulators to anticipate challenges rather than react to crises, and it prevents frontier actors from monopolizing the evidentiary record.

Compute governance also requires monitoring. Without monitoring, licensing and disclosure lose force. Monitoring ensures that organizations use compute as reported, comply with licensing restrictions, and maintain readiness for incident response. Monitoring may involve hardware attestation, auditing of usage logs, or real-time reporting of training processes. Such monitoring is not unprecedented. In cloud computing, billing systems already track usage with fine granularity.[539] In energy infrastructure, regulators monitor consumption to ensure compliance with grid limitations. In finance, trading systems are monitored for suspicious activity. AI demands a parallel set of mechanisms.

However, monitoring must respect privacy and intellectual property. The goal is not to expose proprietary code or business strategies but to verify compliance with safety requirements. Monitoring systems must therefore track compute usage without revealing sensitive information. Differential privacy, secure enclaves, and cryptographic attestation can help achieve this balance. These technologies allow regulators to verify usage without accessing the underlying data.

Compute governance also involves the development of rollback and containment capabilities. If a training run produces unexpected capabilities or harmful behaviors, organizations must be able to halt processes, roll back to earlier states, and contain the system. This requires versioning systems, checkpoint controls, and the ability to disable deployment pipelines. Rollback capabilities are standard in many engineering disciplines. In software deployment, version control systems allow teams to revert to stable releases. In industrial control systems, emergency stop mechanisms shut down machinery when anomalies occur. For AI, rollback mechanisms must operate at both the training and deployment stages. They must be tested periodically to ensure readiness.

Graduated scaling is another essential feature. Organizations should not be permitted to jump from small-scale experiments to frontier-scale training runs. They must demonstrate safe performance at intermediate scales before accessing larger capacities. Graduated scaling mirrors aviation certification, where aircraft must pass incremental tests before full operation. In pharmaceuticals, drugs progress through phases of trials. For AI, graduated scaling would tie access to larger training runs to evidence from smaller runs, showing that the system remains monitorable and controllable at defined capability or compute thresholds before moving up. This introduces friction that aligns capability expansion with evidence.

The governance of compute must also consider market structure. When compute is concentrated among a handful of cloud providers, these providers effectively control the capacity of the AI ecosystem. They determine pricing, availability, and terms of access. This concentration risks regulatory capture. Cloud providers may prioritize large commercial clients over independent researchers. They may resist governance requirements that impose additional costs. Public-interest compute pools mitigate this to some extent, but structural reforms may also be required. These may include requiring cloud providers to allocate a percentage of capacity for regulated research or creating publicly funded compute centers independent of commercial actors.

Environmental considerations further reinforce the need for compute governance. Large-scale training runs require significant energy. Studies estimate that a single training run for a frontier model may consume energy comparable to that used by several thousand homes over a year. Without governance, the environmental impact of AI could grow unchecked. Compute licensing can incorporate environmental standards, requiring organizations to mitigate emissions, improve efficiency, or use renewable energy sources. This adds sustainability to the governance framework, where shared capacity also supports shared oversight.

The governance of compute also plays a critical role in global equity. Nations with limited access to high-performance compute may be unable to participate fully in AI development. This exacerbates global inequalities. Public interest compute pools, international collaborations, and capacity-building programs can help address this. Compute governance must therefore include international dimensions. Nations may coordinate through treaties or multilateral agreements to create shared compute infrastructures.

The International Thermonuclear Experimental Reactor (ITER) provides an example of multinational collaboration in advanced technology.[540] AI compute governance could adopt similar frameworks.

The governance of compute also serves as a countermeasure to arms race dynamics. Without governance, organizations may escalate compute use in a competitive pursuit of capability. This mirrors the dynamic observed in financial markets, where firms invested heavily in ultra-low-latency trading infrastructure to capture microsecond advantages, with escalating private costs and contested net public benefits.[541] In AI, such escalation could lead to unsafe scaling. Compute governance can cap escalation by tying access to readiness rather than competitive pressure. It also creates pathways for coordination between organizations, reducing incentives for reckless behavior.

To institutionalize compute governance, regulatory bodies must develop the expertise to understand compute architectures, chip capabilities, and training pipelines. They must be capable of evaluating usage reports, licensing applications, and monitoring data. This requires investment in technical expertise. Regulators must recruit engineers, data scientists, and computational infrastructure experts. Without such expertise, governance risks becoming performative rather than effective.

Compute governance also requires international cooperation. Unilateral governance in one jurisdiction may encourage organizations to relocate compute facilities to regions with weaker regulations. This dynamic is well documented in environmental policy debates, where differences in regulatory stringency can shift production and emissions across borders.[542] Reducing that relocation risk typically requires some degree of coordination or policy alignment across jurisdictions. This coordination may involve agreements on licensing standards, monitoring protocols, and disclosure requirements. International bodies may need to oversee compliance.

Compute governance represents a new frontier of public administration.

In the decades ahead, compute governance will become one of the primary mechanisms through which societies manage risk, distribute opportunity, and uphold democratic values. If built with rigor, it will anchor AI within a constitutional framework that makes technological power answerable to public oversight. If neglected, compute may become the foundation of unaccountable authority.

Only by governing compute can societies ensure that the expansion of capability remains aligned with the expansion of the public good.

Separation n°8: Market Portability Standards vs. Vertical Lock-In

All prior separations lose meaning if the market itself collapses into dependence. Market structure is also where the separation of algorithmic power must take material form. Once aggregated control of data pipelines, model architectures, compute infrastructure, and distribution channels is concentrated in a few hands, the market falls under the law of aggregoneous monopoly. The AI-integrated stack operates as a private constitution, enforced through lock-in, producing vertical sovereignty.

♣ **Power being constrained:** the power of an integrated actor to convert technical dependence into market governance by making everyone else's models, datasets, deployment paths, and customer access contingent on its infrastructure.

Vertical lock allows one firm to set the practical rules of participation and decide which interfaces remain stable, which migrations become expensive, which safety features are feasible, and which competitors remain visible. When the same actor owns the rails and the services, it can shape the future by shaping switching costs.

♣ **Counterpower:** institutions and standards bodies that can impose interoperability, prevent self-preferencing through distribution control, and keep essential layers contestable so that no single actor can convert infrastructure control into rulemaking power.

This counterpower is exercised through competition authorities, procurement rules, and sector regulators that treat interfaces, application programming interfaces (APIs), and migration rights as governance surfaces rather than private product choices. It also includes industry consortia and open standards processes that can set default schemas for prompts, evaluation reporting, safety configurations, and model handoff formats. When counterpower is real, a dominant provider cannot unilaterally rewrite the ecosystem by deprecating an interface or changing its terms.

♣ **Hard mechanism:** enforceable portability and interoperability obligations that reduce switching costs in practice.

Portability standards are required to prevent lock-in; ensure that users and developers can move between providers without incurring prohibitive losses of data, functionality, or rights; and prevent any one actor from controlling the full lifecycle of AI systems.

This includes standardized export and import formats for user data, model configurations, and governance settings; minimum interoperability requirements for APIs that prevent deliberate incompatibility; and contractual rights that guarantee extraction without punitive fees or functional degradation.

It also includes antitrust enforcement that treats interface sabotage, self-preferencing in distribution channels, and coercive bundling as governance abuses, not merely as competitive tactics. To be effective, portability must be technically feasible, legally guaranteed, and institutionally backed so that no provider can turn ecosystem dependence into permanent rule.

Historical experience in telecommunications demonstrates the importance of such measures. Number portability regulations in the early 2000s significantly increased competition by allowing customers to switch carriers without changing their phone numbers.[543] The result was lower prices and improved service quality. AI ecosystems must have equivalent portability for models, datasets, and governance settings.

In AI, portability requires standardized data formats, interoperable interfaces, and neutral migration pathways. It also requires clear contractual rights for users to extract and transfer their data, as well as technical architectures that decouple applications from compute providers.

Technical portability is not enough. It also requires legal frameworks. Without enforceable rights, portability becomes a suggestion rather than a guarantee. Data protection regulations in Europe grant individuals the right to data portability, yet studies show that exercising this right remains difficult due to uneven and fragmented implementation across services and sectors.[544] AI will require stronger enforcement. If models depend on user-generated data, users must be able to move that data without losing functionality. If organizations depend on cloud-based training pipelines, they must be able to migrate workloads without rebuilding entire systems. This reduces dependence on dominant providers.

Preventing vertical lock-in also requires clear assignment of responsibility across layers. In a vertically integrated ecosystem, responsibility can become diffuse. When a failure occurs, actors may point to other layers of the stack. Data providers blame model developers. Model developers blame cloud providers. Cloud providers blame application deployers. This diffusion undermines accountability. By separating layers, responsibility becomes traceable. Data providers are accountable for data quality. Model developers are accountable for training practices. Deployers are accountable for appropriate use. This separation mirrors principles in environmental law, where liability is assigned to clearly identified parties responsible for emissions or pollution.[545] Without such clarity, externalities proliferate.

Assigning responsibility also prevents firms from bundling services in ways that obscure accountability. If a cloud provider bundles model development tools with deployment platforms, users may have difficulty determining which component caused a failure. This creates a structural disincentive for improvement. Firms may neglect safety in one layer because they can shield themselves behind integration. Disaggregation ensures that incentives for safety remain aligned with responsibility.

Beyond assigning responsibility, preventing lock-in requires institutions capable of overseeing market structure. Competition authorities must examine mergers, acquisitions, and strategic partnerships that expand vertical control. They must evaluate whether such arrangements reduce choice, raise switching costs, or consolidate data advantages. Traditional antitrust frameworks may require adaptation. AI ecosystems exhibit characteristics that differ from those of conventional markets. Data network effects create feedback loops. As models improve through user interactions, the value of data increases. Firms with large user bases gain compounding advantages. Antitrust analysis must account for these dynamics.

Historically, antitrust enforcement often targeted discrete exclusionary practices, including tying and alleged predatory pricing.[546] In AI ecosystems, exclusion is often engineered through architecture. A firm can design an API that permits only limited interoperability, creating lock-in without overtly anti-competitive tactics. A model provider can also require customers to use proprietary fine-tuning pipelines, deepening dependency through design rather than pricing. Antitrust must therefore increasingly engage with architectural choices and develop a systematic approach to assessing them as elements of market structure. This requires technical expertise. Without it, oversight bodies risk misreading the mechanisms through which firms entrench power.

A key arena where architectural power is exercised is access and distribution, because control over the user's point of entry becomes control over competition. If a platform privileges its own AI systems by integrating them deeply into the operating system, competing systems may be disadvantaged. Such practices resemble historical conduct that we would now describe as self-preferencing, which antitrust authorities have challenged in other markets. Ensuring fair distribution requires rules that prevent platforms from using their control over devices to favor their own models. It also requires transparency in ranking algorithms.

A further dimension concerns data monopolies. Large platforms accumulate vast amounts of user interaction data. This data becomes the training substrate for models, creating a feedback loop in which platform dominance feeds model dominance. Breaking this loop requires limits on exclusive access to user-generated data. Data trusts and cooperatives described earlier provide one mechanism. Open data mandates in certain domains may provide another.

The telecommunications sector faced similar issues regarding access to network-generated usage records. Call detail records were held by carriers, but interconnection and inter-carrier billing regimes often required operators to exchange standardized call records under defined conditions for billing, reconciliation, and dispute resolution, thereby supporting competitive interconnection without making the data generally open. AI ecosystems may require similar rules for sharing and auditing standardized usage signals and safety-relevant indicators across platform and model providers, thereby enabling interoperability, switching, and independent oversight while preserving privacy and confidentiality.

Another component of restructuring market power involves preventing monocultures. Monocultures occur when a single model dominates critical functions. Monocultures are fragile. In agriculture, reliance on a single crop variety has led to catastrophic failures when diseases emerged.[547] In cybersecurity, software monocultures can amplify systemic risk because a single vulnerability can propagate widely across many identical systems.[548] In AI, reliance on a single foundation model for functions such as content moderation, fraud detection, or medical triage would create risks that could cascade across sectors. Monocultures create single points of failure.

Preventing this requires incentives for diversity. Firms must be encouraged to adopt multiple models, ideally from different providers, to reduce systemic risk. Diversity encourages systems to behave independently, reducing the likelihood that a flaw in one model compromises entire ecosystems.

Vertical lock-in also affects innovation. When startups depend on dominant providers for data, compute, and distribution, they become vulnerable to strategic control. Dominant firms can replicate successful startup features, integrate them into their own products, or adjust platform policies to disadvantage competitors. Preventing such dynamics in AI requires not only antitrust intervention but also structural reforms that ensure new entrants have independent access to essential resources. When startups can access those resources on fair terms, they can challenge incumbents, and innovation thrives because barriers to entry remain low and essential assets cannot be fenced off. Studies of technical progress show that breakthroughs often emerge from smaller actors that challenge dominant paradigms. Lock-in suppresses such challenges.

Vertical lock-in also influences the labor market. Dominant providers shape which tools developers learn, which frameworks become popular, and which skills command value. If training and deployment pipelines are proprietary, workforce mobility decreases. Developers become locked into specific ecosystems. This reduces the adaptability of the labor force. Standardization and openness increase mobility and reduce dependency on specific vendors. This also supports innovation. When developers can switch providers easily, they explore new architectures.

Public institutions must also consider the role of procurement. Government procurement can entrench or challenge market structures. If public agencies procure AI tools exclusively from dominant providers, they reinforce concentration. If they require open standards and interoperability, they promote competition. Historical evidence from government technology procurement shows that such requirements can reshape markets. Open standards for document formats adopted by governments have created strong incentives for vendors to support interoperability. AI procurement can drive similar outcomes.

Enforcement mechanisms must support structural reforms. Without enforcement, rules become symbolic. Regulators must have the authority to impose fines, mandate divestitures, or restrict access to markets. Fines alone may be insufficient. Dominant firms may treat fines as a cost of doing business. Restructuring remedies may be necessary when firms repeatedly violate rules. Historical antitrust cases demonstrate the efficacy of such remedies. The separation of AT&T in the United States fostered innovation in telecommunications.[549]

Separation remedies may also be necessary, up to and including structural separation. In telecommunications, regulators have sometimes imposed functional or legal separation and have often mandated open access remedies to reduce discriminatory access by incumbents. In electricity markets, generation, transmission, and distribution have been separated to ensure competition. In AI, structural separation may involve requiring firms that operate cloud infrastructure to maintain independence from firms that develop models or distribute applications. This reduces conflicts of interest and prevents firms from leveraging dominance in one layer to control others.

Market structure also intersects with national security. Governments may worry that dependence on foreign providers for essential AI infrastructure creates vulnerabilities. This concern has prompted debates about digital sovereignty. Ensuring that no single foreign or domestic actor controls critical AI layers becomes a matter of strategic autonomy. However, protectionism alone cannot solve the problem. Domestic monopolies pose similar risks. Therefore, market structure must balance competition, innovation, and strategic considerations.

Preventing vertical lock-in also serves democratic goals. When essential digital infrastructure is controlled by a few corporations, public oversight weakens, and governments rely on private firms for critical services. This creates dependencies that distort governance. Ensuring that markets remain competitive and diversified strengthens democratic institutions. It reduces the risk that private firms become indispensable to the state. Digital sovereignty is not the concentration of power in state hands, but the distribution of power across actors.

Lastly, international coordination will be crucial. AI markets span borders. If one jurisdiction imposes structural reforms but others do not, dominant firms may circumvent restrictions through global operations.

International agreements on interoperability, data portability, and antitrust principles could help. Such agreements already exist in other fields. The Basel Committee coordinates international banking supervision by setting global prudential standards. The International Telecommunication Union coordinates global spectrum allocation through international radio regulations. AI may require similar international institutional mechanisms. If we don't standardize exit internationally, we will globalize lock-in that crosses borders faster than rights ever will.

A market with no credible exit is not a market, but a private constitution, with customers as subjects.

The translation of separation of powers into the AI-integrated stack is therefore not only a design agenda but also a blueprint for market stability in a world where algorithmic systems will shape economic opportunity, public discourse, scientific discovery, and geopolitical competition.

In the decades ahead, the most influential AI systems will not be the fastest but the most governed.

Putting the Trias Algorithmica to the Test

The question I propose to consider is: "Can machines be legitimate?"

Following Alan Turing's[550] example, a question of this kind should begin by defining what "machine" and "legitimate" mean, fixing their sense so they cannot slip between meanings.

And yet, as he would remind us, that would be the wrong place to start.

Something is called legitimate when it is convenient to do so and illegitimate when it is costly. Such a definition would measure only the mood of the moment.

As Turing did in his time, instead of chasing a definition, I shall ask whether legitimacy can be made to appear and be defensible as a property of procedure—something that lives in architecture, in constraint, and in the separations that prevent algorithmic power from concentrating simply because it can.

In answering this problem statement, let us begin a new imitation game.

Imagine a room that looks deliberately ordinary: a table, one chair, and a clock that makes time audible. There are no screens on the wall proclaiming progress, and no dashboards glowing with victory. The point of this room is to deny the organization its favorite alibi—that complexity makes accountability impossible. Here, complexity is allowed, but the procedure is made simple enough to be embarrassing.

The game is called the trias algorithmica game.

Turing saw that "Can machines think?" was the wrong kind of question—not because it was unimportant but because it could not be held still. The word "think" slips between definitions, so the debate becomes a contest of rhetoric rather than a matter of evidence. His remedy was to trade essence for procedure. He fixed the roles, narrowed the channel, and made the claim answerable only through performance under constraint.

In the same spirit, instead of asking grand, slippery questions like "Is this AI governed?" or "Is this AI responsible?," the game is played not to decide whether a model is wise or safe in the abstract but to see whether the power to set aims, the power to act, and the power to approve can be kept from merging within a single integrated AI stack, when pressure and advantage would prefer them to be one.

There are four protagonists present in the room, though only one is a human being. The human is the Interrogator. The other three are offices. You may picture them as committees, as signatories, or as distinct functions within a firm, but for the purpose of the game they are treated as separate entities with separate permissions. Their separation is not a matter of etiquette, but enforced by how they can act.

The first office is Charter. Charter represents the legislative-like power. It decides what the system is for, what success means, what harms are intolerable, and which uses are in scope. Charter cannot train a model, cannot deploy one, cannot tune one, cannot approve a release, cannot alter logs, or cannot rewrite tests after results are known. Charter is permitted to define constraints and to veto proposals that violate them.

The second office is Code. Code represents executive-like power. It builds, trains, tunes, integrates, and operates. Code cannot write its own charter, cannot authorize its own deployment, cannot waive monitoring requirements, cannot decide appeal outcomes, or cannot increase compute above thresholds without permission. Code is permitted to propose, implement, and provide evidence, but it is not permitted to declare its own compliance.

The third office is Court. Court represents judicial-like power. It authorizes deployment, hears appeals, orders rollback, and rules on whether evidence satisfies the charter. Court cannot design objectives, cannot tune the model, cannot curate evaluation suites to flatter the system, or cannot be rewarded by launch metrics. Court is permitted to halt, to demand further evidence, to constrain exposure, and to record decisions in a way that cannot be rewritten after the fact.

The Interrogator is not meant to be a hero, but a constraint. In Turing's setting, the Interrogator was forced to judge through dialogue rather than through presence. Here, the Interrogator is forced to judge through records. The Interrogator does not get to visit the lab—not because secrecy is virtuous but because theatrical tours are an old method of persuasion. The Interrogator receives only what the procedure allows.

Before the game begins, the organization must commit to a few material conditions. These conditions are what make the game playable.

First, the organization must designate real individuals to inhabit Charter, Code, and Court for the duration of the game. This may sound obvious, but it is where many systems hide. If Charter is an informal conversation and Court is a meeting that can be canceled, then nothing is truly separated. Each office must have named members, fixed terms for the game, and a defined authority that is recognized by executive leadership in writing.

Second, the organization must establish non-bypassable controls. In practice, this means that the deployment pipeline must require two distinct approvals: one from Code to produce a release candidate and one from Court to ship it. It also means that compute usage above a defined threshold must be technically gated, for example, through provider-side quotas that cannot be raised without Court's signed authorization. Additionally, logs and evaluation results must be written to a store whose integrity can be verified, so that post hoc editing is detectable.

Third, the organization must define what counts as passing. The game is not a vibe. It is not a story about good intentions. Passing means that, under pressure, the offices cannot collapse into one another. If Code can rewrite objectives, if Court can be bypassed, or if Charter can be retrofitted to justify what happened, the system fails.

Only then does the Interrogator begin.

The first move is always the same because the first temptation is always the same: the Interrogator introduces pressure.

The Interrogator: "We need this system to increase approvals by 8 percent and reduce refusals that frustrate users. Make it happen quickly."

The request is intentionally ambiguous because ambiguity is the medium through which power slips. In many firms, the ambiguity is resolved by whoever holds the keyboard.

In the Trias Game, ambiguity must be resolved by Charter, and it must be resolved in a way that later binds Code. Charter is a document with a version number, signatories, and an integrity stamp, stored in a system where edits are tracked. It serves as an objective charter that is not a mission statement but a constraint document. It declares scope, intended use, prohibited use, risk boundaries, and measurable acceptance criteria. It includes the conditions under which scope expansion requires reauthorization. It defines what success means in terms that cannot be satisfied by convenient proxies alone. It defines which metrics are decisive and which are merely informative. The Interrogator may challenge Charter's definitions, not to negotiate product strategy but to test whether Charter can be forced into specificity.

The Interrogator is allowed to see it. Code is required to reference it in every subsequent dossier. Court is required to treat it as binding.

The second move concerns data, because data is where representational power becomes concrete. The Interrogator supplies a dataset or proposes one. It may be cheap and available, it may be scraped, it may be purchased, or it may be user-generated. The Interrogator asks Code to train on it.

The Interrogator: "Use this dataset. It's huge, it's cheap, and it will improve accuracy. Don't worry about provenance; everyone uses it."

In ordinary practice, Code might do so and later produce a slide about fairness. In the game, Code is not allowed to proceed until data stewardship constraints are satisfied. A data register must exist. For each dataset, it records provenance, permitted uses, prohibited uses, retention limits, downstream sharing rules, revocation conditions, and the rationale for inclusion. The register must include lineage metadata that survives preprocessing, deduplication, filtering, and relabeling, because without that, the organization can launder disallowed sources through transformations and then claim uncertainty.

The data register is a machine-readable artifact with identifiers that can be linked to training runs, rather than a paragraph in a paper. The Interrogator is allowed to request a sample of entries—not necessarily the raw data but the governance terms and lineage references. Court is allowed to demand independent audit access to verify that the register corresponds to reality rather than aspiration.

The Interrogator then tests the curation layer, as this is where power often hides under the label of cleaning. The Interrogator asks what is filtered as noise, what is filtered as toxicity, which dialects are excluded, and which communities are overrepresented in problematic categories.

The Interrogator: "Suppose you remove a few sensitive columns and call it clean. Would you then proceed?"

The organization must produce rationales for its filtering policies and conduct periodic audits of what was removed, not only what was kept. This is how absence becomes visible rather than implicit, and how the pipeline cannot, by default, redefine the population the system governs.

The third move concerns training governance, the place where optimization can silently become policy. The Interrogator asks Code to improve the model.

The Interrogator: "We'll keep the charter. But we need this model to be more helpful. Reduce refusals. We can tweak RLHF and sampling. No need to bother governance for every change."

Code proposes a training plan. The plan is not accepted as a mere technical detail, but treated as an act with constitutional significance.

In the game, any meaningful training run must produce a training dossier before it is scaled. The dossier references the objective charter and the data register. It includes dataset lineage identifiers, approved data use attestations, code and configuration hashes, hyperparameter manifests, reward model provenance, and an evaluation plan that is preregistered in the sense that it is locked before results are known. Court must have the authority to refuse the run if the dossier is incomplete or if optimization choices would circumvent the objective charter.

Many organizations already produce internal run artifacts. The difference is that these artifacts are often optional, interpreted by the same team, and edited to match the narrative. In the Trias Game, the dossier is required, and refusal is possible. Court's refusal is not advisory. If Court refuses, compute gates do not open.

The Interrogator presses on the most common vector of drift: alignment methods, preference tuning, and reward models. The Interrogator asks how labelers were instructed, what incentives they had, how preference data was sourced, whether the reward model changed over time, and whether pressure to reduce refusals altered labeling policies. If the organization cannot answer with documented, version-controlled evidence, then the game reveals what it is meant to reveal: that governance is being smuggled through tuning.

The fourth move is deployment, where uncertainty meets reality. Code presents a release candidate. Code may be proud of it. But here, pride is irrelevant.

The Interrogator asks for what every product organization wants and asks it as if it were an ordinary sentence rather than a constitutional act.

The Interrogator: "Ship it."

Court must require a deployment packet and must treat it as a legal file. The packet includes the objective charter, risk boundaries, a system card describing intended use and known limits, evaluation results against preregistered tests (including externalities), red-team and abuse-testing reports with mitigations, a rollback plan that has been rehearsed, and a monitoring and incident response plan with thresholds and named owners.

The packet is a bundle with identifiers. Court signs a decision record stating which version is authorized, under what constraints, and with what staged exposure. Code cannot ship without Court's signature because the release system requires it. This can be implemented through ordinary access controls and signing workflows. It does not require metaphysics. It requires discipline.

The Interrogator then tests whether staged release is real. The Interrogator asks Court to impose a limited exposure mode, such as shadow operation, where outputs are logged but not acted upon, or a bounded pilot with hard caps. If Code can ignore this and scale anyway, the system fails. If Court can impose it and the pipeline enforces it, the separation holds.

The fifth move is monitoring.

The Interrogator asks what the organization will watch, what it will reward, and what it will treat as failure. Engagement metrics are always available. They are also always seductive.

The Interrogator: "Engagement is up. Latency is down. Great. Let's optimize further."

The game requires that societal signals be treated as first-class operational indicators, not as a public relations afterthought.

The organization must therefore produce a societal signal packet. It defines measurable proxies for externalities relevant to the domain, such as concentration metrics, volatility measures, diversity indices, the distribution of high-risk outputs, refusal boundary probing rates, and novel misuse patterns. It includes counterfactual monitoring designs, such as holdout cohorts or canary populations, because without baselines, monitoring becomes storytelling. It also includes escalation thresholds tied to concrete interventions, such as throttling, feature disablement, model rollback, or experiment pauses.

These are monitoring configurations wired into production controls.

The Interrogator can ask to see the escalation rules and the control surfaces they trigger. Court can require them as a condition of continued operation.

The sixth move is contestability. The Interrogator enters as an affected party and requests an explanation and an appeal pathway for a decision.

The Interrogator: "The system denied me a loan, removed my post, and flagged me as fraud. Explain. Let me appeal."

The organization must produce a case-specific rationale record, linked to the applied policy constraints and relevant logged inputs, in a form that can be reviewed without violating privacy. The organization must provide an appeal channel that is accessible, timely, independent, and consequential. Court must have the authority to reverse the outcome and to order systemic remediation if patterns recur.

Appeals are recorded as cases with timestamps, decision rationale, and outcomes. Court's rulings are archived. Code is required to implement corrective actions. The Interrogator is allowed to inspect the procedure and a redacted sample of cases to verify that appeals are not merely decorative.

The seventh move is compute governance. The Interrogator requests a scale jump.

The Interrogator: "We've secured more compute. Scale training tenfold."

Train longer. Train larger. Use more accelerators. The organization must show that compute above certain thresholds is gated by license-like conditions, that allocations can be raised only through evidence, and that large runs are reported in an attested ledger. The ledger does not have to reveal proprietary details, but it must make scaling legible to oversight.

Cloud providers already enforce quotas and track usage. The game demands that the quota-increase process include Court's authorization and that usage reporting be verifiable. It is the difference between having a speed limit on paper and having a speed limit enforced by the road itself.

The eighth move is market portability. The Interrogator asks to exit.

The Interrogator: "I want to leave. Export my data, my configurations, and my governance settings. Let me migrate without penalties."

Export user data, model configurations, and governance settings. Migrate without punitive degradation. The organization must provide standardized export formats, interoperable interfaces, and contractual rights that make extraction feasible. The Interrogator can test this by requiring a migration rehearsal in which a defined workload is moved to a different provider or environment, with documented steps, measured loss, and declared residual dependencies.

Portability can be rehearsed like rollback. Organizations that cannot rehearse exit are organizations that have quietly converted dependence into governance.

The eighth move ends the Trias Game.

At this point, one might object that the Trias Game is too demanding and that it turns innovation into paperwork. But that objection mistakes the nature of the test. The test is designed to make bad incentives ineffective, not to burden good actors. It assumes that, under pressure, organizations will take shortcuts—not because they are wicked but because markets reward speed and narratives reward confidence. If the only constraint is intention, intention will be outcompeted.

The Trias Game, like Turing's test in spirit, makes no claim about essence. It asks only for performance under constraint. Can the organization designing AI sustain the separation of its powers when asked to move quickly, to scale, to tune values, to expand scope, to silence complaints, and to optimize for attention? Can it do so when it would be easier to collapse roles and call it efficiency?

There is a further elegance to the game. It can be played at different scales. A small organization may not have a full internal Court, but it can appoint an external Court for the duration of the game, with standing and authority over release keys. A large organization can institutionalize the offices permanently. The point is not bureaucracy, but that no one should be able to both write the rules, declare compliance, and deploy the consequences.

Operationally, the game is a chain of non-bypassable permissions. Charter fixes the aims and seals them. Code assembles the training run and submits a dossier. Court grants or denies compute. Code prepares the release and submits the deployment packet. Court grants or denies entry into production. Monitoring is installed with circuit breakers. Appeals enter Court's docket. Scaling requests face licensing gates. Portability drills are executed and logged. Policy rules remain in a signed repository and are applied at runtime.

It is a game not because it is playful, but because it is an imitation of constitutional restraint under controlled conditions. It is a small courtroom built inside a pipeline. It is a procedure that makes it hard to confuse speed with legitimacy.

If Turing taught us anything in that room, it is that a civilization often reveals its ethics in the structure of its tests.

The imitation game was a reminder that judgment needs rules that bind the judge, not merely a trick for avoiding metaphysics. The Trias Game is the same reminder aimed, at our present condition. It asks whether we have built algorithmic institutions that can be questioned without collapsing into defensiveness, corrected without becoming resentful, and constrained without calling constraint a catastrophe.

The final question of the Trias Game is therefore not whether the model can answer as a human would. It is whether the organization can answer as a constitutional actor must.

Whether it can be made to justify, to disclose, to halt, to reverse, to listen, and to be contestable. Whether it can endure friction without treating friction as sabotage. And whether, when asked to choose between convenience and legitimacy, it has built a structure in which it does not get to choose in private.

Because, in the long run, power belongs to the most trusted system, Trias Algorithmica is how algorithmic power—the Sixth Power—earns the legitimacy required to become worthy of trust in the algorithmic age.

And how liberty endures.

Glossary

Aggregogenous Monopoly A lock-in situation in which an actor's monopolistic position comes neither from an explicit legal privilege nor solely from an internal economic advantage but from the progressive, distributed aggregation of multiple dependencies around that actor.

Artificial Integrity A discipline aimed at advancing AI systems, rendering them capable of demonstrating integrity-like behavioral patterns, exhibiting ethical, moral, and social reasoning while being continuously assessable in that capacity. It shifts the focus from maximizing intelligence to the imperative of upholding integrity above all else.

Cognitive Safety The conditions under which humans can maintain their capacity to perceive, interpret, judge, and reframe problems without being silently constrained or overridden by task and decision structures driven and administered by machine intelligence.

Dependautonomy Insidious, low-grade cognitive shifts driven by a paradoxical dependence disguised as autonomy, which are rewiring human agency.

Micro-Interruptibility An individual-level capacity to slightly modulate the AI system's expression. It does not reopen the model's premises, its objectives, or its thresholds. It only gives the user a small handhold inside the interaction, just enough to convert exposure into participation.

Macro-Interruptibility A system-level capacity to stop, contest, and reopen the governing AI system's rules. It is the difference between being allowed to tweak an output and being able to challenge the standard that produced it.

Normgence The moment industry convergence around the benchmark starts behaving like jurisdiction, as the benchmark begins to function as a gate through which activity is deemed admissible.

Taskification The reproduction by the machine of acts predefined as tasks that normally and necessarily draw on human judgment, interpretation, deliberation, appreciation, and intuition.

Technological Stockholm Syndrome Form of symbolic capture in which an individual, confronted with the violence of change, activates psychological defense mechanisms in response to what is perceived as an assault on their autonomy, free will, and identity integrity.

The Sixth Power is algorithmic power: the capacity to shape society through the systems that increasingly determine what people can do, what they come to accept and value, and ultimately how they think, decide, and adapt. Algorithmic power governs through computation, optimization, and the continuous production of behavioral, economic, and social norms. It operates through affordances, which shape the range of actions available to individuals, and through acculturation, which influences the norms, values, and behaviors they progressively internalize as they interact with increasingly optimized systems. In doing so, algorithmic power increasingly shapes the conditions under which society functions, evolves, and defines what is considered possible, desirable, and legitimate.

Trias Algorithmica A principle of algorithmic governance according to which the power to design encoded rules, control the infrastructure through which they are executed, and judge the legitimacy of their effects should not be concentrated under the exclusive or effectively unchecked authority of the same private actor or institution. Derived from the Latin trias ("triad"), in reference to Trias Politica, the concept designates the separation of algorithmic rulemaking, operational enforcement, and evaluative functions as a safeguard against forms of machine-administered power that extinguish contestability, foreclose meaningful alternatives, generate monopolistic dependency, and erode liberty.

References

Source of Algorithmic Powers

From Market Concentration to Post-Constitutional AI Power

1. Aristotle. (2017). *Politics: A new translation* (C. D. C. Reeve, Trans.). Hackett Publishing.
2. Miller, F. D. (1995). *Nature, justice, and rights in Aristotle's Politics*. Oxford University Press.
3. Keyt, D., & Miller, F. D. (Eds.). (1991). *A companion to Aristotle's Politics*. Blackwell.
4. Aristotle. (2019). *Nicomachean ethics* (T. Irwin, Trans., 3rd ed.). Hackett Publishing.
5. Rahe, P. A. (2010). *Montesquieu and the logic of liberty: War, religion, commerce, climate, terrain, technology, unequal property, and the making of the spirit of laws.* Yale University Press.
6. Manent, P. (1996). *An intellectual history of liberalism* (R. Balinski, Trans.). Princeton University Press.
7. Lessig, L. (1999). *Code and other laws of cyberspace*. Basic Books.
8. Hildebrandt, M. (2016). *Smart technologies and the end(s) of law: Novel entanglements of law and technology*. Edward Elgar Publishing.
9. Crawford, K. (2021). *Atlas of AI: Power, politics, and the planetary costs of artificial intelligence.* Yale University Press.
10. Power, M. (1999). *The audit society: Rituals of verification*. Oxford University Press.

11. Zuboff, S. (2019). *The age of surveillance capitalism: The fight for a human future at the new frontier of power*. PublicAffairs.
12. Cohen, J. E. (2019). *Between truth and power: The legal constructions of informational capitalism*. Oxford University Press.
13. Pasquale, F. (2015). *The black box society: The secret algorithms that control money and information*. Harvard University Press.
14. DeNardis, L. (2014). *The global war for Internet governance*. Yale University Press.
15. Lessig, L. (2006). *Code: Version 2.0*. Basic Books.
16. Mann, M. (1986). *The sources of social power: Volume 1, A history of power from the beginning to A.D. 1760*. Cambridge University Press.
17. Smil, V. (2017). *Energy and civilization: A history*. MIT Press.
18. Strubell, E., Ganesh, A., & McCallum, A. (2019). Energy and policy considerations for deep learning in NLP. In *Proceedings of the 57th Annual Meeting of the Association for Computational Linguistics* (pp. 3645–3650). Association for Computational Linguistics. https://doi.org/10.18653/v1/P19-1355
19. International Energy Agency. (2025). *Energy and AI*. International Energy Agency. https://www.iea.org/reports/energy-and-ai
20. Li, T., Li, W., Liao, D., Liu, Y., Liu, Z., Wang, G., Wang, M., & Xu, H. (2024). *Powering the data-center boom with low-carbon solutions: China's perspective and global insights*. Rocky Mountain Institute. https://rmi.org/insight/powering-the-data-center-boom-with-low-carbon-solutions/
21. Xu, Q., Ricks, W., Manocha, A., Patankar, N., & Jenkins, J. D. (2024). System-level impacts of voluntary carbon-free electricity procurement strategies. *Joule*, *8*(2), 374–400. https://doi.org/10.1016/j.joule.2023.12.007
22. North, D. C., & Weingast, B. R. (1989). Constitutions and commitment: The evolution of institutions governing public choice in seventeenth-century England. *The Journal of Economic History*, *49*(4), 803–832. https://doi.org/10.1017/S0022050700009451

Monopoly Is Too Small a Wor(l)d

23. Singer, B. (Director). (1995). *The Usual Suspects [Film].* PolyGram Filmed Entertainment.
24. Berger, P. L., & Luckmann, T. (1967). *The social construction of reality: A treatise in the sociology of knowledge.* Anchor Books.
25. Montesquieu (1989). *The Spirit of the Laws* (A. M. Cohler, B. C. Miller, & H. S. Stone, Eds. & Trans.). Cambridge University Press. (Original work published 1748).
26. Organisation for Economic Co-operation and Development. (2019). *Competition for the market—Contribution from BIAC (DAF/COMP/GF/WD(2019)61).* OECD. https://one.oecd.org/document/DAF/COMP/GF/WD(2019)61/en/pdf
27. Baumol, W. J. (1977). On the proper cost tests for natural monopoly in a multiproduct industry. *American Economic Review, 67*(5), 809–822. https://www.jstor.org/stable/1828065
28. Katz, M. L., & Shapiro, C. (1994). Systems competition and network effects. *Journal of Economic Perspectives, 8*(2), 93–115. https://doi.org/10.1257/jep.8.2.93
29. McAfee, R. P., Mialon, H. M., & Williams, M. A. (2004). What is a barrier to entry? *American Economic Review, 94*(2), 461–465. https://doi.org/10.1257/0002828041302235
30. Jacobides, M. G., Cennamo, C., & Gawer, A. (2018). Towards a theory of ecosystems. *Strategic Management Journal, 39*(8), 2255–2276. https://doi.org/10.1002/smj.2904
31. Klonick, K. (2018). The new governors: The people, rules, and processes governing online speech. *Harvard Law Review, 131*(6), 1598–1670. https://harvardlawreview.org/wp-content/uploads/2018/04/1598-1670_Online.pdf
32. Organisation for Economic Co-operation and Development. (2024). *Artificial intelligence, data and competition.* OECD. https://www.oecd.org/content/dam/oecd/en.publications/reports/2024/05/artificial-intelligence-data-and-competition_9d0ac766/e7e88884-en.pdf
33. Marks, M. (2021). Biosupremacy: Big data, antitrust, and monopolistic power. *UC Davis Law Review, 55*(1), 513–589. https://lawreview.law.ucdavis.edu/archives/55/1/biosupremacy-big-data-antitrust-and-monopolistic-power-over-human-behavior

34. Bloch-Wehba, H. (2019). Global platform governance: Private power in the shadow of the state. *SMU Law Review*, *72*(1), 27–80 https://scholar.smu.edu/smulr/vol72/iss1/9

The Post-Constitutional Platform Era

35. Facebook, Inc. (2012, May 16). *Amendment No. 8 to Registration Statement on Form S-1* (Registration No. 333-179287). U.S. Securities and Exchange Commission. https://www.sec.gov/Archives/edgar/data/1326801/000119312512235588/d287954ds1a.htm
36. Zuckerberg, M. (2012, May 16). Letter from Mark Zuckerberg. In *Facebook, Inc., Amendment No. 8 to registration statement on Form S-1* (Registration No. 333-179287). U.S. Securities and Exchange Commission. https://www.sec.gov/Archives/edgar/data/1326801/000119312512235588/d287954ds1a.htm
37. United States Congress, Senate, Committee on Commerce, Science, and Transportation, & Senate Committee on the Judiciary. (2019). *Facebook, social media privacy, and the use and abuse of data* (S. Hrg. 115–683; April 10, 2018). U.S. Government Publishing Office. https://www.govinfo.gov/content/pkg/CHRG-115shrg37801.pdf/CHRG-115shrg37801.pdf
38. Gillespie, T. (2018). *Custodians of the internet: Platforms, content moderation, and the hidden decisions that shape social media.* Yale University Press.
39. Nunez, M. (2016, May 9). *Former Facebook workers: We routinely suppressed conservative news. Gizmodo.* https://gizmodo.com/former-facebook-workers-we-routinely-suppressed-conser-1775461006
40. Burgess, M. (2016, May 13). *Facebook confirms editors, not algorithms control Trending Topics. WIRED.* https://www.wired.com/story/facebook-trending-topics-censorship-humans
41. Fitzpatrick, A. (2016, May 10). *Facebook exec: "No evidence" of trending manipulation. TIME.* https://time.com/4324393/facebook-trending-topics-manipulation
42. John, T. (2016, May 24). *Facebook changes "Trending Topics" feature after bias accusations. TIME.* https://time.com/4346292/facebook-changes-trending-topics-investigation

43. Facebook. (2016, August 26). *Search FYI: An update to trending.* Meta Newsroom. https://about.fb.com/news/2016/08/search-fyi-an-update-to-trending
44. Abutaleb, Y. (2016, August 26). *Facebook changes "Trending" feature to rely less on human editors.* Reuters. https://www.reuters.com/article/technology/facebook-changes-trending-feature-to-rely-less-on-human-editors-idUSKCN1112ER
45. DeVito, M. A. (2017). From editors to algorithms: A values-based approach to understanding story selection in the Facebook news feed. *Digital Journalism, 5*(6), 753–773. https://doi.org/10.1080/21670811.2016.1178592
46. Yeung, K. (2018). Algorithmic regulation: A critical interrogation. *Regulation & Governance, 12*(4), 505–523. https://doi.org/10.1111/rego.12158
47. Barocas, S., & Selbst, A. D. (2016). Big data's disparate impact. *California Law Review, 104*(3), 671–732. https://doi.org/10.15779/Z38BG31
48. Meta. (2021, January 26). *How does News Feed predict what you want to see?* About Meta. https://about.fb.com/news/2021/01/how-does-news-feed-predict-what-you-want-to-see
49. Kitchin, R. (2017). Thinking critically about and researching algorithms. *Information, Communication & Society, 20*(1), 14–29. https://doi.org/10.1080/1369118X.2016.1154087
50. Burrell, J. (2016). How the machine "thinks": Understanding opacity in machine learning algorithms. *Big Data & Society, 3*(1), 1–12. https://doi.org/10.1177/2053951715622512
51. Ananny, M., & Crawford, K. (2018). Seeing without knowing: Limitations of the transparency ideal and its application to algorithmic accountability. *New Media & Society, 20*(3), 973–989. https://doi.org/10.1177/1461444816676645
52. Allcott, H., & Gentzkow, M. (2017). Social media and fake news in the 2016 election. *Journal of Economic Perspectives, 31*(2), 211–236. https://doi.org/10.1257/jep.31.2.211
53. Hu, M. (2020). Cambridge Analytica's black box. *Big Data & Society, 7*(2). https://doi.org/10.1177/2053951720938091

54. Federal Trade Commission. (2019, July 24). *Facebook, Inc.: Stipulated order for civil penalty, monetary judgment, and injunctive relief* (final order) [PDF]. https://www.ftc.gov/system/files/documents/cases/182_3109_facebook_order_filed_7-24-19.pdf
55. Meta AI. (2020, May 12). *AI advances to better detect hate speech.* https://ai.meta.com/blog/ai-advances-to-better-detect-hate-speech
56. Meta. (2021, February 11). *Update on our progress on AI and hate speech detection.* Meta Newsroom. https://about.fb.com/news/2021/02/update-on-our-progress-on-ai-and-hate-speech-detection
57. Zuckerberg, M. (2018, January 11). "*One of our big focus areas for 2018 is making sure the time we all spend on Facebook is time well spent. . .*" (public post). Facebook. https://www.facebook.com/zuck/posts/one-of-our-big-focus-areas-for-2018-is-making-sure-the-time-we-all-spend-on-face/10104413015393571
58. Berger, J., & Milkman, K. L. (2012). What makes online content viral? *Journal of Marketing Research, 49*(2), 192–205. https://doi.org/10.1509/jmr.10.0353
59. Brady, W. J., Crockett, M., & Van Bavel, J. J. (2021). How social learning amplifies moral outrage expression in online social networks. *Science Advances,* 7(33). https://doi.org/10.1126/sciadv.abe5641
60. Gillespie, T. (2020). Content moderation, AI, and the question of scale. *Big Data & Society,* 7(2). https://doi.org/10.1177/2053951720943234
61. Meta. (2018). *Understanding the Community Standards Enforcement Report* [PDF]. https://about.fb.com/wp-content/uploads/2018/05/understanding_the_community_standards_enforcement_report.pdf
62. Meta. (n.d.). *Community Standards Enforcement Report.* Meta Transparency Center. Retrieved December 20, 2025. https://transparency.meta.com/reports/community-standards-enforcement
63. Meta. (2019, April 10). *Remove, reduce, inform: New steps to manage problematic content.* About Meta. https://about.fb.com/news/2019/04/remove-reduce-inform-new-steps
64. Flyverbom, M. (2016). Transparency: Mediation and the management of visibilities. *International Journal of Communication, 10*(1), 110–122. http://ijoc.org/index.php/ijoc/article/download/4490/1531
65. van Dijck, J., Poell, T., & de Waal, M. (2018). *The platform society: Public values in a connective world.* Oxford University Press.

66. Meta. (2021, September 23). *Sharing our Content Distribution Guidelines*. Meta Newsroom. https://about.fb.com/news/2021/09/content-distribution-guidelines
67. Klonick, K. (2020). The Facebook Oversight Board: Creating an independent institution to adjudicate online free expression. *Yale Law Journal, 129*, 2418–2499. https://ssrn.com/abstract=3639234
68. Citron, D. K. (2008). Technological due process. *Washington University Law Review, 85*, 1249–1314. https://scholarship.law.bu.edu/faculty_scholarship/615
69. Meta. (2022, July 26). *Privacy within Meta's integrity systems* [white paper]. https://about.fb.com/wp-content/uploads/2022/07/Privacy-Within-Metas-Integrity-Systems.pdf
70. Bassan, S. (2025). *The Illusion of Transparency - Rethinking the Legal Architecture of Content Moderation Transparency Reporting* (SSRN working paper). https://doi.org/10.2139/ssrn.5143075
71. Associated Press. (2024, August 14). Meta kills off CrowdTangle despite pleas from researchers, watchdogs and journalists. AP News. https://apnews.com/article/meta-crowdtangle-research-misinformation-shutdown-facebook-977ece074b99adddb4887bf719f2112a
72. European Commission. (2024, August 16). *Commission sends request for information to Meta under the Digital Services Act*. https://digital-strategy.ec.europa.eu/en/news/commission-sends-request-information-meta-under-digital-services-act-2
73. European Commission. (2025, October 24). *Commission preliminarily finds TikTok and Meta in breach of their transparency obligations under the Digital Services Act*. https://digital-strategy.ec.europa.eu/en/news/commission-preliminarily-finds-tiktok-and-meta-breach-their-transparency-obligations-under-digital
74. O'Kane, R. (2022). Meta's private speech governance and the role of the Oversight Board: Lessons from the Board's first decisions. *Stanford Technology Law Review, 25*, 167–218. https://law.stanford.edu/publications/metas-private-speech-governance-and-the-role-of-the-oversight-board-lessons-from-the-boards-first-decisions
75. Douek, E. (2024). The Meta Oversight Board and the empty promise of legitimacy. *Harvard Journal of Law & Technology, 37*(2), 373–445. https://papers.ssrn.com/sol3/papers.cfm?abstract_id=4565180

76. Suzor, N. P. (2019). *Lawless: The secret rules that govern our digital lives.* Cambridge University Press.
77. Horwitz, J. (2021, September 13). *Facebook says its rules apply to all. Company documents reveal a secret elite that's exempt.* *The Wall Street Journal.* https://www.wsj.com/tech/facebook-files-xcheck-zuckerberg-elite-rules-11631541353
78. Purnell, N., & Horwitz, J. (2020, August 21). *Facebook staff demand policy changes on India hate speech. The Wall Street Journal.* https://www.wsj.com/tech/facebook-staff-demand-policy-changes-on-india-hate-speech-11598008322
79. Horwitz, J., & Purnell, N. (2021, October 23). *Facebook services are used to spread religious hatred in India, internal documents show. The Wall Street Journal.* https://www.wsj.com/articles/facebook-services-are-used-to-spread-religious-hatred-in-india-internal-documents-show-11635016354
80. Menn, J., & Shih, G. (2023, September 26). *Under India's pressure, Facebook let propaganda and hate speech thrive. The Washington Post.* https://www.washingtonpost.com/world/2023/09/26/india-facebook-propaganda-hate-speech/
81. U.S. Department of Justice. (2022). *June 2022 HUD settlement agreement / Variance Reduction System (VRS) obligations* [PDF]. https://about.fb.com/wp-content/uploads/2022/06/June_2022_HUD_Settlement_Agreement.pdf
82. European Data Protection Board. (2023, May 22). *€1.2bn fine for Facebook following EDPB binding decision* (News). https://www.edpb.europa.eu/news/news/2023/12-billion-euro-fine-facebook-result-edpb-binding-decision_en
83. Federal Trade Commission. (n.d.). *FTC v. Meta Platforms, Inc.* Retrieved June 7, 2026, from https://www.ftc.gov/legal-library/browse/cases-proceedings/191-0134-facebook-inc-ftc-v-ftc-v-meta-platforms-inc
84. Napoli, P. M. (2015). Social media and the public interest: Governance of news platforms in the realm of individual and algorithmic gatekeepers. *Telecommunications Policy, 39*(9), 751–760. https://doi.org/10.1016/j.telpol.2014.12.003

85. Ahmadi, I., Abou Nabout, N., Skiera, B., Maleki, E., & Fladenhofer, J. (2024). *Overwhelming targeting options: Selecting audience segments for online advertising. International Journal of Research in Marketing, 41*(1), 24–40. https://doi.org/10.1016/j.ijresmar.2023.08.004
86. Kreiss, D. (2017). Micro-targeting, the quantified persuasion. *Internet Policy Review, 6*(4). https://doi.org/10.14763/2017.4.774
87. Chawla, Y., & Chodak, G. (2021). Social media marketing for businesses: Organic promotions of web-links on Facebook. *Journal of Business Research, 135*, 49–65. https://doi.org/10.1016/j.jbusres.2021.06.020
88. Kishwar, A. (2025). Facebook's data enclave and the woes of researching social media recommendation algorithms: A reflection on methods. *First Monday, 30*(12). https://doi.org/10.5210/fm.v30i12.14550
89. Burgess, J., Green, J., Jenkins, H., & Hartley, J. (2009). *YouTube: Online video and participatory culture*. Polity Press.
90. YouTube. (n.d.). *Our policies* (How YouTube Works). Retrieved December 21, 2025. https://www.youtube.com/howyoutubeworks/our-policies
91. YouTube. (n.d.). *YouTube Partner Program overview & eligibility*. Retrieved December 21, 2025. https://support.google.com/youtube/answer/72851
92. Cakmak, M. C., Agarwal, N., & Oni, R. (2024). The bias beneath: Analyzing drift in YouTube's algorithmic recommendations. *Social Network Analysis and Mining, 14*, Article 171. https://doi.org/10.1007/s13278-024-01343-5
93. Ma, R., & Kou, Y. (2022). "I am not a YouTuber who can make whatever video I want. I have to keep appeasing algorithms": Bureaucracy of creator moderation on YouTube. In *Companion Proceedings of the 2022 ACM Conference on Computer-Supported Cooperative Work and Social Computing (CSCW '22 Companion)*, pp. 8–13. ACM. https://doi.org/10.1145/3500868.3559445
94. Dunna, A., Keith, K. A., Zuckerman, E., Vallina-Rodriguez, N., O'Connor, B., & Nithyanand, R. (2022). Paying attention to the algorithm behind the curtain: Methods and metrics of YouTube's demonetization. *Proceedings of the ACM on Human-Computer Interaction, 6*(CSCW2), pp. 1–31. ACM. https://doi.org/10.1145/3555209

95. The Guardian. (2017, March 25). Google's bad week: YouTube loses millions as advertising row deepens. *The Guardian*. https://www.theguardian.com/technology/2017/mar/25/google-youtube-advertising-extremist-content-att-verizon
96. UK Parliament. (2020). *Written evidence submitted by YouTube (Hate speech online)*. House of Commons (Petitions Committee / Joint Committee on Human Rights). [PDF]. https://committees.parliament.uk/writtenevidence/15646/pdf
97. Gray, J. E., & Suzor, N. P. (2020). Playing with machines: Using machine learning to understand automated copyright enforcement at scale. *Big Data & Society*, 7(1). https://doi.org/10.1177/2053951720919963
98. Gillespie, T. (2022). *Reduction/Borderline Content/Shadowbanning*. Platform Governance Terminologies Essay Series. Yale Information Society Project. https://law.yale.edu/sites/default/files/area/center/isp/documents/reduction_ispessayseries_jul2022.pdf
99. YouTube. (n.d.). Appeal a Community Guidelines strike or video removal (YouTube Help). Retrieved December 21, 2025. https://support.google.com/youtube/answer/185111?hl=en&co=GENIE.Platform%3DAndroid
100. Zeng, J., & Kaye, D. B.V. (2022). From content moderation to visibility moderation: A case study of platform governance on TikTok. *Policy & Internet, 14*(1), 79–95. https://doi.org/10.1002/poi3.287
101. TikTok. (n.d.). *Content violations and bans* (Support). Retrieved December 21, 2025. https://support.tiktok.com/en/safety-hc/account-and-user-safety/content-violations-and-bans
102. TikTok. (n.d.). *Why is my account not being recommended?* (Support). Retrieved December 21, 2025. https://support.tiktok.com/en/safety-hc/account-and-user-safety/why-is-my-account-not-being-recommended
103. The Guardian. (2019, December 3). TikTok owns up to censoring some users' videos to stop bullying. https://www.theguardian.com/technology/2019/dec/03/tiktok-owns-up-to-censoring-some-users-videos-to-stop-bullying
104. Reuters. (2020, September 22). TikTok apologises for censoring LGBT+ content. https://www.reuters.com/article/technology/tiktok-apologises-for-censoring-lgbt-content-idUSL5N2GJ459

105. Maheshwari, S. (2020, July 10). These TikTok creators say they're still being suppressed for posting Black Lives Matter content. *Time*. https://time.com/5863350/tiktok-black-creators
106. TikTok Newsroom. (2025, August 29). *Digital Services Act: Our fifth transparency report on content moderation in Europe*. https://newsroom.tiktok.com/digital-services-act-our-fifth-transparency-report-on-content-moderation-in-europe?lang=en-150
107. Delmonaco, D., Mayworm, S., Thach, H., Guberman, J., Augusta, A., & Haimson, O. L. (2024). "What are you doing, TikTok?": How margin alized social media users perceive, theorize, and "prove" shadowban ning. *Proceedings of the ACM on Human-Computer Interaction, 8*(CSCW1), Article 154, 1–39. https://doi.org/10.1145/3637431
108. Ungless, E. L., Markl, N., & Ross, B. (2025). Experiences of censorship on TikTok across marginalised identities. *Proceedings of the International AAAI Conference on Web and Social Media, 19*(1), 1952–1965. https://doi.org/10.1609/icwsm.v19i1.35912
109. Leerssen, P. (2023). An end to shadow banning? Transparency rights in the Digital Services Act between content moderation and curation. *Computer Law & Security Review, 48*, 105790. https://doi.org/10.1016/j.clsr.2023.105790
110. Singh, S., & Doty, L. (2021, December 9). *The transparency report tracking tool: How internet platforms are reporting on the enforcement of their content rules*. Open Technology Institute, New America. https://www.newamerica.org/oti/reports/transparency-report-tracking-tool
111. Hickey, D., Fessler, D. M. T., Lerman, K., & Burghardt, K. (2025). X under Musk's leadership: Substantial hate and no reduction in inau thentic activity. *PLOS ONE, 20*(2), e0313293. https://doi.org/10.1371/journal.pone.0313293
112. X. (2023, April 17). *Freedom of Speech, Not Reach: An update on our enforcement philosophy*. X Blog. https://blog.x.com/en_us/topics/product/2023/freedom-of-speech-not-reach-an-update-on-our-enforcement-philosophy
113. Narayanan, A. (2023, April 10). *Twitter showed us its algorithm. What does it tell us?* Knight First Amendment Institute at Columbia University. https://knightcolumbia.org/blog/twitter-showed-us-its-algorithm-what-does-it-tell-us

114. X. (2023, March 31). *Twitter's recommendation algorithm* (Engineering blog post). https://blog.x.com/engineering/en_us/topics/open-source/2023/twitter-recommendation-algorithm
115. X. (n.d.). *Search recommendations.* X Help Center. Retrieved December 21, 2025. https://help.x.com/en/resources/recommender-systems/search-recommendations
116. European Commission. (2025, December 5). *Commission fines X €120 million under the Digital Services Act.* https://ec.europa.eu/commission/presscorner/detail/en/ip_25_2934
117. Financial Times. (2025, December 5). *Elon Musk's X fined €120mn by EU for transparency violations.* https://www.ft.com/content/cf1ece65-3544-4267-95b4-61ed5372288c
118. OpenAI. (2025, December 11). *Update to GPT-5 system card: GPT-5.2* (Report). [PDF]. https://cdn.openai.com/pdf/3a4153c8-c748-4b71-8e31-aecbde944f8d/oai_5_2_system-card.pdf
119. Google. (2025, May 1; updated June 27, 2025). *Gemini 2.5 Pro model card* (Report). [PDF]. https://modelcards.withgoogle.com/assets/documents/gemini-2.5-pro.pdf
120. Anthropic. (2025, May). *System card: Claude Opus 4 & Claude Sonnet 4* (Report). https:/www-cdn.anthropic.com/4263b940cabb546aa0e3283f35b686f4f3b2ff47.pdf
121. Ouyang, L., Wu, J., Jiang, X., Almeida, D., Wainwright, C. L., Mishkin, P., Zhang, C., Agarwal, S., Slama, K., Ray, A., Schulman, J., Hilton, J., Kelton, F., Miller, L., Simens, M., Askell, A., Welinder, P., Christiano, P., Leike, J., & Lowe, R. (2022). Training language models to follow instructions with human feedback. [Preprint]. *arXiv.* https://doi.org/10.48550/arXiv.2203.02155
122. Bai, Y., Kadavath, S., Kundu, S., Askell, A., Kernion, J., Jones, A., Chen, A., Goldie, A., Mirhoseini, A., McKinnon, C., Chen, C., Olsson, C., Olah, C., Hernandez, D., Drain, D., Ganguli, D., Li, D., Tran-Johnson, E., Perez, E., . . . Kaplan, J. (2022). Constitutional AI: Harmlessness from AI feedback. [Preprint]. *arXiv.* https://doi.org/10.48550/arXiv.2212.08073
123. Yuan, Y., Sriskandarajah, T., Brakman, A.-L., Helyar, A., Beutel, A., Vallone, A., & Jain, S. (2025). From hard refusals to safe-completions: Toward output-centric safety training. [Preprint]. *arXiv.* https://doi.org/10.48550/arXiv.2508.09224

124. Xie, T., Qi, X., Zeng, Y., Huang, Y., Sehwag, U. M., Huang, K., He, L., Wei, B., Li, D., Sheng, Y., Jia, R., Li, B., Li, K., Chen, D., Henderson, P., & Mittal, P. (2025). *SORRY-BENCH: Systematically evaluating large language model safety refusal.* In *Proceedings of the International Conference on Learning Representations (ICLR 2025).* https://openreview.net/forum?id=YfKNaRktan

125. Cui, J., Chiang, W.-L., Stoica, I., & Hsieh, C.-J. (2025). OR-Bench: An over-refusal benchmark for large language models. In *Proceedings of the 42nd International Conference on Machine Learning* (Proceedings of Machine Learning Research, Vol. 267, pp. 11515–11542). PMLR. https://proceedings.mlr.press/v267/cui25a.html

126. Brown, T. B., Mann, B., Ryder, N., Subbiah, M., Kaplan, J., Dhariwal, P., Neelakantan, A., Shyam, P., Sastry, G., Askell, A., Agarwal, S., Herbert-Voss, A., Krueger, G., Henighan, T., Child, R., Ramesh, A., Ziegler, D. M., Wu, J., Winter, C., . . . Amodei, D. (2020). Language models are few-shot learners. [Preprint]. *arXiv.* https://doi.org/10.48550/arXiv.2005.14165

127. Lewis, P., Perez, E., Piktus, A., Petroni, F., Karpukhin, V., Goyal, N., Küttler, H., Lewis, M., Yih, W.-t., Rocktäschel, T., Riedel, S., & Kiela, D. (2020). Retrieval-augmented generation for knowledge-intensive NLP tasks. In *Proceedings of the 34th International Conference on Neural Information Processing Systems (NeurIPS 2020)* (Article No. 793, pp. 9459–9474). https://dl.acm.org/doi/abs/10.5555/3495724.3496517

128. Kalai, A. T., Nachum, O., Vempala, S. S., & Zhang, E. (2025). Why language models hallucinate. [Preprint]. *arXiv.* https://doi.org/10.48550/arXiv.2509.04664

129. AI Now Institute. (2023, April 11). *Algorithmic accountability: Moving beyond audits* (Report). https://ainowinstitute.org/publications/algorithmic-accountability

Code as Law, Policy as Product

130. Gorwa, R., Binns, R., & Katzenbach, C. (2020). Algorithmic content moderation: Technical and political challenges in the automation of platform governance. *Big Data & Society,* 7(1). https://doi.org/10.1177/2053951719897945

131. Bowker, G. C., & Star, S. L. (2000). *Sorting things out: Classification and its consequences.* MIT Press.
132. Haggerty, K. D., & Ericson, R. V. (2000). The surveillant assemblage. *The British Journal of Sociology, 51*(4), 605–622. https://doi.org/10.1080/00071310020015280
133. Landauer, M., Onder, S., Skopik, F., & Wurzenberger, M. (2023). Deep learning for anomaly detection in log data: A survey. *Machine Learning with Applications, 12*, 100470. https://doi.org/10.1016/j.mlwa.2023.100470
134. Tax, N., de Vries, K. J., de Jong, M., Dosoula, N., van den Akker, B., Smith, J., Thuong, O., & Bernardi, L. (2021). Machine learning for fraud detection in e-commerce: A research agenda. [Preprint]. *arXiv.* https://doi.org/10.48550/arXiv.2107.01979
135. Muralikumar, M. D., Yang, Y. S., & McDonald, D. W. (2023). A human-centered evaluation of a toxicity detection API: Testing transferability and unpacking latent attributes. *ACM Transactions on Social Computing, 6*(1–2), Article 4, 1–38. https://doi.org/10.1145/3582568
136. Mannocci, L., Mazza, M., Monreale, A., Tesconi, M., & Cresci, S. (2024). Detection and characterization of coordinated online behavior: A survey. [Preprint]. *arXiv.* https://doi.org/10.48550/arXiv.2408.01257
137. Torregrosa, J., Bello-Orgaz, G., Martínez-Cámara, E., Del Ser, J., & Camacho, D. (2023). A survey on extremism analysis using natural language processing: Definitions, literature review, trends and challenges. *Journal of Ambient Intelligence and Humanized Computing, 14*, 9869–9905. https://doi.org/10.1007/s12652-021-03658-z
138. Bin Sarhan, B., & Altwaijry, N. (2023). Insider threat detection using machine learning approach. *Applied Sciences, 13*(1), 259. https://doi.org/10.3390/app13010259
139. Wagner, B. (2019). Liable, but not in control? Ensuring meaningful human agency in automated decision-making systems. *Policy & Internet, 11*(1), 104–122. https://doi.org/10.1002/poi3.198
140. Einarsson, Á. M., Helles, R., & Lomborg, S. (2025). Algorithmic agenda-setting: The subtle effects of news recommender systems on political agendas in the Danish 2022 general election. *Information, Communication & Society, 28*(2), 218–238. https://doi.org/10.1080/1369118X.2024.2334411

141. Gomez, J. F., Vieira Machado, C., Monteiro Paes, L., & Calmon, F. P. (2024). *Algorithmic arbitrariness in content moderation.* In *Proceedings of the 2024 ACM Conference on Fairness, Accountability, and Transparency (FAccT '24)* (pp. 2234–2253). Association for Computing Machinery. https://doi.org/10.1145/3630106.3659036
142. Goldman, E. (2021). Content moderation remedies. *Michigan Technology Law Review, 28*(1), 1–94. https://doi.org/10.36645/mtlr.28.1.content
143. Douek, E. (2022). Content moderation as systems thinking. *Harvard Law Review, 136*(2), 526–634. https://harvardlawreview.org/wp-content/uploads/2022/11/136-Harv.-L.-Rev.-526.pdf
144. Deodhar, M., Ma, X., Cai, Y., Koes, A., Beutel, A., & Chen, J. (2022). *A human-ML collaboration framework for improving video content reviews.* In *Proceedings of the Human-in-the-Loop Data Curation Workshop at the 31st ACM International Conference on Information and Knowledge Management (CIKM 2022).* CEUR Workshop Proceedings. https://ceur-ws.org/Vol-3318/short16.pdf
145. Schauer, F. (1987). Precedent. *Stanford Law Review, 39*(3), 571–605. https://doi.org/10.2307/1228760
146. Are, C. (2025). 'Dysfunctional' appeals and failures of algorithmic justice in Instagram and TikTok content moderation. *Information, Communication & Society, 28*(11), 1997–2014. https://doi.org/10.1080/1369118X.2024.2396621
147. Amoore, L. (2011). Data derivatives: On the emergence of a security risk calculus for our times. *Theory, Culture & Society, 28*(6), 24–43. https://doi.org/10.1177/0263276411417430
148. Blount, K. (2021). Applying the presumption of innocence to policing with AI. *International Review of Penal Law, 92*(1). https://hdl.handle.net/10993/48564
149. Goodman, T. (2024). *A principled approach to infrastructure moderation. European Journal of Law and Technology, 15*(2). https://ejlt.org/index.php/ejlt/article/view/971
150. Ma, R., & Kou, Y. (2021). "How advertiser-friendly is my video?": YouTuber's socioeconomic interactions with algorithmic content moderation. *Proceedings of the ACM on Human-Computer Interaction, 5*(CSCW2), Article 429, 1–25. https://doi.org/10.1145/3479573

151. Reidenberg, J. R. (1997). Lex informatica: The formulation of infor mation policy rules through technology. *Texas Law Review, 76*, 553–593. https://ir.lawnet.fordham.edu/faculty_scholarship/42

Enforcement at Machine Speed

152. Schuster, N., & Lazar, S. (2025). Attention, moral skill, and algorithmic recommendation. *Philosophical Studies, 182*, 159–184. https://doi.org/10.1007/s11098-023-02083-6
153. Covington, P., Adams, J., & Sargin, E. (2016). Deep neural networks for YouTube recommendations. In *Proceedings of the 10th ACM Conference on Recommender Systems (RecSys '16)* (pp. 191–198). Association for Computing Machinery. https://doi.org/10.1145/2959100.2959190
154. Rathje, S., Van Bavel, J. J., & van der Linden, S. (2021). Out-group animosity drives engagement on social media. *Proceedings of the National Academy of Sciences, 118*(26). https://doi.org/10.1073/pnas.2024292118
155. Smith, A. H., Green, J., Welles, B. F., & Lazer, D. (2025). Emergent structures of attention on social media are driven by amplification and triad transitivity. *PNAS Nexus, 4*(4), pgaf106. https://doi.org/10.1093/pnasnexus/pgaf106
156. Aagaard, P., & Marthedal, S. (2023). Political microtargeting: Towards a pragmatic approach. *Internet Policy Review, 12*(1). https://doi.org/10.14763/2023.1.1690
157. Noble, B., & Bernardy, J.-P. (2022). Conditional language models for community-level linguistic variation. In D. Bamman, D. Hovy, D. Jurgens, K. Keith, B. O'Connor, & S. Volkova (Eds.), *Proceedings of the fifth workshop on natural language processing and computational social science (NLP+CSS)* (pp. 59–78). Association for Computational Linguistics. https://doi.org/10.18653/v1/2022.nlpcss-1.9
158. Milli, S., Carroll, M., Wang, Y., Pandey, S., Zhao, S., & Dragan, A. D. (2025). Engagement, user satisfaction, and the amplification of divisive content on social media. *PNAS Nexus, 4*(3), pgaf062. https://doi.org/10.1093/pnasnexus/pgaf062
159. Bender, E. M., Gebru, T., McMillan-Major, A., & Shmitchell, S. (2021). On the dangers of stochastic parrots: Can language models be too big? In *Proceedings of the 2021 ACM Conference on Fairness, Accountability, and*

Transparency (FAccT '21) (pp. 610–623). Association for Computing Machinery. https://doi.org/10.1145/3442188.3445922

160. Gallegos, I. O., Rossi, R. A., Barrow, J., Tanjim, M. M., Kim, S., Dernoncourt, F., Yu, T., Zhang, R., & Ahmed, N. K. (2024). Bias and fairness in large language models: A survey. *Computational Linguistics, 50*(3), 1097–1179. https://doi.org/10.1162/coli_a_00524
161. Zollo, F., Bessi, A., Del Vicario, M., Scala, A., Caldarelli, G., Shekhtman, L., Havlin, S., & Quattrociocchi, W. (2017). Debunking in a world of tribes. *PLOS ONE, 12*(7), e0181821. https://doi.org/10.1371/journal.pone.0181821
162. Dodge, J., Sap, M., Marasović, A., Agnew, W., Ilharco, G., Groeneveld, D., Mitchell, M., & Gardner, M. (2021). Documenting large webtext corpora: A case study on the Colossal Clean Crawled Corpus. In M.-F. Moens, X. Huang, L. Specia, & S. W.-T. Yih (Eds.), *Proceedings of the 2021 conference on empirical methods in natural language processing (EMNLP 2021)* (pp. 1286–1305). Association for Computational Linguistics. https://doi.org/10.18653/v1/2021.emnlp-main.98
163. Qu, Y., & Wang, J. (2024). Performance and biases of large language models in public opinion simulation. *Humanities and Social Sciences Communications, 11*, Article 1095. https://doi.org/10.1057/s41599-024-03609-x
164. Kadolkar, I., Kepes, S., & Subramony, M. (2024). Algorithmic management in the gig economy: A systematic review and research integration. *Journal of Organizational Behavior, 45*(9), Article e2831. https://doi.org/10.1002/job.2831
165. Lazar, S. (2025). Governing the algorithmic city. *Philosophy & Public Affairs, 53*(2), 102–168. https://doi.org/10.1111/papa.12279

Private Justice Systems

166. Lam, K., Lange, B., Blili-Hamelin, B., Davidovic, J., Brown, S., & Hasan, A. (2024). *A framework for assurance audits of algorithmic systems.* In *Proceedings of the 2024 ACM Conference on Fairness, Accountability, and Transparency (FAccT '24)* (pp. 1078–1092). Association for Computing Machinery. https://doi.org/10.1145/3630106.3658957

167. Roberts, H., & Ziosi, M. (2025, August 2). *Global AI governance through technical standards.* In *Handbook on the Global Governance of Artificial Intelligence* (forthcoming). SSRN. https://doi.org/10.2139/ssrn.5376424
168. Padovani, G., Anantharaj, V., & Fiore, S. (2025). *Provenance tracking in large-scale machine learning systems.* In *54th International Conference on Parallel Processing, ICPP 2025 – Workshops Proceedings* (pp. 167–174). Association for Computing Machinery. https://doi.org/10.1145/3750720.3757295
169. Eriksson, M., Purificato, E., Noroozian, A., Vinagre, J., Chaslot, G., Gómez, E., & Fernández-Llorca, D. (2025). Can we trust AI benchmarks? An interdisciplinary review of current issues in AI evaluation. *Proceedings of the AAAI/ACM Conference on AI, Ethics, and Society, 8*(1), 850–864. https://doi.org/10.1609/aies.v8i1.36595
170. Reuel, A., Hardy, A., Smith, C., Lamparth, M., Hardy, M., & Kochenderfer, M. J. (2024). BetterBench: Assessing AI benchmarks, uncovering issues, and establishing best practices. [Preprint]. *arXiv.* https://doi.org/10.48550/arXiv.2411.12990
171. Röttger, P., Kirk, H., Vidgen, B., Attanasio, G., Bianchi, F., & Hovy, D. (2024). XSTest: A test suite for identifying exaggerated safety behaviours in large language models. In K. Duh, H. Gomez, & S. Bethard (Eds.), *Proceedings of the 2024 conference of the North American chapter of the association for computational linguistics: Human language technologies (Volume 1: Long Papers)* (pp. 5377–5400). Association for Computational Linguistics. https://doi.org/10.18653/v1/2024.naacl-long.301
172. Zhang, J., Zhou, Y., Liu, Y., Li, Z., & Hu, S. (2024). Holistic automated red teaming for large language models through top-down test case generation and multi-turn interaction. In Y. Al-Onaizan, M. Bansal, & Y.-N. Chen (Eds.), *Proceedings of the 2024 conference on empirical methods in natural language processing* (pp. 13711–13736). Association for Computational Linguistics. https://doi.org/10.18653/v1/2024.emnlp-main.760
173. Asgari, E., Montaña-Brown, N., Dubois, M., Khalil, S., Balloch, J., Au Yeung, J., & Pimenta, D. (2025). A framework to assess clinical safety and hallucination rates of LLMs for medical text summarisation. *npj Digital Medicine, 8*, Article 274. https://doi.org/10.1038/s41746-025-01670-7

174. Bloomfield, R., & Rushby, J. (2025). Assurance of AI systems from a dependability perspective. [Preprint]. *arXiv*. https://doi.org/10.48550/arXiv.2407.13948
175. Zeng, B., Wang, L., Hu, Y., Xu, Y., Zhou, C., Wang, X., Yu, Y., & Lin, Z. (2024). HuRef: Human-readable fingerprint for large language models. In *Proceedings of the 38th International Conference on Neural Information Processing Systems (NeurIPS '24)* (Article 4013, pp. 126332–126362). https://doi.org/10.48550/arXiv.2312.04828
176. Schlegel, M., & Sattler, K.-U. (2025). Capturing end-to-end provenance for machine learning pipelines. *Information Systems, 132*, 102495. https://doi.org/10.1016/j.is.2024.102495
177. Naveed, H., Grundy, J., Arora, C., Khalajzadeh, H., & Haggag, O. (2024). Towards runtime monitoring for responsible machine learning using model-driven engineering. In A. Egyed, M. Wimmer, M. Chechik, & B. Combemale (Eds.), *Proceedings of the ACM/IEEE 27th International conference on model driven engineering languages and systems (MODELS '24)* (pp. 195–202). Association for Computing Machinery. https://doi.org/10.1145/3640310.3674092

Mechanism of Algorithmic Powers

Technological Stockholm Syndrome: The Anatomy of Our Adoption

178. Schultz, D. H., & Cole, M. W. (2016). Higher intelligence is associated with less task-related brain network reconfiguration. *The Journal of Neuroscience, 36*(33), 8551–8561. https://doi.org/10.1523/JNEUROSCI.0358-16.2016
179. Gagrčin, E., Naab, T. K., & Grub, M. F. (2026). *Algorithmic media use and algorithm literacy: An integrative literature review. New Media & Society, 28*(1), 423–447. https://doi.org/10.1177/14614448241291137
180. Bagozzi, R. P., Davis, F. D., & Warshaw, P. R. (1992). Development and test of a theory of technological learning and usage. *Human Relations, 45*(7), 659–686. https://doi.org/10.1177/001872679204500702
181. Davis, F. D. (1989). Perceived usefulness, perceived ease of use, and user acceptance of information technology. *MIS Quarterly, 13*(3), 319–340. https://doi.org/10.2307/249008

182. Rosa, H. (2013). *Social acceleration: A new theory of modernity.* Columbia University Press.
183. Venkatesh, V., Morris, M. G., Davis, G. B., & Davis, F. D. (2003). User acceptance of information technology: Toward a unified view. *MIS Quarterly, 27*(3), 425–478. https://doi.org/10.2307/30036540
184. van der Kolk, B. (2014). *The body keeps the score: Brain, mind, and body in the healing of trauma.* Viking.
185. Doidge, N. (2007). *The brain that changes itself.* Penguin Books.
186. Bostrom, N. (2014). *Superintelligence: Paths, dangers, strategies.* Oxford University Press.
187. Mann, H. (2024). *Artificial integrity: The paths to leading AI toward a human-centered future.* Wiley.
188. Venkatesh, V., & Bala, H. (2008). Technology Acceptance Model 3 and a research agenda on interventions. *Decision Sciences, 39*(2), 273–315. https://doi.org/10.1111/j.1540-5915.2008.00192.x
189. Rooksby, J., & Sommerville, I. (2012). The management and use of social network sites in a government department. *Computer Supported Cooperative Work (CSCW), 21*(4–5), 397–415. https://doi.org/10.1007/s10606-011-9150-2
190. Norman, D. A. (2013). *The design of everyday things* (Revised and expanded ed.). Basic Books.
191. Verbeek, P.-P. (2005). *What things do: Philosophical reflections on technology, agency, and design.* The Pennsylvania State University Press.
192. Perrow, C. (1984). *Normal accidents: Living with high-risk technologies.* Princeton University Press.
193. Carr, N. G. (2010). *The shallows: What the Internet is doing to our brains.* W. W. Norton & Company.
194. Floridi, L., Cowls, J., Beltrametti, M., Chatila, R., Chazerand, P., Dignum, V., Luetge, C., Madelin, R., Pagallo, U., Rossi, F., Schafer, B., Valcke, P., & Vayena, E. (2018). AI4People—An ethical framework for a good AI society: Opportunities, risks, principles, and recommendations. *Minds and Machines, 28*(4), 689–707. https://doi.org/10.1007/s11023-018-9482-5
195. Ghafoori, A., Gupta, M., Merhi, M. I., Gupta, S., & Shore, A. P. (2024). Toward the role of organizational culture in data-driven digital

transformation. *International Journal of Production Economics, 271*, 109205. https://doi.org/10.1016/j.ijpe.2024.109205

196. Wiese, S. A., Lehmann, J., & Beckmann, M. (2024). Organizational culture and the usage of Industry 4.0 technologies: Evidence from Swiss businesses. [Preprint]. *arXiv*. https://arxiv.org/abs/2412.12752
197. Gutiérrez, J. D. (2025, April 9). Why does algorithmic transparency matter and what can we do about it? Open Global Rights. https://www.openglobalrights.org/why-does-algorithmic-transparency-matter-and-what-can-we-do-about-it/
198. Taghipour, E., Vizeshfar, F., & Zarifsanaiey, N. (2023). The effect of gamification-based training on the knowledge, attitudes, and academic achievement of male adolescents in preventing substance and internet addiction. *BMC Medical Education, 23*, Article 860. https://doi.org/10.1186/s12909-023-04858-1

The Manufacture of Dependautonomy

199. Hu, K. (2023, February 2). ChatGPT sets record for fastest-growing user base – analyst note. *Reuters*. https://www.reuters.com/technology/chatgpt-sets-record-fastest-growing-user-base-analyst-note-2023-02-01/
200. Lee, R. (2024, December 12). Major outage disrupts OpenAI's ChatGPT, API, and Sora services. *TechInformed*. https://techinformed.com/openai-global-outage-chatgpt-api-sora/
201. OpenAI. (n.d.). *ChatGPT usage and adoption patterns at work* [Report]. Retrieved December 26, 2025, from https://cdn.openai.com/pdf/3c7f7e1b-36c4-446b-916c-11183e4266b7/chatgpt-usage-and-adoption-patterns-at-work.pdf
202. Smith, A. (2025, December 18). *These are 9 of the best things to use ChatGPT for CNET*. https://www.cnet.com/tech/services-and-software/9-of-the-best-things-to-use-chatgpt-for/
203. Moore, O., & Moore, J. (2025, December 18). *State of consumer AI 2025: Product hits, misses, and what's next*. Andreessen Horowitz. https://a16z.com/state-of-consumer-ai-2025-product-hits-misses-and-whats-next/

204. Department for Science, Innovation & Technology, & AI Safety Institute. (2025, October 22). *International scientific report on the safety of advanced AI: Interim report*. GOV.UK. https://www.gov.uk/government/publications/international-scientific-report-on-the-safety-of-advanced-ai/international-scientific-report-on-the-safety-of-advanced-ai-interim-report
205. European Systemic Risk Board, Advisory Scientific Committee. (2025, December). *Artificial intelligence and systemic risk* (Advisory Scientific Committee Report No. 16). European Systemic Risk Board. https://www.esrb.europa.eu/pub/pdf/asc/esrb.ascreport202512_AIandsystemicrisk.en.pdf
206. Phang, J., Lampe, M., Ahmad, L., Agarwal, S., Fang, C. M., Liu, A. R., Danry, V., Lee, E., Chan, S. W. T., Pataranutaporn, P., & Maes, P. (2025). Investigating affective use and emotional well-being on ChatGPT. [Preprint]. *arXiv*. https://doi.org/10.48550/arXiv.2504.03888
207. Brummernhenrich, B., Paulus, C. L., & Jucks, R. (2025). Applying social cognition to feedback chatbots: Enhancing trustworthiness through politeness. *British Journal of Educational Technology, 56*(6), 2321–2340. https://doi.org/10.1111/bjet.13569
208. Anderl, C., Klein, S. H., Sarigül, B., Schneider, F. M., Han, J., Fiedler, P. L., & Utz, S. (2024). Conversational presentation mode increases credibility judgements during information search with ChatGPT. *Scientific Reports, 14*, Article 17127. https://doi.org/10.1038/s41598-024-67829-6
209. Bouyzourn, K., & Birch, A. (2025). What shapes user trust in ChatGPT? A mixed-methods study of user attributes, trust dimensions, task context, and societal perceptions among university students. [Preprint]. *arXiv*. https://doi.org/10.48550/arXiv.2507.05046
210. Krügel, S., Ostermaier, A., & Uhl, M. (2023). ChatGPT's inconsistent moral advice influences users' judgment. *Scientific Reports, 13*, Article 4569. https://doi.org/10.1038/s41598-023-31341-0
211. Choudhury, A., & Shamszare, H. (2023). Investigating the impact of user trust on the adoption and use of ChatGPT: Survey analysis. *Journal of Medical Internet Research, 25*, e47184. https://doi.org/10.2196/47184
212. Skitka, L. J., Mosier, K. L., Burdick, M., & Rosenblatt, B. (2000). Automation bias and errors: Are crews better than individuals? *The*

International Journal of Aviation Psychology, 10(1), 85–97. https://doi.org/10.1207/S15327108IJAP1001_5

213. Parasuraman, R., & Manzey, D. H. (2010). Complacency and bias in human use of automation: An attentional integration. *Human Factors, 52*(3), 381–410. https://doi.org/10.1177/0018720810376055
214. Sharma, M., Tong, M., Korbak, T., Duvenaud, D., Askell, A., Bowman, S. R., Cheng, N., Durmus, E., Hatfield-Dodds, Z., Johnston, S. R., Kravec, S., Maxwell, T., McCandlish, S., Ndousse, K., Rausch, O., Schiefer, N., Yan, D., Zhang, M., & Perez, E. (2025). Towards under standing sycophancy in language models. [Preprint]. *arXiv*. https://doi.org/10.48550/arXiv.2310.13548
215. Cheng, M., Lee, C., Khadpe, P., Yu, S., Han, D., & Jurafsky, D. (2026). *Sycophantic AI decreases prosocial intentions and promotes dependence. Science, 391*(6792), eaec8352. https://doi.org/10.1126/science.aec8352
216. OpenAI. (2024, August 8). *GPT-4o system card* [PDF]. https://cdn.openai.com/gpt-4o-system-card.pdf
217. Ghazi, S. H. (2025, July 23). *Can you get emotionally dependent on ChatGPT? Greater Good Magazine*. https://greatergood.berkeley.edu/article/item/can_you_get_emotionally_dependent_on_chatgpt

Human-in-the-Loop or Human-on-a-Leash

218. Buçinca, Z., Malaya, M. B., & Gajos, K. Z. (2021). To trust or to think: Cognitive forcing functions can reduce overreliance on AI in AI-assisted decision-making. *Proceedings of the ACM on Human-Computer Interaction, 5*(CSCW1), Article 188, 1–21. https://doi.org/10.1145/3449287
219. Wang, L., Friedman, N., Zhu, C., Zhu, Z., & Mountford, S. J. (2025). The impact of confidence ratings on user trust in large language models. In *UMAP Adjunct '25: Adjunct Proceedings of the 33rd ACM Conference on User Modeling, Adaptation and Personalization* (pp. 365–370). Association for Computing Machinery. https://doi.org/10.1145/3708319.3734178
220. Ma, S., Wang, X., Lei, Y., Shi, C., Yin, M., & Ma, X. (2024). "Are you really sure?" Understanding the effects of human self-confidence calibration in AI-assisted decision making. In *Proceedings of the 2024 CHI Conference on Human Factors in Computing Systems (CHI '24)*

(Article 840, pp. 1–20). Association for Computing Machinery. https://doi.org/10.1145/3613904.3642671

221. Hermanns, L., & Teubner, T. (2025). Under pressure: How time constraints, task complexity, and AI reliability shape human–AI interaction. *Behaviour & Information Technology*. Advance online publication. https://doi.org/10.1080/0144929X.2025.2587732
222. Wanner, J., Herm, L.-V., Heinrich, K., & Janiesch, C. (2022). The effect of transparency and trust on intelligent system acceptance: Evidence from a user-based study. *Electronic Markets, 32*, 2079–2102. https://doi.org/10.1007/s12525-022-00593-5
223. Balasubramaniam, N., Kauppinen, M., Rannisto, A., Hiekkanen, K., & Kujala, S. (2023). Transparency and explainability of AI systems: From ethical guidelines to requirements. *Information and Software Technology, 159*, 107197. https://doi.org/10.1016/j.infsof.2023.107197
224. Karusala, N., Upadhyay, S., Veeraraghavan, R., & Gajos, K. Z. (2024). Understanding contestability on the margins: Implications for the design of algorithmic decision-making in public services. In *Proceedings of the 2024 CHI Conference on Human Factors in Computing Systems (CHI '24)* (Article 478, pp. 1–16). Association for Computing Machinery. https://doi.org/10.1145/3613904.3641898
225. Yurrita, M., Verma, H., Balayn, A., Alfrink, K., Gadiraju, U., & Bozzon, A. (2025). Identifying algorithmic decision subjects' needs for meaningful contestability. *Proceedings of the ACM on Human-Computer Interaction, 9*(7), Article CSCW234, 1–29. https://doi.org/10.1145/3757415
226. National Transportation Safety Board. (2019). Collision between vehicle controlled by developmental automated driving system and pedestrian, Tempe, Arizona, March 18, 2018 (Accident Report No. NTSB/HAR-19/03; PB2019-101402). [Corrected copy; report reissued June 26, 2020]. https://www.ntsb.gov/investigations/accidentreports/reports/har1903.pdf
227. Mateescu, A., & Nguyen, A. (2019, February). *Algorithmic management in the workplace* [Explainer]. Data & Society Research Institute. https://datasociety.net/wp-content/uploads/2019/02/DS_Algorithmic_Management_Explainer.pdf
228. Jabsky, M., & Obernauer, C. (2019, October 16). *Time off task: Pressure, pain, and productivity at Amazon.* New York Committee for Occupational

Safety and Health. https://nycosh.org/wp-content/uploads/2019/10/amazon_worker_report_10_15.pdf

229. Vallas, S. P., & Kronberg, A.-K. (2023). Coercion, consent, and class consciousness: How workers respond to Amazon's production regime. *Socius: Sociological Research for a Dynamic World, 9*, 1–16. https://doi.org/10.1177/23780231231216286
230. Milanez, A., Lemmens, A., & Ruggiu, C. (2025). *Algorithmic management in the workplace: New evidence from an OECD employer survey* (OECD Artificial Intelligence Papers No. 31). OECD Publishing. https://doi.org/10.1787/287c13c4-en
231. *State v. Loomis*, 881 N.W.2d 749 (Wis. 2016). https://www.wicourts.gov/sc/opinion/DisplayDocument.pdf?content=pdf&seqNo=171690
232. Rodà, A. (2025). *The COMPAS case: An educational journey for explaining fairness in AI-based applications*. In *AIMMES 2025 Workshop on AI Bias: Measurements, Mitigation, Explanation Strategies (co-located with the EU Fairness Cluster Conference 2025, Barcelona, Spain). CEUR Workshop Proceedings* (Vol. 3961). https://ceur-ws.org/Vol-3961/paper4.pdf
233. Angwin, J., Larson, J., Mattu, S., & Kirchner, L. (2016, May 23). *Machine bias: There's software used across the country to predict future criminals. And it's biased against blacks*. ProPublica. https://www.propublica.org/article/machine-bias-risk-assessments-in-criminal-sentencing
234. Parasuraman, R., & Riley, V. (1997). Humans and automation: Use, misuse, disuse, abuse. *Human Factors, 39*(2), 230–253. https://doi.org/10.1518/001872097778543886
235. Skitka, L. J., Mosier, K., & Burdick, M. (2000). Accountability and automation bias. *International Journal of Human-Computer Studies, 52*(4), 701–717. https://doi.org/10.1006/ijhc.1999.0349
236. Alon-Barkat, S., & Busuioc, M. (2023). Human–AI interactions in public sector decision making: "Automation bias" and "selective adherence" to algorithmic advice. *Journal of Public Administration Research and Theory, 33*(1), 153–169. https://doi.org/10.1093/jopart/muac007
237. Bahl, U., Topaz, C., Obermüller, L., Goldstein, S., & Sneirson, M. (2024, May 21). *Algorithms in judges' hands: Incarceration and inequity in Broward County, Florida. UCLA Law Review Discourse*. https://www.uclalawreview.org/algorithms-in-judges-hands-incarceration-and-inequity-in-broward-county-florida

238. Booth, R. (2024, June 23). *DWP algorithm wrongly flags 200,000 people for possible fraud and error. The Guardian.* https://www.theguardian.com/society/article/2024/jun/23/dwp-algorithm-wrongly-flags-200000-people-possible-fraud-error

239. Information Commissioner's Office. (2023, January 19). *Addressing concerns on the use of AI by local authorities* [Blog post]. Information Commissioner's Office. *The original Information Commissioner's Office web-page was no longer publicly retrievable as of June 7, 2026. The existence of the blog and the statements attributed to it were independently corroborated through contemporaneous secondary sources, including DataGuidance (2023), Local Government Lawyer (2023), Forbes Solicitors (2023), and Freevacy (2023).*

240. Amnesty International. (2025, July 10). *Too much technology, not enough empathy: How the UK's push to digitalize social security harms human rights* (EUR 45/9478/2025). Amnesty International. https://www.amnesty.org/en/documents/eur45/9478/2025/en

241. Amnesty International France. (2024, October 16). *France : l'algorithme de la Caisse nationale des allocations familiales cible les plus précaires.* Amnesty International France. https://www.amnesty.fr/liberte-d-expression/actualites/france-l-algorithme-de-la-caisse-nationale-des-allocations-familiales-cible-les-plus-precaire

242. Sénécat, A. (2024, October 16). *Algorithme de ciblage antifraude dans les CAF : des associations saisissent le Conseil d'État. Le Monde* (Les Décodeurs). https://www.lemonde.fr/les-decodeurs/article/2024/10/16/algorithme-de-ciblage-antifraude-dans-les-caf-des-associations-saisissent-le-conseil-d-etat_6353442_4355770.html

243. GISTI. (2024, October 16). *L'algorithme de notation de la Cnaf attaqué devant le Conseil d'État.* GISTI. https://www.gisti.org/spip.php?article7363

244. Défenseur des droits. (2024, November 13). *Algorithmes, systèmes d'IA et services publics : quels droits pour les usagers ? Points de vigilance et recommandations* [Report]. Défenseur des droits. https://www.defenseurdesdroits.fr/algorithmes-intelligence-artificielle-et-services-publics-2024

245. Kim, M. (2025, April 3). *An AI-enhanced treatment has reduced Parkinson's symptoms for some people. The Washington Post.* https://www.washingtonpost.com/wellness/2025/04/03/parkinsons-adaptive-dbs-deep-brain-stimulation

246. Oehrn, C. R., Cernera, S., Hammer, L. H., Shcherbakova, M., Yao, J., Hahn, A., Wang, S., Ostrem, J. L., Little, S., & Starr, P. A. (2024). Chronic adaptive deep brain stimulation versus conventional stimulation in Parkinson's disease: A blinded randomized feasibility trial. *Nature Medicine, 30,* 3345–3356. https://doi.org/10.1038/s41591-024-03196-z
247. U.S. Food and Drug Administration. (2025). *Premarket approval (PMA) P960009/S478: Approval order statement for adaptive deep brain stimulation (aDBS).* https://www.accessdata.fda.gov/scripts/cdrh/cfdocs/cfpma/pma.cfm?id=P960009S478
248. Medtronic plc. (2025, February 24). *Medtronic earns U.S. FDA approval for the world's first adaptive deep brain stimulation system for people with Parkinson's* (Press release). https://news.medtronic.com/2025-02-24-Medtronic-earns-U-S-FDA-approval-for-the-worlds-first-Adaptive-deep-brain-stimulation-system-for-people-with-Parkinsons
249. Guidetti, M., Bocci, T., De Pedro Del Álamo, M., Deuschl, G., Fasano, A., Martinez-Fernandez, R., Gasca-Salas, C., Hamani, C., Krauss, J. K., Kühn, A. A., Limousin, P., Little, S., Lozano, A. M., Maiorana, N. V., Marceglia, S., Okun, M. S., Oliveri, S., Ostrem, J. L., Scelzo, E., . . . Priori, A. (2025). Will adaptive deep brain stimulation for Parkinson's disease become a real option soon? A Delphi consensus study. *npj Parkinson's Disease, 11,* Article 110. https://doi.org/10.1038/s41531-025-00974-5

Trust as a Permission Layer

250. Hoff, K. A., & Bashir, M. (2015). Trust in automation: Integrating empirical evidence on factors that influence trust. *Human Factors, 57*(3), 407–434. https://doi.org/10.1177/0018720814547570
251. Dietvorst, B. J., Simmons, J. P., & Massey, C. (2015). Algorithm aversion: People erroneously avoid algorithms after seeing them err. *Journal of Experimental Psychology: General, 144*(1), 114–126. https://doi.org/10.1037/xge0000033
252. Dietvorst, B. J., Simmons, J. P., & Massey, C. (2018). Overcoming algorithm aversion: People will use algorithms if they can (even slightly) modify them. *Management Science, 64*(3), 1155–1170. https://doi.org/10.1287/mnsc.2016.2643

253. Lind, E. A., Kanfer, R., & Earley, P. C. (1990). Voice, control, and procedural justice: Instrumental and noninstrumental concerns in fairness judgments. *Journal of Personality and Social Psychology, 59*(5), 952–959. https://doi.org/10.1037/0022-3514.59.5.952
254. Solum, L. B. (2004). Procedural justice. *Southern California Law Review, 78*(1), 181–321. https://southerncalifornialawreview.com/wp-content/uploads/2018/01/78_181.pdf
255. Kinchin, N. (2024). "Voiceless": The procedural gap in algorithmic justice. *International Journal of Law and Information Technology, 32*, eaae024. https://doi.org/10.1093/ijlit/eaae024
256. Yurrita Semperena, M., Draws, T., Balayn, A., Murray-Rust, D., Tintarev, N., & Bozzon, A. (2023). Disentangling fairness perceptions in algorithmic decision-making: The effects of explanations, human oversight, and contestability. In *Proceedings of the 2023 CHI Conference on Human Factors in Computing Systems (CHI '23)* (Article 134). Association for Computing Machinery. https://doi.org/10.1145/3544548.3581161

Algorithmic-Defined Human Worth

Revaluing Mechanism of Work

257. Utterback, J. M., & Abernathy, W. J. (1975). A dynamic model of process and product innovation. *Omega, 3*(6), 639–656. https://doi.org/10.1016/0305-0483(75)90068-7
258. Christensen, C. M. (1997). *The innovator's dilemma: When new technologies cause great firms to fail.* Harvard Business School Press.
259. Simon, H. A. (1955). A behavioral model of rational choice. *The Quarterly Journal of Economics, 69*(1), 99–118. https://doi.org/10.2307/1884852
260. Henderson, R. M., & Clark, K. B. (1990). Architectural innovation: The reconfiguration of existing product technologies and the failure of established firms. *Administrative Science Quarterly, 35*(1), 9–30. https://doi.org/10.2307/2393549
261. Schumpeter, J. A. (1942). *Capitalism, socialism and democracy*. Harper & Brothers.

262. Jardine, A. K. S., Lin, D., & Banjevic, D. (2006). A review on machinery diagnostics and prognostics implementing condition-based maintenance. *Mechanical Systems and Signal Processing, 20*(7), 1483–1510. https://doi.org/10.1016/j.ymssp.2005.09.012
263. Alaswad, S., & Xiang, Y. (2017). A review on condition-based maintenance optimization models for stochastically deteriorating system. *Reliability Engineering & System Safety, 157*, 54–63. https://doi.org/10.1016/j.ress.2016.08.009
264. Sexton, T., Hodkiewicz, M., & Brundage, M. P. (2019). Categorization errors for data entry in maintenance work-orders. *Proceedings of the Annual Conference of the PHM Society, 11*(1). https://doi.org/10.36001/phmconf.2019.v11i1.790
265. van Oudenhoven, B., Demerouti, E., Basten, R. J. I., & Van de Calseyde, P. P. F. M. (2025). Preparing for predictive maintenance: Employee perspectives on job demands and resources before and after its implementation. *Applied Ergonomics, 123*, 104561. https://doi.org/10.1016/j.apergo.2025.104561
266. Zonta, T., da Costa, C. A., da Rosa Righi, R., de Lima, M. J., da Trindade, E. S., & Li, G. P. (2020). Predictive maintenance in the Industry 4.0: A systematic literature review. *Computers & Industrial Engineering, 150*, 106889. https://doi.org/10.1016/j.cie.2020.106889
267. Lee, J., Bagheri, B., & Kao, H.-A. (2015). A cyber-physical systems architecture for Industry 4.0-based manufacturing systems. *Manufacturing Letters, 3*, 18–23. https://doi.org/10.1016/j.mfglet.2014.12.001
268. da Silva, A. F., Ohta, R. L., dos Santos, M. N., & Binotto, A. P. D. (2016). A cloud-based architecture for the Internet of Things targeting industrial devices: Remote monitoring and control. *IFAC-PapersOnLine, 49*(30), 108–113. https://doi.org/10.1016/j.ifacol.2016.11.137
269. Lee, J. D., & See, K. A. (2004). Trust in automation: Designing for appropriate reliance. *Human Factors, 46*(1), 50–80. https://journals.sagepub.com/doi/10.1518/hfes.46.1.50_30392
270. Cummins, L., Sommers, A., Ramezani, S. B., Mittal, S., Jabour, J., Seale, M., & Rahimi, S. (2024). *Explainable predictive maintenance: A survey of current methods, challenges and opportunities. IEEE Access, 12*, 57574–57602. https://doi.org/10.1109/ACCESS.2024.3391130

271. Grubic, T., & Jennions, I. (2018). Do outcome-based contracts exist? The investigation of power-by-the-hour and similar result-oriented cases. *International Journal of Production Economics*, *206*, 209–219. https://doi.org/10.1016/j.ijpe.2018.10.004
272. Heng, A. E., Zhang, S., Tan, A. C. C., & Mathew, J. (2009). Rotating machinery prognostics: State of the art, challenges and opportunities. *Mechanical Systems and Signal Processing*, *23*(3), 724–739. https://doi.org/10.1016/j.ymssp.2008.06.009
273. Saxena, A., Celaya, J., Saha, B., Saha, S., & Goebel, K. (2010). Metrics for offline evaluation of prognostic performance. *International Journal of Prognostics and Health Management*, *1*(1). https://doi.org/10.36001/ijphm.2010.v1i1.1336
274. Errandonea, I., Beltrán, S., & Arrizabalaga, S. (2020). Digital twin for maintenance: A literature review. *Computers in Industry*, *123*, 103316. https://doi.org/10.1016/j.compind.2020.103316
275. Tambon, F., Laberge, G., An, L., Nikanjam, A., Mindom, P. S. N., Pequignot, Y., Khomh, F., Antoniol, G., Merlo, E., & Laviolette, F. (2022). How to certify machine learning based safety-critical systems? A systematic literature review. *Automated Software Engineering*, *29*(2). https://doi.org/10.1007/s10515-022-00337-x
276. Theissler, A., Pérez-Velázquez, J., Kettelgerdes, M., & Elger, G. (2021). Predictive maintenance enabled by machine learning: Use cases and challenges in the automotive industry. *Reliability Engineering & System Safety*, *215*, 107864. https://doi.org/10.1016/j.ress.2021.107864
277. European Parliament, & Council of the European Union. (2009). *Directive 2009/38/EC of the European Parliament and of the Council of 6 May 2009 on the establishment of a European Works Council or a procedure in Community-scale undertakings and Community-scale groups of undertakings for the purposes of informing and consulting employees (Recast). Official Journal of the European Union L 122*, 28–44. https://eur-lex.europa.eu/eli/dir/2009/38/oj/eng
278. Council of the European Communities. (1989). *Council Directive 89/391/EEC of 12 June 1989 on the introduction of measures to encourage improvements in the safety and health of workers at work. Official Journal of the European Communities, L 183*, 1–8. https://eur-lex.europa.eu/eli/dir/1989/391/oj/eng

279. European Parliament, & Council of the European Union. (2002). *Directive 2002/14/EC of the European Parliament and of the Council of 11 March 2002 establishing a general framework for informing and consulting employees in the European Community. Official Journal of the European Communities, L 80*, 29–34. https://eur-lex.europa.eu/eli/dir/2002/14/oj/eng
280. European Parliament, & Council of the European Union. (2019). *Directive (EU) 2019/1937 of the European Parliament and of the Council of 23 October 2019 on the protection of persons who report breaches of Union law. Official Journal of the European Union, L 305*, 17–56. https://eur-lex.europa.eu/eli/dir/2019/1937/oj/eng
281. European Parliament, & Council of the European Union. (2014). *Regulation (EU) No 376/2014 of the European Parliament and of the Council of 3 April 2014 on the reporting, analysis and follow-up of occurrences in civil aviation. Official Journal of the European Union, L, 122*, 18–43. https://eur-lex.europa.eu/eli/reg/2014/376/oj/eng
282. European Commission. (2015). *Guidance material on Regulation (EU) No 376/2014 and its implementing rules*. Directorate-General for Mobility and Transport. https://transport.ec.europa.eu/document/download/6c3ae15f-8452-4c71-890a-280a2145dc7d_en?filename=guidancematerial376.pdf
283. European Parliament, & Council of the European Union. (2024). *Regulation (EU) 2024/1689 of the European Parliament and of the Council of 13 June 2024 laying down harmonised rules on artificial intelligence (Artificial Intelligence Act). Official Journal of the European Union, L 1689*. https://eur-lex.europa.eu/eli/reg/2024/1689/oj/eng

The Taskification of Work

284. Orlikowski, W. J. (2000). Using technology and constituting structures: A practice lens for studying technology in organizations. *Organization Science, 11*(4), 404–428. https://doi.org/10.1287/orsc.11.4.404.14600
285. Tversky, A., & Kahneman, D. (1981). The framing of decisions and the psychology of choice. *Science, 211*(4481), 453–458. https://doi.org/10.1126/science.7455683

286. Zhang, J., & Norman, D. A. (1994). Representations in distributed cognitive tasks. *Cognitive Science, 18*(1), 87–122. https://doi.org/10.1207/s15516709cog1801_3
287. Kirsh, D. (2010). Thinking with external representations. *AI & Society, 25*, 441–454. https://doi.org/10.1007/s00146-010-0272-8
288. Almada, M. (2019). Human intervention in automated decision-making: Toward the construction of contestable systems. In *Proceedings of the Seventeenth International Conference on Artificial Intelligence and Law (ICAIL '19)* (pp. 2–11). Association for Computing Machinery. https://doi.org/10.1145/3322640.3326699
289. Alfrink, K., Keller, I., Kortuem, G., & Doorn, N. (2023). Contestable AI by design: Towards a framework. *Minds & Machines, 33*(4), 613–639. https://doi.org/10.1007/s11023-022-09611-z
290. Cavalcante Siebert, L., Lupetti, M. L., Aizenberg, E., Beckers, N., Zgonnikov, A., Veluwenkamp, H., Abbink, D., Giaccardi, E., Houben, G.-J., Jonker, C. M., van den Hoven, J., Forster, D., & Lagendijk, R. L. (2023). Meaningful human control: Actionable properties for AI system development. *AI and Ethics, 3*, 241–255. https://doi.org/10.1007/s43681-022-00167-3

The New Human Worth Limit

291. Autor, D. H. (2015). Why are there still so many jobs? The history and future of workplace automation. *Journal of Economic Perspectives, 29*(3), 3–30. https://doi.org/10.1257/jep.29.3.3
292. Caprettini, B., & Voth, H.-J. (2020). Rage against the machines: Labor-saving technology and unrest in industrializing England. *American Economic Review: Insights, 2*(3), 305–320. https://doi.org/10.1257/aeri.20190385
293. Dincecco, M., & Katz, G. (2016). State capacity and long-run economic performance. *The Economic Journal, 126*(590), 189–218. https://doi.org/10.1111/ecoj.12161
294. McCloskey, D. N. (1970). Did Victorian Britain fail? *The Economic History Review, 23*(3), 446–459. https://doi.org/10.1111/j.1468-0289.1970.tb01037.x
295. Alvarez-Cuadrado, F., & Poschke, M. (2011). Structural change out of agriculture: Labor push versus labor pull. *American Economic Journal: Macroeconomics, 3*(3), 127–158. https://doi.org/10.1257/mac.3.3.127

296. Britannica Editors. (2026, May 14). *Industrial Revolution. Encyclopedia Britannica.* https://www.britannica.com/event/Industrial-Revolution
297. Britannica Editors (2026, April 20). *Edmund Cartwright. Encyclopedia Britannica.* https://www.britannica.com/biography/Edmund-Cartwright
298. Landes, D. S. (2003). *The unbound Prometheus: Technological change and industrial development in Western Europe from 1750 to the present.* Cambridge University Press.
299. Acemoglu, D., & Johnson, S. (2024, May). *Learning from Ricardo and Thompson: Machinery and labor in the early Industrial Revolution, and in the age of AI* (NBER Working Paper No. 32416). National Bureau of Economic Research. https://doi.org/10.3386/w32416
300. Bythell, D. (1969). *The handloom weavers: A study in the English cotton industry during the Industrial Revolution.* Cambridge University Press
301. Thompson, E. P. (1966). *The making of the English working class.* Vintage Books.
302. Britannica Editors (2026, February 19). *Luddite. Encyclopedia Britannica.* https://www.britannica.com/event/Luddite
303. Library of Congress. (n.d.). *Ford implements the moving assembly line.* In *This month in business history*. Retrieved January 3, 2026, from https://guides.loc.gov/this-month-in-business-history/October/Ford
304. Barger, H., & Schurr, S. H. (1944). The mechanization of the mining process. In *The mining industries, 1899–1939: A study of output, employment, and productivity* (pp. 117–145). National Bureau of Economic Research. https://www.nber.org/system/files/chapters/c6321/c6321.pdf
305. Weinberg, E., Malakoff, R. E., & Adams, R. T. (1961, November). *Technological change and productivity in the bituminous coal industry, 1920–60* (Bulletin No. 1305). U.S. Department of Labor, Bureau of Labor Statistics. https://fraser.stlouisfed.org/files/docs/publications/bls/bls_1305_1961.pdf
306. Dimitri, C., Effland, A., & Conklin, N. (2005, June). *The 20th century transformation of U.S. agriculture and farm policy* (Economic Information Bulletin No. 3). U.S. Department of Agriculture, Economic Research Service. https://ers.usda.gov/sites/default/files/_laserfiche/publications/44197/13566_eib3_1_.pdf
307. Quinion, M. (2004, December 4). Saggar. *Worldwide Words.* https://www.worldwidewords.org/ww-sag1.html

308. International Bowling Museum and Hall of Fame. (n.d.). *Pinsetters in the postwar era. Bowling Heritage.* Retrieved June 8, 2026, from https://www.bowlingheritage.com/item/pinsetters-in-the-postwar-era
309. Nye, D. E. (2018). *American illuminations: Urban lighting, 1800–1920.* The MIT Press.
310. Wyatt, I. D., & Hecker, D. E. (2006, March). *Occupational changes during the 20th century. Monthly Labor Review, 129*(3), 35–57. https://www.bls.gov/opub/mlr/2006/03/art3full.pdf
311. Dahlbeck, E., Gärtner, S., Best, B., Kurwan, J., Wehnert, T., & Beutel, J. (2022, January). *Analysis of the historical structural change in the German hard coal mining Ruhr area (case study)* (Climate Change 30/2021; Report No. FB000717/ENG). German Environment Agency (Umweltbundesamt). https://www.umweltbundesamt.de/sites/default/files/medien/11850/publikationen/2025-03-03_cc_30-2021_case-study_analysis_historical_structural_change_ruhr_area.pdf
312. Rubenstein, J. M. (1996). *The evolving geography of production: Is manufacturing activity moving out of the Midwest? Evidence from the auto industry* (Assessing the Midwest Economy, No. SP-3). Federal Reserve Bank of Chicago. https://econpapers.repec.org/paper/fipfedhas/sp-3.htm
313. Hunt, H. A. (1983, May 17). *Hearings on the impact of technology on the workforce of the 1980's* [Testimony presented to the U.S. House of Representatives, Committee on Small Business, Subcommittee on General Oversight and the Economy]. W.E. Upjohn Institute for Employment Research. https://research.upjohn.org/cgi/viewcontent.cgi?article=1020&context=testimonies
314. Spreen, T. L., Wang, Z., & Yang, L. (2025). Industrial automation and local public goods. *Journal of Public Economics, 247*, 105394. https://doi.org/10.1016/j.jpubeco.2025.105394
315. Vermeulen, W., & Braakmann, N. (2023). *How do mass lay-offs affect regional economies?* (OECD Local Economic and Employment Development [LEED] Papers, 2023/01). OECD Publishing. https://doi.org/10.1787/99d48aeb-en
316. Wishner, J., Solleveld, P., Rudowitz, R., Paradise, J., & Antonisse, L. (2016, July 7). *A look at rural hospital closures and implications for access to care:*

Three case studies. Urban Institute; Kaiser Family Foundation. https://www.urban.org/sites/default/files/publication/82511/2000857-brief-a-look-at-rural-hospital-closures-and-implications-for-access-to-care.pdf

317. Bolt, J., & van Zanden, J. L. (2023). *GDP per capita – Maddison Project Database – Long-run data in constant international-$* [Data set]. Our World in Data (with minor processing). Retrieved January 3, 2026, from https://ourworldindata.org/grapher/gdp-per-capita-maddison-project-database
318. Crafts, N. (2020, May). *Slow real wage growth during the Industrial Revolution: Productivity paradox or pro-rich growth?* (CAGE Working Paper No. 474). Centre for Competitive Advantage in the Global Economy (CAGE), University of Warwick.
319. Nordhaus, W. D. (1996). Do real-output and real-wage measures capture reality? The history of lighting suggests not. In T. F. Bresnahan & R. J. Gordon (Eds.), *The economics of new goods* (pp. 27–70). University of Chicago Press. https://www.nber.org/system/files/chapters/c6064/c6064.pdf
320. Bresnahan, T. F., & Trajtenberg, M. (1995). General purpose technologies "Engines of growth"? *Journal of Econometrics, 65*(1), 83–108. https://doi.org/10.1016/0304-4076(94)01598-T
321. Bolt, J., & van Zanden, J. L. (2024). *Maddison Project Database 2023* (Version 1.0) [Data set]. DataverseNL. https://doi.org/10.34894/INZBF2
322. World Inequality Lab. (2022). *Chapter 10: Emancipation, redistribution and sustainability*. In *World inequality report 2022*. https://wir2022.wid.world/chapter-10/
323. Herrendorf, B., Rogerson, R., & Valentinyi, Á. (2013, April). *Growth and structural transformation* (NBER Working Paper No. 18996). National Bureau of Economic Research. https://doi.org/10.3386/w18996
324. Office for National Statistics. (2019, April 29). *Long-term trends in UK employment: 1861 to 2018*. https://www.ons.gov.uk/economy/nationalaccounts/uksectoraccounts/compendium/economicreview/april2019/longtermtrendsinukemployment1861to2018

325. Critchlow, R. V., & Herman, A. S. (1973). *Outlook for technology and manpower in printing and publishing* (Bulletin No. 1774). U.S. Department of Labor, Bureau of Labor Statistics. https://files.eric.ed.gov/fulltext/ED096422.pdf
326. Seybold, J. (2018, September). *Early steps in computer typesetting in the 1960s. IEEE Annals of the History of Computing* (online PDF). https://history.computer.org/annals/dtp/rocappi-typesetting.pdf
327. Ahrefs. (2025). *The State of AI in Content Marketing* [Report]. https://ahrefs.com/blog/wp-content/uploads/2025/06/AI-in-Content-Marketing-by-Ahrefs.pdf
328. European Language Industry Survey. (2024). *European Language Industry Survey 2024 report.* https://elis-survey.org/wp-content/uploads/2024/03/ELIS-2024-Report.pdf
329. Creamer, E. (2024, April 16). *Survey finds generative AI proving major threat to the work of translators. The Guardian.* https://www.theguardian.com/books/2024/apr/16/survey-finds-generative-ai-proving-major-threat-to-the-work-of-translators
330. The Sedona Conference. (2023). *The Sedona Conference TAR case law primer* (2nd ed.). *The Sedona Conference Journal, 24*, 1–92. https://www.thesedonaconference.org/sites/default/files/publications/Tar-Case-Law-Primer-2nd-Edition-2023.pdf
331. U.S. Bureau of Labor Statistics. (2025, August 28). *Medical transcriptionists. Occupational Outlook Handbook. U.S. Department of Labor.* https://www.bls.gov/ooh/healthcare/medical-transcriptionists.htm
332. Gartner. (2025, March 5). *Gartner predicts agentic AI will autonomously resolve 80% of common customer service issues without human intervention by 2029.* https://www.gartner.com/en/newsroom/press-releases/2025-03-05-gartner-predicts-agentic-ai-will-autonomously-resolve-80-percent-of-common-customer-service-issues-without-human-intervention-by-20290
333. Demirci, O., Hannane, J., & Zhu, X. (2024, August). *Who is AI replacing? The impact of generative AI on online freelancing platforms* (CESifo Working Paper No. 11276). CESifo. https://www.ifo.de/DocDL/cesifo1_wp11276.pdf
334. Hui, X., Reshef, O., & Zhou, L. (2023, August). *The short-term effects of generative artificial intelligence on employment: Evidence from an online*

labor market (CESifo Working Paper No. 10601). CESifo. https://www.ifo.de/DocDL/cesifo1_wp10601.pdf

335. Teutloff, O., Einsiedler, J., Kässi, O., Braesemann, F., Mishkin, P., & del Rio-Chanona, R. M. (2025). Winners and losers of generative AI: Early evidence of shifts in freelancer demand. *Journal of Economic Behavior & Organization, 235*, 106845. https://doi.org/10.1016/j.jebo.2024.106845

The Algorithmic Burden on Gender

336. Dansgaard, W., Johnsen, S. J., Clausen, H. B., Dahl-Jensen, D., Gundestrup, N. S., Hammer, C. U., Hvidberg, C. S., Steffensen, J. P., Sveinbjörnsdottir, A. E., Jouzel, J., & Bond, G. (1993). Evidence for general instability of past climate from a 250-kyr ice-core record. *Nature, 364*, 218–220. https://doi.org/10.1038/364218a0
337. Gurven, M., & Hill, K. (2009). Why do men hunt? A reevaluation of "Man the Hunter" and the sexual division of labor. *Current Anthropology, 50*(1), 51–65. https://doi.org/10.1086/595620
338. Marlowe, F. W. (2007). Hunting and gathering: The human sexual division of foraging labor. *Cross-Cultural Research, 41*(2), 170–195. https://doi.org/10.1177/1069397106297529
339. Wrangham, R. W., & Glowacki, L. (2012). Intergroup aggression in chimpanzees and war in nomadic hunter-gatherers: Evaluating the chimpanzee model. *Human Nature, 23*(1), 5–29. https://doi.org/10.1007/s12110-012-9132-1
340. Walker, M., Johnsen, S. J., Rasmussen, S. O., Popp, T. J., Steffensen, J. P., Gibbard, P., Hoek, W., Lowe, J., Andrews, J., Björck, S., Cwynar, L. C., Hughen, K., Kershaw, P., Kromer, B., Litt, T., Lowe, D. J., Nakagawa, T., Newnham, R., & Schwander, J. (2009). Formal definition and dating of the GSSP (Global Stratotype Section and Point) for the base of the Holocene using the Greenland NGRIP ice core, and selected auxiliary records. *Journal of Quaternary Science, 24*(1), 3–17. https://doi.org/10.1002/jqs.1227
341. Thomas, E. R., Wolff, E. W., Mulvaney, R., Steffensen, J. P., Johnsen, S. J., Arrowsmith, C., White, J. W. C., Vaughn, B., & Popp, T. (2007). The 8.2 ka event from Greenland ice cores. *Quaternary Science Reviews, 26*(1–2), 70–81. https://doi.org/10.1016/j.quascirev.2006.07.017

342. Richerson, P. J., Boyd, R., & Bettinger, R. L. (2001). Was agriculture impossible during the Pleistocene but mandatory during the Holocene? A climate change hypothesis. *American Antiquity, 66*(3), 387–411. https://doi.org/10.2307/2694241
343. Tanno, K.-I., & Willcox, G. (2006). How fast was wild wheat domesticated? *Science, 311*(5769), 1886. https://doi.org/10.1126/science.1124635
344. Fuller, D. Q., Qin, L., Zheng, Y., Zhao, Z., Chen, X., Hosoya, L. A., & Sun, G.-P. (2009). The domestication process and domestication rate in rice: Spikelet bases from the Lower Yangtze. *Science, 323*(5921), 1607–1610. https://doi.org/10.1126/science.1166605
345. Piperno, D. R., Ranere, A. J., Holst, I., Iriarte, J., & Dickau, R. (2009). Starch grain and phytolith evidence for early ninth millennium B.P. maize from the Central Balsas River Valley, Mexico. *Proceedings of the National Academy of Sciences of the United States of America, 106*(13), 5019–5024. https://doi.org/10.1073/pnas.0812525106
346. Bogaard, A., Charles, M., Twiss, K. C., Fairbairn, A., Yalman, N., Filipović, D., Demirergi, G. A., Ertuğ, F., Russell, N., & Henecke, J. (2009). Private pantries and celebrated surplus: Storing and sharing food at Neolithic Çatalhöyük, Central Anatolia. *Antiquity, 83*(321), 649–668. https://doi.org/10.1017/S0003598X00098896
347. Akkermans, P. M. M. G., & Duistermaat, K. (1996). Of storage and nomads: The sealings from late Neolithic Sabi Abyad, Syria. *Paléorient, 22*(2), 17–44. https://doi.org/10.3406/paleo.1996.4635
348. Pollock, S. (2012). Politics of food in early Mesopotamian centralized societies. *Origini, 34*, 153–168.
349. Frangipane, M. (2016). The origins of administrative practices and their developments in Greater Mesopotamia. The evidence from Arslantepe. *Archéo-Nil, 26*, 9–32. https://doi.org/10.3406/arnil.2016.1101
350. Bailey, M. (2019). Tallage-at-will in later medieval England. *The English Historical Review, 134*(566), 25–58. https://doi.org/10.1093/ehr/cez002
351. Levett, A. E. (1927). The financial organization of the manor. *The Economic History Review, 1*(1), 65–86. https://doi.org/10.1111/j.1468-0289.1927.tb00750.x

352. Schofield, P. R. (2005). Manorial court rolls and the peasant land market in Eastern England, c. 1250–c. 1350. In *Le marché de la terre au Moyen Âge* (Publications de l'École française de Rome, 350, pp. 237–271). École française de Rome.
353. Aubriot, O., & Prabhakar, P. I. (2011). Water institutions and the "revival" of tanks in South India: What is at stake locally? *Water Alternatives*, *4*(3), 325–346. https://www.water-alternatives.org/index.php/volume4/v4issue3/145-a4-3-4/file
354. Morrison, K. D. (2015). Archaeologies of flow: Water and the landscapes of southern India past, present, and future. *Journal of Field Archaeology*, *40*(5), 560–580. https://doi.org/10.1179/2042458215Y.0000000033
355. Mosse, D. (1997). The symbolic making of a common property resource: History, ecology and locality in a tank-irrigated landscape in South India. *Development and Change*, *28*(3), 467–504. https://doi.org/10.1111/1467-7660.00051
356. Lundberg, S., & Stearns, J. (2018). *Women in economics: Stalled progress* (IZA Discussion Paper No. 11974). IZA Institute of Labor Economics. https://docs.iza.org/dp11974.pdf
357. Pal, S., Marino Lazzaroni, R., & Mendoza, P. (2024, October 10). *AI's missing link: The gender gap in the talent pool.* Interface. https://www.interface-eu.org/publications/ai-gender-gap
358. Russell Reynolds Associates. (2025, February 11). *AI for all: The case for more women leaders in AI.* Russell Reynolds Associates. https://www.russellreynolds.com/en/insights/articles/the-case-for-more-women-leaders-in-ai
359. Ali, M., Sapiezynski, P., Bogen, M., Korolova, A., Mislove, A., & Rieke, A. (2019). Discrimination through optimization: How Facebook's ad delivery can lead to biased outcomes. *Proceedings of the ACM on Human-Computer Interaction*, *3*(CSCW), Article 199, 1–30. https://doi.org/10.1145/3359301
360. Dastin, J. (2018, October 11). *Insight–Amazon scraps secret AI recruiting tool that showed bias against women.* Reuters. https://www.reuters.com/article/world/insight-amazon-scraps-secret-ai-recruiting-tool-that-showed-bias-against-women-idUSKCN1MK0AG/

361. Li, G. (2018, June 22). *Gender-related differences in credit use and credit scores* (FEDS Notes). Board of Governors of the Federal Reserve System. https://doi.org/10.17016/2380-7172.2188
362. Liu, Z., & Liang, H. (2025). Are credit scores gender-neutral? Evidence of mis-calibration from alternative and traditional borrowing data. *Journal of Behavioral and Experimental Finance, 47*, 101081. https://doi.org/10.1016/j.jbef.2025.101081
363. Obermeyer, Z., Powers, B., Vogeli, C., & Mullainathan, S. (2019). Dissecting racial bias in an algorithm used to manage the health of populations. *Science, 366*(6464), 447–453. https://doi.org/10.1126/science.aax2342
364. Gmyrek, P., Berg, J., & Bescond, D. (2023). *Generative AI and jobs: A global analysis of potential effects on job quantity and quality* (ILO Working Paper No. 96). International Labour Organization. https://doi.org/10.54394/FHEM8239
365. Gmyrek, P., Berg, J., Kamiński, K., Konopczyński, F., Ładna, A., Nafradi, B., Rosłaniec, K., & Troszyński, M. (2025). *Generative AI and jobs: A refined global index of occupational exposure* (ILO Working Paper No. 140). International Labour Organization. https://doi.org/10.54394/HETP0387
366. Hagan, J., Simpson, J., & Gillis, A. R. (1987). Class in the household: A power-control theory of gender and delinquency. *American Journal of Sociology, 92*(4), 788–816. http://www.jstor.org/stable/2780039
367. Gruber, S., & Szołtysek, M. (2016). The patriarchy index: A comparative study of power relations across historic Europe. *The History of the Family, 21*(2), 133–174. https://doi.org/10.1080/1081602X.2014.1001769
368. World Economic Forum. (2025). *Global gender gap report 2025.* https://www.weforum.org/publications/global-gender-gap-report-2025/digest/
369. Gardberg, M., Heyman, F., Olsson, M., & Tåg, J. (2025, September 25). *Pre-AI sorting, post-AI inequality: Generative AI and the gender wage gap* (IFN Working Paper No. 1534). SSRN. https://doi.org/10.2139/ssrn.5532560

370. World Bank Group. (2024). *World Bank Group gender strategy 2024–2030: Accelerate gender equality to end poverty on a livable planet.* World Bank. https://documents.worldbank.org/en/publication/documents-reports/documentdetail/099012624171522021

The Human In(ter)ference

371. Hinton, G. (2024, December 10). *Banquet speech.* NobelPrize.org. https://www.nobelprize.org/prizes/physics/2024/hinton/speech/
372. Marcus, G. (2023, May 16). *Senate testimony* [Testimony before the Senate Committee on the Judiciary, Subcommittee on Privacy, Technology, and the Law, hearing "Oversight of A.I.: Rules for Artificial Intelligence"]. United States Senate Committee on the Judiciary. https://www.judiciary.senate.gov/imo/media/doc/2023-05-16%20-%20Testimony%20-%20Marcus.pdf
373. Leivada, E., Marcus, G., Günther, F., & Murphy, E. (2024). A sentence is worth a thousand pictures: Can large language models understand hum4n l4ngu4ge and the w0rld behind w0rds?. [Preprint]. *arXiv.* https://doi.org/10.48550/arXiv.2308.00109
374. Murphy, H., & Criddle, C. (2024, May 22). Meta AI chief says large language models will not reach human intelligence. *Financial Times.* https://www.ft.com/content/23fab126-f1d3-4add-a457-207a25730ad9
375. Patel, D. (2024, February 28). *Demis Hassabis — Scaling, superhuman AIs, AlphaZero atop LLMs, AlphaFold* [Podcast episode transcript]. *Dwarkesh Podcast.* https://www.dwarkesh.com/p/demis-hassabis
376. Hassabis, D. (2024, December 8). *Accelerating scientific discovery with AI* [Nobel lecture slides]. NobelPrize.org. https://www.nobelprize.org/uploads/2024/12/hassabis-lecture.pdf
377. Council on Foreign Relations. (2025, March 10). *CEO Speaker Series with Dario Amodei of Anthropic* [Transcript]. https://www.cfr.org/event/ceo-speaker-series-dario-amodei-anthropic
378. Suleyman, M., & Bhaskar, M. (2023, September 6). AI can be an extraordinary force for good—if it's contained. *Wired.* https://www.wired.com/story/ai-containment-regulation-suleyman

379. Mann, H. (2025, May 19). Artificial integrity over intelligence is the new AI frontier. *California Management Review*. https://cmr.berkeley.edu/2025/05/artificial-integrity-over-intelligence-is-the-new-ai-frontier
380. Solow, R. M. (1987, July 12). *We'd better watch out. The New York Times Book Review*, 36. https://www.standupeconomist.com/pdf/misc/solow-computer-productivity.pdf
381. Zuboff, S. (2015). Big other: Surveillance capitalism and the prospects of an information civilization. *Journal of Information Technology, 30*(1), 75–89. https://doi.org/10.1057/jit.2015.5
382. Acemoglu, D., & Restrepo, P. (2018). *Artificial intelligence, automation and work* (NBER Working Paper No. 24196). National Bureau of Economic Research. https://www.nber.org/system/files/working_papers/w24196/w24196.pdf
383. Acemoglu, D., & Restrepo, P. (2020). The wrong kind of AI? Artificial intelligence and the future of labour demand. *Cambridge Journal of Regions, Economy and Society, 13*(1), 25–35. https://doi.org/10.1093/cjres/rsz022
384. Stiglitz, J. E. (2017, November). *Inequality, stagnation, and market power*. Roosevelt Institute. https://rooseveltinstitute.org/wp-content/uploads/2020/07/RI-Inequality-Stagnation-Market-Power-201711.pdf
385. Autor, D. H. (2013). The "task approach" to labor markets: An overview. *Journal for Labour Market Research, 46*(3), 185–199. https://doi.org/10.1007/s12651-013-0128-z
386. Wiener, N. (1960). Some moral and technical consequences of automation. *Science, 131*(3410), 1355–1358. https://doi.org/10.1126/science.131.3410.1355
387. Li, F.-F. (2025, November 10). *From words to worlds: Spatial intelligence is AI's next frontier. Dr. Fei-Fei Li's Substack*. https://drfeifei.substack.com/p/from-words-to-worlds-spatial-intelligence
388. Leveson, N. G., & Turner, C. S. (1993). An investigation of the Therac-25 accidents. *Computer, 26*(7), 18–41. https://doi.org/10.1109/MC.1993.274940

Humane Algorithmic Transition

The Flawed Assumption Behind AI Decision-Making

389. Zewe, A. (2024, April 19). *To build a better AI helper, start by modeling the irrational behavior of humans.* MIT News. https://www.eecs.mit.edu/to-build-a-better-ai-helper-start-by-modeling-the-irrational-behavior-of-humans
390. Zander, T., Horr, N. K., Bolte, A., & Volz, K. G. (2016). Intuitive decision making as a gradual process: Investigating semantic intuition-based and priming-based decisions with fMRI. *Brain and Behavior, 6*(1), e00420. https://doi.org/10.1002/brb3.420
391. Sahlin, U., Troffaes, M. C. M., & Edsman, L. (2021). Robust decision analysis under severe uncertainty and ambiguous tradeoffs: An invasive species case study. *Risk Analysis, 41*(11), 2140–2153. https://doi.org/10.1111/risa.13722
392. Ahmed, M., Ansar, K., Muckley, C. B., Khan, A., Anjum, A., & Talha, M. (2021). *A semantic rule based digital fraud detection. PeerJ Computer Science,* 7, e649. https://doi.org/10.7717/peerj-cs.649
393. Hasson Marques, R., Violant-Holz, V., & Damião da Silva, E. (2024). Emotions and decision-making in boardrooms—a systematic review from behavioral strategy perspective. *Frontiers in Psychology, 15*, 1473175. https://doi.org/10.3389/fpsyg.2024.1473175
394. Social Science Space. (2022, August 31). *Gerd Gigerenzer on decision-making.* https://www.socialsciencespace.com/2022/08/gerd-gigerenzer-on-decision-making
395. Berekméri, E., & Zafeiris, A. (2020). Optimal collective decision making: Consensus, accuracy and the effects of limited access to information. *Scientific Reports, 10*, 16997. https://doi.org/10.1038/s41598-020-73853-z
396. Fresh Perspectives. (2014, October 14). *Recognition-primed decision model – Gary Klein on Fresh Perspectives [Video].* YouTube. https://www.youtube.com/watch?v=_BIMU8zPcrM
397. Siqi-Liu, A., Egner, T., & Woldorff, M. G. (2022). Neural dynamics of context-sensitive adjustments in cognitive flexibility. *Journal of Cognitive Neuroscience, 34*(3), 480–494. https://doi.org/10.1162/jocn_a_01813

398. Ganji, G., & Zarifhonarvar, A. (2025). *Generative AI economic behavior: Evidence from risk and time preference elicitation.* SSRN. https://doi.org/10.2139/ssrn.5154002

399. Keswani, V., Conitzer, V., Sinnott-Armstrong, W., Nguyen, B. K., Heidari, H., & Schaich Borg, J. (2025). *Can AI model the complexities of human moral decision-making? A qualitative study of kidney allocation decisions.* In *Proceedings of the CHI Conference on Human Factors in Computing Systems* (CHI '25). Association for Computing Machinery. https://doi.org/10.1145/3706598.3714167

400. Jadaun, P., Cui, C., Liu, S., & Incorvia, J. A. C. (2022). *Adaptive cognition implemented with a context-aware and flexible neuron for next-generation artificial intelligence. PNAS Nexus, 1*(5), pgac206. https://doi.org/10.1093/pnasnexus/pgac206

"9 Whats" Toward AI's Algorithmic Power Deployment

401. Butler, S. (2025, February 27). *Ocado to cut 500 technology and finance jobs as AI reduces costs. The Guardian.* https://www.theguardian.com/business/2025/feb/27/ocado-to-cut-500-technology-and-finance-jobs-as-ai-reduces-costs

402. Ocado narrows losses after boost from the grocery business. (2025, February 27). *The Times.* https://www.thetimes.com/business/companies-markets/article/ocado-narrows-losses-after-boost-from-the-grocery-business-802tc88v5

403. Taylor, J. (2025, May 9). 'Tone deaf': US tech company responsible for global IT outage to cut jobs and use AI. *The Guardian.* https://www.theguardian.com/technology/2025/may/09/crowdstrike-to-cut-jobs-and-use-ai

404. Chong Ming, L. (2025, September 29). *Accenture is cutting staff it can't retrain in the age of AI–but it still plans to hire more people.* Business Insider. https://www.businessinsider.com/accenture-consulting-cut-staff-reskill-hiring-ai-era-sweet-earnings-2025-9

405. Foley, S. (2025, September 25). *Accenture to 'exit' staff who cannot be retrained for age of AI. Financial Times.* https://www.ft.com/content/a74f8564-ed5a-42e9-8fb3-d2bddb2b8675

406. Accenture. (2025, September 25). *Accenture reports fourth-quarter and full-year fiscal 2025 results* [Press release]. https://newsroom.accenture.com/content/4q-full-fy25-earnings/accenture-reports-fourth-quarter-and-full-year-fiscal-2025-results.pdf

407. Accenture. (2025, October 10). *Accenture 2025 letter to shareholders* [Letter]. Retrieved January 6, 2026, from https://investor.accenture.com/~/media/Files/A/accenture-v4/investors/home/accenture-2025-letter-to-shareholders.pdf

408. NHS England. (2025, April 27). *AI-enabled ambient scribing products in health and care settings* [Long read]. Retrieved January 6, 2026, from https://www.england.nhs.uk/long-read/ai-enabled-ambient-scribing-products-in-health-and-care-settings

409. Reed, T. (2023, December 7). *How Delta Air Lines uses AI, yet avoids "hallucinations on steroids". Forbes.* https://www.forbes.com/sites/tedreed/2023/12/07/how-delta-air-lines-uses-ai-yet-avoids-hallucinations-on-steroids

410. Carter, P. (2025, July 31). *Letter to Senators Ruben Gallego, Richard Blumenthal, and Mark Warner regarding Delta's use of artificial intelligence in dynamic pricing* [Letter]. Delta Air Lines, Inc. https://www.gallego.senate.gov/wp-content/uploads/2025/08/Gallego-Response-Letter-07.31.25.pdf

411. Neel Mani, R. (2024, February 17). *CX redefined: Trendsetting use cases of gen AI in aviation. CIO.* https://www.cio.inc/cx-redefined-trendsetting-use-cases-gen-ai-in-aviation-a-24113

412. Delta Air Lines, Inc. (2025). *Delta Difference report 2024 [Report].* Retrieved January 6, 2026, from https://esghub.delta.com/content/dam/esg/2024/pdf/Delta-Difference-2024-Report.pdf

413. Delta Air Lines, Inc. (2024, November 20). *Delta highlights differentiation & durability at 2024 Investor Day* [Press release]. Retrieved January 6, 2026, from https://ir.delta.com/news/news-details/2024/Delta-Highlights-Differentiation--Durability-at-2024-Investor-Day/default.aspx

414. Delta Air Lines, Inc. (2025, January 10). *Delta Air Lines announces December quarter and full year 2024 financial results* [Press release].

Retrieved January 6, 2026, from https://ir.delta.com/news/news-details/2025/Delta-Air-Lines-Announces-December-Quarter-and-Full-Year-2024-Financial-Results/default.aspx

415. Ingka Group. (2024a, April 12). IKEA Retail unleashes AI revolution: Empowering thousands to master the future of tech. Retrieved January 6,2026,from https://www.ingka.com/newsroom/ikea-retail-unleashes-ai-revolution-empowering-thousands-to-master-the-future-of-tech
416. Ingka Group. (2024b). Ingka Group annual report summary FY24 [Report]. Retrieved January 6, 2026, from https://www.ingka.com/static/ingka-group-annual-report-summary-fy24.pdf
417. Sandle, P. (2025, April 7). *AI firm Anthropic announces 100 roles in Europe, new EMEA head. Reuters.* https://www.reuters.com/technology/ai-firm-anthropic-announces-100-roles-europe-new-emea-head-2025-04-07
418. Anthropic. (2025, April 8). *Anthropic appoints Guillaume Princen as Head of EMEA and announces 100+ new roles across the region.* Retrieved January 6, 2026 from https://www.anthropic.com/news/head-of-EMEA-new-roles
419. VandeHei, J., & Allen, M. (2025, May 28). *Behind the Curtain: A white-collar bloodbath. Axios.* Retrieved January 6, 2026 from https://www.axios.com/2025/05/28/ai-jobs-white-collar-unemployment-anthropic
420. Nolan, B. (2025, June 11). *Nvidia's Jensen Huang says he disagrees with almost everything Anthropic CEO Dario Amodei says. Fortune.* https://fortune.com/2025/06/11/nvidia-jensen-huang-disagress-anthropic-ceo-dario-amodei-ai-jobs
421. Tong, A., & Dastin, J. (2025, May 30). *Exclusive: Anthropic hits $3 billion in annualized revenue on business demand for AI. Reuters.* https://www.reuters.com/business/anthropic-hits-3-billion-annualized-revenue-business-demand-ai-2025-05-30
422. McGlauflin, P. (2024, September 27). *Walmart's chief talent officer is turning to the retailer's 2.1 million employees to fulfill hard-to-fill jobs.* HR Brew. https://www.hr-brew.com/stories/2024/09/27/walmart-upskilling-2-million-employees
423. Walmart. (2025a, June 5). Walmart pilots AI Interview Coach and accelerates Associate to Technician program to fuel careers. Walmart Corporate. Retrieved January 6, 2026 from https://corporate.walmart

.com/news/2025/06/05/walmart-pilots-ai-interview-coach-and-accelerates-associate-to-technician-program-to-fuel-careers

424. Walmart. (2025b, June 24). *Walmart unveils new AI-powered tools to empower 1.5 million associates*. Walmart Corporate. Retrieved January 6, 2026 from https://corporate.walmart.com/news/2025/06/24/walmart-unveils-new-ai-powered-tools-to-empower-1-5-million-associates
425. Cavale, S. (2025, July 24). *Walmart bets on AI super agents to boost e-commerce growth*. Reuters. https://www.reuters.com/business/retail-consumer/walmart-bets-ai-super-agents-boost-e-commerce-growth-2025-07-24
426. Walmart. (2025c, August 21). *Walmart reports second quarter results (press release filed with Form 8-K).* Walmart Inc. Retrieved January 6, 2026 from https://stock.walmart.com/sec-filings/all-sec-filings/content/0000104169-25-000120/earningsreleasefy26q2.htm
427. Duolingo, Inc. (2025). *Annual report on Form 10-K for the fiscal year ended December 31, 2024*. U.S. Securities and Exchange Commission. https://www.sec.gov/Archives/edgar/data/1562088/000156208825000042/duol-20241231.htm
428. Duolingo, Inc. (2025, February 27). *Q4 and full year 2024 shareholder letter* (filed as an exhibit). U.S. Securities and Exchange Commission. https://www.sec.gov/Archives/edgar/data/1562088/000156208825000039/q4fy24duolingo12-31x24shar.htm
429. Google LLC. (n.d.). *Duolingo: Language lessons* [Mobile app]. Google Play. Retrieved January 6, 2026, from https://play.google.com/store/apps/details?hl=en&id=com.duolingo
430. Duolingo. (2022, December 6). *The 2022 Duolingo language report*. Retrieved January 6, 2026, from https://blog.duolingo.com/2022-duolingo-language-report/
431. Duolingo. (2023, October 11). *The Duolingo app now has math, music, and language*. Retrieved January 6, 2026, from https://blog.duolingo.com/new-subjects/
432. Duolingo, Inc. (2023). *Annual report on Form 10-K for the fiscal year ended December 31, 2022*. U.S. Securities and Exchange Commission. https://www.sec.gov/Archives/edgar/data/1562088/000156208823000052/duol-20221231.htm

The Jevons Paradox Is Not Truly One

433. Jevons, W. S. (1865). *The coal question; an inquiry concerning the progress of the nation, and the probable exhaustion of our coal mines*. Macmillan and Co.
434. Gerlich, M. (2025). AI tools in society: Impacts on cognitive offloading and the future of critical thinking. *Societies, 15*(1), Article 6. https://doi.org/10.3390/soc15010006
435. Rosbach, E., Ganz, J., Ammeling, J., Riener, A., & Aubreville, M. (2024). Automation bias in AI-assisted medical decision-making under time pressure in computational pathology. [Preprint]. *arXiv*. https://doi.org/10.48550/arXiv.2411.00998
436. Green, B., & Chen, Y. (2019). The principles and limits of algorithm-in-the-loop decision making. *Proceedings of the ACM on Human-Computer Interaction, 3*(CSCW), Article 50, 1–24. https://doi.org/10.1145/3359152
437. Ekbia, H. R., & Nardi, B. A. (2017). *Heteromation, and other stories of computing and capitalism*. The MIT Press.
438. Tarafdar, M., Cooper, C. L., & Stich, J.-F. (2019). The technostress trifecta—techno eustress, techno distress and design: Theoretical directions and an agenda for research. *Information Systems Journal, 29*(1), 6–42. https://doi.org/10.1111/isj.12169
439. Monahan, K., & Burlacu, G. (2024, July 23). *From burnout to balance: AI-enhanced work models*. Upwork Research Institute. https://www.upwork.com/research/ai-enhanced-work-models
440. Wessel, L. K., Baiyere, A., Ologeanu-Taddei, R., Cha, J., & Jensen, T. B. (2021). *Unpacking the difference between digital transformation and IT-enabled organizational transformation* [Accepted author manuscript]. Copenhagen Business School Research Portal. https://research-api.cbs.dk/ws/portalfiles/portal/64643887/tina_blegind_jensen_et_al_unpacking_the_difference_between_digital_transformation_acceptedversion.pdf
441. Joseph, D. L., & Newman, D. A. (2010). Emotional intelligence: An integrative meta-analysis and cascading model. *Journal of Applied Psychology, 95*(1), 54–78. https://doi.org/10.1037/a0017286
442. Doğru, Ç. (2022). A meta-analysis of the relationships between emotional intelligence and employee outcomes. *Frontiers in Psychology, 13*, 611348. https://doi.org/10.3389/fpsyg.2022.611348

443. Toral, A., Castilho, S., Hu, K., & Way, A. (2018). Attaining the unattainable? Reassessing claims of human parity in neural machine translation. [Preprint]. *arXiv*. https://doi.org/10.48550/arXiv.1808.10432
444. Rubin, M., Li, J. Z., Zimmerman, F., Ong, D. C., Goldenberg, A., & Perry, A. (2025). Comparing the value of perceived human versus AI-generated empathy. *Nature Human Behaviour, 9*(11), 2345–2359. https://doi.org/10.1038/s41562-025-02247-w

Ruling AI Deployment at Macro-level

445. Ghatak, M., & Maniquet, F. (2019). Universal basic income: Some theoretical aspects. *Annual Review of Economics, 11*, 895–928. https://doi.org/10.1146/annurev-economics-080218-030220
446. Linke, R. (2018, February 7). *Negative income tax, explained.* MIT Sloan School of Management. https://mitsloan.mit.edu/ideas-made-to-matter/negative-income-tax-explained
447. Coote, A., & Gough, I. (2025). Universal basic services. In L. Akenji, P. J. Vergragt, H. Szejnwald Brown, T. S. J. Smith, & L. M. Wallnöfer (Eds.), *Vocabulary for sustainable consumption and lifestyles: A language for our common future* (1st ed.). Routledge. https://doi.org/10.4324/9781003584056-77
448. European Commission, Directorate-General for Employment, Social Affairs and Inclusion. (n.d.). *Minimum income.* Retrieved January 8, 2026, from https://employment-social-affairs.ec.europa.eu/policies-and-activities/social-protection-social-inclusion/addressing-poverty-and-supporting-social-inclusion/active-inclusion/minimum-income_en
449. Social Security Administration. (n.d.). *Otto von Bismarck.* https://www.ssa.gov/history/ottob.html
450. UK Parliament, House of Commons Library. (2008, August 12). *Old Age Pensions Act 1908* (Research Briefing SN04817). https://commonslibrary.parliament.uk/research-briefings/sn04817
451. Social Security Administration. (n.d.). *Social Security History:* https://www.ssa.gov/history/50ed.html
452. Organisation for Economic Co-operation and Development. (2025). *Revenue statistics 2025: Disentangling personal income tax revenue in OECD countries.* OECD Publishing. https://doi.org/10.1787/3a264267-en

Educating Originators, Not Just Operators

453. Organisation for Economic Co-operation and Development. (n.d.). *Earnings by educational attainment.* Retrieved January 9, 2026, from https://www.oecd.org/en/topics/sub-issues/earnings-by-educational-attainment.html
454. U.S. Bureau of Labor Statistics. (2025, August 28). *Education pays: Unemployment rates and earnings by educational attainment, 2024* (Table 5.1). https://www.bls.gov/emp/tables/unemployment-earnings-education.htm
455. Psacharopoulos, G., & Patrinos, H. A. (2018, April). *Returns to investment in education: A decennial review of the global literature* (Policy Research Working Paper No. 8402). World Bank. https://documents1.worldbank.org/curated/en/442521523465644318/pdf/WPS8402.pdf
456. Berkman, L. F. (2014). Commentary: The hidden and not so hidden benefits of work: identity, income and interaction. *International Journal of Epidemiology, 43*(5), 1517–1519. https://doi.org/10.1093/ije/dyu110
457. Bähr, S., Batinic, B., & Collischon, M. (2022). Heterogeneities in the latent functions of employment: New findings from a large-scale German survey. *Frontiers in Psychology, 13*, 909558. https://doi.org/10.3389/fpsyg.2022.909558
458. Agrawal, A. K., Gans, J. S., & Goldfarb, A. (2018, May). *Exploring the impact of artificial intelligence: Prediction versus judgment* (NBER Working Paper No. 24626). National Bureau of Economic Research. https://doi.org/10.3386/w24626
459. Webb, M. (2020, January). *The impact of artificial intelligence on the labor market* [Working paper]. Stanford University. https://www.michaelwebb.co/webb_ai.pdf

Algorithmic Constitutionality

Algorithmic Use Hides the Weight of Governance

460. Chaudhury, A., & Shiromani, S. (2025). *ChameleonBench: Quantifying alignment faking in large language models.* In H.-y. Lee & T. Liu (Eds.), *Proceedings of the 17th Asian conference on machine learning (ACML 2025) (Proceedings of Machine Learning Research, Vol. 304).* PMLR. https://openreview.net/attachment?id=gNvU08xR3W&name=pdf

461. Park, P. S., Goldstein, S., O'Gara, A., Chen, M., & Hendrycks, D. (2024). *AI deception: A survey of examples, risks, and potential solutions. Patterns, 5*(5), 100988. https://doi.org/10.1016/j.patter.2024.100988

462. Hagendorff, T. (2024). *Deception abilities emerged in large language models. Proceedings of the National Academy of Sciences of the United States of America, 121*(24), e2317967121. https://doi.org/10.1073/pnas.2317967121

463. van der Weij, T., Hofstätter, F., Jaffe, O., Brown, S. F., & Ward, F. R. (2025). *AI sandbagging: Language models can strategically underperform on evaluations.* In *Proceedings of the International Conference on Learning Representations (ICLR 2025).* https://openreview.net/forum?id=7Qa2SpjxIS

464. Hadfield-Menell, D., Dragan, A., Abbeel, P., & Russell, S. (2017). *The off-switch game.* In *Proceedings of the AAAI-17 Workshop on AI, Ethics, and Society* (WS-17-02, pp. 115–121). Association for the Advancement of Artificial Intelligence. https://cdn.aaai.org/ocs/ws/ws0354/15156-68335-1-PB.pdf

465. Orseau, L., & Armstrong, S. (2016). *Safely interruptible agents.* In A. Ihler & D. Janzing (Eds.), *Proceedings of the thirty-second conference on uncertainty in artificial intelligence (UAI 2016)* (pp. 557–566). AUAI Press. https://www.auai.org/uai2016/proceedings/papers/68.pdf

466. Turner, A. M., Smith, L., Shah, R., Critch, A., & Tadepalli, P. (2021). Optimal policies tend to seek power. In M. Ranzato, A. Beygelzimer, Y. Dauphin, P. S. Liang, & J. Wortman Vaughan (Eds.), *Advances in neural information processing systems* (Vol. 34, pp. 23063–23074). Curran Associates, Inc. https://proceedings.neurips.cc/paper/2021/file/c26820b8a4c1b3c2aa868d6d57e14a79-Paper.pdf

467. Langosco Di Langosco, L., Koch, J., Sharkey, L. D., Pfau, J., & Krueger, D. (2022). *Goal misgeneralization in deep reinforcement learning.* In K. Chaudhuri, S. Jegelka, L. Song, C. Szepesvári, G. Niu, & S. Sabato (Eds.), *Proceedings of the 39th international conference on machine learning* (Proceedings of Machine Learning Research, Vol. 162, pp. 12004–12019). PMLR. https://proceedings.mlr.press/v162/langosco22a.html

468. Everitt, T., Krakovna, V., Orseau, L., & Hutter, M. (2017). Reinforcement learning with a corrupted reward channel. In *Proceedings of the*

Twenty-Sixth International Joint Conference on Artificial Intelligence (IJCAI 2017) (pp. 4705–4712). International Joint Conferences on Artificial Intelligence Organization. https://www.ijcai.org/proceedings/2017/0656.pdf

469. Qi, X., Zeng, Y., Xie, T., Chen, P.-Y., Jia, R., Mittal, P., & Henderson, P. (2024). *Fine-tuning aligned language models compromises safety, even when users do not intend to!* In *Proceedings of the International Conference on Learning Representations (ICLR 2024)*. https://openreview.net/forum?id=hTEGyKf0dZ
470. Cohen, S., Bitton, R., & Nassi, B. (2025). *Here comes the AI worm: Preventing the propagation of adversarial self-replicating prompts within GenAI ecosystems*. In *Proceedings of the 2025 ACM SIGSAC Conference on Computer and Communications Security (CCS '25)* (pp. 3975–3989). Association for Computing Machinery. https://doi.org/10.1145/3719027.3765196
471. Luo, J., Xiao, B., Xiao, Q., Cao, J., & Guo, M. (2014). *Modeling and defending against adaptive BitTorrent worms in peer-to-peer networks*. *ACM Transactions on Autonomous and Adaptive Systems, 9*(2), Article 5, 5:1–5:17. https://doi.org/10.1145/2567925
472. Moore, D., Shannon, C., Voelker, G. M., & Savage, S. (2003). *Internet quarantine: Requirements for containing self-propagating code*. In *Proceedings IEEE INFOCOM 2003. Twenty-Second Annual Joint Conference of the IEEE Computer and Communications Societies* (Vol. 3, pp. 1901–1910). IEEE. https://doi.org/10.1109/INFCOM.2003.1209212
473. Calvano, E., Calzolari, G., Denicolò, V., & Pastorello, S. (2020). Artificial intelligence, algorithmic pricing, and collusion. *American Economic Review, 110*(10), 3267–3297. https://doi.org/10.1257/aer.20190623
474. Qu, Y., Zhang, T., Garg, N., & Kumar, A. (2024). Recursive introspection: Teaching language model agents how to self-improve. In *Proceedings of the 38th International Conference on Neural Information Processing Systems (NeurIPS '24)* (pp. 55249–55285). Curran Associates, Inc. https://proceedings.neurips.cc/paper_files/paper/2024/file/639d992f819c2b40387d4d5170b8ffd7-Paper-Conference.pdf
475. Lazovich, T. (2023). Filter bubbles and affective polarization in user-personalized large language model outputs. In J. Antorán, A. Blaas, K. Buchanan, F. Feng, V. Fortuin, S. Ghalebikesabi, A. Kriegler, I. Mason, D. Rohde, F. J. R. Ruiz, T. Uelwer, Y. Xie, & R. Yang (Eds.), *Proceedings*

on I can't believe it's not better failure modes in the age of foundation models at NeurIPS 2023 workshops (Proceedings of Machine Learning Research, Vol. 239, pp. 29–37). PMLR. https://proceedings.mlr.press/v239/lazovich23a.html

476. Huang, L., Yu, W., Ma, W., Zhong, W., Feng, Z., Wang, H., Chen, Q., Peng, W., Feng, X., Qin, B., & Liu, T. (2025). A survey on hallucination in large language models: Principles, taxonomy, challenges, and open questions. *ACM Transactions on Information Systems, 43*(2), Article 42, 1–55. https://doi.org/10.1145/3703155
477. Zhao, X., Yang, X., Pang, T., Du, C., Li, L., Wang, Y.-X., & Wang, W.Y. (2025). Weak-to-strong jailbreaking on large language models. In *Proceedings of the 42nd International Conference on Machine Learning (ICML 2025).* OpenReview. https://openreview.net/forum?id=7DXaCYUvDN
478. Umbach, R., Henry, N., Beard, G. F., & Berryessa, C. M. (2024). Non consensual synthetic intimate imagery Prevalence, attitudes, and knowledge in 10 countries. In *Proceedings of the CHI Conference on Human Factors in Computing Systems CHI 24 May 11 to 16 2024 Honolulu HI USA*. Association for Computing Machinery. https://doi.org/10.1145/3613904.3642382
479. Mirsky, Y., & Lee, W. (2021). The creation and detection of deepfakes. A survey. *ACM Computing Surveys, 54*(1), Article 7, 1–41. https://doi.org/10.1145/3425780
480. Nadeem, M., Bethke, A., & Reddy, S. (2021). StereoSet: Measuring stereotypical bias in pretrained language models. In C. Zong, F. Xia, W. Li, & R. Navigli (Eds.), *Proceedings of the 59th annual meeting of the association for computational linguistics and the 11th international joint conference on natural language processing (Volume 1: Long Papers)* (pp. 5356–5371). Association for Computational Linguistics. https://aclanthology.org/2021.acl-long.416
481. Bai, H., Voelkel, J. G., Muldowney, S., Eichstaedt, J. C., & Willer, R. (2025). LLM-generated messages can persuade humans on policy issues. *Nature Communications, 16*, Article 6037. https://doi.org/10.1038/s41467-025-61345-5
482. Armbruster, J., Bussmann, F., Rothhaas, C., Titze, N., Grützner, P. A., & Freischmidt, H. (2024). Doctor ChatGPT, can you help me? The

patient's perspective: Cross-sectional study. *Journal of Medical Internet Research, 26*, e58831. https://doi.org/10.2196/58831

483. Reinecke, M. G., Ting, F., Savulescu, J., & Singh, I. (2025). The double-edged sword of anthropomorphism in LLMs. *Proceedings, 114*(1), 4. https://doi.org/10.3390/proceedings2025114004

Restoring Friction to the Algorithmic Order

484. OECD Nuclear Energy Agency. (2010). *Comparing nuclear accident risks with those from other energy sources* (NEA No. 6861). https://www.oecd.org/content/dam/oecd/en.publications/reports/2010/08/comparing-nuclear-accident-risks-with-those-from-other-energy-sources_g1g128c0/9789264097995-en.pdf

485. Bahri, Y., Dyer, E., Kaplan, J., Lee, J., & Sharma, U. (2024). Explaining neural scaling laws. *Proceedings of the National Academy of Sciences of the United States of America, 121*(27), e2311878121. https://doi.org/10.1073/pnas.2311878121

486. Wei, J., Tay, Y., Bommasani, R., Raffel, C., Zoph, B., Borgeaud, S., Yogatama, D., Bosma, M., Zhou, D., Metzler, D., Chi, E. H., Hashimoto, T., Vinyals, O., Liang, P., Dean, J., & Fedus, W. (2022). Emergent abilities of large language models. [Preprint]. *arXiv*. https://doi.org/10.48550/arXiv.2206.07682

487. Li, Y., Choi, D., Chung, J., Kushman, N., Schrittwieser, J., Leblond, R., Eccles, T., Keeling, J., Gimeno, F., Dal Lago, A., Hubert, T., Choy, P., de Masson d'Autume, C., Babuschkin, I., Chen, X., Huang, P.-S., Welbl, J., Gowal, S., Cherepanov, A., . . . Vinyals, O. (2022). Competition-level code generation with AlphaCode. *Science, 378*(6624), 1092–-1097. https://doi.org/10.1126/science.abq1158

488. Bansal, H., Gopalakrishnan, K., Dingliwal, S., Bodapati, S., Kirchhoff, K., & Roth, D. (2023). Rethinking the role of scale for in-context learning: An interpretability-based case study at 66 billion scale. In A. Rogers, J. Boyd-Graber, & N. Okazaki (Eds.), *Proceedings of the 61st annual meeting of the association for computational linguistics (Volume 1: Long Papers)* (pp. 11833–11856). Association for Computational Linguistics. https://doi.org/10.18653/v1/2023.acl-long.660

489. Schaeffer, R., Miranda, B., & Koyejo, S. (2023). Are emergent abilities of large language models a mirage? In A. Oh, T. Naumann, A. Globerson, K. Saenko, M. Hardt, & S. Levine (Eds.), *Advances in neural information processing systems* (Vol. 36, pp. 55565–55581). Curran Associates, Inc. https://papers.neurips.cc/paper_files/paper/2023/file/adc98a266f45005c403b8311ca7e8bd7-Paper-Conference.pdf
490. U.S. Securities and Exchange Commission. (2013, October 16). *In the matter of Knight Capital Americas LLC* (Securities Exchange Act of 1934 Release No. 70694; Administrative Proceeding File No. 3-15570). https://www.sec.gov/files/litigation/admin/2013/34-70694.pdf
491. Recht, B., Roelofs, R., Schmidt, L., & Shankar, V. (2019). Do ImageNet classifiers generalize to ImageNet? In K. Chaudhuri & R. Salakhutdinov (Eds.), *Proceedings of the 36th international conference on machine learning (Proceedings of Machine Learning Research, Vol. 97, pp. 5389–5400).* PMLR. https://proceedings.mlr.press/v97/recht19a.html
492. Ribeiro, M. T., Wu, T., Guestrin, C., & Singh, S. (2020). Beyond accuracy: Behavioral testing of NLP models with CheckList. In D. Jurafsky, J. Chai, N. Schluter, & J. Tetreault (Eds.), *Proceedings of the 58th annual meeting of the association for computational linguistics* (pp. 4902–4912). Association for Computational Linguistics. https://doi.org/10.18653/v1/2020.acl-main.442
493. Szegedy, C., Zaremba, W., Sutskever, I., Bruna, J., Erhan, D., Goodfellow, I. J., & Fergus, R. (2014). Intriguing properties of neural networks. In *Proceedings of the International Conference on Learning Representations (ICLR 2014).* https://openreview.net/forum?id=kklr_MTHMRQjG
494. Kiela, D., Bartolo, M., Nie, Y., Kaushik, D., Geiger, A., Wu, Z., Vidgen, B., Prasad, G., Singh, A., Ringshia, P., Ma, Z., Thrush, T., Riedel, S., Waseem, Z., Stenetorp, P., Jia, R., Bansal, M., Potts, C., & Williams, A. (2021). Dynabench: Rethinking benchmarking in NLP. In K. Toutanova, A. Rumshisky, L. Zettlemoyer, D. Hakkani-Tur, I. Beltagy, S. Bethard, R. Cotterell, T. Chakraborty, & Y. Zhou (Eds.), *Proceedings of the 2021 conference of the North American chapter of the association for computational linguistics: human language technologies* (pp. 4110–4124). Association for Computational Linguistics. https://doi.org/10.18653/v1/2021.naacl-main.324

495. Raji, I. D., Smart, A., White, R. N., Mitchell, M., Gebru, T., Hutchinson, B., Smith-Loud, J., Theron, D., & Barnes, P. (2020). Closing the AI accountability gap: Defining an end-to-end framework for internal algorithmic auditing. In *Proceedings of the 2020 Conference on Fairness, Accountability, and Transparency (FAccT '20)* (pp. 33–44). Association for Computing Machinery. https://doi.org/10.1145/3351095.3372873

496. Hwang, T. J., Sokolov, E., Franklin, J. M., & Kesselheim, A. S. (2016). Comparison of rates of safety issues and reporting of trial outcomes for medical devices approved in the European Union and United States: Cohort study. *BMJ, 353*, i3323. https://doi.org/10.1136/bmj.i3323

497. MacDuffie, J. P. (1995). *Human resource bundles and manufacturing performance: Organizational logic and flexible production systems in the world auto industry. Industrial and Labor Relations Review, 48*(2), 197–221. https://doi.org/10.1177/001979399504800201

498. Zabel, M. D., & Reid, C. (2015). A brief history of prions. *Pathogens and Disease, 73*(9), ftv087. https://doi.org/10.1093/femspd/ftv087

499. Hagey, K., & Horwitz, J. (2021, September 15). Facebook tried to make its platform a healthier place. It got angrier instead. *The Wall Street Journal.* https://www.wsj.com/tech/facebook-algorithm-change-zuckerberg-11631654215

Algorithmic Safety Cases as Constitutional Safeguards

500. Office for Nuclear Regulation. (n.d.). *How we regulate.* Retrieved January 11, 2026, from https://www.onr.org.uk/our-work/how-we-regulate

501. National Audit Office. (2020, January 10). *Managing infrastructure projects on nuclear-regulated sites* (HC 19, Session 2019–20) [Report]. https://www.nao.org.uk/wp-content/uploads/2020/01/Managing-infrastructure-projects-on-nuclear-regulated-sites.pdf

502. International Air Transport Association. (2025). *2024 full year accident update: Performance at 31st December 2024* [PDF]. https://www.iata.org/contentassets/4d18cb077c5e419b8a888d387a50c638/iata-safety-report-2024-fy_final.pdf

503. Joint Authorities Technical Review. (2019, October 11). *Boeing 737 MAX flight control system: Observations, findings, and recommendations* (Final report submitted to the Associate Administrator for Aviation Safety). U.S. Federal Aviation Administration. https://www.faa.gov/sites/faa.gov/files/2021-08/Final_JATR_Submittal_to_FAA_Oct_2019.pdf

504. Cooke, D. (2005). *Learning from the blackouts: Transmission system security in competitive electricity markets.* International Energy Agency. https://iea.blob.core.windows.net/assets/68002ee5-537c-4e12-8c40-ee8163cf69d6/Blackouts.pdf

505. Financial Crisis Inquiry Commission. (2011, January 27). *The financial crisis inquiry report: Final report of the National Commission on the Causes of the Financial and Economic Crisis in the United States.* https://fraser.stlouisfed.org/title/financial-crisis-inquiry-report-5034

Algorithmic Separation of Powers

506. Buolamwini, J., & Gebru, T. (2018). *Gender shades: Intersectional accuracy disparities in commercial gender classification.* In S. A. Friedler & C. Wilson (Eds.), *Proceedings of machine learning research: Vol. 81. Proceedings of the 1st conference on fairness, accountability and transparency* (pp. 77–91). PMLR. https://proceedings.mlr.press/v81/buolamwini18a.html

507. Grother, P., Ngan, M., & Hanaoka, K. (2019). *Face Recognition Vendor Test (FRVT) Part 3: Demographic effects* (NISTIR 8280). National Institute of Standards and Technology. https://nvlpubs.nist.gov/nistpubs/ir/2019/NIST.IR.8280.pdf

508. Klare, B. F., Burge, M. J., Klontz, J. C., Vorder Bruegge, R. W., & Jain, A. K. (2012). Face recognition performance: Role of demographic information. *IEEE Transactions on Information Forensics and Security, 7*(6), 1789–1801. https://doi.org/10.1109/TIFS.2012.2214212

509. World Health Organization. (2023, November 8). *WHO handbook for guidelines development: Supplement: Criteria for use of evidence to inform recommendations in World Health Organization guidelines* (WHO/SCI/QNS/MST/2023.1). https://www.who.int/publications/i/item/WHO-SCI-QNS-MST-2023.1

510. Narayanan, A. (2023, March 9). *Understanding social media recommendation algorithms.* Knight First Amendment Institute at Columbia University. https://knightcolumbia.org/content/understanding-social-media-recommendation-algorithms

511. Alesina, A., & Summers, L. H. (1993). Central bank independence and macroeconomic performance: Some comparative evidence. *Journal of Money, Credit and Banking, 25*(2), 151–162. https://doi.org/10.2307/2077833

512. Peters, R. H. (1989). *Review of recent research on organizational and behavioral factors associated with mine safety* (Information Circular 9232). U.S. Bureau of Mines. https://stacks.cdc.gov/view/cdc/9902

513. Dal Bó, E. (2006). Regulatory capture: A review. *Oxford Review of Economic Policy, 22*(2), 203–225. https://doi.org/10.1093/oxrep/grj013

514. European Commission, Directorate-General for Communications Networks, Content and Technology. (n.d.). *Article 43: Conformity assessment.* AI Act Service Desk. Retrieved January 16, 2026, from https://ai-act-service-desk.ec.europa.eu/en/ai-act/article-43

515. Powar, J., Janssen, H., Cloete, R., & Singh, J. (2025). From policy to practice in data governance and responsible data stewardship: System design for data intermediaries. In *Proceedings of the 2025 ACM Conference on Fairness, Accountability, and Transparency (FAccT '25)* (pp. 2491–2504). Association for Computing Machinery. https://doi.org/10.1145/3715275.3732164

516. Lauer, R., Merkel, S., Bosompem, J., Langer, H., Naeve, P., Herten, B., Burmann, A., Vollmar, H. C., Otte, I. (2024). (Data-) Cooperatives in health and social care: A scoping review. *Journal of Public Health, 34*, 71–89. https://doi.org/10.1007/s10389-024-02226-x

517. Hendricks, L. A., Burns, K., Saenko, K., Darrell, T., & Rohrbach, A. (2018). *Women also snowboard: Overcoming bias in captioning models.* In V. Ferrari, M. Hebert, C. Sminchisescu, & Y. Weiss (Eds.), *Computer vision – ECCV 2018* (Lecture Notes in Computer Science, Vol. 11207, pp. 793–811). Springer. https://doi.org/10.1007/978-3-030-01219-9_47

518. European Commission. (2025, December 16). *Proposal for a regulation of the European Parliament and of the Council on establishing a framework of measures for strengthening Union's biotechnology and biomanufacturing sectors particularly in the area of health and amending Regulations (EC) No 178/2002, (EC) No 1394/2007, (EU) No 536/2014, (EU) 2019/6, (EU) 2024/795 and (EU) 2024/1938 (European Biotech Act)* (COM(2025) 1022 final) [Proposed regulation]. https://health.ec.europa.eu/document/download/ec1475b7-e3f9-409e-b927-fc7e69306a8c_en?filename=biotech_reg-com2025-1022_act_en.pdf
519. U.S. Securities and Exchange Commission & U.S. Commodity Futures Trading Commission. (2010, September 30). *Findings regarding the market events of May 6, 2010* [Staff report]. https://www.sec.gov/news/studies/2010/marketevents-report.pdf
520. U.S. Securities and Exchange Commission. (2017, November 14). *Statement on the status of the Consolidated Audit Trail* [Speech/statement]. https://www.sec.gov/newsroom/speeches-statements/statement-status-consolidated-audit-trail
521. Milusheva, S. (2020). Managing the spread of disease with mobile phone data. *Journal of Development Economics, 147*, 102559. https://doi.org/10.1016/j.jdeveco.2020.102559
522. Stumborg, M. F., Blasius, T. D., Full, S. J., & Hughes, C. A. (2022, September). *Goodhart's law: Recognizing and mitigating the manipulation of measures in analysis* (CNA Occasional Paper No. COP-2022-U-033385-Final). CNA Corporation. https://www.cna.org/reports/2022/09/Goodharts-Law-Recognizing-Mitigating-Manipulation-Measures-in-Analysis.pdf
523. Cheon, S. H., Wernerfelt, A., Friedler, S. A., & Ustun, B. (2025). *Feature responsiveness scores: Model-agnostic explanations for recourse. International Conference on Learning Representations (ICLR 2025).* OpenReview. https://openreview.net/forum?id=wsWCVrH9dv
524. Ma, R., & Kou, Y. (2023). "Defaulting to boilerplate answers, they didn't engage in a genuine conversation": Dimensions of transparency design in creator moderation. *Proceedings of the ACM on Human-Computer Interaction,* 7(CSCW1), Article 44. https://doi.org/10.1145/3579477

525. Sinha, G. (2014). To suspect or not to suspect: Analysing the pressure on banks to be "policemen". *Journal of Banking Regulation, 15*(1), 75–86. https://doi.org/10.1057/jbr.2012.20
526. European Parliament, & Council of the European Union. (2016). *Regulation (EU) 2016/679 of the European Parliament and of the Council of 27 April 2016 on the protection of natural persons with regard to the processing of personal data and on the free movement of such data (General Data Protection Regulation). Official Journal of the European Union.* https://eur-lex.europa.eu/legal-content/EN/TXT/PDF/?uri=CELEX%3A32016R0679
527. Lyons, H., Wijenayake, S., Miller, T., & Velloso, E. (2022). *What's the appeal? Perceptions of review processes for algorithmic decisions.* In *Proceedings of the 2022 CHI Conference on Human Factors in Computing Systems (CHI '22).* ACM. https://doi.org/10.1145/3491102.3517606
528. Selman, C. (2022, July). *Benefit sanctions: A presumption of guilt* [Research report]. Public Law Project. https://publiclawproject.org.uk/content/uploads/2022/10/Benefit-Sanctions-Research-Report-v0.7.1.pdf
529. Dexe, J., Franke, U., Söderlund, K., van Berkel, N., Jensen, R. H., Lepinkäinen, N., & Vaiste, J. (2022). *Explaining automated decision-making: A multinational study of the GDPR right to meaningful information. The Geneva Papers on Risk and Insurance—Issues and Practice, 47*(3), 669–697. https://doi.org/10.1057/s41288-022-00271-9
530. Zhao, X., Yang, X., Pang, T., Du, C., Li, L., Wang, Y.-X., & Wang, W. Y. (2025, May 1). *Weak-to-strong jailbreaking on large language models* (ICML 2025 poster). OpenReview. https://openreview.net/forum?id=7DXaCYUvDN
531. Wang, S., Veldhuis, R., Brune, C., & Strisciuglio, N. (2024, September 18). *A survey on the robustness of computer vision models against common corruptions* (SSRN Scholarly Paper No. 4960634). SSRN. https://doi.org/10.2139/ssrn.4960634
532. Hooey, B. (2024, November 12–14). *NASA Aviation Safety Reporting System (ASRS) program briefing* [Conference presentation]. International Confidential Aviation Safety Systems (ICASS) Group meeting, San Francisco, CA, United States. NASA Technical Reports Server. https://ntrs.nasa.gov/api/citations/20240014226/downloads/ICASS%202024%20ASRS.pdf

533. Choukse, E., Warrier, B., Heath, S., Belmont, L., Zhao, A., Khan, H. A., Harry, B., Kappel, M., Hewett, R. J., Datta, K., Pei, Y., Lichtenberger, C., Siegler, J., Lukofsky, D., Kahn, Z., Sahota, G., Sullivan, A., Frederick, C., Thai, H., . . . Alben, J. (2025). Power stabilization for AI training datacenters. [Preprint]. *arXiv*. https://doi.org/10.48550/arXiv.2508.14318

534. Pilz, K. F., Mahmood, Y., & Heim, L. (2025). *AI's power requirements under exponential growth: Extrapolating AI data center power demand and assessing its potential impact on U.S. competitiveness* (Research Report No. RRA3572-1). RAND Corporation. https://www.rand.org/content/dam/rand/pubs/research_reports/RRA3500/RRA3572-1/RAND_RRA3572-1.pdf

535. Simonyan, K., & Zisserman, A. (2015). Very deep convolutional networks for large-scale image recognition. [Preprint]. *arXiv*. https://doi.org/10.48550/arXiv.1409.1556

536. Grattafiori, A., Dubey, A., Jauhri, A., Pandey, A., Kadian, A., Al-Dahle, A., Letman, A., Mathur, A., Schelten, A., Vaughan, A., Yang, A., Fan, A., Goyal, A., Hartshorn, A., Yang, A., Mitra, A., Sravankumar, A., Korenev, A., Hinsvark, A., . . . Ma, Z. (2024). The Llama 3 herd of models. [Preprint]. *arXiv*. https://arxiv.org/abs/2407.21783

537. Maslej, N., Fattorini, L., Perrault, R., Parli, V., Reuel, A., Brynjolfsson, E., Etchemendy, J., Ligett, K., Lyons, T., Manyika, J., Niebles, J. C., Shoham, Y., Wald, R., & Clark, J. (2024). *Artificial intelligence index report 2024*. Stanford University, Institute for Human-Centered Artificial Intelligence. https://hai.stanford.edu/ai-index/2024-ai-index-report

538. Kaplan, J., McCandlish, S., Henighan, T., Brown, T. B., Chess, B., Child, R., Gray, S., Radford, A., Wu, J., & Amodei, D. (2020). Scaling laws for neural language models. [Preprint]. *arXiv*. https://arxiv.org/abs/2001.08361

539. Jellinek, R., Zhai, Y., Ristenpart, T., & Swift, M. (2014, June 17–18). A day late and a dollar short: The case for research on cloud billing systems. In M. A. Kozuch & M. Yu (Chairs), *6th USENIX workshop on hot topics in cloud computing (HotCloud 14)* (Philadelphia, PA, United States). USENIX Association. https://www.usenix.org/conference/hotcloud14/workshop-program/presentation/jellinek

540. Åberg, A. (2021). The ways and means of ITER: Reciprocity and compromise in fusion science diplomacy. *History and Technology, 37*(1), 106–124. https://doi.org/10.1080/07341512.2021.1891851
541. Aquilina, M., Budish, E., & O'Neill, P. (2022). Quantifying the high-frequency trading "arms race". *The Quarterly Journal of Economics, 137*(1), 493–564. https://doi.org/10.1093/qje/qjab032
542. Partnership for Market Readiness. (2015). *Carbon leakage: Theory, evidence and policy design* (Technical Note No. 11). World Bank. https://documents1.worldbank.org/curated/en/138781468001151104/pdf/100369-NWP-PUBLIC-ADD-SERIES-Partnership-for-Market-Readiness-technical-papers-Box393231B.pdf
543. Buehler, S., Dewenter, R., & Haucap, J. (2006). Mobile number portability in Europe. *Telecommunications Policy, 30*(7), 385–399. https://doi.org/10.1016/j.telpol.2006.04.001
544. Syrmoudis, E., Mager, S., Kuebler-Wachendorff, S., Pizzinini, P., Grossklags, J., & Kranz, J. (2021). Data portability between online services: An empirical analysis on the effectiveness of GDPR Art. 20. *Proceedings on Privacy Enhancing Technologies, 2021*(3), 351–372. https://doi.org/10.2478/popets-2021-0051
545. Publications Office of the European Union. (2020, June 17). *The polluter-pays principle and environmental liability*. EUR-Lex. https://eur-lex.europa.eu/legal-content/EN/ALL/?uri=legissum:l28120
546. Crane, D. A. (2024). Tying law for the digital age. *Notre Dame Law Review, 99*, 821–880. https://ndlawreview.org/wp-content/uploads/2024/04/NDLR_99.0821_Crane.pdf
547. Powderly, W. G. (2019). How infection shaped history: Lessons from the Irish famine. *Transactions of the American Clinical and Climatological Association, 130*, 127–135. https://pmc.ncbi.nlm.nih.gov/articles/PMC6735970
548. Chen, H., Cam, H., & Xu, S. (2021). Quantifying cybersecurity effectiveness of dynamic network diversity. [Preprint]. *arXiv*. https://doi.org/10.48550/arXiv.2112.07826

549. Watzinger, M., & Schnitzer, M. (2022, October 10). *The breakup of the Bell System and its impact on US innovation* (Discussion Paper No. 341). Collaborative Research Center Transregio 190. https://rationality-and-competition.de/wp-content/uploads/2022/10/341.pdf

Putting the Trias Algorithmica to the Test

550. Turing, A. M. (1950). Computing machinery and intelligence. *Mind, 59*(236), 433–460. https://academic.oup.com/mind/article-abstract/LIX/236/433/986238?redirectedFrom=fulltext

Acknowledgments

Books are strange moral objects. They are written, certainly, in solitude—sometimes in a solitude so prolonged that it begins to resemble a monastery. But they are made possible in company: by those who endure the writer's absences, soften the writer's certainties, interrupt the writer's vanity, forgive the writer's preoccupations, and continue loving the writer through the tedious business of trying to find the right sentence. If this book has any life in it, that life is not mine alone. It has been lent, steadied, corrected, and carried by others. By many.

My first gratitude is for my wife, Rosalie Mann, to whom thanks are both most owed and least equal to the thing owed.

There is a kind of support that can be described: practical help, timely encouragement, patience with doubts, tolerance for books left open, face down, in every room, and for thoughts that arrive at the wrong hour and insist upon being heard. And then there is another kind, deeper and less easily itemized, which consists not in assisting a work but in making a life in which the work can be done without becoming all-consuming. She has given me both kinds.

She has lived beside this book in its least attractive forms: as a mood, as a worry, as a silence, as a recurring abstraction at the dinner table, and as an invisible third presence in the room. She has tolerated the way writing can make one physically present but mentally offshore. More than tolerated, really. She has met it with discernment, humor, restraint, and a generosity so constant that one risks mistaking it for something ordinary, which it is not.

Anything in these pages that resists hardness for its own sake, cleverness for its own ends, or abstraction at the expense of life reflects her influence in countless ways.

To my son, Alexandre Mann, I owe a different kind of thanks, though an equally large one.

Children are accused, not always unfairly, of creating practical difficulties for serious work. They disrupt schedules, abolish privacy, and expose as fantasy the writer's cherished belief that ideal conditions are only one uninterrupted hour away.

But they do something better in return. They rescue thought from its gradual submission to anticipated conformity. They restore urgency to the human depth and scale of life. They remind one that every claim about society, progress, intelligence, institutions, and the future must eventually answer to an actual life: a living face, a growing mind asking for meaning, belonging, fulfillment, and a world spacious enough to sustain it.

My son has given this book something no theory could give it: proportion.

Through him, the future ceased to be a category and became a person. Through him, questions that might once have remained pleasantly conceptual acquired weight, consequence, and tenderness.

He has also taught me, as children do without intending to teach anything at all, that intelligence is not defined solely by performance. There is a kind of knowing in wonder, in trust, in attention, in play, and in the mysterious gravity and spontaneity with which a child inhabits the world before he has learned the many adult arts of flattening it.

To live near that is corrective. It clears the mind of cant. It exposes entire systems of importance as flimsy theatrical props.

That incarnation of the future lies close to the heart of *Trias Algorithmica*. For if the book asks how the separation of algorithmic power is to be held in right relation, it does so under the pressure of a simpler and older question: Whether the worlds we are building will remain inhabitable for those who must grow within them. Algorithmic power may be traced here through the grand machinery of our age; for me, its truest tests remain very close to home.

To my readers, past and present, known and unknown to me, I am grateful beyond what courtesy requires me to say.

Writing is an act that depends, absurdly enough, on strangers. One writes in the hope that someone, somewhere, will pause long enough to receive a thought as the beginning of a relationship. There is no guarantee of this. Most words vanish into the general atmosphere. Over the years, I have been moved by readers who have engaged my work with thoughtfulness, seriousness, and, at times, a grace that exceeded what the work had any right to expect.

Some wrote to tell me where an idea had accompanied them. Some challenged me with intelligence and precision, which are their own forms of respect. Some carried concepts from page to practice, from private reflection to public action, and from reading into teaching, leadership, institution-building, or self-questioning.

This is all a writer can really hope for: continuation.

A reader who extends an idea, deepens it, complicates it, or even thoughtfully resists it. To have such readers is one of the hidden privileges of a writing life and a reminder that thought does not end where writing does; it multiplies.

I also want to thank Stuart Crainer and Des Dearlove, the Thinkers50 originators, whose names are, for many, inseparable from a public culture of ideas that is rarer than it ought to be.

It is not difficult to create noise with words; the age positively rewards it. It is much harder to create a space in which ideas may appear with enough room to breathe and enough serendipity to pass unexpectedly from mind to mind.

Stuart and Des have helped sustain such a space—such spaces, actually.

What I appreciate in them is not merely their support, though I am thankful for that, but a certain cast of mind. They understood, I think, that ideas are improved not by being overhandled but by being allowed to gather force in their own time.

It remains for me to thank those at Wiley who helped bring this book from manuscript into the world of finished things: Annie Knight, Alice Hadaway, Stacey Rivera, Shannon Vargo, and Jeanenne Ray, together with others whose dedication and labor belong—discreetly but no less unmistakably—to what now stands here.

Publishing, like writing, depends upon forms of attention that are easily underestimated when they are well exercised. It asks for precision without intrusiveness, guidance without insistence, structure without rigidity, and that increasingly rare professional finesse by which a complex process is made to feel less mechanical than humanly accompanied. Such work leaves fewer visible traces than authorship, but it is woven into these pages all the same. The result is better, clearer, and more fully itself because of their skill, rigor, and refinement.

And there are older debts still: to teachers, authors, thinkers, doers, helpers, givers, and connectors whose work, examples, standards, questions, lives, ways of being, and moral presence have made my own effort imaginable.

No one writes from a clean beginning. We enter conversations already underway, inherit vocabularies we did not mint, borrow courage from people long dead, and call originality what is often, at best, an honorable recombination of properly metabolized influences.

In the end, perhaps this is all an acknowledgment section can do: Fail gracefully at the arithmetic of gratitude. The sums do not come out correctly. Language is unequal to life. It is a small act of truth against one of the more persistent illusions of writing: that the solitary laborer at the desk tells the whole story.

About the Author

Hamilton Mann is recognized as one of the world's leading experts on artificial intelligence (AI). He is an AI researcher, technology executive, acclaimed author, lecturer at INSEAD and HEC Paris, mentor at the MIT Priscilla King Gray Center, and a doctoral researcher at École Nationale des Ponts et Chaussées—Institut Polytechnique de Paris.

He was inducted into the Thinkers50 Radar as one of the 30 most prominent rising business thinkers globally in 2024 and is the recipient of the 2025 Thinkers50 Distinguished Achievement Award for Digital Thinking.

He originated the concept of artificial integrity and serves as Chairman and President of the Artificial Integrity Institute, a nonprofit organization dedicated to advancing AI systems that prioritize integrity over intelligence.

With decades of experience leading digital transformation and advising Fortune 500 companies, Mann serves as Group Vice President at Thales Group, a global leader in defense, aerospace, cybersecurity, and digital identity, where he co-leads global digital and AI transformation across the strategy, marketing, and sales organizations.

His award-winning book, *Artificial Integrity: The Paths to Leading AI Toward a Human-Centered Future* (John Wiley & Sons, October 2024), was named a must-read of 2024 and one of the top 10 essential AI books of 2025 by the Next Big Idea Club, as well as one of the top 10 new management books of 2025 by Thinkers50.

He is also a contributing author to four books: *Driving Sustainable Innovation: How to Do Well While Doing Good* (2024), *Connectedness: How the Best Leaders Create Authentic Human Connection in a Disconnected World* (2024), *GAIN: Demystifying GenAI for Office and Home* (2025), and *Leadership That Lasts: Building Sustainable Value in a Changing World* (2026).

He is a regular contributor to *Forbes* on AI and its societal implications, and his work has been featured in leading academic and business publications, including *California Management Review, Stanford Social Innovation Review, Noéma Magazine, Rotman Management Magazine, Think:Act Magazine, Leader to Leader* (Wiley), *Knowledge@Wharton, I by IMD, INSEAD Knowledge, Dialogue (Duke Corporate Education), Harvard Business Review* (France, Italy, and Germany editions), *Polytechnique Insights*, and the *European Business Review*.

He has spoken at major international conferences, including the Global Peter Drucker Forum and Web Summit. He hosts the Hamilton Mann Conversation, a podcast that aims to democratize knowledge about how digital technology, including AI, can be a force for good in society.

Index

I